PAPISTS AND PURITANS
UNDER ELIZABETH I

BLANDFORD HISTORY SERIES
(General Editor R. W. Harris)

PROBLEMS OF HISTORY

HISTORY OF EUROPE

THE HISTORY OF ENGLAND

Papists and Puritans Under Elizabeth I

PATRICK McGRATH
Reader in History, University of Bristol

BLANDFORD PRESS
LONDON

First published in 1967
© 1967 Blandford Press Ltd,
167 High Holborn, London W.C.1

DEDICATION

To Sara and Veronica

*Set in 11pt Times, Printed in Great Britain by
Richard Clay (The Chaucer Press) Ltd,
Bungay, Suffolk*

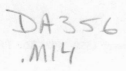

DA356
.MI4

CONTENTS

Acknowledgments

Acknowledgment is due to the following for their kind permission to reproduce illustrations:

Bodleian Library, Oxford: Nos. 6, 10, 14, 15, 16
Country Life: No. 17
Emmanuel College, Cambridge: No. 18
Radio Times Hulton Picture Library: Nos. 1, 2, 3, 4, 7, 8, 12, 19
Victoria and Albert Museum (Crown Copyright): No. 11

List of Illustrations

MAPS

Preface

BOTH the Papists and the Puritans in Elizabethan England have received a great deal of attention from historians, but for the most part the two groups have been considered in isolation from each other and treated as though they had little or nothing in common except, perhaps, hostility to the Elizabethan religious settlement. Although in many ways they differed as much as chalk from cheese, they had in fact more in common than they would have cared to admit. It is the purpose of this book to give some account of both movements and to suggest some of the ways in which they resembled each other as well as some of the ways in which they differed.

The first two chapters examine in a general way the problem of religious unity in the Elizabethan period and the difficulties which faced the government when it attempted to impose uniformity on Papist and Puritan deviationists who found unacceptable the doctrine and liturgy of the established church. There were considerable differences in the ranks of those who opposed the establishment, and it is misleading to think of either Papists or Puritans as completely homogeneous groups with clear-cut party lines. The term 'Puritan' raises special difficulties since so many different meanings have been attached to it both by sixteenth-century writers and by later historians. Some of these different interpretations are examined in the second chapter, and an attempt is made to find a working definition which will cover the kind of Puritanism examined in this book.

The history of the Papists and the Puritans is then treated chronologically in four rough and ready divisions of time. In each division the two groups are considered separately, but an attempt is made to draw attention to similarities and differences. The chronological divisions which are significant in the history of the Papists do not, of course, always correspond exactly with the significant chronological divisions in the history of the Puritans, but nevertheless this fourfold division of the Elizabethan period will, it is hoped, provide a reasonably satisfactory framework within which these developments can be studied.

The Hampton Court Conference of 1604 and the Gunpowder Plot

of 1605 provide useful points at which to conclude the story of the two groups of deviationists whose fortunes under the Stuarts were so different from what they had been in the days of Elizabeth I.

In the concluding chapter some attempt is made to compare and contrast the developments of Papists and Puritans in Elizabethan England. There is still much that is unknown about national, regional and local religious history, and little has been done in the way of a comparative study of the distribution, organisation and religious outlook of these two groups which found themselves in conflict with the policy of the established church. The conclusions must therefore be very tentative, but it is hoped they may nevertheless be of some value.

*   *   *

A general survey of this nature must obviously draw heavily on the very considerable literature relating to religious developments in the Elizabethan age, and I have tried to indicate in the footnotes something of my debt to numerous writers, living and dead, who have contributed to our understanding of this highly complex subject. I should like particularly to acknowledge my debt to the work of Dr. Patrick Collinson whose fascinating and scholarly studies have in recent years added new dimensions to our knowledge of Elizabethan Puritanism. His authoritative book on *The Elizabethan Puritan Movement* appeared while this work was going through the press, but I have been able to alter a number of footnote references so that they refer to his book instead of to his thesis on 'The Puritan Classical Movement'.

I should like to express my gratitude to Dr. D. M. Rogers of the Bodleian Library and to Dr. A. F. Alison of the British Museum for their advice and help with the illustrations, and to Mr. R. W. Harris and Mr. Peter Gwyn for a number of valuable comments and criticisms. Miss Kathleen Hek and Miss E. Stayt-Harris patiently typed the manuscript, and Mr. David Large and Mrs. Frances Stuart kindly assisted with the proof reading. The Blandford Press and its staff have been extremely helpful on all occasions.

Finally, I gratefully acknowledge the comments, both relevant and irrelevant, which I have received from my wife and children during the long period in which this book was coming into existence.

Nether Stowey, April 1967

PATRICK MCGRATH

1

The Problem of Church Unity in Elizabethan England

This liberty, that men may openly profess diversity of religion, must needs be dangerous to the Commonwealth. What stirs diversity of religion hath raised in nations and kingdoms, the histories are so many and so plain, and our times in such sort have told you, that with further proof I need not trouble your ears. One God, one king, one faith, one profession, is fit for one monarchy and commonwealth. . . . Let conformity and unity in religion be provided for; and it shall be as a wall of defence unto this realm.
Sermon of Edwin Sandys[1]

UNDER Henry VII and during the first half of the reign of Henry VIII all Englishmen were required to be members of the Church of Rome. After the break with the papacy in the 1530's, they were legally bound to accept the peculiarly national but mainly Catholic church of which Henry VIII was Supreme Head. During Edward VI's reign the state church became increasingly Protestant. Mary restored Roman Catholicism for a few years, but Elizabeth I replaced it by a Church of England of which she was the Supreme Governor. These violent and bewildering changes in a period of less than thirty years demonstrate the unstable and fluctuating nature of Tudor religious policy, but in one thing at least it was consistent and unchanging—all Englishmen must belong to one church, the church officially recognised by the state.

In this the Tudors were no different from most other rulers in sixteenth-century Europe, Catholic or Protestant, and no different from the Christian princes of the Middle Ages who, with few exceptions,

[1] *The Sermons of Edwin Sandys*, edit. J. Ayre, Parker Society, Cambridge, 1841, p. 49.

had insisted on religious uniformity among their subjects. They were in line, too, with all the great religious leaders of their time, for neither the Roman Catholic Church nor the various Protestant Churches were prepared to allow religious toleration. The Churches believed that those who would not accept their teaching were heretics and were guilty men, since they refused to believe the truth when it was clearly presented to them. If heretics persisted in their errors, their obstinacy and pride deserved to be punished, even with death. If they were allowed to spread their views, they would not only lose their own souls, but they would infect others and lead them to damnation.

Many sixteenth-century princes were convinced of the truth of the religion they imposed on their subjects, but even when they were not whole-heartedly committed to its teaching, they insisted on religious unity for political and social reasons. Nonconformity in religion threatened the unity of the state; it meant that the subject was defying in a matter of great importance the authority of the ruler. If the subject could differ from the prince in religion, he might easily differ from him in politics. He might question not only the established form of religion but also the established form of society. Elizabeth I in the later stages of her reign seems to have toyed with the possibility of allowing some kind of toleration to her loyal Roman Catholic subjects, but she decided that it was not practical politics.[1] In Spain her great opponent Philip II would not even have considered such a possibility, for he would have thought it morally wrong to tolerate error within his dominions. There were, it is true, a few countries in Europe in the sixteenth century where, at least for a time, more than one religion was tolerated within the same state, but it was usually because neither of the opposing parties within the state was sufficiently strong to win an outright victory and to impose its religion on every one. The Edict of Nantes in 1598 gave limited toleration to Huguenots within the French Catholic state, but it had taken forty years of inconclusive religious wars to make such a settlement acceptable to Frenchmen.

This insistence on religious unity by sixteenth-century governments is difficult for us to understand in twentieth-century England where religion is regarded as a private matter about which the individual is free to make up his own mind. Nevertheless, in the modern

---

[1] As Professor Hurstfield puts it in *Elizabeth 1 and the Unity of England*, p. 214: '...there *was* a theme in Elizabeth's life and reign, and that was the unremitting search to bind the nation in unity after two decades of discord...'

world religious toleration is not universal, and religious minorities can still be hampered and penalised in a number of ways. Even if there is no insistence on religious uniformity, society may seek, directly or indirectly, to impose political and social beliefs on all its citizens. Things can be made intolerable for people whose way of life is markedly different from that of their neighbours. In some occupations in England a man is not allowed to be employed unless he belongs to the appropriate trade union, even though he may have genuine conscientious objections to joining. In some areas there has been strong prejudice against minority groups and immigrants from other countries. It is not unknown in the United States of America for people who disagree with commonly accepted views to be stigmatised by their neighbours as 'un-American' or as 'commies'. Nor do communist states allow freedom of conscience to deviationists—they label them 'capitalist and imperialist hyenas' in very much the same way as the Elizabethan government labelled popish recusants 'spies and intelligencers . . . for her Majesty's foreign enemies' and Puritan dissenters as 'seditious sectaries and disloyal persons'. For many people in the sixteenth century there was an unanswerable case on religious, political and social grounds for enforcing religious uniformity, and neither the Catholic nor the Puritan opponents of the queen could justifiably complain against the principle on which the government acted. Like the government, Catholics and Puritans both wanted religious uniformity. They were not prepared to tolerate error.

Thus, when Elizabeth I became queen on 17 November 1558 the question for her and for her advisers was not whether there should be one religion in England, but what that religion should be. The religious changes in England during the last thirty years had furnished them with several different models from which they could, if they so decided, take their pick. Alternatively, they could shop in the European market and consider the possibilities of some of the religious patterns which Englishmen returning from Zurich or Frankfurt or Geneva were only too anxious to sell to them.

But the queen and her advisers in 1558 were political realists. They were not beginning from scratch and they could not do just what they liked. There were many clashing interests both at home and abroad which had to be taken into account, and when they made a choice they would have to choose wisely and stand by their decision. There might well be a limit to the number of times Englishmen would be prepared to change their religion on orders from above. Nine years later the duke of Norfolk advised the queen against marrying a Habsburg archduke who wanted freedom to practise his religion in England, 'for lette your hyenesse assure your selfe that Ingland cane beare no more changys in relygyon, ytt hathe been bowyd so ofte that yff ytt schuld be bente ageyn ytt wolde breke'.[1] In 1558 breaking point had not yet been reached, but clearly if the religious policy of the government continued to oscillate as violently as it had in the last two decades, it might be brought into contempt and might cease to be taken seriously.

One possibility, which should not perhaps be dismissed out of hand, would have been for the new government to continue with the religion then established, that of the Roman Catholic Church recently restored by Mary. This would not have required new legislation, and Elizabeth herself was nominally a Catholic. She had conformed outwardly and gone to mass. Such a policy would have raised complications in that, according to the canon law of the Roman Church, Elizabeth I was illegitimate. For that matter, she was illegitimate by English law, but Henry VIII's Act of Succession had fixed the succession on her,[2] and there was no support in England for her possible rival. Mary of Scotland was in France, married to the dauphin and shortly to become Queen of France.[3] Only a successful conquest of England by invading French troops could give her the crown, and Spain would have supported England in resisting the invaders. If Elizabeth I had been a convinced Catholic seriously determined to come to terms with the papacy, she could no doubt have made some arrangement with the pope in spite of her illegitimacy.[4]

Professor Dickens maintains that: 'As the daughter of Anne Boleyn, as a child of the Protestant humanism which had nourished Edward and Lady Jane, above all as the idol of the anti-Marian Londoners, the new queen was deeply committed to reverse the religious settlement of her predecessor.'[5] It is quite true that Elizabeth's upbringing and background inclined her towards some form of

[1] Historical Manuscripts Commission: *MSS of the Marquis of Bath*, II. 18.
[2] *Statutes of the Realm*, III. 955 (35 Henry VIII, c. 1), 1543.
[3] Her husband, Francis II, died at the end of 1560 and she returned to Scotland in August 1561. The problem of succession to the throne is examined in Mortimer Levine, *The early Elizabethan succession Question 1558-1568*, Stanford University Press, 1966.
[4] The pope was very anxious to come to terms with Elizabeth. See pp. 67, 68.
[5] A. G. Dickens, *The English Reformation*, 1964, p. 294.

Protestantism, but it did not seem quite so obvious to contemporaries as it does to historians that she must inevitably adopt the kind of policy which she did in fact choose to adopt. There is considerable uncertainty about what Elizabeth I really did believe in religion, and she was not, it would seem, deeply committed theologically in the great disputes over doctrine which divided men at this time. If in 1558 there had been a strong case on other grounds for her outwardly accepting Roman Catholicism, it is conceivable that she would have done so, for England was worth a mass, just as under Mary life had been worth a mass. Neither Edward VI nor Lady Jane Grey would have come to terms with Anti-Christ, but Elizabeth was not of the stuff of which religious martyrs are made. If she had been, the course of English history would have been profoundly changed, because in the sixteenth century the personality of the ruler still counted for so much. As it is, we shall never know what would have happened if Mary had been succeeded by a committed Catholic or by a Protestant zealot.

Even if Elizabeth's own history had not inclined her to adopt some form of Protestantism, there was a very strong case against continuing the policy of her predecessor. If she wished to do so, she would have to go as a suitor to the pope for recognition, and she would have to rely on the support and goodwill of Philip of Spain. She might even have to accept his reluctant offer of marriage. A pro-Catholic policy would inevitably be associated with a pro-Spanish policy—and none knew better than Elizabeth how unpopular that policy had been and how near Mary had been to losing her throne.[1] She would need for whatever policy she adopted the consent of the majority of the ruling class, the nobility and gentry without whom Tudor England could not be governed. She might conceivably have won their reluctant consent to a Catholic settlement, as Mary had done, but it would not have been whole-hearted consent, and there would have been formidable opposition. She would have had to form a government from the same kind of people as had formed the incompetent and inefficient privy council under Mary, and she would have alienated the able and vigorous men in the country. Cecil had conformed under Mary and no doubt he would have gone on conforming under a Catholic Elizabeth, but he would not have played that major constructive rôle in government that he was destined to play under a Protestant

[1] For Mary's difficulties, see D. M. Loades, *Two Tudor Conspiracies*, Cambridge, 1965.

Elizabeth. His heart would not have been in his work. There would have been no room in a Catholic England for the Marian exiles such as Elizabeth's Lord Keeper, Sir Nicholas Bacon, or her cousin and Vice-Chamberlain, Sir Francis Knollys, or Cecil's father-in-law, Sir Anthony Cooke.

If Elizabeth had wanted to maintain Catholicism, she would have met with considerable resistance in parliament, but presumably she would have been able to deal with it, at any rate for a time. All Tudor rulers had so far been able to obtain parliamentary support for their religious policies. Even Mary had managed to get the House of Commons to approve, with only one dissenting vote, the restoration of the pope's authority. Nevertheless, Elizabeth knew that many of the gentry who had accepted the Marian restoration were not enthusiastic about it. She also knew that she could count on a good deal of support if she decided to break with Rome, and she calculated that although parliament had restored papal authority in 1555 it would be very willing to abolish it in 1559 if the government gave a lead. What she probably did not anticipate was the strength of the radical Protestant minority returned to her first parliament. It was so effective that the Commons took a much more extreme line in religion than the queen really wanted, and the settlement of 1559 was something she had to accept by way of compromise, not something she had planned from the beginning.[1]

Although she may well have been surprised and, indeed, disconcerted, by the determination of the radical Protestants in her first parliament, Elizabeth must have been well aware at the very beginning of her reign that religious enthusiasm and intellectual ability were to be found in the Protestant rather than in the Catholic camp. Mary's reign had been of short duration, and the reform of Catholicism which Cardinal Pole had put in hand had been brief and ineffectual. The Counter-Reformation had, as yet, made little impact on England. As it turned out, Catholicism was to produce a number of able men in the 1560's, but at the beginning of the reign the vigour, the enthusiasm and the intellectual ability seemed to be on the other side and Elizabeth would have been reluctant to reject and to drive into opposition the small but very influential group of Protestant enthusiasts.

[1] The classical account of this parliament is in J. E. Neale, *Elizabeth I and her Parliaments*, 1953, vol. i.

In assessing the situation at the beginning of the reign, Elizabeth had to take into account the existence in a number of European cities of groups of English Protestant refugees who had left the country during Mary's reign but who began to return to their native country as soon as they received the news of Mary's death.[1] The numbers were relatively small, less than 800, including women and children, but their importance was out of all proportion to their numbers. They were composed mainly of gentlemen, clergy, merchants and young men studying for the ministry, and they included some very able men who would, given the opportunity, inevitably play a leading rôle in state and church. The exiles had established organised churches in a number of cities, including Frankfurt, Strassburg, Zurich and Geneva, and they had been subjected to the influence of continental reformers far more than those who remained in England. In general, they had moved a considerable way to the left of the position set out in the Second Prayer Book of Edward VI, and a number of them had adopted the full Calvinist doctrine and form of worship. The exiles had quarrelled among themselves and there were considerable differences between them about what should now be done in England, but they were united in their fierce hatred of popery. They could not be ignored by anyone who wanted to break with Rome. The queen needed the help of such able and enthusiastic supporters. Only time would show whether or not she would be able to control them.

Whether the church to be established by the queen was Catholic or Protestant, it would need for its work the service of many thousands of clergy. It was not easy to supply satisfactory ministers in a hurry, and the government had to consider the possible reactions of the existing Marian priests. As far as the ordinary parish clergy were concerned, it might reasonably calculate that they would not give a great deal of trouble. They had, with relatively few exceptions, accepted the changes of Henry VIII, of Edward VI and of Mary. It might be thought that a clergy which could accept so many momentous alterations in religion in so short a time would accept anything. The priests were unlikely to protest if they were told that the religion of the new government was still Catholicism; they would conform without too much fuss if the government decided on a change of

---

[1] For an account of the Protestant exiles under Mary, see Christina Hallowell Garrett, *The Marian Exiles, A Study in the Origins of Elizabethan Puritanism*, Cambridge, 1938.

B

policy. There were, of course, exceptions. There are various estimates of those who refused to conform in the early years of Elizabeth, but whatever estimate one accepts, it is clear that the number of those who were prepared to give up their livings was very small.[1] If the ordinary clergy had offered even passive resistance the government would not have succeeded in manning its new church. But only a few hundred were willing to risk deprivation, let alone martyrdom. Like most of their parishioners, the parish clergy were bewildered and confused by frequent changes in religion. Like their parishioners, they were often poor men who had to live. Their standard of education was low, and they had been untouched by any Catholic revival. They were not the sort of men who could stand up to their social superiors, the gentry, and they were very ill-equipped to argue with convinced Protestants. They included a number who had been compelled under Mary to put away their wives and many of them were by no means enthusiastic supporters of clerical celibacy.

The higher clergy were potentially much more dangerous. Elizabeth was not in fact able to carry with her the surviving Marian bishops, although she hoped for a time that she would be able to do so. Fortunately for her, the episcopal bench was considerably under strength at her accession, and there were few bishops who were able to give a really effective lead to the Catholic opposition. Some of them did what they could to resist change, but they were generals without an army. In February 1559, the Lower House of Convocation proclaimed its belief in Catholic doctrine and asserted that 'to the apostle Peter, and to his lawful successors in the apostolic see, there has been given, as vicars of Christ, the supreme power of pasturing the church militant of Christ . . .',[2] but it soon became apparent that the clergy were not prepared to come forward in their thousands to refuse the royal supremacy. It is true that as the 1560's went on and it became increasingly apparent that the break with Rome was final, there was a trickle of emigrés to Catholic centres abroad and that this included university men like Allen, Stapleton, Harding, Vaux and Nicholas Sander. Such men could have been invaluable to the newly established church, but the danger of losing very large numbers

[1] Estimates vary between 200 and 800. The probability is that they were nearer 200 than 800. The total number of livings in the church was about 9,000 but the actual number of ordained clergy at the beginning of the reign was probably about 7,000.

[2] For an English translation of the protest, see Philip Hughes, *Rome and the Counter-Reformation in England*, 1942, pp. 138–9.

in this way cannot have seemed so very great to those who had to estimate the chances of opposition, and the number of emigrés was in fact even smaller than might have been anticipated.

It has already been suggested that Elizabeth could reasonably expect considerable support from the most active and energetic of the gentry. How would the ordinary people in the towns and villages react to the strong lead given from above? What they really thought about the numerous religious changes is one of the hardest questions to answer. Except on rare occasions, the majority of them were inarticulate. Religious feeling could flare up in particular areas, often mingled with other grievances in a way which makes it extraordinarily difficult to assess. The Pilgrimage of Grace of 1536 and the Prayer Book Rebellion of 1549 had shown that the common people could not be completely ignored and that they were not always indifferent to religious changes imposed by their betters, but in her long reign of forty-five years Elizabeth did not in fact have to face a religious rebellion. Religion played a part in the Rising of the Northern Earls in 1569, but this was not in origin a rebellion about religion.[1] In 1559 few Catholics were prepared to die for the pope or the mass. The government calculated that as far as the people of England were concerned there was likely to be little really active resistance. Indeed, it seemed probable that there would be more violent opposition to retaining a Catholic settlement than there would be to introducing a Protestant one. The fact that under Mary something like three hundred people had died for their Protestant beliefs—and they were mostly from relatively humble sections of the community—must have strengthened the opinion of the government that it could successfully impose some form of Protestantism. In terms of martyrs the record of the Protestant minority was overwhelmingly superior to that of the nominally Catholic majority. If the leaders among the nobility and gentry were willing to support the queen's policy, and if active and zealous men could be put into positions of influence in the Church, then the ordinary people might in time be induced not merely to acquiesce but to give a measure of active support to the religion established by law.

It was comparatively easy for the queen to decide that the religion of Elizabethan England should not be Roman Catholicism. It was more difficult to decide what it should be. Political as well as religious

---

[1] See pp. 65–67.

factors had to be taken into account. What the queen wanted was some form of religion which would not in any way weaken the power of the crown. Roman Catholicism would mean that her subjects owed allegiance to the pope as well as to the queen, but a well-organised Calvinist church might be equally dangerous. Calvinists, like Catholics, asserted the supremacy of the spiritual over the temporal power, and if they thought it was the will of God, they were prepared to challenge the authority of the prince. It is true that Calvinism had not yet shown in France or in the Netherlands its full potentialities as an independent force within the state, but a warning was close at hand in Scotland. Elizabeth had no desire to find herself in the position of Mary of Guise struggling to uphold her power against factious nobles and a Kirk with a direct mandate from God. She was not prepared to tolerate either a pope of Rome or a pope who had learnt his business in Geneva.

Elizabeth at one time told the Spanish ambassador that she was thinking of a church settlement like her father's. A settlement on Henrician lines would certainly have ensured that spiritual authority was adequately controlled by royal authority. But in 1558 there was little support for such a proposal, and it is unlikely that Elizabeth seriously considered it as a permanent policy. She may have had some such arrangement in mind as a temporary measure while she took stock of the situation and consolidated her position. It seems that her original intention was simply to restore the royal supremacy and to allow communion in both kinds as a gesture to the Protestants. Her own feelings appear to have inclined towards a moderate Protestant theology, possibly on the lines of the 1549 Prayer Book, and towards the retention of many of the externals of Catholic practice. There was a good deal to be said for establishing a church which should represent a *via media* between Catholicism and Protestantism, and Elizabeth has often been given the credit for doing precisely this; but whatever she originally intended to do, this is not what she was allowed to do. Although Elizabeth more than any other single individual determined the shape of her church, she had to take into account the wishes of others. This did not mean simply, or even primarily, the wishes of the mass of her subjects. Obviously they could not be ignored, and whatever was done must be acceptable, or at least capable of being made acceptable in the long run, to as many people as possible. But far more important were the wishes of the politically active and the intellectually active minorities whose services were essential in running state and church. Here the influence of the returning Marian exiles was very considerable, and they found able allies in England, including some of Elizabeth's closest advisers. When he preached Mary's funeral sermon, Bishop White of Winchester had warned his hearers against 'the wolves . . . coming out of Geneva and other places of Germany'. The wolves from Geneva were in fact rather slow in returning and were not back in time to have much direct influence on the initial settlement, but the men who had formed the English Protestant communities in Zurich and Frankfurt and other cities abroad were certainly not 'lambs' from Elizabeth's point of view, and in the parliament of 1558–9 the queen was faced by a formidable minority which was not prepared to accept a moderate *interim* settlement limited to the re-introduction of the royal supremacy and a few concessions to Protestants.

Professor Neale has convincingly shown that in 1559 the government had to change its plans and bring in an Act of Uniformity and not merely an Act of Supremacy as had originally been intended.[1] The Act of Uniformity imposed on the nation not the relatively moderate Prayer Book of 1549, which might have been acceptable to the majority of Englishmen, but the much more Protestant Second Prayer Book of 1552.[2] The queen, it is true, saved something from the wreck which parliament made of her original plans. In the communion service the words used in the administration of the sacrament in the 1549 Prayer Book, which could be interpreted in a Catholic sense, were inserted before the words used in the 1552 Prayer Book, which seemed to make the eucharist simply a commemoration.[3] The 'Black Rubric' with regard to kneeling when receiving the sacrament, which had been inserted without parliamentary authority into the Prayer Book of 1552, was omitted in the Elizabethan Prayer Book. This rubric stated that kneeling did not imply adoration of the sacramental bread and wine or of 'any Corporal Presence of Christ's

[1] *Elizabeth I and her Parliaments* I: Chapters I and II (The Religious Settlement Before Easter; The Religious Settlement: After Easter).

[2] For a discussion of the Elizabethan Prayer Book, see Carl S. Meyer, *Elizabeth I and the Religious Settlement of 1559*, St. Louis, 1960, Chapter IV, 'The Prayer Book of Queen Elizabeth'.

[3] 'The Body of our Lord Jesus Christ, which was given for thee, preserve thy body and soul into everlasting life' (1549). 'Take and eat this in remembrance that Christ died for thee, and feed on him in thy heart with thanksgiving' (1552).

natural Flesh and Blood'. That would be 'Idolatry' since 'the natural Body and Blood of our Saviour Christ are in Heaven and not here . . .' This omission was not welcome to those Protestants who denied the Real Presence, and they would have much preferred to retain the Rubric; nor did they see any reason for removing from the Litany the words: 'From the tyranny of the Bishop of Rome and all his detestable enormities, good Lord, deliver us.'

The queen also retained considerable freedom of action with regard to the rites and ceremonies of her Church. The Act of Uniformity stated that the 'ornaments of the church and of the ministers' should be as established by parliament in 1549 'until other order shall be therein taken by the authority of the Queen's Majesty, with the advice of her commissioners . . . for causes ecclesiastical or of the metropolitan of this realm . . .' If any irreverence or contempt arose by misuse of the Prayer Book, 'the Queen's Majesty may, by the like advice . . . ordain and publish such further ceremonies or rites as may be most for the advancement of God's glory, the edifying of his Church, and the due reverence of Christ's holy mysteries and sacraments'.[1] Much would depend on the way in which the queen used her powers. The extreme Protestants were not pleased that the Church of England still retained what they regarded as the remnants of popery, but they hoped that this was merely a holding operation until such time as the queen ordained further ceremonies and rites. It was some time before they realised how big a difference of opinion there could be about what was 'for the advancement of God's glory and the edifying of his Church'.

The settlement of 1559 was thus not what Elizabeth had wanted. In so far as it was more extreme than she had wished, it would be more difficult to impose on all her subjects. We must remember that in 1559 the committed Protestants were only a minority of her people and that those who gave unqualified approval to the new Prayer Book were probably only a minority within a minority. Neither the queen nor those who forced these concessions upon her were fully satisfied with what had been done. Even the more moderate among the returning exiles had, while they were abroad, become accustomed to forms of religious worship considerably more Protestant than the Prayer Book of 1552, while the Calvinists from Geneva would in the long run be satisfied with nothing less than the full Genevan form of worship.

[1] Act of Uniformity, 1559: 1 Elizabeth c. 2, xiii.

Thus there is a good deal to be said for the view that the Elizabethan settlement was a *via media*, not between Catholicism and Protestantism, but between different forms of Protestantism, a half-way house between the Prayer Book of 1549 and the Genevan order of service. It was the highest common denominator among the various Protestant groups. For many of them it was only a beginning, the first step on the road that would lead to the establishment of the church of Christ on earth, but for the queen it was as far as she wished to go on what she saw was a very dangerous road. She was not prepared to be pushed any further, partly because she was personally not deeply committed to any particular theological system,[1] partly because she realised that the more she moved in the direction of extreme Protestantism, the smaller would be the hope of bringing everyone into her national church. Perhaps it might have been easier to win support for her church from the mass of Englishmen if she had not been compelled to go so far, but on the other hand a more cautious and conservative settlement would have been unacceptable to a potentially very dangerous and very active minority.[2] Looking back on the reign at the end of her forty-five years as queen, she could feel that the decision of 1559 was the right one. She had not in fact succeeded in imposing complete religious unity or in destroying the threats from Catholics and from Puritans. There were still formidable dissenting minorities, and, like Macbeth, the queen might well have said:

We have scotch'd the snake, not kill'd it

as far as religious nonconformity was concerned, but at least the challenge had been contained within limits beyond which it seemed unlikely to break, and the Church established in 1559 had, through long familiarity and through the development of its own ethos, become in some sense acceptable to the majority of Englishmen. An Edward VI or a Lady Jane Grey would have gone much further to the left in religion, and the political and religious unity of England might have

[1] The quite extraordinary tenacity with which the queen resisted attempts to make her church more 'Protestant' was no doubt influenced by her assessment of the views of her people, but it may also be the result of strong personal feelings. She stubbornly resisted such attempts even when it seemed politically wiser to give way.

[2] Time was not on her side. Professor Neale writes: 'In giving way to the Protestant divines Elizabeth had been wise. Thereby she obtained as conservative and comprehensive a Church as was possible. . . . No subsequent Elizabethan House of Commons would have agreed to the Prayer Book of 1559—without, indeed, the most bitter struggle and a degree of coercion fatal to harmony . . .' [*Elizabeth I and her Parliaments*: I. 82–3].

been as seriously threatened as it had been under the Catholic Mary.

The national church which was established by the Acts of Uniformity and Supremacy in 1559 was national only in the sense that all Englishmen were required by law and under various penalties to adhere publicly to it and to attend its services. The government and the parliament which imposed it spoke in the name of the people of England, and in theory all Englishmen gave their assent to laws passed in the parliament. But in fact only a small minority of Englishmen had the right to vote for those who nominally represented them. In 1559 it was still an open question whether the members of parliament spoke even for the majority of the governing class, let alone for the man in the street or the man behind the plough. There were no public opinion polls by which the views of the different sections of the community could be tested. Those who made the settlement must have thought that there was a reasonable chance that it would be accepted, but only time could show whether they were right, and the new church faced a difficult and uncertain future.

When we look back at the early days of the Elizabethan Church with the knowledge of the way in which it established itself in the four centuries after 1559, it is only too easy to think of it in terms of what it was to become in the course of time; to regard it as being from the very beginning the Church of England, with a developed theology, liturgy and organisation; a church in which the majority of men and women were baptised, brought up, married and buried; a church holding a unique place in national life. It is only too easy to forget that in 1558 it did not exist at all, that on Mary's death on 17 November 1558 and for some months after, England was still officially a Roman Catholic country in communion with the see of Rome. There was, of course, a long tradition of dissent from Roman Catholicism going back to Wyclif and the Lollards. There were, too, a number of English Protestants both at home and abroad; there was a considerable Protestant literature built up over the years and there was the memory of the break with Rome under Henry VIII and of a national Protestant Church under Edward VI. The vigour of the Protestant underground movement had recently been displayed for all to see by the three hundred martyrs, mostly humble people, who died for their faith under Mary. But although there were various Protestant traditions, there was no organised English Protestant Church with a clearly defined body of doctrine and form of worship, able and ready to take over once Elizabeth became queen, in the way that the Church of England was able to take over again in 1660 when Charles II was restored and the religious experiments of the Commonwealth came to an end.

The infant church which came into being in 1559 as a result of the Acts of Uniformity and Supremacy was handicapped by a number of serious weaknesses—some of them temporary and capable of being remedied, at least in part, before the queen's long life had run its course; others of a much more lasting and fundamental nature which were destined to become even more serious with the passing of time. But if there was weakness, there was also strength, and a Church which was in 1559 a rather sickly baby which might easily succumb to the many dangers which threatened a sixteenth-century childhood had acquired by the end of the reign a vigour and a vitality which carried it through fresh perils in the seventeenth century. The history of Elizabethan Catholicism and of Elizabethan Puritanism can be properly understood only against this background of weakness and strength in the established church. The weakness in the Church of England made it very vulnerable to attack both from the right and the left; the strength meant that these attacks could not be successfully pressed home against the solid ranks of those who supported the queen and the religious settlement to which she was committed.

One of the very serious deficiencies of the Church of England in 1559 was that there was considerable uncertainty about what kind of church it was. The Book of Common Prayer, it is true, gave some indication of its doctrinal position, and the Thirty Nine Articles of 1563 were to give more definite form to its theology, but the Prayer Book and the Articles were not without ambiguity, and it was to become only too clear that they could mean different things to different men. Indeed for most of the Elizabethan period the Church of England failed to develop a theology of its own. Professor Chadwick points out that: 'During the whole of what might be called the formative period of reformed theology there is not something which one might call an English school of theology, but only English theologians influenced by Wittenberg, or Zurich, or Geneva, or Strasbourg.'[1] Not until right at the end of the reign did the Church produce in Hooker anyone who might be called a really great constructive and original

[1] *The English Church and the Continent*, edit. C. R. Dodwell, 1959, p. 61.

thinker.[1] This official theological vagueness was, it is true, an advantage from the point of view of a government anxious above all things to include as many people as possible within a single established church, but it was not a desirable state of affairs from the point of view of zealous ecclesiastics and laymen anxious to establish in England the true church of Christ. Comprehensiveness based on wide differences in belief was not a virtue to those who believed that theological truth could be known with certainty, and the committed Protestant who had strengthened his faith in Zurich or in Frankfurt or in Geneva could hardly be expected to accept with enthusiasm the view that what men believed in their hearts was no business of the state provided they conformed outwardly and went to church. He might well feel that if Elizabeth did not make windows in men's souls she was failing in her duty as a Christian Prince.

Nor was it easy in 1559 to be enthusiastic about a settlement which few expected to last. For a great many ordinary people it must have appeared merely as one more of the bewildering changes in religion imposed from above. In towns and villages there were many who could be relied upon to do as they were told and to attend the official services in their parish churches. For most of them there was nowhere else where they could worship, and it must be remembered that the habit of public worship on Sundays and holy days had centuries of tradition behind it and was too deeply ingrained in sixteenth-century men and women to be lightly rejected—quite apart from the temporal and spiritual risks involved if they did reject it. But passive acceptance of what was laid down by law was a very different thing from active commitment. In 1559 there were few committed Anglicans. People can only be committed to something they have learnt to know and love—and the Church of England was at the beginning of the reign still an unknown quantity.

Nor could the Church of England in its early stages count on the enthusiastic support of those who had deep religious convictions. The committed Catholics naturally hoped that it would in due course pass away and be replaced by the old religion. In England, or in exile abroad, they waited patiently for better times to come. Among the committed Protestants there was also a hope that the arrangements of 1559 would be only temporary. To them the Church was only a half-

---

[1] This is not intended to suggest that Bishop Jewel's contribution was of little importance. See pp. 50–52.

way house. Much survived within it that smacked of popery and superstition. Concessions had to be made, they felt, to the evil state of the times; the godly reformation could not be completed all at once. The nightmare of Mary's reign had passed, much had been achieved, and more would follow as soon as their godly princess saw the way clear amidst the perils at home and abroad. Some of them were restless and thought that the strict letter of the law need not be followed too closely. Many of the bishops were ready to turn a blind eye to practices which were not strictly legal, and so, like the Catholics, the Protestant enthusiasts bided their time, made temporary concessions in non-essentials and looked hopefully for the day when the work of reforming the church could be completed and all relics of popery and superstition could be swept away.

The Elizabethan Church had the misfortune to be deprived of the services of many able men who in different circumstances might have made a tremendously important contribution to its organisation, its theology and its spiritual life. It alienated Catholics such as Thomas Stapleton, Gregory Martin, Nicholas Sander, Edmund Campion, Robert Southwell, Robert Parsons and John Gerard; it was unable to win the undivided loyalty of Puritans such as Thomas Cartwright, Walter Travers, John Field, Thomas Wilcox and the zealous and courageous men who composed and circulated the Marprelate Tracts. If men like these, with their great abilities and their profound religious convictions, had supplemented the work of Jewel and of Hooker, of Parker, Grindal and Whitgift, then the Church of England might have enjoyed a flowering of religious thought and religious life even more spectacular than the great achievements of the Elizabethan secular world. But comprehensiveness proved impossible, and all too often those who occupied high positions in the Church were markedly inferior intellectually and spiritually to their Catholic and to their Puritan critics.

There have been differences of opinion among historians concerning the character of the Elizabethan bishops. Professor Trevor-Roper has described them as 'earnest, Protestant-minded, worried men, burdened with duties, uncertain of their position in a society which was both revolutionary and conservative, and labouring under a double disapproval: of the queen, who disliked their wives, and of the Puritans, who disliked their doctrines'.[1] Dr. A. L. Rowse writes of

[1] H. R. Trevor-Roper, *Historical Essays*, 1957, p. 130.

them: 'I do not know a single Elizabethan bishop who was a bad man . . . The great majority of them were conscientious hard-working men struggling in difficult circumstances with a heavy burden of administrative toil'.[1] He thinks that: 'On the whole, the bishops were a respectable lot, for all that they were traduced by their enemies at the time . . . and for all that some of the mud has stuck.'[2] There is certainly need for a thorough study of the bishops as a group,[3] and generalisation is difficult when we take into account that there were nearly eighty individuals spread over two generations who at one time or another held bishoprics under Queen Elizabeth. In their ranks were certainly to be found time-servers and ambitious men, and Dr. Rowse's statement that none of them was bad can only be upheld if one applies to them rather different standards from those usually applied to spiritual leaders. There are indications, too, that the bishops appointed in the early part of the reign were more deeply committed to the cause of religion than the second generation of Elizabethan bishops. As the Church became more securely established, there were plenty of ambitious and intelligent men hastening to jump on the band-waggon; there were fewer men anxious to establish Christ's Kingdom on earth and more whose main qualification was academic ability and a capacity to act as good administrators in a state church.

The position of Elizabethan bishops was indeed difficult. Not only did they have to face resistance and insults from Catholics and from Puritans, but their authority in relation to the state and to secular society was by no means unquestioned. They held office by virtue of authority given to them by the Supreme Governor of the Church. They could not govern the church as they liked. They had to keep one eye on the queen and another on parliament. For them, there could be no appeal to Rome against the civil power. Archbishop Parker continually found himself in embarrassing positions as he compared what ought to be done with what the state allowed him to do, and when Archbishop Grindal acted in accordance with his conscience, he found himself suspended for years from the exercise of his office.[4] Elizabeth I did not encourage her bishops to take an independent line.

[1] A. L. Rowse, *The England of Elizabeth*, 1950, p. 389.
[2] *Ibid.*, p. 408.
[3] For a series of short lives of the bishops, see F. O. White, *Lives of the Elizabethan Bishops of the Anglican Church*, 1898.
[4] See p. 155.

The higher clergy were made to realise that the Church could not run its own affairs, whether it was a question of ecclesiastical wealth or of more fundamental matters like doctrine and liturgy. They had to accept the fact that major policy decisions affecting religion were made by laymen, that religious enthusiasm and the desire for religious reformation could be tolerated only within the bounds laid down by a government which was not concerned solely to promote the cause of true religion. It was not easy to draw the line between the things that were God's and the things that were Caesar's, and any bishop who wanted to continue in office had to accept official policy in a way that left him open to attack from Catholics and Puritans alike.

As for the ordinary clergy, the priests and curates in the parishes, they too had serious weaknesses which made the Church particularly vulnerable. It is true, as Fr. Hughes has noted, that the clerical proletariat in the sixteenth century did not give much trouble to the state and that there were plenty of vicars of Bray. Of the many thousands of priests who had accepted the pope and the mass under Mary, there were only a few hundred who refused to accept the Acts of Supremacy and Uniformity and the new Prayer Book of 1559, but outward conformity was a very different thing from spiritual commitment. There must have been a great many in the early stages of the reign who conformed because they were in the habit of doing what they were told to do.

Moreover, at the beginning of the period standards of clerical education were pitifully low, and the majority of parish priests were quite unable to preach. These 'dumb dogs' were to provide a fruitful source of complaint to critics of the church. In addition, there were other weaknesses. Inevitably, there were in such a poorly-paid profession a considerable number of men whose conduct gave scandal to those who were only too ready to be scandalised. Drunkenness, gambling, brawling, tavern haunting and wenching were common enough among the clergy in Elizabethan as in earlier times. Many of the parishioners must have taken such weaknesses for granted in their clergy, but the deficiencies of its ministers made the Church increasingly vulnerable in an age when there was a growing body of critics, both Puritan and Catholic, using such information for propaganda purposes against the establishment. The systematic and critical surveys of the clergy made by Puritans need not always be taken too seriously,[1] but the

[1] See p. 226 ff.

image of the Church of England cannot have been improved by long lists of the deficiencies of its ministers in which one parson was summed up as 'a drunckard, loden with these three benefices'; another as 'a notorious swearer, a dicer, a carder, a hawker and hunter, a verie careless person, he had a childe by a maid', and yet another as 'very drunke, unlearned, and idle, unsound in religion, and a secreat perswader of the simple to poperie, one that praieth for the dead . . . vicious and licentious of life, a companion at all games, an alehouse haunter'.[1]

The Elizabethan Church had to face the fact that there existed an increasingly educated and self-conscious laity very ready to criticise defects in its ministers and determined to keep the church in its proper place. The governing class, including the queen, the nobility, the gentry and the little groups of wealthier citizens who controlled the towns, did not mean to let the bishop or the parson lord it over them. There was a strong erastian tradition and a strong anti-clerical tradition which wanted the wings of the clergy to be kept clipped, and in matters of doctrine and ritual there were many laymen who thought themselves as good as or better than their ministers. It is doubtful whether there were many parsons in the established church who could command anything like the respect which the zealous Catholic gave to the seminary priests and the Jesuit, or which the numerous Puritan congregations were willing to give to their chosen leaders. It was partly a question of education. It was also a matter of men speaking with authority. The Catholic priest and the Puritan preacher were confident that they taught the truth. The Anglican parson was not always so sure of himself.

Although its powers were drastically limited in comparison with those which the Church of Rome had enjoyed before the Reformation, the Elizabethan Church was nevertheless allowed to retain an elaborate organisation of church courts which gave it considerable authority in men's lives. The efficient working of these courts was, however, made difficult by the fact that for the whole of Elizabeth's reign the Church of England failed to develop a satisfactory code of ecclesiastical law. The need for such a code to replace the canon law of the medieval Church was all too clear. Earlier on, Cranmer had

---

[1] These are but a few of the many similar comments in 'A Survey of the Ministry', 1586, to be found in *The Seconde Parte of a Register*, edit. A. E. Peel, 2 vols., Cambridge, 1915.

drawn up an elaborate new code, but it had not been promulgated, and there were many laymen and common lawyers who viewed with misgiving any proposals to give the Church a new canon law which might make its courts more efficient and more powerful. Moreover, the Church had inherited from the past not only much of the machinery of the church courts but also many of the abuses which had been so fruitful a source of anti-clericalism. The disgruntled layman who had fallen foul of the spiritual power, who had been harassed in the archdeacon's court or threatened with excommunication in a tithes dispute, was likely to listen with sympathy to the Puritan critics of the establishment, even when he was not himself particularly concerned with the theological questions which led to the criticism.

Mr. Christopher Hill has shown convincingly and with a wealth of illustration the importance of what he calls 'non-doctrinal reasons for disliking the established church'.[1] Even among those who did not dislike the church, there were many who were prepared to weaken it economically whenever it was to their advantage to do so. The queen herself, the nobility, the gentry, the universities, the wealthy townsmen and many of the bishops and the higher clergy were ready to enrich themselves at the expense of an institution which lacked the power to defend itself. Lands of bishoprics and dean and chapter lands were fair game to those with influence and patronage. The Supreme Governor of the Church of England got her share of the plunder, and it was not concern for the spiritual welfare of the realm that led her to keep the see of Oxford vacant for 41 years; that of Ely for 19 years, and that of Bristol for 14 years.[2] Mr. Hill notes that: 'In 1591, and again in 1598, the see of Salisbury was hawked around to the highest bidder. The successful purchasers had to gratify Ralegh and Sir Robert Cecil.'[3] Archbishop Whitgift complained: 'The temporalty seek to make the clergy beggars, that we may depend upon them.' He might have added that a considerable number of his brother bishops were determined not to become paupers and were highly successful in enriching themselves, as well as their friends and relations, at the expense of the church. Edwin Sandys who was given the see of Worcester in 1559 has been described as 'a spoliator, who robbed the Church for self-enrichment, impoverishing his successors by leasing out the

---

[1] Christopher Hill, *Economic Problems of the Church from Archbishop Whitgift to the Long Parliament*, Oxford, 1956.
[2] *Ibid.*, p. 15.   [3] *Ibid.*, p. 16.

estates of the see to his own family and dependents';[1] Dr. A. L. Rowse writes of Bishop John Scory of Hereford that he 'was not a pretty piece of work though he had a pretty financial sense; he presented three sinecure prebends to his wife, and his son to a prebend in his cathedral: a convenient arrangement for the family';[2] and Mr. Hill comments on Bishop Hughes of St. Asaph he held an archdeaconry and sixteen benefices *in commendam*, and that he was reported to have leased episcopal manors for long periods to his wife, children, sisters and cousins.[3]

There were a great many ways in which the laity could take advantage of the weakness of the church.[4] There was increasing resistance to the payment of tithes and a great deal of evasion, particularly by those most capable of paying. Impropriation of livings by laymen and by corporations had gone on to such a degree that Grindal in 1576 complained to the Queen that 'this church of England hath been by appropriations . . . spoiled of the livings, which at the first were appointed to the offices of preaching and teaching . . . So as at this day, in my opinion, where one church is able to yield sufficient living for a learned preacher, there be at least seven churches unable to do the same'.[5] The deficiencies of the system were obvious, but there was a vast vested interest in it, including many of the bishops and wealthier clergy as well as the universities and the laity. No one wanted reforms which might damage his property rights.

When so many livings were poor, the standard of education of many of the parish clergy was bound to be low. Pluralism flourished not only as a means by which the more fortunate and influential of the clergy accumulated wealth but also because livings were in themselves often too poor to provide for the needs of a priest.[6] The figures for Lincoln in 1576 show that 77 out of 466 ministers were pluralists.

[1] F. O. White, *Lives of the Elizabethan Bishops*, 1898, p. 100. Sandys became bishop of London in 1570 and archbishop of York in 1577.

[2] A. L. Rowse, *The England of Elizabeth*, 1950, p. 410.

[3] Christopher Hill, *Economic Problems of the Church*, pp. 18–19. There are very many other examples.

[4] They are examined in great detail in Mr. Hill's *Economic Problems of the Church*.

[5] Christopher Hill, *Economic Problems of the Church*, p. 139. In Chapter VI Mr. Hill examines the many complications arising from impropriation of livings. The owner of the impropriation received the income and paid only a part, often a very small part, to the vicar. By the end of the century something like one third of all livings were impropriated.

[6] *Ibid.*, Chapter X, 'Pluralism and non-residence'.

At least 1 in 8 of the ministers were non-resident, and less than 1 in 6 were licensed to preach.[1] Attempts in 1563 and 1581 to augment the livings of poor parishes came to nothing.[2] There were too many influential people determined to maintain the *status quo*. The laity did not want to surrender their pickings, and the higher clergy naturally resisted any suggestion that poor parishes should be financed at the expense of bishops' lands and dean and chapter lands; nor did the Church show any enthusiasm for Puritan proposals to establish salaried clergy. The laity with its rights of patronage and presentation had already encroached deeply on the independence of the church; if laymen paid the salaries of the clergy they would be even more influential in controlling the pulpits.

One must not exaggerate the poverty of the Church. There were plenty of wealthy clerics. Archbishop Parker, spending £448 a year on servants' wages, and Archbishop Whitgift, attended by 1,000 servants, 40 of them gentlemen wearing chains of gold, did not present a public image of clerical poverty, although they did offer a target to their critics who suggested that this ostentatious wealth might be better used for other purposes. Taking the church as a whole its total wealth during the Elizabethan period may not have fallen, but it fell relatively to that of other sections of society, and this meant loss of prestige. In that materialist world there was no admiration for holy poverty. Moreover, the wealth was badly distributed, and if there were a number of rich clerics, there were many who were very poor. There was nothing new in this. It was characteristic of the medieval church as well as of the sixteenth-century church, but the division between rich and poor clergy was increasingly serious at a time when the organisation of the church was being subjected to fierce criticism. There was a body of have-nots among the clergy who had economic as well as religious reasons for wanting to reform the Church.[3]

Few historians would disagree with Mr. Christopher Hill's conclusion that 'there was a whole complex of causes, apart from the narrowly doctrinal, which might make men hostile to the ruling hierarchy in the Church of England.'[4] Mr. Hill was concerned particularly with the period from 1583, when Whitgift became Archbishop

---

[1] Christopher Hill, *Economic Problems of the Church*, p. 225.   [2] *Ibid.*, pp. 245–6.
[3] See Christopher Hill, *Economic Problems of the Church*, Chapter IX, 'Social and Economic Status of the Clergy'.
[4] *Ibid.*, p. 351.

C

of Canterbury, to the outbreak of the Civil War, but the causes which he examines were operative from the beginning of Elizabeth's reign, and indeed many of them went back far beyond 1558. The leaders of the church under Elizabeth were faced with a situation in which economic, social, political and religious factors made the institution they served vulnerable to attack from many directions. They were not, for the most part, fools or knaves, and many of them were genuinely anxious to put things right. They achieved a good deal, but many of their difficulties were of such a nature that they could not meet them without creating for themselves even more serious problems. These 'earnest, Protestant-minded, worried men' had plenty of things to worry about, and it is hardly surprising that Dr. Rowse, looking at 'their atrabilious, constipated expressions, always grave, often sour', does not find them congenial.

Yet the fact remains that in spite of all the difficulties and in spite of the very serious threats to the church from within and from without, it achieved a remarkable measure of success. The queen did not succeed in destroying either the Puritan or the Catholic threat, and the economic and social problems of the Church were certainly not decreasing, but the fragile plant of 1559 had established deep roots by 1603. Even the tempest of the Civil War could not destroy it. It had not succeeded in imposing complete religious unity in England. The minorities which rejected it, or which wished to reform it in such a way that it would become something entirely different, were formidable minorities, but for all that, the remarkable thing was not the extent to which the Church of England had failed to become the accepted religion of Englishman, but the extent to which it had succeeded.

Some of the reasons why this was so will become clear as we examine the Papists and the Puritans and see how they too had their problems which prevented them from pushing home their attacks as effectively as they wanted to. We must bear in mind too that the Church of England had built-in advantages—the backing of the state, the support of the whole official machinery of propaganda, and the tremendous benefit of being associated in men's minds with a remarkably successful government and a tremendously popular queen. It was in possession of magnificent cathedrals and beautiful parish churches, and the noble and dignified English of its Prayer Book was in time to become the birth-right of Englishmen. To some extent it realised the desirability of involving the laity directly in its services, so that they were not merely passive spectators of ceremonies performed by the minister. In 1560, Bishop Jewel wrote enthusiastically to Peter Martyr: 'The people are everywhere exceedingly inclined to the better part. The practice of joining in church music has very much conduced to this. For as soon as they had once commenced singing in public, in only one little church in London, immediately not only the churches in the neighbourhood, but even the towns far distant, began to vie with each other in the same practice . . . This sadly annoys the mass-priests, and the devil.'[1] Jewel was, perhaps, too optimistic about the immediate future, but in the long run his optimism was justified.

By the end of the reign the Church of England was for the majority of Elizabeth's subjects the only form of religion of which they had first-hand experience. Catholic priests might say mass in secret in many places, but they could reach only a small section of the community; Puritan preachers and lecturers might operate like a fifth-column within the church and hope to change it; but the Catholic priest worked under very great difficulties and the Puritan preacher had to tread warily to avoid trouble. The majority of Englishmen attending the parish church on Sundays and holy days probably never saw a Catholic priest and probably never heard a Puritan sermon. They listened instead, week after week, to the services of the Book of Common Prayer; they were baptised in the Church of England, married according to its rites, and came to it for the last time for the burial service. As long as they conformed outwardly and did not openly speak against its teaching, they were left alone, and there was then, as now, a wide range of doctrinal beliefs among the members of the church. There seems to have been comparatively little heresy-hunting as far as the ordinary people were concerned. They did not find the official religion too demanding or too repressive.

Thus by the end of Elizabeth's reign the church established in 1559 had become in fact, as well as in name, the Church of England. In a period of over forty years it had grown in self-confidence; it had found able apologists, and the great Hooker, building on the foundation of earlier writers, had succeeded in making it appear intellectually respectable and reasonable. It had survived the violent attacks of

[1] *The Zurich Letters*, edit. the Rev. Hastings Robinson, Parker Society, 1842, I. 71, 5 March 1560.

Catholics and Puritans; it had apparently entered calm waters in the last years of the queen's reign, and it faced with self-confidence a new age. Many were aware of its unsolved problems, but few would have expected that within forty years it would meet with a major disaster.

2

The Deviationists

And as to ... the Observation of the uniform Order in Religion;
you are to endeavour your selves to the best of your powers and
understandings ... to further, set forth and maintain the same ...
And here great Observations and watch should be had of the with-
drawers and hinderers thereof ... Amongst these I mean to
comprehend, as well those that be too swift, as those that be too
slow ...

Sir Nicholas Bacon, 8 May 1559

IT has often been assumed that the Elizabethans can be neatly
divided into three parts—Anglicans, Papists and Puritans—and that
each group held more or less recognisable views which distinguished
it sharply from the others. The Anglicans are seen as the orthodox
officially-approved centre party which was being attacked from the
right by the Papists, who wanted to destroy the Church of England,
and from the left by the Puritans, who wanted to seize control of the
church and change it into something different. The work of historians
would be very much easier if all Elizabethans could be labelled in this
way and put in the appropriate religious boxes, but the reality is not
so simple as this threefold division suggests. Sixteenth-century reference to 'Church Papists' who attended the services of the Church of
England but who were Papists at heart, and modern references to
'Anglican Puritans' and to 'the Puritan character of the Elizabethan
Church'[1] remind us that the dividing lines between the groups were
not clearly drawn. We must never forget that in this period of over
forty years there was considerable variety and continual change both

[1] A. G. Dickens, *The English Reformation*, pp. 313, 314.

27

among the 'orthodox' groups in the Church and among those who differed from them.

Of the three main religious groupings the Papists were the most easily recognisable and the least subject to change. A Papist or Roman Catholic was a member of a church which, he believed, had been founded by Christ and which was governed by bishops whose authority had been handed down in direct succession from the Apostles. Its head on earth was the bishop of Rome, the vicar of Christ and the successor of St. Peter whom Christ had made head of his Church. The central act of worship in this church was the mass during which the priest, who could be made a priest only by the power invested in a bishop, used the words which changed the bread and wine into the Body and Blood of Christ. In this church a considerable and complicated theology had been developed over the centuries, and there had also grown up a great variety of devotions and 'pious practices'. For the Roman Catholic there was only one true church of Christ, and outside it there was no salvation. The English Roman Catholic regarded himself as belonging to that part of the universal church which had been established in the sixth century by St. Augustine who had been sent to England for this purpose by Pope Gregory the Great. This church—the *Ecclesia Anglicana*—had continued for nearly a thousand years until in the 1530's King Henry VIII had broken with the pope and led his people into schism by repudiating the authority of the bishop of Rome and cutting the church in England off from the body of the universal church. Later, this English church had become not only schismatical, but also heretical; that is to say, it not only denied the authority of the pope but it also taught false doctrine.

The distinction between Papists and members of the Church of England should, at least in theory, have been absolutely clear from the very beginning of the Elizabethan period. The Act of Supremacy of 1559 expressly forbade any subject of the queen to recognise the authority, spiritual or temporal, of any foreign prince, and the Act of Uniformity prohibited the use of any forms of service except those in the Book of Common Prayer. All subjects of the queen were required under penalty to attend their parish church on Sundays and holy days. Thus, if they obeyed the law, Roman Catholics could not legally recognise the spiritual authority of the pope, that is to say, they could not legally remain Roman Catholics; nor could they participate in the central act of worship of their religion—the mass. The government had from the beginning no intention of officially permitting two forms of religion, although in practice it knew it could not hope to compel everyone to conform immediately. Its policy and its intentions were clearly stated by the Lord Keeper, Sir Nicholas Bacon, at the end of the parliament in May 1559 when he urged the M.P.s to further the Observation of the Uniform Order in Religion 'which by great and deliberate advice in Parliament hath been established'. He issued a special warning against 'those, that subtilly, by indirect means, seek to procure the contrary'. Offenders were to be given 'sharp and severe correction . . . and that in the very beginning, without respect of persons'.[1]

Logically, every committed Roman Catholic should have refused to recognise in any way the newly established church; and from very early in the reign there were Papists who fled from the country in which they could no longer legally practise their religion. Others remained in England but consistently absented themselves from the parish church in which heretical services were now held. Nevertheless, there were very many who were prepared to conform to the extent of attending the official services on Sundays and holy days, even though they did not accept the authority of the Church of England or recognise it as a true church. Many of them believed that they could attend the parish church with a good conscience, provided they did not give internal consent but merely appeared as a formality to avoid the penalties which the law could impose on absentees. Some thought it desirable to show what they really thought by ostentatiously ignoring what was going on, by reading Catholic books of devotion during the service, or by going to sleep. The question of whether a good Roman Catholic might conform in this way was still being debated as late as the 1580's, and only slowly did the stricter view prevail. Even when it did, there were still many who preferred to conform outwardly rather than face the possible consequence of refusing. The existence of an unknown number of these 'Church Papists' complicates the problem of deciding how many Englishmen did or did not accept the teaching of the established church. There were probably many nominal members of the Church of England who were really Catholic at heart and Catholic in their general outlook.

[1] *The Journal of all the Parliaments during the Reign of Queen Elizabeth*, collected by Sir Simonds D'Ewes, London, 1682, p. 34.

Some have even put William Shakespeare in this category. It is hardly surprising that there was among the Protestants of Tudor and Stuart England an ever-present fear that many who outwardly conformed would become Roman Catholics again whenever it was safe to do so.

The situation was further complicated by the papal bull of excommunication of 1570[1] and the subsequent attempts to enforce it. The right of the pope to depose an heretical ruler was not an Article of Faith of the Roman Church, but it was a right which the papacy had repeatedly exercised in the Middle Ages and which it was unwilling to abandon in the sixteenth century. It obstinately clung to this right, just as in the nineteenth century it obstinately asserted its temporal power over the Papal States. The sixteenth-century Catholic who questioned the papal deposing power did so at his peril. In practice the vast majority of Papists in England ignored the papal bull of excommunication,[2] but there was a small but very influential group of English Catholics in exile, including William Allen, Robert Parsons and Nicholas Sander,[3] who were committed whole-heartedly to the view that when circumstances became favourable, the pope had the right and the duty of declaring the bull of excommunication to be in force and of calling on Catholic princes to depose the heretical queen with the assistance, it was hoped, of a Catholic rising in England. It is clear that if an invasion had come, most English Catholics would have supported their queen against the invaders, but in a way they would have been acting illogically in so doing, since from their point of view the Church of England was an heretical church which the government was seeking to impose by force on all Englishmen. Unless the papacy would openly or tacitly abandon its deposing power, English Catholics might find themselves faced with a conflict of loyalties. The government exploited this dilemma with great skill, and the desperate anxiety of English Papists to show their loyalty to the queen, combined with their habit of attending the official services in order to avoid legal penalties, gradually pushed over into the ranks of the established church many who would have remained Roman Catholics if they had not been subjected to these pressures.

---

[1] See pp. 69–71.

[2] In 1580 it was officially stated that it was not binding on the consciences of Catholics 'as things now stand' but that it was still binding on heretics. See p. 162.

[3] See pp. 61, 69, 199 ff.

The effect of all this was to blur the clear line of division which ought to have existed between the members of the Church of Rome and the members of the Church of England. There existed under Elizabeth I a large group of people consisting of 'Church Papists', nominal members of the Church of England who were neither fully committed Catholics nor fully committed Protestants. From this group there was continual movement to the right and to the left. The Catholic revival associated with the seminary priests and the Jesuits won large numbers of them over to the committed Catholic position, but many finally settled down in the Church of England where their sympathies would presumably incline them to adopt a moderate 'Anglican' rather than an extreme 'Protestant' or 'Puritan' position.[1]

Although it is not always possible in the case of particular individuals to say where their real religious allegiance lay, there is no difficulty in seeing the sharp differences in theology and in form of worship which divided the Church of England from the Church of Rome. It is much more difficult to draw a line between what for convenience may be called the 'Anglican' position and the position of the 'Puritans'. Indeed, we are confronted with the problem of whether in the Elizabethan period we ought to draw a line at all.

Before discussing 'Puritanism' it is desirable to consider what we mean by 'Anglicanism'. The word has been used in two different ways. It has been employed to describe the religious settlement established by the Acts of Supremacy and Uniformity in 1559, and the Church of England then established has been commonly referred to as 'The Anglican Church'. The word has also been used to refer, not to the whole Elizabethan Church, but to a particular religious tradition within it which was becoming of increasing importance in the later Elizabethan period and which was to become very influential indeed in the seventeenth century. This tradition was partly a reaction against European Protestant theology, especially Calvinism; partly a reaction against extreme Protestant and Puritan religious practices which

---

[1] It is conceivable that the growth of 'anglo-Catholic' and anti-calvinist views at the expense of the strongly 'Protestant' traditions in the Church of England in the later sixteenth and early seventeenth century may have been influenced, directly or indirectly, by the existence within the Church of a body of 'Church Papists' and 'pseudo-papists' who had finally ended up as committed members of the Church of England. This is no more than a suggestion. The matter requires further investigation. The reaction against Calvinism was not, of course, merely an English phenomenon.

sought to sweep away all the 'relics of popery' within the Church of England; and partly a stressing of those 'Catholic' elements which were contained in the original settlement but which had hitherto been undervalued. The 'Anglican' was prepared to retain many of the ancient beliefs and ceremonies provided they were not directly in conflict with the teaching of the Bible and provided there was a case for them on rational grounds. The apologist of this tradition was Richard Hooker who in 1593 published the first four volumes of his great 'Anglican' apologia—*the Laws of Ecclesiastical Polity*. When the word is used in this restricted sense, 'Anglicanism' cannot be said to have been really important much before the last decade of Elizabeth's reign.[1]

In this book the word has normally been used in its wider sense to mean the religion established by law at the beginning of Elizabeth's reign. In order to avoid confusion it has been used as sparingly as possible, and the Elizabethan Church has been usually referred to as the Church of England.

The problem which confronts us is the relationship of the 'Puritans' to the Church of England, and this raises a whole series of questions. Was a Puritan a member of the Church of England? Were there major differences in theology, in religious practices and in views about church government between Puritans and non-Puritans within the Church, and if so, what were they? Did all those who were labelled 'Puritans' share a common set of beliefs, and were they all agreed about what they wanted done? Is 'Puritanism' solely or primarily a term with a religious significance, or can it legitimately be used in a much wider sense to include 'political Puritans' and that large group of people who had grievances against the established church for reasons which were not mainly religious? Those who write about the Puritans have given very different answers to such questions because they are not agreed about what a 'Puritan' was. The question is in fact highly complex and there is no simple and satisfactory answer. All we can do here is to examine some of the reasons why it is so difficult to define Puritanism, to look at the way in which a number of

---

[1] 'Here first the Anglican Communion was made aware of itself as an independent branch of the Church Universal, neither Roman nor Calvinist, but at once Catholic and Protestant, with a positive doctrine and discipline of its own and a definite mission in the wide economy of grace . . . The publication of the *Ecclesiastical Polity* is thus the given *terminus a quo* for any compilation designed to illustrate the specific genius of Anglicanism.' *Anglicanism*, edit. P. E. More and F. L. Cross, 1935, p. xix.

historians have treated the problem, and to try to find a working definition which we can use in this book.[1]

The first thing to bear in mind is that, apart from a very small body of separatists who left the Church, the Puritans of the Elizabethan age regarded themselves as members of the Church of England. Their aim was not to leave it but to reform it from within, to make *their* church what they believed it ought to be. Cartwright and Travers and Field saw themselves as teachers of true doctrine in a church which had not yet accepted the whole truth of the Gospel. Both the bishops who harried the Puritans and the Puritans who attacked the bishops maintained that they were members of the established church. They were like members of one family who quarrelled savagely with each other but who quickly formed a united front when outsiders like the Papists tried to take advantage of their division.

One of the difficulties in deciding at what point a Puritan ceased in fact to be an orthodox member of the Church of England was that orthodoxy was by no means clearly defined.[2] It was hard then, as it is now, to say when an Anglican was not an Anglican. The Acts of Supremacy and Uniformity, the Prayer Book of 1559 and the Thirty-Nine Articles of 1563 laid down a framework of belief, but they were not without ambiguity, and their authority was not unchallenged. Very quickly the English began one of their favourite sports—arguing about the meaning of the Prayer Book and the Articles. The Church of England during Elizabeth's reign was still very immature and was experiencing the difficulties and the excitements of adolescence. There was plenty of room for debate about its theology, its organisation and its liturgy. The need for discipline conflicted with the claims of freedom and, like Mrs. Tabitha Twitchit, Queen Elizabeth often found herself in the position of an anxious parent of an unruly family. The Church included within itself a number of different, and often conflicting, religious traditions. The pre-Reformation Wycliffite heritage and the formative work of Archbishop Cranmer mingled with the teachings of continental reformers. The doctrinal influence of the great John Calvin was very powerful and much of his teaching was accepted as orthodoxy by the bishops and the clergy, particularly in

---

[1] For further discussion, see Basil Hall, 'Puritanism: the Problem of Definition' in *Studies in Church History II*, edit. G. J. Cuming, Ecclesiastical History Society, 1965.

[2] In the Canons of 1604 the Church of England did attempt to say what was meant by membership of the church. See p. 357 ff.

the University of Cambridge which was the creative theological centre and the most important seminary of the Elizabethan Church. But although he was the most important, Calvin was not the only continental reformer who influenced English theological thinking. There was a rich legacy from Luther, and in addition many of the bishops had in exile made personal friendships with Henry Bullinger, Peter Martyr and other great Protestant reformers whose advice they continued to seek when they ended their Marian wanderings and came to the promised land ruled over by a godly queen. Finally, these many streams of thought were joined by the powerful current flowing from the mind of the Judicious Hooker[1] who in the last decade of the reign, elaborated a peculiarly English or 'Anglican' view of the nature of the Church. When there were so many different traditions, it was not easy to say what was 'orthodox' and what was not.

But if the Church of England had in the early years of the reign only a confused and undeveloped theology, the Puritans within the church had no common creed at all. There was no Confession of Faith to which they all subscribed, no set of Articles of which it could be said: 'This is the Puritan Credo.' It is true that they had God's Word in the scriptures, but even the Papists—and the Devil—could quote scripture. Puritanism may have been a Religion of the Book, but its members disagreed about what the Book meant. In the course of the reign Puritan theology, like Anglican theology, underwent growth and change. There were to be a number of fierce controversies which piled up a vast theological literature stressing opposing views. Jewel and Hooker, Cartwright, Travers, Field and Perkins were but a few of the voluminous writers who kept the licensed and unlicensed printing presses busy turning out massive theological works and thousands of pamphlets. The question which we have to ask is whether as a result of all these controversies there emerged a recognisable Puritan creed (or creeds) distinguishing those who accepted it from the 'non-Puritans' within the Church of England.

It would certainly be convenient if we could find some theological test which we could apply when we want to know whether an Elizabethan should or should not be classified as a 'Puritan',[2] but the

---

[1] See p. 315 ff.

[2] We really need a set of questions, on the lines familiar to magazine-readers, headed 'How Puritan are you?' The questions would have to cover a wide field and carry marks weighted according to their importance. They would range from 'What are your views on prevenient grace and double election?' to 'May Christians bow at the name of Jesus?';

difficulty about trying to distinguish between 'Puritans' and 'non-Puritans' on theological lines is admirably illustrated by two recent works which ask the question whether this can be done, and give fundamentally different answers.[1] No one, of course, denies that there were differences of emphasis and a number of points of conflict. If there had not been such differences, there would have been no 'Puritan Problem' in Elizabethan England. The argument turns on whether these differences were of comparatively minor importance or whether they were about fundamental theological issues.

In *The Protestant Mind of the English Reformation* Charles and Katherine George examine, over a very wide field, the views held by those who are labelled 'Puritan' and by those who are Protestant but who are not considered to be within the Puritan camp.[2] The Georges reject emphatically the view that the characteristic note of 'Puritanism' was its Calvinist theology and, in particular, its unique interpretation of the doctrine of predestination.[3] They find that on many of the major issues there was a basic agreement between 'Puritan' and 'non-Puritan' Protestants. They sum up by saying: 'In our effort to find a distinguishing line between "Puritan" and Anglican, we have found no issue, doctrinal or ecclesiastical, of which we can speak in other than relative terms. The so-called "Puritans" never either monopolize the concept or viewpoint in question or universally exhibit it. . . .'[4] The Georges stress the variety of different religious traditions which existed

---

from 'Should the Church be governed by presbyteries?' to 'May ministers wear the surplice?'. If questions on these lines could have been put to those commonly called Elizabethan Puritans, the marks would have varied very widely, and a considerable number would probably have failed to pass the test.

[1] Charles and Katherine George, *The Protestant Mind of the English Reformation 1570–1640*, Princeton, 1961; and John F. W. New, *Anglican and Puritan. The Basis of their Opposition 1558–1640*, 1964.

[2] There is, of course, the further problem that before you can begin to examine what the Puritans held, you have to make up your mind who should be classified as Puritans. If you use a very wide definition of the term, your conclusions about what Puritans believed may be very different from what they would be if you used a narrower definition.

[3] C. and K. George, *op. cit.*, p. 7. The practice of identifying Puritanism with Calvinism is a long-established one. It is still commonly assumed that if an Elizabethan can be shown to hold Calvinist views, he can be regarded as a 'Puritan'. Professor Dickens notes that when Daniel Neal and Benjamin Brook compiled their immense biographical collections of great Puritans, they were very largely writing about Calvinist clergymen of the Anglican Church. If Calvinist doctrine is the test of Puritanism, then Archbishop Whitgift, who persecuted the Puritans, must himself have been a Puritan, and so must many of the leaders of the Elizabethan church.

[4] C. and K. George, *op. cit.*, p. 405.

within the one church, and they see the leaders and spokesmen of that church as striving, in pursuit of their ideal of a comprehensive national church, 'to maintain the seamless coat, the unbroken body of their society.'[1]

If, as the Georges suggest, 'Puritans' and 'non-Puritans' within the Church of England were not divided over profound theological issues, what were they divided about, and what were the special characteristics of 'Puritans' distinguishing them from others within the church? Some writers have made great play with the idea of 'a Puritan spirit' or 'a Puritan temper'. Thus, the Georges note that 'the "Puritan" thinks of himself as simply more intensely religious, Christian, and Protestant (and specifically more English Protestant) than the ordinary churchgoer, and especially more than those who oppose him'.[2] No one would deny the intense religious convictions and emotions displayed in many of the writers and preachers who are generally agreed to be 'Puritans', and it may possibly be true to say that one can recognise a 'Puritan' from his words and his actions.[3] Nevertheless, a 'spirit' or a 'temper' is not easy to pin down, and the Elizabethan Puritans were not harried by the authorities because they had a particular 'spirit' or 'temper'. They were harried because they came into conflict with the authorities on a number of specific issues, including the liturgy, the ceremonies and the government of the church. Those who deny that the conflicts were over major theological difference suggest that the cause of the trouble was that Elizabeth's bishops and ministers, while allowing a great difference of doctrinal views within the Church, nevertheless insisted on fixed and unchanging ceremonial and liturgical detail. According to Dr. Marchant: 'The result was not a lessening of party strife, but the diverting of it to disputes over unessentials—the wearing of the surplice, the use of the cross in baptism, bowing at the name of Jesus and the like', and he argues that 'these matters, secondary in themselves, were magnified into spiritual issues of profound significance.'[4] Even the great dispute over whether the church should be governed by bishops or by presbyteries, which at first sight seems to be a major conflict, appears to lose

---

[1] C. and K. George, *op. cit.*, p. 397.   [2] *Ibid.*, p. 404.

[3] Thus, the Georges, after quoting a sermon of Thomas Adams, comment: 'This then, is undoubtedly "puritanism". The sermon . . . could have been written by no one other than a "puritan".' *Ibid.*, p. 406.

[4] R. Marchant, *The Puritans and the Church Courts in the Diocese of York 1560–1642*, 1960, pp. 205, 206.

much of its theological significance once one realises that the Elizabethan Church took the view that episcopacy was a convenient method of government but not one which Christ had established for all time and for all places. The Church of England recognised as 'true churches' a number of Protestant churches outside England which did not in fact have bishops.

One of the objections to this view that the conflict between 'Puritans' and 'non-Puritans' within the Church of England was merely about 'non-essentials' is that many Elizabethan Puritans fiercely denied that this was the case. The great Puritan manifesto of 1572—*An Admonition to the Parliament*—argued: 'Neither is the controversie betwixt them and us, as they would have the world in hand, as for a cap, a tippet, or a surplesse, but for great matters concerning a true ministerie, and the regiment of the churche, according to the word.'[1] Here, then, is an explicit assertion that the conflict was about 'great matters' and not about trivialities, and if this is so we have one more illustration of Cardinal Manning's generalisation that 'all great quarrels between men are at bottom theological'.

In his book *Anglican and Puritan: The Basis of their Opposition* Mr. New attempts to examine these 'great matters' which were alleged to be at the heart of the disputes.[2] Unlike the Georges, he thinks that the quarrel between 'Puritans' and 'non-Puritans' in the church was a conflict between irreconcilable theologies. He argues that subtle doctrinal differences existed from the very outset and developed over the years. It is impossible here to consider in detail all these 'subtle doctrinal differences', but some of them must be briefly noted.

Mr. New thinks there is a basic difference in the 'Anglican' and the 'Puritan' conception of man and of God's relations with man. The 'Puritan' believed that fallen human nature was totally evil, and that all man's faculties were affected, including his reason. The 'Anglican', while believing that man could do nothing on his own to merit salvation, nevertheless assigned to human reason an important rôle in deciding the way in which man should behave in this life. Both groups believed that the Bible contained the word of God and that all beliefs

---

[1] *Puritan Manifestoes: a study in the origin of the Puritan revolt*, edit. W. H. Frere and C. E. Douglas, 1907. Another edition with a new preface, 1954.

[2] For a critical review of Mr New's book, see Patrick Collinson in *The English Historical Review*, lxxx.

and actions must be tested by it, but for the 'Puritan' God's word in Sacred Scripture provided *all* the answers. For him anything which it did not permit, expressly or by implication, was unlawful, whereas the 'Anglicans', particularly after Hooker, were inclined to the view that if a belief or practice could be supported by reason, by custom or by tradition, then it was permissible to hold it, provided it was not expressly contrary to Scripture.

With regard to the highly complicated and involved question of whether God has from the beginning of time selected some people for salvation and others for damnation, many 'Anglican' churchmen, like many 'Puritans', subscribed to one version or another of the doctrine of predestination. Nevertheless, Mr. New thinks, there was a difference of emphasis between the two groups. The 'Anglican' did not think that salvation depended upon his own choice, but he believed that he had his God-given reason, and that he could be further perfected by grace dispensed through the church. He tended, too, to stress the kindness and mercy of God rather than His awful majesty, and the frightening Calvinist doctrine became, in the words of the Prayer Book of 1559, 'full of sweet, pleasant, and unspeakable comfort to godly persons'.

There were differences, too, in the attitudes of both groups to the sacraments. They were much more important for the 'Anglican' than they were for the 'Puritan'. Baptism, for example, was of vital significance to the 'Anglican' as the means by which people entered God's House. It was necessary for salvation, and the infant in danger of death must be baptised at all costs, if necessary in private, if necessary by a woman. Cartwright, however, held that infants would not be condemned because they were unbaptised and quoted Calvin: 'The truth is . . . that if he were no Christian before he came to receive baptism, baptism can make him no Christian, which is only the seal of the grace of God before received'. It was 'the grace of God before received' (or, in the case of those predestined to damnation, 'not received') that really counted, not merely the formal conferment of the sacrament. Similarly, there were differences about the sacrament of the Lord's Supper. The 'Anglican' saw it as a means by which the sinner received grace; the 'Puritan' thought it was only for the worthy, and that the unworthy in the congregation should be weeded out by the minister and excluded from it.

The different emphasis on the part played by the sacraments went hand in hand with a different emphasis on the rôle of the minister. For the 'Puritan' the most important function of the minister was to preach the Word of God. Even the efficacy of the eucharist depended to a considerable extent on preaching. Thus Thomas Cartwright wrote: ' . . . When as the life of the sacrament dependeth on the preaching of the Word of God, there must of necessity the Word of God be, not read, but preached unto the people amongst whom the sacraments are ministered.'[1] For the 'Anglican', too, preaching was of great importance, and he, like the 'Puritan', was very concerned about the existence of so many 'dumb dogs' or non-preaching ministers in the Church. Nevertheless, he thought that even the 'dumb dog' had a vital work to do—he could read the services in the Book of Common Prayer, read the Homilies if he could not compose his own sermons, and, above all, he could administer the sacraments. The difference of outlook is made plain in one of the canons of the Church of England, approved in 1604, which stated that 'divers persons, seduced by false teachers, do refuse to have their children baptised by a minister that is no preacher, and to receive communion at his hands in the same respect; as though the virtue of the sacraments did depend upon his ability to preach'. The canon explicitly laid down that both sacraments were equally effectual 'whether they be ministered by a minister that is no preacher, or by one that is a preacher'.

Different views about the sacraments and the priesthood led to differences about ceremonies and clerical dress. Although these might appear to be quarrels about non-essentials, the outward symbols aroused fierce passions because of the ideas which they symbolised. For the 'Anglican' who regarded the communion service and the eucharist as of very special significance, it was only fitting that there should be an appropriate and dignified ritual, that there should be a decent communion table properly covered, and that the sacred elements of the consecrated bread and wine should be received kneeling and not sitting or standing. It was right, too, that ministers should wear appropriate dress when performing their sacred functions and should be decently attired for all occasions. Even those 'Anglicans' like Bishop Jewel and other Marian exiles who were unhappy about these 'ornaments' felt they must put up with them since they were prescribed by lawful authority. As the 'vestiarian controversy'

[1] For an examination of the rôle of the Puritan preacher, see Irvonwy Morgan, *The Godly Preachers of the Elizabethan Church*, 1965.

D

showed,[1] 'Puritans' were not prepared to regard these things as having little theological significance. They protested against them in no uncertain terms: 'Copes, caps and surplesses, tippets and such lyke baggage, the preachyng signes of popyshy priesthode . . . are as the garments of the Idole, to which we should . . . say, avaunt and get thee hence. They are as the garments of the Balamites, of popishe priestes, enemies to God and all Christians. They serve not to edification, they have the shewe of evyll . . . they worke discorde . . . they bryng the ministerie into contempte, they offende the weake, they encourage the obstinate.'[2] Those who do not take account of the significance of symbolism in men's lives may feel that this protest was an example of Much Ado about Nothing, but the 'Puritan' might argue that such a charge could, with equal lack of justice, be brought against the early Christian martyrs who had died rather than burn a grain of incense before a statue of the Divine Emperor.

It can also be claimed that there were serious differences of view about the relations of Church and State. Both groups agreed that the Church ought to include within itself every one within the state, but the 'Puritan' often gave much more authority and much more independence to the Church than did the 'Anglican'. Cartwright, for example, held that 'the civil magistrate hath not to ordain ceremonies pertaining to the church'. His opponent, Archbishop Whitgift, thought that the Puritans made a false distinction between the powers of the Church and of the State. He would not in the least have minded the accusation Cartwright brought against him 'that he (Whitgift) cannot put a difference between the church and the commonwealth . .' 'Anglicans' thought of Church and State as part of one commonwealth, and in spite of the experience of Protestants under Mary, they did not think in terms of a possible conflict between the orders of the ruler and the demands of 'true religion'. They remembered that they were members of a church which had been established by law, and the bishops were not allowed to forget that they had been appointed by a secular ruler who was Supreme Governor of their church and who could, if she chose, remove them from office. The 'Puritans' on the other hand were much less ready to obey the commands of the Supreme Governor. If they had obeyed her, there would have been no Puritan conflict under Elizabeth I.

[1] See p. 86 ff.
[2] *Puritan Manifestoes*, edit. W. H. Frere and C. E. Douglas, 1907, p. 35.

It is possible, then, for people to hold diametrically opposed views about whether the differences between 'Anglicans' and 'Puritans' were along clearly marked theological lines. Certainly there were a great many different varieties of 'Anglicanism' and of 'Puritanism' and, in an age of development and change, it is not easy to decide what is 'orthodox'. Indeed it may well be that what was 'orthodox' at the beginning of the period differed considerably from what was 'orthodox' at the end. Much work still remains to be done on the theology and history of the Church of England in Elizabeth I's reign. Nevertheless, one is left with the impression that throughout these years there were growing differences within the Church on theological questions and that the seamless robe was being torn. A broad division was appearing between 'Puritan' theologies, which differed one from another but which had a good deal in common, and what may be called 'Anglican' or official theologies. At the heart of the matter lay a growing divergence of views about the meaning of the Sacred Scriptures and about the nature and teaching of the true church.

Although there were these considerable differences within the Church of England, the civil and ecclesiastical authorities were not heresy-hunters. In order to keep the established church as comprehensive as possible, they were prepared to permit a diversity of theological views. In that sense Elizabeth I did not seek to make windows into Puritan any more than she did into Catholic souls. There was room within the one church for men with such different outlooks as Parker, Grindal, Jewel, Cartwright, Travers and Hooker, but only on certain conditions. Whatever they believed, they must conform outwardly with official policy and not challenge what was laid down by law. Those who held 'Puritanical' views would not necessarily find themselves in trouble if they confined themselves to academic discussion, but there was a limit to the toleration they could expect if they took action, or directly or indirectly incited others to action, which threatened the authority of the State Church or the orders of its Supreme Governor.

Unfortunately for themselves many of those who held 'Puritanical' theological views were not prepared to divorce belief from action. They felt bound in conscience to do what they could to put things right in the Church of which they were members. It was their actions more than their beliefs that got them into trouble with authority.

There is much to be said for restricting the term 'Puritan' in the

Elizabethan period to those who held the kind of theological views which we have been considering above, for regarding 'Puritanism' as a body of opinion within the church which wanted to emphasise and develop the 'Protestant' elements embodied in the settlement of 1559 and to minimise, or even remove altogether, the 'Catholic' elements which that settlement also contained. Puritans could then be seen as the left-wing of the church, anxious to purge the establishment of all relics of popery and to move further in the direction of the 'reformed' churches abroad. It would be necessary always to insist that they were not one group but a number of groups, that they varied very much in their theological beliefs and religious practices, that there were 'conservative Puritans' who wanted only minor changes and 'radical Puritans' who wanted to alter fundamentally the nature of the establishment. Nevertheless, although they were not agreed about ultimate aims, they had enough in common to work together for particular and limited purposes. Such a view of Puritanism would emphasise what can only too easily be forgotten—that Puritanism was basically something concerned with religion, even though Mr. Hill has made admirably clear how much of the support given to it was for non-religious reasons.

Unfortunately many historians of Puritanism have been anxious to give the word such a wide and comprehensive meaning that it has become a very imprecise and positively confusing term. In his classic study of Tudor Puritanism, Dr. Knappen begins in 1524 when William Tyndale left London for Germany in order to prepare an English translation of the Bible.[1] Professor Haller, the writer of another standard work on the Puritans, includes in their ranks people like Chaucer's Poor Parson.[2] Some historians find room under the same umbrella for Presbyterians and for Independents, for separatists and non-separatists. Professor Dickens thinks that to the end of Elizabeth's reign Puritanism can be said to have commanded a majority in the House of Commons, to have dominated the Elizabethan pulpit and to have as its active lay leaders some of the most influential in the land. The late G. M. Trevelyan defined Puritanism as 'the religion of all those who wished either to purify the usage of the established

---

[1] M. M. Knappen, *Tudor Puritanism*, Chicago, 1939. Reprinted 1963.
[2] W. Haller, *The Rise of Puritanism or, the Way to the New Jerusalem as set forth in pulpit and press from Thomas Cartwright to John Lilburne and John Milton, 1570–1643*, New York, 1938.

Church from the taint of popery, or to worship separately by forms of worship so purified'.[1] Such definitions do at least consider Puritanism as a religious phenomenon, but it might be suggested that they are so wide that they amount simply to using 'Puritan' as another word for 'Protestant'.

The bounds of Mr. Christopher Hill's Puritan Empire extend even further. He considers Puritanism as a body of opinion which had 'a core of doctrine about religion and Church government, aiming at purifying the Church from inside' and which for a variety of reasons won the support of a substantial and growing group of laymen.[2] He stresses the many non-religious reasons for criticism of the Church of England and insists that it is important to remember that 'for contemporaries the word had no narrowly religious connotation'. We must avoid the temptation to see it simply as a movement concerned with religion and 'always we must remember the broader, looser sense in which the word was used to describe any opponents of the policies pursued by hierarchy and court'. Mr. Hill illustrates with a wealth of examples the great variety of meanings which the word had for contemporaries, but insists that Puritanism can nevertheless be considered as a body of opinion held by people who adopted comparable attitudes to a large number of problems, attitudes which appealed to a large body of lay opinion which we can conveniently describe as Puritan.[3]

Some of the objections to omnibus definitions of Puritanism have been ably stated by Dr. Kearney. Criticising Mr. Hill's view that a single meaning can be attributed to the word, he argues: 'There are

[1] G. M. Trevelyan's definition has been widely used. Its weakness seems to be that it defines Puritanism primarily in negative terms, it suggests that the dispute was merely about 'forms of worship' and it ignores the fundamental question as to whether there were major theological differences between Puritans and 'non-Puritans'. It is too comprehensive, for it includes under one umbrella separatists and non-separatists, and it stamps as 'Puritan' many whose only qualification for being so labelled was that they disliked popery.

[2] Christopher Hill, *Society and Puritanism in Pre-Revolutionary England*, 1964, p. 28. Elsewhere, Mr. Hill defines it as 'that body of opinion which was opposed to the general religious policy of the hierarchy but which did not carry its opposition to the point of raising separatism to a principle' (*Economic Problems of the Church*, p. xii). It might be suggested that it would be better to amend this to read: 'which was opposed *for religious reasons* to the general religious policy of the hierarchy...' Those whose reasons for supporting the Puritans were non-religious might be better described as 'Puritan sympathizers'.

[3] Christopher Hill, *Society and Puritanism in Pre-Revolutionary England*, especially Chapter I, 'The Definition of a Puritan'.

as many "Puritanisms" as there are "socialisms" and "romanticisms". In short, to describe some one as a Puritan is not really to tell us very much about his specific views.' To Dr. Kearney, Puritanism consists of 'various cross-currents of thought and emotion'. He says 'much Puritan thought was clerical in colour, much of it anti-clerical. Some of it was academic, some opposed to learning. Many Puritans were Presbyterians, others were Independents . . . Puritanism is nearer a flavour, a tone of voice, a loose set of not always consistent assumptions than a precise and unambiguous concept which can be sharply defined. If we must have a definition, I would define Puritanism as the growing circle of discontent both within and without the Established Church from the 1560's onwards . . . Basically I suppose what was common to all of them was a vision of what the Church of Christ ought to be if it were stripped of externals and unessentials. Where they differed (and their differences were not insignificant) was in their view of what was external and unessential. Their vision varied as much as the nineteenth century socialist vision itself.'[1]

The use of the word 'Puritan' to describe a wide range of very different reactions can be seriously misleading. Those who wanted relatively minor changes and certain much-needed reforms in the Elizabethan Church have been treated by historians as fellow-travellers with those who wanted to impose undiluted Calvinist doctrine and replace government by bishops with a godly Presbyterian discipline. Archbishop Grindal, who was lukewarm about enforcing the regulations concerning clerical dress and unwilling to suppress 'prophesyings' which, he thought, were helpful in raising the standards of clerical education, is put in the same boat as the writer of the Martin Marprelate Tracts which savagely attacked bishops.

There is serious injustice, too, in regarding the Puritans as the only people who were anxious to 'purify' and reform the church. The Puritans had no monopoly in this matter, and many who genuinely wanted to remove abuses cannot in any sense be regarded as 'Puritans'. Others besides the 'Puritans' were concerned about the low standards of clerical education and clerical behaviour and about the number of non-preaching clergy. Many bishops were troubled by these serious weaknesses and did what they could to bring about an improvement.

[1] H. F. Kearney, 'Puritanism and Science: Problems of Definition', *Past and Present*, No. 31, July 1965, pp. 104–10.

It is too easily overlooked that what the Puritans really wanted was not a preaching clergy but preachers who would preach theological views of which they themselves approved. Concern for stricter observance of the sabbath was another characteristic of Puritanism, but this too was not limited to Puritans. Nor was the Church of England wedded to the belief that pluralism, which the Puritans attacked, was an essential feature of the true church. The failure to deal effectively with the abuse was not by any means the fault of the hierarchy alone. If bishops were often hostile to 'lecturers' whom the Puritans favoured, it was the contents of their lectures and sermons rather than practice in itself which produced conflict. The wish to purify the church of the relics of popery was certainly not restricted to one group in the Church and was something found at all levels, among the proud prelates as well as among the godly ministers.

Everyone feels that he knows what Puritanism means and that he can recognise it when he sees it, but estimates of the extent of Elizabethan Puritanism vary considerably because in fact the word means different things to different writers. There are almost as many Puritanisms as there are writers about Puritanism. No attempt will be made here to add yet another definition, but since the word 'Puritan' appears in the title of this book it is necessary to comment briefly on the way in which the term is used. We shall be concerned primarily with those people in Elizabethan England whose ideas and actions on matters concerning religious belief, religious practice, church government or church organisation brought them into conflict with the church established by law and with the policy of its Supreme Governor. We shall not to any great extent be concerned with 'Anglican Puritans' or with Calvinist Anglicans unless we find them in the category of those in trouble with the establishment. This approach may appear to restrict unduly the meaning of the word Puritanism, but at least it makes it easier to recognise the people whose activities we are trying to examine. They make up a considerable and varied collection of individuals and of groups inside the established church who, like the Papists outside the church, followed their consciences and refused to obey unquestioningly the orders of those in authority. They published their views from the pulpit, they wrote thousands of books and pamphlets, and their words and their actions were regarded as dangerous, or potentially dangerous, by the Supreme Governor and others in power in the State Church. Some of them were guilty of only minor offences and received only minor punishment. Some conformed under pressure. Many, no doubt, remained undiscovered, while others escaped punishment owing to protection received from a sympathetic bishop or a powerful lay patron. Others challenged the authorities on major issues and were persistent and determined offenders, even when it cost them their liberty or their lives. To the leaders and to the committed men must be added the much larger groups of those who showed varying degrees of sympathy with the views they put forward. Some of these genuinely shared, to a greater or lesser degree, the religious beliefs of those they supported. Others had non-religious reasons for giving their support and should perhaps be labelled 'sympathisers with Puritanism' rather than 'Puritans'.

When we consider Puritanism in this way we shall still find that its keynote is variety rather than uniformity. What unites these people is not so much what they want to create as what they want to destroy. The common factor is not so much a 'Puritan spirit' as a dislike of the *status quo*. There was considerable agreement about what ought to be swept away, but much less agreement about what to put in its place.

3

The Years of Uncertainty 1558–1570: The Consolidation of the Church of England

From the very beginning of her reign she has treated all religious questions with so much caution and incredible prudence that she seems both to protect the Catholic religion and at the same time not entirely to condemn or outwardly reject the new Reformation ... In my opinion, a very prudent action, intended to keep the adherents of both creeds in subjection, for the less she ruffles them at the beginning of her reign the more easily will she enthral them later on.

Count von Helffstein to the Emperor,
16 March 1559[1]

... every day men look for a change and prepare for the same.

The bishop of Carlisle to William Cecil,
14 January 1562[2]

A DOZEN years separate the accession of Queen Elizabeth I from the papal bull of excommunication of 1570 and from the famous lectures which Thomas Cartwright delivered that same year in Cambridge, outlining a system of church government radically different from that which had been established by law. They are years of expectancy and uncertainty when men watched to see whether the new régime would establish itself successfully and on what lines its religious policy would develop. The whole situation might so easily be radically changed by circumstances which no one could predict. Everyone expected that the queen would marry, and the personality and the religion of her husband would certainly influence policy. Again, there was always the possibility that she might die, as she nearly did in 1562,

[1] *Queen Elizabeth and Some Foreigners*, edit. Victor von Klarwill, 1928, p. 47.
[2] Quoted in H. N. Birt, *The Elizabethan Religious Settlement*, 1907, p. 311.

and then the obvious heir was the Catholic Mary Stuart. And all the time it was necessary to take into account the dangerous and continually changing international situation in which the small English state had to steer a perilous course in a world dominated politically by the great Catholic powers of France and Spain. England could not remain isolated from the political and religious upheavals in Europe, nor could she ignore what was going on across the Scottish border.

For the committed Catholic there was in these years always the hope that better days might come. Bishop Jewel commented to Peter Martyr in 1562 that the Papists were thought to be 'expecting something, I know not what, no less than the Jews do their Messiah'.[1] Many Protestants were also full of expectancy. They were convinced that the arrangements made in 1559 could not possibly be final and that in due course the queen would complete the work of reformation which she had begun so well. They realised that there were difficulties and that it was 'no easy matter to drag the chariot without horses, especially up hill'.[2] They, too, knew from bitter experience under Mary how drastically things could alter if there were a change of ruler. Many of them were prepared as far as religious policy was concerned to accept the second-best, but they lived in hope.[3]

This atmosphere of uncertainty made Papists and Puritans reluctant to take definite steps to challenge the régime, and since the government proceeded cautiously and in practice allowed a good deal of latitude to deviationists, partly from policy and partly because it had no option, these years were a time of relative peace. As an astute German observer noted, Elizabeth refrained from ruffling too much the religious susceptibilities of her people. She hoped to cast her spell over Papists and Protestants alike. Meanwhile the established church could consolidate its position and, if charm failed, the queen would then be in a position to take a stronger line with nonconformists.

The task of giving some shape to the new church, of imposing some kind of order on the religious chaos and of making the official religion intellectually respectable, was entrusted to the unwilling but very capable hands of Matthew Parker whom the queen chose as her first archbishop of Canterbury. A recent biographer has commented with

[1] *The Zurich Letters*, I. 102, 7 February 1562.

[2] *The Zurich Letters*, I. 45. Jewel to Peter Martyr, 2 November 1559.

[3] *Ibid.*, I. 103. 'O how wretched are we, who cannot tell under what sovereign we are to live! God will, I trust, long preserve Elizabeth to us in life and safety, and that will satisfy us.' 7 February 1562.

justice: 'It is not easy to imagine a man better suited to nurse the Elizabethan church in its early and perilous days.'[1] Parker had been born in 1504 and ordained priest in 1527 when the mass was still the central act of worship for Englishmen. He had a distinguished career as a scholar in the University of Cambridge, he had been chaplain to Elizabeth's mother, and he was known to be an efficient and practical administrator. He had not joined the Protestant exiles abroad under Mary, but neither had he conformed to Catholicism. He had been deprived of his offices, but for reasons not entirely clear he seems to have escaped serious persecution. He was a happily married man and he had no desire to take on the heavy responsibilities that were bound to face the first Elizabethan archbishop of Canterbury. He would have preferred to return to the life of a scholar and to use his considerable administrative talents in the narrower field of university affairs, but from the government's point of view he was just the man needed to put the church on its feet. He had not been subjected to the full and direct influence of the continental Reformation as had the returning exiles, and he was unlikely to be carried away by the fierce enthusiasm which characterised so many of them. His background and his experience were wholly English. He was a sincere and honest man who could on occasions stand up to the queen on matters of principle, but he was not the type to take a violently independent line. His reasonableness, his tact and his respect for royal authority ensured that there were no serious clashes between Elizabeth and her bishops, even though some of them were very restless at the slow progress of true religion in England. By a combination of firmness and moderation Parker sought to put down the old religion and to keep the Protestant zealots in check. No one has ever called him a Puritan. He performed the remarkable feat of securing a measure of agreement among the bishops, many of them hot Protestants, on 'the principal articles of our religion', and in 1563 he successfully steered through convocation the famous Thirty Nine Articles.[2] By visitations and other means he kept up the pressure on Roman Catholics and he also sought to impose a measure of uniformity on the Puritans. He gave to the new church a tradition of scholarship, of moderation and of co-operation with the state. He died in 1575 sadly aware that the opponents of what he stood for were becoming more vigorous and more vocal and that the problem of

---

[1] V. J. K. Brook, *A Life of Archbishop Parker*, Oxford, 1962, p. 345.
[2] V. J. K. Brook, *A Life of Archbishop Parker*, pp. 103, 134.

religious unity had not been solved, but if he had failed to bring all Englishmen into one church, he had at least succeeded in making the Church of England more acceptable to more people than any other man could have done.

Parker's main achievement was to give form and shape to the Church of England and to construct the solid foundations on which others could build, but the chief defender of the new institution in its early perilous years was another great Elizabethan bishop, John Jewel, an extremely able controversialist whose achievement was to make the Church of England appear intellectually respectable at home and abroad. He was a Devon man, born in 1522 and educated in Barnstaple before proceeding to Oxford. In 1548 he was appointed Reader in Humanity and Rhetoric, and he was very much influenced by the continental reformer Peter Martyr Vermigli who was appointed Regius Professor of Divinity at Oxford in the same year. He was ordained in 1550. Under Mary he was deprived of his fellowship and he signed articles accepting the teaching of the Roman Church on a number of points. Later he fled abroad and played a modest part in supporting the party among the exiles which maintained the Prayer Book of 1552 against those who wanted to replace it by a book based on Calvinist practice. In 1559 Jewel was appointed bishop of Salisbury, and on 26 November of that year he preached his famous Challenge Sermon at St. Paul's Cross. In it he took the offensive against Papists and challenged them on the vital question of authority for religious beliefs. 'If any learned man of all our adversaries', he said, 'or if all the learned men that be alive, be able to bring any one sufficient sentence out of any old catholic doctor, or father, or out of any old general council, or out of the holy scriptures of God, or any one example of the primitive church, whereby it may be clearly and plainly proved that there was any private mass in the whole world at that time, for the space of six hundred years after Christ . . . (I will) give over and subscribe unto him.'[1] And so he continued through a whole series of articles of belief held by Papists, extending eventually to the number of twenty-seven. It was a bold self-confident challenge which could have been made only by a man who was completely sure of his own position and whose study of the Scriptures, of the early fathers and of early church history had left him convinced that the Church of

---

[1] *The Works of John Jewel*, edit. J. Ayre, Parker Society, 1845, I. 20, 21; W. M. Southgate, *John Jewel and the Problem of Doctrinal Authority*, Harvard, 1962, p. 50.

Rome differed in fundamentals from the primitive church, and that the Church of England had stripped away the errors of centuries and returned to the beliefs and practices of early Christianity. This was the kind of self-confidence that the government liked to see, and Jewel was called upon to repeat his sermon at court.

In 1562 Jewel published his very important book *Apologia Ecclesiae Anglicanae*.[1] It appeared originally in Latin because it was meant to be read abroad by Papists and by Protestants and to explain the nature of the established church both to its enemies and to its somewhat puzzled friends among the reformed churches of Europe. To the claim that the Church of England was heretical and divided, he answered, ' . . . we do show it plain that God's Holy Gospel, the ancient bishops, and the primitive church do make on our side' and that 'we have not without just cause left these men (the Papists), and rather have returned to the apostles and the old catholic fathers'. He provided his readers with an exposition of the faith of the Church of England in a form which embodied much of the teaching of the earlier English reformers but which was also of a kind likely to be acceptable to the continental reformed churches. The big issues which divided the reformers abroad were not stressed, for Jewel wanted to emphasise the essential unity of the reformed churches. 'We believe', he wrote, 'that there is one church of God . . . that it is catholic and universal and dispersed throughout the whole world.'

Jewel faced and tried to find an answer to the problem confronting all religious thinkers in the sixteenth century—by what authority could they know the truth. For Jewel the answer lay in the Scriptures rightly interpreted with the help of the Holy Spirit and with reference to the writings of the early Christian Fathers and the practices of the primitive church.

Jewel's book supplied the standard defence of the Church of England for most of Elizabeth's reign. Within a couple of years of its appearance there were two English translations and it was later translated also into French, Italian, Dutch and Spanish. It is difficult to assess the influence of the printed word, but there seems little doubt that Jewel's *Apologia* provided a large number of educated Englishmen with an explanation and a justification of the beliefs of the church to which they were bound by law to belong.

[1] *An Apology of the Church of England by John Jewel*, edited by J. E. Booty, Cornell University Press, 1963.

Jewel's main battle was with the Papists and not with the Puritans. The early Puritans indeed attached considerable weight to his writings, and it has even been claimed that he was a Puritan at heart. Certainly he was disturbed by some of the 'vestiges of popery' still retained in the church, but he appealed to the Puritans not to destroy religious unity for the sake of non-essentials. He died in 1571 before the full force of the Puritan attack had broken on the institution which he had served with such ability, and he did not have to face in debate the arguments which the Puritans later pressed home against him and the other bishops of the Church of England—'You will neither re-forme Gods church yourselves for feare of losing your pomp and honor, neither will you suffer those which would, even with the loss of liberty, living, and life, that the beautiful face and purity of the Apostolicke Church might once shine in England . . .'[1]

Parker and Jewel and others in positions of authority in the Church had in these early years to put flesh and blood on the skeleton framework of the new Church set up in 1559 and to make it into a living organisation acceptable to as many people as possible. They had behind them the considerable resources of the state, and they could also exercise coercion through the church courts. They controlled the printing presses and they had a machinery for propaganda largely denied to their opponents, but they had an uphill and never-ending task. After nearly twenty years of work one of them commented that the church was still 'struggling with that old disease, under which she has laboured even from her infancy: for she will not entirely recover from popery before the last coming of that great physician, Jesus Christ'.[2]

In the first dozen years of the new régime there was a twofold effort to deal with the tremendous problem of securing religious uniformity. The authorities in state and church used the weapons of coercion and of propaganda. An attempt was made to ensure a measure of outward conformity from as many people as possible, and at the same time the ecclesiastical authorities did their best to see that the new religion was preached throughout the country so that there might be another conversion of England. The government refrained from using excessive violence. It tried to remove from key positions those who might give trouble and to replace them by reliable men. It tolerated a good deal

---

[1] *The Seconde Parte of a Register*, edit. A. E. Peel, I. 80.
[2] *The Zurich Letters* I. 320. Bishop Horne to Gualter, 10 August 1576.

which it did not like, and it hoped that time was on its side, that there would eventually grow up a new generation which had been brought up in the Church of England and which had never known any other religion. Meanwhile, it was enough to secure active commitment from the people who mattered in the state and passive acceptance from the nation at large. As Bishop Horne put it to Cecil: 'The common sort of people . . . may easily be brought to conform themselves to the better sort of them in dignity and reputation, as they see them bent to set forward.'[1]

Active commitment to the religious settlement was from the very beginning required from the most important sections of the community. The oath of supremacy acknowledging the queen as 'the only supreme governor . . . as well in all spiritual or ecclesiastical things or causes as temporal', and affirming that no foreign prince or prelate 'hath or ought to have any jurisdiction, power, superiority, pre-eminence or authority ecclesiastical or spiritual within this realm', could be administered to all ecclesiastics, to all judges, mayors and temporal officers, to everyone receiving the queen's fee or wages, to all persons suing livery of lands and doing homage, and to anyone taking holy orders or degrees at the universities. Those who refused the oath were to be deprived of their office and disabled from holding office for life.[2] The punishment may seem light to us today. It would not have seemed light to the office-holders of Tudor England for whom it could mean loss of livelihood and of reputation.

There were sharper penalties under this Act for those who 'by writing, printing, teaching, preaching, express words, deed or act' maintained and defended the spiritual or ecclesiastical jurisdiction of any foreign prince or prelate. For them, the penalty for the first offence could be loss of all goods and chattels; for the second offence, loss of all property and imprisonment for life; and for the third offence the penalties as for high treason. The Papist who defended the pope's spiritual authority now did so at his peril.

The Act of Uniformity[3] similarly distinguished between the key men, who must commit themselves fully, and the masses, who were merely required to conform outwardly. The beneficed clergy who

[1] Bishop Horne to Cecil, 29 August 1561. Quoted in H. N. Birt, *The Elizabethan Religious Settlement*, p. 527, note.

[2] The Act is printed in G. R. Elton, *The Tudor Constitution*, Cambridge, 1960, pp. 363–8.

[3] See G. R. Elton, *The Tudor Constitution*, pp. 401–4.

refused to use the new Prayer Book or who used any other form of service or who spoke 'in derogation' of the Prayer Book could be punished for the first offence with loss of a year's income and six months' imprisonment; for a second offence with prison for a year and loss of all benefices; and for a third offence with life imprisonment. Unbeneficed clergy could receive a year's imprisonment for a first offence and prison for life for a second offence. Anyone who spoke in derogation of the Prayer Book or caused any clergyman to use any other service or who interrupted or hindered the service could be fined 100 marks for a first offence, 400 marks for a second offence, and could lose all his goods and suffer life imprisonment for a third offence. Anyone absent from church on Sundays or holy days could be fined 12d. for each offence or suffer 'censure of the church'.[1]

It has often been argued that the Elizabethan government began by adopting a mild policy and was driven to more severe measures later because of the papal attempts to overthrow the régime. Although it is true that the penalties imposed in 1559 were mild compared with the penalties imposed on heretics under Mary and compared with what was done later in Elizabeth's reign, they were nevertheless severe, and they affected some of the most important groups in the community. The martyrs might regard them as trifling, but the number of members in any religion who will die for their beliefs is always limited, and for the Elizabethan gentleman or scholar or priest the price he might have to pay for adhering to the old religion must have seemed very high indeed. Even though the penalties were not systematically and universally imposed, their mere presence on the statute book was a very powerful inducement to conform. Active propaganda against the new régime might involve very considerable dangers. The intention clearly was to silence opposition.

We shall never know whether the government would in any case have imposed more severe penalties if there had been no papal bull of excommunication. Its alleged mildness in these early years was certainly influenced by the fact that it had to proceed cautiously until it had made sure of a considerable measure of support and given its propaganda time to take effect. What is clear is that it had no intention

---

[1] This might involve lesser or greater excommunication. Excommunication could be a very serious punishment. Among other things an excommunicated person's evidence in a court was considered worthless; his opponent in a lawsuit might plead excommunication as a bar to any further action; he could not receive Christian burial and he might find himself in trouble with High Commission.

1 MATTHEW PARKER, ARCHBISHOP OF CANTERBURY 1559–1575
Elizabeth's first archbishop who nursed her church in its early and critical
years and who wrote in 1573 'Both papists and precisians have one mark to
shoot at, plain disobedience. . . .'

2 JOHN JEWEL, BISHOP OF SALISBURY 1559–1571
Jewel's *Challenge Sermon* in 1559 sparked off a tremendous controversy with English Catholic writers abroad. His *Apologia Ecclesiae Anglicanae* in 1562 provided the standard defence of the Church of England for the greater part of Elizabeth's reign—'we do show it plain that God's Holy Gospel, the ancient bishops, and the primitive church do make on our side'.

of allowing more than one religion to be practised in the state, and when it eventually became evident that Roman Catholicism was not going to die quietly, it would almost certainly have had to proceed to more severe measures than those laid down in the legislation of 1559.

Even those who were not required formally to repudiate the papacy by taking the oath of supremacy were required to accept the settlement outwardly by going to church. Elizabeth has often been given credit because she did not, as the Inquisition did, make windows into men's souls to find out what they really believed in their hearts. Cecil claimed in 1570 that provided the queen's subjects obeyed the law they would not suffer molestation 'by way of examination or inquisition of their secret opinions in their consciences, for matters of faith'.[1] It is true that Elizabeth's treatment of her Catholic subjects in this respect does compare very favourably with the way in which Philip II treated his Protestant subjects, but it is nonsense to suggest that it shows her readiness to tolerate religious differences or to allow liberty of conscience. The situation is summed up by a modern Catholic historian in less favourable terms. As Fr. Hughes puts it: 'The queen's subjects may continue to be Catholics so long as they pretend to be Protestants, and to live as Protestants and to use the new rites as though they are Protestants. They do not need to believe anything of what they profess to believe.'[2] They could, however, be grateful that the House of Commons did not get its way in 1559 and compel them to commit themselves still further by requiring them to receive communion.

The policy of compelling those in key positions to commit themselves formally to the new régime was carried a stage further by parliament in 1563.[3] The obligation to take the oath of supremacy was extended to include all taking holy orders, all university graduates, all schoolmasters, lawyers and Members of Parliament. The punishment for a first offence could be loss of lands and goods and imprisonment during the queen's pleasure, and for a second refusal the penalty of treason. The same penalties could also be imposed on those who defended the pope's spiritual jurisdiction. In the House of Lords, Viscount Montague protested that the law was unnecessary, since 'the Catholics of this realm disturb not, nor hinder the public affairs of the realm, neither spiritual nor temporal'. He asked: 'What man is there

---

[1] Quoted in V. J. Brook, *A Life of Archbishop Parker*, pp. 256–7.
[2] Philip Hughes, *The Reformation in England*, 3 vols., 1954, III. 75.
[3] 5 Eliz. c. 1. *Statutes of the Realm*, IV. 402–5.

E

so without courage and stomach, or void of all honour, that can consent . . . to receive an opinion and new religion by force and compulsion?'[1] The Act nevertheless passed the Lords and received the royal assent, and at the end of the session the Lord Keeper Bacon officially endorsed what had been done when he said: 'Her Majesty considereth how wisely you have done for the abolishing of the Romish power, the common enemy of this realm . . .'[2] The government had in 1559 declared war on papal authority in England, and although the queen would have preferred to use gentler methods than those urged on her by the Commons, it was a difference about means, not about the end which they both desired.

In these years the attempt to impose religious uniformity slowly gathered momentum. The oath of supremacy was administered to those influential groups of people named in the Acts,[3] and the committed Catholics were gradually weeded out from positions where they might be dangerous. Sound men were appointed whenever available to office in the church and in the universities. The newly appointed bishops were hard at work removing the relics of the old religion and spreading the teaching of the new. There was much to be done, and hope and despair alternate in the reports and letters which these busy Protestant bishops sent to Cecil and Parker and to their friends at home and abroad. They administered the oath, they reported on who was hostile to and who supported the religion established by law; they ordained ministers, they licensed preachers and saw that those who could not preach read the homilies setting forth the teaching of the Church. Clergy had to be disciplined and churchwardens prodded into activity. Four times a year all with the cure of souls were required to preach that 'all usurped and foreign power' had no warrant in God's word. Schoolmasters had to be approved and to take the oath, books had to be licensed, and children had to be taught the catechism of the new church. Thus the formidable machinery of the church and of the state was directed against the Roman religion, which in these early years was seen as the main danger to the Church of England. Those in authority hoped that in time Roman Catholicism would quietly die.

[1] J. E. Neale, *Elizabeth I and her Parliaments*, I. 120.

[2] *Ibid.*, p. 126.

[3] See Philip Hughes, *The Reformation in England*, III. 38 ff. for a discussion about the form of the oath administered to the clergy and the suggestion that what they were asked to subscribe to was not the oath laid down in the Act.

4

The Years of Uncertainty 1558–70: The Reactions of the Papists

THE Papists in the early years of Elizabeth's reign were singularly ill-equipped to deal with the critical situation which confronted them. What proportion of the nation can be considered Catholic or Catholic 'at heart', we do not know. Catholics must have greatly exceeded in numbers the small minority of committed Protestants which was imposing its will on the nation, but they were weak in the places that mattered. Their bishops made a stand, but they were quickly disposed of by the government. There was a small number among the nobility who did what they could for the Catholic cause in parliament, but they were a minority fighting a defensive action without much hope of success. As far as the House of Commons was concerned, Catholic influence was for all practical purposes completely absent, and one of the most remarkable features of the parliament summoned in 1558 was the way in which it was prepared not simply to acquiesce in the religious policy of the government but to force upon the queen a much more Protestant settlement than she herself had chosen. The rôle of the Catholic gentry in national affairs in these years was very largely passive. They were anxious to keep quiet and not to make themselves conspicuous. And if the gentry did not give a lead, neither did the priests. The great majority conformed and thus deprived Catholicism of its means of life.[1] In many parts of the country it must from a very

---

[1] Those who do not appreciate the vital rôle of the priests in the Roman Catholic religion tend to underestimate the consequences of their early submission to the Elizabethan government. We need to know a lot more about the Marian priests who still said mass in secret, but their number must have been small, and few of them acted as missionaries. For all practical purposes English Catholicism from 1559 was largely a Catholicism without priests. The seminary priest did not begin to come to England until 1574.

early date have been impossible for a Catholic to go to mass or to receive the sacraments. When the parish priest was ready to use the Book of Common Prayer and the squire publicly appeared at the new services, it was hardly surprising that the ordinary people followed the examples of their social superiors. Lack of leadership from Rome, the example of the gentry, the conformity of the priests, the dangers of breaking the law and a sense of helplessness in the face of the official machinery of state and church, undermined a Catholicism which had not as yet received spiritual and intellectual stimulus from the Counter-Reformation.

Possibly the greatest mistake made on the Catholic side in these early and critical years was the failure to give a strong lead on the question of attending the services of the new church. The matter had been referred to a committee of the Council of Trent in 1562. It decided that Catholics might not conform in this way. Pope Pius V in 1566 spoke strongly against the practice, and some attempt was made by Laurence Vaux[1] to make the pope's views known in England. Earlier on, William Allen had carried on a one-man crusade to persuade Catholics that they might not attend the heretical services. But such efforts had only a very limited and local success. The views of Allen and Vaux were known only to a small part of the Catholic community, and of those who knew them, many would not regard them as authoritative or binding. Outward conformity was widespread, and in the long run many of those who conformed were likely to part company permanently with the Church of Rome.[2] The strong line taken in these early years by Allen and Vaux is one factor in the survival of Catholicism in strength in Lancashire. They realised that in the circumstances any kind of compromise was fatal to their cause.

Although the Papists in England were so ill-organised and ineffective, those whose job it was to spread the new gospel seem to have found their task very formidable. The novelty of the new religion was

[1] *Infra*, p. 62. In a letter to his Lancashire friends, 2 November 1566, Vaux stated that he was 'charged to make a defynytyve sentence, that all suche as offer chyldren to the baptisme nowe used, or be present at the communion of servise nowe used in churches in Englande . . . Dow not walke in the state of Salvacion . . .' His letter is printed in the introduction to an edition of his catechism, edited by T. G. Law, Chetham Society, vol. 4, New Series, 1885, p. xxxii ff.

[2] A. C. Southern, *Elizabethan Recusant Prose*, 1950, p. 136 ff; Philip Hughes, *The Reformation in England*, III, p. 247 ff.

faced by the innate conservatism of many parts of England. The reports of the Elizabethan bishops in the 1560's are full of the difficulties which were encountered and are evidence of the obstinate survival of 'superstition'. Thus, Bishop Jewel in 1563 speaks of 'the popish satellites, who are giving us as much disturbance as they can in their corners and hiding places . . . '[1]; a visitation report on the diocese of Chichester in 1569 dealing with Battle states 'when a preacher dothe come, and speake any thinge agaynst the pope's doctrine, they will not abide, but get them oute of the churche . . . ' It adds that ' . . . the scholemaster is the cause of theire goinge oute which afterwardes, in corners among the people dothe gayne saie the preachers . . . ' Still more ominous was the comment: 'In many places they kepe yit still theire chalices lookinge for to have mas agayne . . . '[2] In 1570 the bishop of Carlisle remarked of Lancashire 'on all hands the people fall from religion, revolt to Popery, refuse to come at Church; the wicked popish priests reconcile them to the Church of Rome and cause them to abjure this (religion); and that openly and unchecked'.[3] These are but a few illustrations from the many that can be produced. It is not possible to make any quantitative estimate of the strength of Catholicism in the sixties. We do not even know how many people were fined or imprisoned in these years. We must perhaps make some allowance for the anxiety of the Elizabethan bishops and other officials to impress on the central government the tremendous difficulties with which they were confronted. Men anxious to see Christ's gospel established in a hurry may well have been depressed when they found that the country did not immediately rally with enthusiasm to the truth now preached to it, but it does seem that the passive resistance of Catholicism and its capacity to survive in the face of great pressure was very considerable. However, if progress in many parts of the country was slow, the establishment was nevertheless winning, and time did seem to be on its side.

In the 1560's when the fortunes of the Papists were at a low ebb in England, the real vitality of English Catholicism was to be found among the exiles. The total number of those who left England for religious reasons during the reign of Elizabeth I is not known. It cannot

---

[1] *The Zurich Letters*, I. 127. Jewel to Josiah Simler, 23 March 1563.
[2] Quoted by F. X. Walker, 'The Implementation of the Elizabethan Statutes against Recusants 1581–1603', unpublished London Ph.D. Thesis, 1961, pp. 27–8.
[3] Quoted in Philip Hughes, *The Reformation in England*, III. 126.

have been much more than a few thousand, but the importance of the exiles, like that of the Protestants who went abroad under Mary, was out of all proportion to their numbers.[1] They settled in a number of towns abroad, particularly in those which had easy communications with England. Like the Marian exiles they were for the most part scholars or gentlefolk and their dependents. They included distinguished university men like Richard Smith, Regius Professor of Divinity in Oxford, who later became Chancellor of Douay University; William Soane, Regius Professor of Civil Law in Cambridge; and Owen Lewis, later bishop of Cassano, and Richard White who became Professor of Canon and Civil Law in Douay, two of the twenty-five Fellows of New College, Oxford, who had resigned or been expelled. One of the exiles commented that 'the very flower of the two Universities, Oxford and Cambridge, was carried away, as it were by a storm and scattered in foreign lands'.[2] He was being over-enthusiastic, but certainly their departure meant a heavy loss to the Church of England.

Although the Catholic exiles were scattered over a number of towns in Europe, the centre which was of particular importance in the 1560's was Louvain where a number of scholars were busy lecturing, teaching and publishing their works with the object of presenting the Catholic case against Protestantism in general and against its English manifestation in particular. The names of these scholars are little remembered now, even by their co-religionists. Much of their work was bound to be ephemeral since it was concerned with contemporary theological issues which lost their relevance in subsequent ages, but at the time these men were of the great importance since they were engaged in a battle for men's minds.

Among the Louvainists was the Sussex man, Thomas Stapleton (1535–98), who had the reputation of being 'the most learned

---

[1] See Peter Guilday, *The English Catholic Refugees on the Continent, 1558–1795*, London, 1914; A. C. Southern, *Elizabethan Recusant Prose*, 1950; Thomas H. Clancy, *Papist Pamphleteers*, Chicago, 1964; A. C. F. Beales, *Education under Penalty*, 1963.

[2] Edward Rishton, quoted in A. C. Southern, *Elizabethan Recusant Prose*, p. 22. Professor A. C. F. Beales notes: 'To Louvain Oxford lost its Regius Professor of Divinity (William Soane), its Vice-Chancellor (Francis Babington), its reader in Greek (John Bavant of St. John's), its proctor from Oriel (Richard Barrett), and dozens of college fellows, including over twenty from New College led by Owen Lewis. Cambridge lost Richard Hale of Pembroke, John Seton of St. John's, Thomas Bailey the Master of Clare Hall, George Bullock the Master of St. John's, Thomas Sedgwick the Regius Professor of Divinity and many more.' *Education under Penalty*, p. 32.

Roman Catholic of all his time'.[1] His voluminous writings in English and Latin included an English translation of Bede's *Ecclesiastical History; Tres Thomae*, dealing with St. Thomas the Apostle, Becket and More; and a mass of controversial writing against English and European Protestants. The titles of two of his works are indicative of the rôle he played in the English controversies—*A Fortresse of the Faith First planted amonge us Englishmen, and continued hitherto in the universall Church of Christ. The faith of which time Protestants call, Papistry*, published at Antwerp in 1565; and a reply to Bishop Horne entitled *A Counterblast to M. Hornes vayne blaste against M. Fekenham . . . touching the Othe of Supremacy. By perusing whereof shall appeare, besides the holy scriptures, as it were a Chronicle of continual practise of Christes Churche in al ages and Countries . . . Prouing the Popes and Bisshops Supremacy in Ecclesiastical causes and Disprouing the Princes Supremacy*, published at Louvain in 1567.

Stapleton was a scholar all his life, but another Louvainist whose career took a very different turn was Nicholas Sander or Sanders. He had been Regius Professor of Canon Law in Oxford and, along with Thomas Harding, another Fellow of New College, he played the leading rôle among the exiled English clergy in the 1560's. His many publications included *The Supper of our Lord set forth in six Bookes, according to the truth of the gospel, and the faith of the Catholike Church*, Louvain, 1565; *The Rocke of the Churche wherein the Primacy of St. Peter and his successors the Bishops of Rome is proved out of Gods Worde*, Louvain, 1567; and a work on the history of the Reformation in England later published as *The Rise and Growth of the Anglican Schism*.[2] Sander was regarded as one of the most dangerous of the exiles and was described as 'a most wicked Englishman who has set forth two most detestable works'. He was one of the first to take the view that the only hope for English Catholicism was a foreign invasion—a view he later summarised in a letter to the Duke of Alva: 'The state of Christendom depends upon the stout assailing of England.' In 1570 he wrote a defence of the bull of excommunication but was persuaded to withdraw it. Nevertheless, he recorded the terms of the bull in his book *De Visibili monarchia Ecclesiae* published in 1571.

---

[1] See Marvin R. O'Connell, *Thomas Stapleton and the Counter Reformation*, Yal University Press, 1964; A. C. Southern, *Elizabethan Recusant Prose*.

[2] *De origine et progressu schismatis Anglicani*, first published in 1585. An English translation by David Lewis was published in 1877.

He left Louvain in the next year and, as we shall see, this notable scholar eventually became a man of action and died as a result.[1]

Another of this group whose fortunes we may briefly note was Laurence Vaux. Like William Allen he was a Lancashire man. He had been a Fellow of Corpus Christi, Oxford, and of an important collegiate church in Manchester. He refused the oath of Supremacy and went to Louvain where he kept a school. Like Allen, he returned to England for a time in the 1560's and endeavoured to persuade his coreligionists not to attend the services of the established church. In 1567 he published a catechism which he had originally made for his pupils in Louvain and which became extremely popular among English Catholics. Later, he was one of the party, including Campion and Parsons, who came to England in 1580, but he was soon taken and he died after five years in prison.[2]

Much of the writings of the Louvainists dealt with religious controversy, but we must not forget that these people were also very concerned with devotional works and with the development of the spiritual life. Richard Hopkins relates how another great Louvainist, Thomas Harding,[3] persuaded him to translate Spanish spiritual writers into English 'affirminge, that more spirituall profite wolde undoubtedlie ensewe thereby to the gayninge of Christian sowles in our countrie from Schisme, and Heresie, and from all sinne, and iniquitie, than by bookes that treate of controversies in Religion: wich (as experience hath nowe plainelie tried) doe nothinge so well dispose the common peoples myndes to the feare, love, and service of almightie God, as bookes treatinge of devotion and howe to leade a vertuous life doe'.[4]

These are but a few of the notable Catholic scholars who were at work abroad in the 1560's. The Louvain group produced over 40 books and pamphlets between 1564 and 1568 dealing with theology, history and the development of the Christian life. Bishop Jewel's

---

[1] *Infra*, p. 163. T. N. Veech, *Dr. Nicholas Sander and the English Reformation*, Louvain, 1935.

[2] *A Catechisme of Christian Doctrine necessarie for Children and ignorante people*, . . . edited by T. G. Law, with an introduction, Chetham Society, vol. 4, New Series, 1885.

[3] Harding, like his antagonist Bishop Jewel, was a Devon man. He had been a distinguished scholar at New College, Oxford, had joined the reformers under Edward VI and returned to Catholicism under Mary. He refused to conform under Elizabeth and was deprived of his living. He was one of the most distinguished Catholic contributors to the controversy over Jewel's Challenge Sermon.

[4] Quoted in A. C. Southern, *Elizabethan Recusant Prose*, p. 181.

famous Challenge Sermon alone sparked off a controversy to which there were over 60 contributions from both sides. Nicholas Sander later estimated, perhaps optimistically, that some 20,000 copies of the works of the exiles were smuggled into England before 1580.

The output of the exiles was remarkable, and they were taken very seriously by the authorities who were well aware of the importance of the printed word in the battle for men's minds. 'The popish exiles', wrote Jewel in 1565, 'are disturbing us and giving us all the trouble in their power . . . '[1] The work they produced no doubt strengthened the faith and, still more, the morale of the limited number of English Catholics who had access to it, but it might be argued that the production of Catholic literature abroad was a poor substitute for direct action in England itself. Public protests and underground missionary efforts in the early critical years might have achieved much better results as far as the ordinary Englishman was concerned. A number of martyrdoms might have worked wonders, particularly as the cause would have appeared much more obviously to be one of religion than it did after the papal bull of excommunication and the struggle with Spain completely changed the public image of Roman Catholicism.

Since Roman Catholicism was a religion whose survival depended so much on priests and bishops, it is astonishing that there was such a long delay before anything was done to ensure that English needs were met. It can be partly explained in terms of the uncertainty about the whole situation which might so easily change, partly in terms of difficulty of communication and lack of definite information, partly in terms of a failure to foresee how important this small country was to become in the future. To many European Catholics at the time England must have seemed a somewhat insignificant battlefield in relation to the world-wide conflict between the Reformation and the Counter-Reformation. The total resources available in terms of men, money and energy were limited. Even so, it is not easy to understand why the situation was allowed to deteriorate for so long. A seminary for the training of priests for work in England was not founded until 1568, and it was another six years before the products of the seminary began to arrive in this country.

The man who was the first to realise the needs of English Catholics was a Lancashire man, William Allen, who made a greater contribution to preserving Roman Catholicism in England than any other

[1] *The Zurich Letters*, I. 138. Jewel to Bullinger, 1 March 1565.

individual. He came of a gentry family and he seemed destined for a distinguished career in Oxford, where he became principal of St. Mary's Hall in 1556. He resigned early in Elizabeth's reign and eventually joined the exiles in Louvain. Later, he returned for a time to England and was one of the few who actively strove to persuade English Catholics that they might not in good conscience attend the services of the established church. His active and uncompromising attitude meant that he was in danger from the authorities, and in 1565 he once again went into exile. He studied theology at Louvain and was ordained priest two years later. In 1568, with the advice and help of Jean Vendeville, one of the professors at Douay, he established in that city a college which was intended to be a centre for English Catholic scholars abroad, a training place for the priests who would restore the Catholic religion in England when the right time came, and an educational establishment for English youths. Allen gathered round him in the years that followed a remarkably able group of men. The first ordinations took place in 1573 and the first Douay priests to come to England arrived in 1574. It is a comment on the lack of vision of the Roman Catholic ecclesiastical authorities and of European Catholics generally that this vitally important college was founded simply as the result of a piece of private enterprise and that through much of its early history it had to operate on a shoe-string budget. Only Allen's great personal charm and courage kept it going in the face of considerable opposition and criticism from both Catholics and non-Catholics. Its achievement was very great, but it came too late to do much more than salvage some of the pieces from the wreck of English Catholicism.

Douay was to be a source of immense strength to the English Catholics, but another event in the same year was to be a source of tremendous embarrassment. In 1568 Mary Queen of Scots fled to England where she was held a prisoner. For some years Elizabeth was actively considering restoring her to Scotland, provided suitable terms could be arranged, but many difficulties arose and she was not set free. If Elizabeth died or was assassinated, Mary would presumably become Queen of England, and English Catholics as well as Protestants were well aware what effect this would have on religion in England. Philip II of Spain, although anxious to further the Catholic cause in England, did not regard with any enthusiasm the prospect of a pro-French queen and the danger that might face him from an

Anglo-French alliance. Inevitably, the Queen of Scots became the centre of complicated international politics and the focus of schemes and plots among Catholic exiles abroad and discontented Catholics in England. Her activities and the propaganda directed against her helped to identify the cause of Catholicism with attempts to overthrow the Elizabethan government.[1]

Yet another damaging blow to English Catholics came in the next year, 1569, with the Rising of the Northern Earls. This was not initially a religious rebellion. There were plans on the part of a number of the English nobility to put pressure on Elizabeth to end the imprisonment of Mary Queen of Scots, to recognise her as heir-presumptive to the throne, and to arrange for her to marry the Protestant Duke of Norfolk. Among those implicated in varying degrees were the earl of Leicester, the earl of Arundel, the earl of Pembroke, the earl of Westmorland and the earl of Northumberland, who was married to the duke of Norfolk's sister. Contact was made with France, and also with Spain through the Italian banker, Ridolfi, who was resident in London. Although it was not a Catholic plot, if it had succeeded it would have benefited the Catholic cause. Moreover, William Cecil would presumably have been removed, since the scheme was in some measure a movement of the nobility against an upstart whom they considered was pursuing a dangerous policy.[2]

The plans failed hopelessly. The queen got to know what was in the wind, Leicester and others made their peace with her, and the duke of Norfolk was given an opportunity to confess all. He hesitated, then fled to his East Anglian estates, and made no further move. Elizabeth had conclusive evidence of his marriage negotiations with Mary, and by 11 October 1569 he was a prisoner in the Tower. He had already written to his brother-in-law, the earl of Westmorland, urging him not to rise. The danger of concerted action by an important group of the nobility was now over, but there was a widespread investigation of all who were suspected of being involved. The earls of Northumberland and Westmorland, who were Papists, met the President of the Council of the North, the earl of Sussex, on 8 October 1569 and

---

[1] There is a vast literature about Mary Queen of Scots. Two recent works by Jesuits argue in great detail that she was the victim of 'double-agents'. See Francis Edwards, *The Dangerous Queen*, 1964, and L. Hicks, *An Elizabethan Problem*, 1964.

[2] We still await a detailed modern study of this neglected rebellion. Some of the documents in the case are printed in *Memorials of the Rebellion of 1569*, edit. Cuthbert Sharpe, 1841.

pledged themselves to help put down any rising. They were not planning rebellion once Norfolk had been arrested, but the queen summoned them to court, and they were faced with a very difficult decision. They feared that if they obeyed the summons, they would be in the hands of their enemies. They were reluctant to rebel, but there were plenty of gentry who urged them on, and as a result Elizabeth had to face the only serious rebellion of her reign.

As in most rebellions, the motives of those who took part were mixed. The queen had for some years been taking steps to weaken the power of the great northern nobles, and they resented the control of the government by upstarts like Cecil. There was the age-old resentment of the North against the South, and a genuine dislike of the treatment given to Mary Queen of Scots. The leaders had their own financial difficulties, and there were the economic problems of the comparatively poor cattle and sheep-raising areas. The West Riding cloth industry had been damaged by government policy which had led to a stoppage of trade with the Low Countries. Again, there were many in the North who would follow a Percy or a Neville wherever they led. There were many reasons for this rebellion, which was not initially about religion, but the religious reason was certainly very important and became increasingly so once the trouble had begun. Richard Norton, sheriff of Yorkshire, bearing the banner of the five wounds of Christ, symbolised the protest of 'the owlde religion' against the new order, and a contemporary Protestant writer saw the rebellion in terms of ' . . . a conspiracy premeditated by them (the earls of Northumberland and Westmorland) against the religion and doctrine proved by the holy scriptures, and established by the authority of our most serene queen, at least ten years since . . . '[1]

On 14 November 1569 the rebels entered Durham Cathedral and restored the altars and the mass. Fortunately for the queen, they were badly led, they did not attempt to take York, and their effort to free Mary was ineffectual. The main rebel force was disbanded without fighting, and the earls of Northumberland and Westmorland fled across the Scottish border. The government had received an unpleasant shock, and the North was now given a sharp lesson. Several hundred rebels were hanged, and the rebellious areas were treated with great severity by the queen's troops. Later, Leonard Dacres, who had kept out of the original rebellion for personal reasons, raised a

[1] *The Zurich Letters*, I. 213. Richard Hilles to Henry Bullinger, 6 February 1570.

force of 3,000 men and attempted to surprise the royal troops under Lord Hunsdon. Dacres was defeated on 19 February 1570 and fled to Scotland.

The Rising of the Northern Earls had not been supported by Papists in other parts of the country; they had no desire to be involved in a rebellion. Nevertheless, it underlined in the eyes of the government the potential danger from Catholic opposition. It provided Cecil with excellent material which could be used as propaganda against all English Catholics, the more so since the rising was related to the decisive step about to be taken by the pope—the excommunication of the queen.

For a number of reasons the popes during the 1560's had refrained from taking any public action against Elizabeth I.[1] The early years of her reign corresponded with the pontificate of Pius IV (1559–65), a friendly, cheerful and vivacious man whose main concern was to re-open the Council of Trent and complete the work of reform which it had begun in its earlier sessions. There was pressure on him from Spain and from some of the English exiles not to take strong measures, and it was widely believed that an arrangement could be made with the queen, who was thought to be under the influence of evil counsellors. Pius IV wrote to Elizabeth in May 1560 saying he would do all he could for the salvation of her soul and to assure her position as queen. The letter was entrusted to Vincenzo Parpaglia, but Philip II arranged for Parpaglia to be detained in Brussels and persuaded the pope not to proceed. The pope made another attempt in 1561 to send a representative to England to invite the queen to be represented at the Council of Trent. There were lengthy discussions about whether the pope's representative should be received, and after much hesitation it was decided that he should not be allowed to enter the country. The question of excommunication then became acute. Philip II was strongly opposed to such action and pointed out that there was no prospect of any Catholic ruler deposing her. In 1563, some of the Catholic exiles in Flanders suggested that the Council of Trent should at least declare that the queen ought to be excommunicated, but the Emperor and the King of Spain were opposed to this, and Pius IV eventually accepted their point of view. Even as late as the end of 1563, he was still considering whether there was any chance of a papal

[1] For an examination of papal policy in these years, see Ludwig von Pastor, *The History of the Popes*, edit. R. F. Kerr, 1928, vols. XV, XVI.

nuncio being admitted into England. When he died in 1565, seven years after Elizabeth's accession, the papacy had not yet taken any official action against her or her church, and the pope had not even publicly forbidden attendance of Catholics at the services of the Church of England.

Pius IV was succeeded early in 1566 by Pius V, a former Dominican friar and a theologian, a man who came from a poor family and who regarded the papacy as a heavy cross which he had to bear. He drove himself hard, he ate and drank little, and his chief delight was in prayer. He was little moved by worldly considerations or by 'reasons of state', and he is one of the few popes who have been canonised. Like his predecessor he at first had some hopes that Elizabeth might be converted, but as early as May 1566 he referred to her publicly as one 'who pretended to be queen of England'. The possibility of ex-communication now began to be taken seriously once more. One of the difficulties was that if Elizabeth was deposed, her probable successor was Mary Stuart, and Mary's conduct had caused a good deal of concern in Rome. By 1569 Mary had made her peace with the papacy, and in March of that year Pius V asked the duke of Alva about the possibility of a joint invasion of England by France and Spain. Alva thought that there was no chance of this, and suggested that the solution was either for Philip to conquer England himself or for the pope to confer the kingdom on some Catholic nobleman who would marry Mary. The pope sent Nicholas Morton to England to find out what sort of reception would be given by English Catholics to a papal excommunication. Morton's report was apparently en-couraging. In November 1569 when rumours began to reach Rome of a possible attempt by the duke of Norfolk to secure the throne for Mary, the pope urged Alva to protect the Catholic religion in England and, if possible, to free Mary with assistance from Spain. Everything now seemed to indicate that the time for papal action had arrived. On 7 November 1569 the earls of Northumberland and Westmorland wrote asking for papal support. The letter did not arrive in Rome until 16 February and it was answered on 22 February 1570. The pope said that it was possible God had chosen them to restore England to the unity of the church. It was better to die than to live a shameful life under a woman like Elizabeth who was the slave of her passion. He had already arranged for money to be sent to England to help the nobles who had taken up arms for the Catholic religion in a just war.

There was pressure, too, from Nicholas Sander in Louvain who on 14 February 1570 asked Rome to support the rebels. He said that if the pope came out openly against Elizabeth, the English nobility and people would stand up for their faith.

It seems that it was in the mistaken belief that English Catholics were only too anxious to overthrow Elizabeth but were troubled in conscience about the morality of taking up arms against their lawful ruler that Pius V opened the process against the 'pretended' Queen of England. It was a simple matter to go through the formal procedure of collecting evidence from refugee witnesses that Elizabeth had assumed the position of Head of the Church, had deposed and imprisoned Catholic bishops and priests, had authorised the preaching of heresy and had imposed an oath against the papacy. Then, on 25 February 1570 Pius V signed the bull *Regnans in Excelsis* excommunicating and deposing the queen.[1]

The bull of excommunication was a stark, uncompromising document. It left no room for doubt about the powers which the pope claimed or about the consequences of his use of those powers. God had committed the one holy Catholic and apostolic Church, outside which there was no salvation, to Peter and his successor, the Pope of Rome whom 'alone He has made ruler over all peoples and Kingdoms, to pull up, destroy, scatter, disperse, plant and build, so that he may preserve His faithful people . . . in the unity of the Spirit and present them safe and spotless to their Saviour'. The pope had spared no pains to preserve that unity and the Catholic religion, but the number of the ungodly had grown, and there was no place in the world which they had not tried to corrupt. Elizabeth, 'the pretended queen of England and the servant of crime', had assisted in this, and 'having seized the crown and monstrously usurped the place of supreme head of the Church in all England' had reduced the kingdom to a miserable ruin. She had embraced the errors of heretics, removed the royal Council, composed of the nobility, and filled it with obscure heretics; she had oppressed the followers of the Catholic faith, instituted false preachers, abolished the mass, celibacy and Catholic ceremonies. She had ordered heretical books to be propounded and impious Calvinist rites to be observed by her subjects. She had ejected bishops and Catholic priests, had forbidden her clergy and people to

---

[1] For the Latin version and an English translation, see G. R. Elton, *The Tudor Constitution*, pp. 414–18.

acknowledge the Church of Rome, and had forced them to accept her on oath as 'their only lady in matters temporal and spiritual'. She had imprisoned prelates. She had despised the pious prayers and admonitions of Catholic princes and refused to admit papal nuncios. 'Therefore', the bull continues, ' . . . we do out of the fullness of our apostolic power declare the foresaid Elizabeth to be a heretic and favourer of heretics, and her adherents in the matters aforesaid to have incurred the sentence of excommunication . . . And moreover [we declare] her to be deprived of her pretended title to the aforesaid crown and of all lordship, dignity and privilege whatsoever.' The bull then goes on to declare 'the nobles, subjects, and people of the said realm, and all others who have in anyway sworn oaths to her, to be forever absolved from such an oath . . . ' Not only is Elizabeth deprived of her pretended title, but her subjects are commanded not to obey her. 'We charge and command all and singular the nobles, subjects, people and others aforesaid that they do not dare obey her orders, mandates and laws. Those who shall act to the contrary we include in the like sentence of excommunication.'

There are a great many problems in connection with this remarkable and belated condemnation of the queen. No provision was made for its enforcement by Catholic princes. They were not even officially informed that it had been issued. No steps were taken to publish it in England, although arrangements were made to make it public in the seaports of the Netherlands and France from whence the news would presumably be carried to England. Everything seems to point to the idea that it was not meant to be a general invitation to Catholic rulers to take action against Elizabeth but was intended simply to reassure the consciences of Englishmen, who were thought to be eager to rise in rebellion. It was issued in ignorance of the fact that a rebellion had already taken place and had ended in disaster. If this had been known in Rome, the question would have arisen whether there was any point in issuing it at all at this particular point in time.

But although the bull was probably intended to deal only with a particular situation, it was in fact an uncompromising general condemnation of the queen which made no reference at all to the circumstances which led to its promulgation. It did not cease to be valid merely because the Rising of the Northern Earls had failed. It could be used to justify the actions of anyone who wanted to overthrow the queen, and it presented English Catholics with a serious problem,

3 CARDINAL WILLIAM ALLEN 1532–1594
The Lancashire man who made perhaps the biggest single contribution to the survival of English Catholicism by founding at Douay in 1568 a seminary for the training of priests for the English mission. He was later heavily involved in plans for saving English Catholicism by means of a Spanish invasion.

4 POPE PIUS V 1566–1572
The Pope who in 1570 issued the bull *Regnans in Excelsis*—'we do out of the
fulness of our apostolic power declare the foresaid Elizabeth to be a heretic
. . . And moreover we (declare) her to be deprived of her pretended title to the
aforesaid crown. . . .'

since it expressly forbade them to obey her orders. It is true that most English Catholics ignored it. The vast majority never saw it, and it could always be argued that it had not been officially communicated to them. They remained loyal to Elizabeth, but it was hardly surprising that the government used the bull with great effect to argue that Papists were henceforth bound to be traitors. The government's case was strengthened by the fact that the bull was not withdrawn and that from 1569 onwards the papacy undoubtedly strove to overthrow the queen. A number of English Catholic exiles were heavily involved in these efforts. English Catholics might take the line that they were loyal to the pope in religion and loyal to the queen as their temporal ruler, but the popes themselves did not accept this division of loyalty, and the most they would concede at any time was that the bull did not bind English Catholics 'as things now stand'.[1]

It has often been argued that by issuing this bull the papacy declared war on England. In a sense this is true, but it must not be forgotten that the English government had been waging war on the papacy ever since 1559. Elizabeth clearly intended to destroy Roman Catholicism in England, and Englishmen were forbidden under heavy penalties to recognise the pope's spiritual authority or to practise their religion. As Pius V saw the situation, it was necessary for him at long last to issue an official condemnation of the queen's policy and to take what steps he could, by virtue of his deposing power, to prevent her achieving her objective. It would be a betrayal of his spiritual responsibilities if he allowed the situation to deteriorate even further and failed to take advantage of what seemed a favourable opportunity. The papal policy was logical, but it was in fact unsuccessful. We can see now that the cause of Catholicism in England would have gained immensely in the sixteenth century if the popes had concentrated all their efforts on employing spiritual rather than temporal weapons, and if, instead of devoting so much energy to trying to secure armed intervention, they had devoted themselves to training priests and sending them to convert England. But they could not foresee that the sword would break in their hands, and that what they believed to be a fully justified attempt to save English Catholicism by force of arms would prove both ineffective and extremely harmful to their cause.

Regnans in Excelsis was not only mistimed in the sense that it came

[1] *Infra*, p. 162.

F

too late to help the northern rebels, but it was also mistimed in that it came too late to rally Catholic opinion in England. If such a condemnation had been issued by the papacy before the government and the established church had had time to consolidate their position, then there would have been at least a chance that Catholicism in England would have become a much more effective force. By 1570 the battle had to a large extent been lost. If the Papists later became much more formidable than they had been in the sixties, it was not because *Regnans in Excelsis* put fresh heart into them and halted the drift towards the established church, but because the missionary priests from Douay and the other seminaries brought the Counter-Reformation to England for the first time. Their efforts were not assisted and indeed were gravely hampered by *Regnans in Excelsis* which was not withdrawn, even though its application was modified in an attempt to help their work.[1]

[1] See p. 162.

5

The Years of Uncertainty 1558–70: The Rise of Puritan Resistance

THE main drive of the Elizabeth government in the 1560's was directed against the Papists. These nonconformists on the right were numerically much stronger and potentially more dangerous than the nonconformists on the left. The government had no desire to fight a war on two fronts if it could avoid it, and enthusiastic Protestants were obviously very valuable allies in a war against Rome.

Although it was some years before serious conflict broke out between the established Church and the more extreme Protestants within its fold, the seeds of trouble were present from the very beginning of the reign. The Marian exiles returning from abroad and their like-minded supporters in England did not regard the settlement of 1559 as final. The Elizabeth Prayer Book was much more conservative, much less 'reformed', than that used even by the moderate Marian exiles in Frankfurt or Zurich, and it fell far short of what was wanted by those who had adopted the model of Geneva. For such people 1559 was only the beginning. The first battle had been won, and they hoped, with God's help, to win the campaign. They were the more confident because the queen had no alternative but to offer many of them important posts in the Church. They were prepared to wait, to make allowances for the difficulties facing their ruler, and to look forward to the day when their godly princess would complete the work so gloriously begun.[1]

---

[1] Jewel to Peter Martyr, 7 February 1562: '. . . many things are often tolerated by sovereigns by reason of the times. And this at first, probably, was not attended with inconvenience; but now that the full light of the gospel has shone forth, the very vestiges of error must, as far as possible, be removed together with the rubbish and, as the saying is, with the very dust.' *The Zurich Letters*, I. 100.

73

But if such men regarded the settlement of 1559 as only the begin-ning, Elizabeth regarded it as the end. It has been said of her that 'Religiously she was in 1603 what she was in 1558, a huge boulder in the path of Puritanism, unavoidable, insurmountable, immovable.'[1] For her the question was not so much theological truth as what could, with time and good fortune, be made acceptable to as many English-men as possible. In 1559 she had been forced to make big concessions to the determined Protestants in the House of Commons, and Pro-fessor Neale suggests that 'she detested Puritanism the more for having wrested so much from her in this Parliament'.[2] After this early and considerable defeat, she was the chief obstacle to the further pro-gress of 'true religion'. Fortunately for her, most of the Protestants whom she opposed continued to regard her as 'a wise and religious Queen', and they directed their criticism not against her but against her bishops and other evil advisers. Thomas Sampson wrote to Peter Martyr in January 1560 saying 'she is indeed a child of God' but, he added, princes 'have many friends in their temporal concerns, and but few who are concerned for their souls'.[3] The Papists who began by thinking that the queen was well disposed and that it was her council-lors who were to blame were disillusioned fairly quickly; many of the Puritans kept their illusions to the end.

In the early years of the reign there was little or nothing that could be called an organised Puritan movement. There were, however, indi-viduals and groups who were very uneasy in their consciences about whether they could accept so imperfect a church as that established by law. Their bitterness and disillusionment was noted by Bishop Jewel who told a friend: 'It is idly and scurrilously said, by way of joke, that as heretofore Christ was *cast out* by his enemies, so he is now *kept out* by his friends.'[4] Thomas Sampson, writing to Peter Martyr in December 1558 expressing his doubts about whether he could accept ecclesiastical office, noted, with reference to the bishops, 'the degeneracy from the primitive institution, as regards their elec-tion, (for there is required neither the consent of the clergy, nor of the people)'. He pointed to 'the unseemliness of their superstitious dresses', and he added, 'I cannot take upon myself the government of the

---

[1] M. M. Knappen, *Tudor Puritanism*, p. 168.
[2] J. E. Neale, *Elizabeth I and her Parliament*, I. 83.
[3] *The Zurich Letters*, I. 64.
[4] *The Zurich Letters*, I. 17, 6 April 1559.

church, until, after having made an entire reformation in all ecclesiastical functions, she will concede to the clergy the right of ordering
all things according to the word of God, both as regards doctrine and
discipline, and the property of the Church . . . '[1] Even Bishop Jewel,
outraged by the fact that the queen retained a silver cross and candle-
sticks in her chapel, contemplated resignation in 1560 when he wrote
to Peter Martyr ' . . . as far as I can conjecture, I shall not again write
to you as a bishop. For matters are come to that pass, that either the
crosses of silver and tin, which we have every where broken in pieces,
must be restored, or our bishopricks relinquished.'[2]

The desire to bring the Elizabethan Church more into line with
'the best reformed churches' was naturally found in its most intense
form among the different groups of exiles who had gone abroad under
Mary. They had acquired first-hand experience of what a true reformation meant. What they had seen and done in Emden, Wesel, Zurich,
Strasbourg, Frankfurt, Arau, Basel and Geneva was very different
from what they found in the new English Church. About a quarter of
them, including some of the most distinguished, had come under the
direct influence of Geneva and had adopted a Calvinist form of worship. At Frankfort, where lived the largest group of exiles, an attempt
had been made to secure the adoption of a form of service much more
advanced than the Book of Common Prayer of 1552. The leaders of
this movement had been William Whittingham, later one of the most
important of the early Elizabethan Puritans, and John Knox. They
had been successfully resisted by two future Elizabethan bishops,
Richard Cox and John Jewel. Cox had argued that 'they would do as
they had done in England, and they would have the face of an English
church'. Knox's reply—'The Lord grant it to have the face of Christ's
church'—anticipated the criticism which the Puritans were later to
make of the Elizabethan establishment. Knox and Whittingham had
led a secession movement to Basel and Geneva, where they adopted a
full-blooded Calvinist form of worship. But even the exiles who had
stuck by the Second Prayer Book of Edward VI had become used to
a much simpler and more 'Protestant' form of worship than that used
in England in the later years of Edward VI. They had made big concessions and had given up private baptism, confirmation of children,

---

[1] *The Zurich Letters*, I. 1–2, 17 December 1558. He refused a bishopric but in the end
accepted the office of dean of Christ Church, Oxford. For his later difficulties, see p. 86 ff.
[2] *The Zurich Letters*, I. 68, 4 February 1560.

saints' days, kneeling at communion, and the use of the surplice. Many of them were to find the Elizabethan settlement a retrograde step in the search for 'true religion'.

The returning exiles not unnaturally hoped to play a major part in the making of the Elizabethan settlement. They were, after all, the Protestant theological experts and they had in foreign lands drunk the pure milk of the gospel. In fact, they found themselves given only a minor rôle. Jewel, not yet a bishop, complained plaintively to his friend Peter Martyr, *'we* are not consulted'.[1] Even the more moderate of the exiles were uneasy at this settlement imposed on them by authority of queen and parliament without consultation. One can see their hopes and fears, their hesitations and uncertainties, expressed in the fascinating collection of letters which they wrote to their friends abroad.[2] What they were compelled to accept was clearly not what they wanted. They were desperately anxious to explain that it did not differ in principle from the doctrines they had held in exile, and that if their church was not as yet perfect, it was because of the need to proceed cautiously, lest all should be undone. They were clearly struggling to justify the settlement both to themselves and to others, to get their continental friends to agree that they were not sacrificing principles for expediency and that the compromises which they had made were only over matters which were in themselves 'indifferent'. Many of them gradually came to terms with their doubts and were able eventually to accept and justify what initially they did not approve, but some found it increasingly difficult to put up with what was from their point of view the second-best, and such men were potentially a threat to the religion established by law.

The group which found it hardest to come to terms with political reality was that which had accepted Calvinist doctrine and forms of worship. 'The wolves . . . coming out of Geneva', to whom the bishop of Winchester had referred at Mary's funeral, found the new church a good deal less satisfactory than did the wolves from Frankfurt and Zurich. We have already seen that Thomas Sampson had so many scruples that he refused the bishopric of Norwich,[3] and although he

---

[1] *The Zurich Letters*, I. 23.

[2] *The Zurich Letters, comprising the Correspondence of several English Bishops and others with some of the Helvetian Reformers during the early part of the reign of Queen Elizabeth*, edited for the Parker Society by the Rev. Hastings Robinson, Cambridge, 1842, 2 vols.

[3] See p. 74.

eventually accepted a deanery, he was to run into trouble later in the vestiarian controversy.[1] William Whittingham another Geneva exile, did not immediately return to England, but stayed on to complete his famous translation of the Bible. Later he became dean of Durham through the influence of Robert and Ambrose Dudley, but he too was to fall foul of the ecclesiastical authorities.[2] Miles Coverdale, whose translation of the Bible had earned him a very high reputation and who might reasonably have expected a bishopric, did not get one, partly because of his links with John Knox, who was himself very much *persona non grata* in Elizabeth's England. Christopher Goodman, who had been Lady Margaret Professor in Oxford from 1548 to 1554 and who had worked abroad with Knox and Whittingham, was also not welcome and did not return to England until 1565. Even John Foxe, whose *Book of Martyrs* was to become one of the most influential books in the history of English Protestantism, got very little in the way of preferment in the Church.

In his study of Thomas Wood, another very important person in the early history of English Puritanism, Dr. Collinson shows how his letters 'provide an insight into that still mysterious sector of Elizabethan society, "the godly" '. He suggests that 'The Genevan emigrés were isolated almost as a distinct sect in the early Elizabethan Church both by the official disfavour which Knox and Goodman's political teaching had brought upon them and their consequent failure to find promotion, and by the exercise of tight internal discipline.'[3]

These English Protestants returning from abroad constituted a very serious potential threat to the Church set up in 1559, and some of them were in fact to provide a nucleus for a Puritan movement. Their numbers were not large, but what they lacked in quantity they made up for in quality and in determination. Fortunately for Elizabeth, the danger was lessened by the fact that they were not united about what ought to be done.[4] Their effectiveness as a pressure group was considerably reduced by the fact that a number of them accepted high office in the Church. Jewel as bishop of Salisbury, Sandys as bishop

---

[1] See p. 86 ff.   [2] See pp. 86, 88 note 1.

[3] *Letters of Thomas Wood, Puritan, 1566–1577*, edited by Patrick Collinson, *Bulletin of the Institute of Historical Research*, Special Supplement No. 5, November 1960, p. ix.

[4] *The Zurich Letters*, I. 21. Jewel to Peter Martyr, 28 April 1559. 'We . . . have not departed in the slightest degree from the confession of Zurich . . . although your friend (Sir Anthony Cook) defends some scheme of his own, I know not what, most obstinately, and is mightily angry with us.'

of Worcester, Grindal in London, Cox in Ely, Pilkington in Durham and Scory in Hereford proved far less radical than they had been in exile. Inevitably the responsibilities of office made them more conservative, limited their freedom of speech and action, and inclined them to the view that rather than desert their flocks and leave them a prey to Romish wolves, it was better to accept the considerable gains already made and not to risk everything by demanding what the queen would certainly refuse to grant. Bishop Pilkington of Durham argued, 'We propose to submit ourselves to such orders as shall be established by Authority, being not of themselves wicked'. He pointed out: 'We are under authority and can innovate nothing without the Queen; nor can we alter the laws; the only thing left to our choice is whether we will bear these things, or break the peace of the Church.'[1] Bishops, like politicians, do not find resignation comes easily to them, and they felt that something must be sacrificed for the sake of unity. When some of these bishops took action against the Puritans and for the sake of the peace of the church enforced regulations laid down by the state, they naturally exposed themselves to the comment: 'What talke they of their being beyond the seas in quene Maries dayes because of the persecution, when they in queene Elizabethes days, are come home to raise a persecution?'[2] The former poachers had turned into quite efficient gamekeepers, and when they arrested those who had once been their companions on the run, they could hardly expect that their motives would be interpreted correctly by the victims.

It also became increasingly clear that there would be no official welcome in England for the European Protestant theologians from whom the returning emigrés had learnt so much. The exiles had hoped that their friends would be invited to give a hand in putting the church on its feet, as they had been in the days of Edward VI. In January 1559, Jewel wrote to Peter Martyr telling him how his friends 'desire for you at present nothing more than England',[3] and in November he told him that he had heard from the archbishop of Canterbury that Peter had been invited to come over and that his old lectureship at Oxford had been kept open for him,[4] but the invitation was never sent. Earlier in the year, Jewel had written to Henry

[1] Quoted in H. C. Porter, *Reformation and Reaction in Tudor Cambridge*, Cambridge, 1958, p. 89.
[2] *Puritan Manifestoes*, edit. W. H. Frere and C. E. Douglas, p. 112.
[3] *The Zurich Letters*, I. 9.
[4] *Ibid.*, I. 45.

Bullinger commenting on the depressed and ruined state of Oxford. He added ' . . . although it would give me the greatest pleasure, under other circumstances, to see even a dog from Zurich in England, yet I cannot at this time recommend you to send your young men to us, either for a learned or religious education, unless you would have them sent back to you wicked and barbarous'.[1] Whatever Jewel might think, the government was no more enthusiastic about welcoming dogs from Zurich than it was about welcoming unmuzzled wolves from Geneva. The former exiles had to be content with discussing their problems with their European friends by correspondence.

Thus the impact of the returning emigrés was considerably reduced, and water was added to the pure milk of the gospel. Those who had learnt abroad how to purify religion were uneasy about the Elizabethan adulteration. The time would come when some of them would see that compromise with the establishment was as fatal to their cause as attending the parish church was for the Catholics. Meanwhile, like the Catholics, they carried on as best they could. Their lot was easier because a number of bishops sympathised with their views and did not harry them, even when they broke the law.

A number of the returning emigrés sat in Elizabeth's first parliament. They included Sir Anthony Cooke, father-in-law to Sir William Cecil and Sir Nicholas Bacon; Sir Francis Knollys, the queen's cousin and a member of the Privy Council; and Sir Edward Rogers, Vice-Chamberlain. We do not as yet know how many of them were there, but Professor Neale suggested that there was 'a vital core of at least twelve and probably sixteen'.[2] They were an influential and powerful group, but some of them were hampered by holding office, and they would not have been able to achieve much but for the existence in the house of a much larger body of determined Protestants. A reasonable and perhaps over-cautious estimate of the number of M.P.s whose sympathies were whole-heartedly with the emigrés puts the figure at one hundred out of a House of four hundred members.[3] If the other three hundred Members of the Commons were less committed, they were at least willing to support the minority in forcing upon the queen a more Protestant settlement than she wanted. The outcome was less radical than the House desired, for if the queen had to make con-

---

[1] *The Zurich Letters*, I. 33, 22 May 1559.
[2] J. E. Neale, *Elizabeth I and her Parliaments*, I. 57.
[3] J. E. Neale, *op. cit.*, I. 58.

cessions, so did the Members of the Commons. Thus there were many M.P.s who were dissatisfied with the settlement and who regarded it merely as a first step.

Apart from the M.P.s there were a number of other gentlemen scattered about the country who sympathised with the views of their representatives in parliament and who were prepared to give protection to Protestant zealots. Ministers with uneasy consciences were to enjoy a considerable measure of help from lay patrons, many of them in positions of importance and influence, who could find employment for those who did not fit in easily into the religious strait-jacket of the Acts of Supremacy and Uniformity. The debt of the Puritans to the earl of Leicester, to the earl of Huntingdon, the earl of Bedford, the earl of Warwick, Lord Rich, the duchess of Suffolk and a number of other patrons among the nobility and gentry, was very considerable.[1] Dr. Collinson claims that 'the strength of the patronage which the puritans were able to command determined the rise and fall of their fortunes'.[2] The lay patron could not only help in appointments to livings, to chaplaincies, to lectureships and to university posts, but he could also protect his protégés from the persecution of bishops anxious to enforce uniformity.

Another breeding ground for Puritanism was the universities, especially the University of Cambridge.[3] Of 472 Marian exiles listed by Miss Garrett, 76 had been members of Cambridge colleges, and another 10 are known to have been educated in the university. Only about a dozen of these returned to Cambridge after 1558, but the earlier tradition of dissent was continued, and Cambridge very quickly produced a crop of young Fellows who wanted more radical reform. Under the sympathetic Chancellorship of William Cecil, the university enjoyed a greater measure of freedom of discussion and a greater diversity of religious practice than was to be found outside. It was no accident that the vestiarian controversy was sparked off here[4]

[1] L. Stone, *The Crisis of the Aristocracy 1558–1641*, Oxford, 1965, p. 733 ff. For a brief but admirable summary of Leicester's influence, exercised over a long period and over a wide field, in support of 'moderate Puritans', see *Letters of Thomas Wood*, edited by Patrick Collinson, *Bulletin of the Institute of Historical Research*, Special Supplement, No. 5 November 1960.

[2] Patrick Collinson, 'The Puritan Classical Movement in the Reign of Elizabeth I', unpublished London Ph.D. thesis, 1957, p. xi.

[3] H. C. Porter, *Reformation and Reaction in Tudor Cambridge*, C. H. Garrett, *The Marian Exiles*.

[4] See p. 86.

and that it was in Cambridge that Thomas Cartwright issued his Presbyterian challenge to the Church of England.

Another potential centre of resistance to the establishment was London. Here the Protestant congregations which had operated underground in Mary's reign were reinforced by a number of exiles returning from Geneva. As early as September 1559 at St. Antholin's Church there was held an exercise 'after Geneva fassyon' with psalm singing and sermons two mornings a week.[1] Dr. Collinson suggests that in London the Puritans formed quite early in the reign a closely associated faction, a 'Genevan brotherhood' of the godly, and that there was a 'small but effectively organized group of puritan activists who laboured to bring the English Reformation to what they conceived to be its logical conclusion'.[2] Although there were comparatively few of them, their influence, like that of the Jesuits later, was out of all proportion to their number.

It is clear, then, that from the very beginning there was discontent and dissatisfaction with the established church. Those who wanted further change were not united and they did not, generally speaking, constitute 'a movement' but rather 'a climate of opinion'. Some of their complaints would receive support not only from zealous Protestant laymen but from bishops and pious churchmen who were aware that all was not well with a church in which there were many pseudo-papists, many absentee and pluralistic clergy, many ill-educated ministers who could not preach, and many relics of popery. The determination of the queen to go no further and to insist on uniformity was bound to run into serious opposition from critics who held widely differing views about what constituted 'true religion' but who were united in believing that the Church of England was not, as yet, a fully reformed church.

An important influence in creating a climate of opinion favourable to more radical change was the publication in 1560 of what was to be a standard work for Elizabethans—the Geneva Bible. It was the work mainly of William Whittingham, Anthony Gilby and Thomas Sampson, all of whom have a prominent place in the history of Elizabethan Puritanism. For the first time Englishmen had a complete Bible in Roman type and with numbered verses. It has been said of it that it

---

[1] Patrick Collinson, 'The Puritan Classical Movement,' p. 36; *The Elizabethan Puritan Movement*, p. 84 ff.
[2] *Letters of Thomas Wood*, edit. Patrick Collinson, pp. viii–ix.

was 'a book undertaken at the instance of a Calvinist congregation, by Calvinist scholars, for Calvinist readers'.[1] Its explanatory notes were Calvinist in tone and were not approved by the Elizabethan bishops, who brought out their own version—the Bishops' Bible—in 1568, but the Geneva Bible was nevertheless the best selling of all English translations before the Authorised Version of 1611.

The influence of Calvinism was further increased by the publication in 1561 of the Genevan *Forme of Prayer*. The printer, Rowland Hall, had been one of the Marian exiles in Geneva, and he set up in London a press which produced English editions of Calvin's works.[2] Another printer, Thomas Norton, brought out in the same year an English edition of Calvin's authoritative and most influential book—*The Institutes of the Christian Religion*.

Calvin was not the only European Protestant theologian to influence Elizabethan religious thinking. The debt to Zurich and to other foreign churches was considerable. Peter Martyr, Henry Bullinger and Rudolph Gualter had been close friends of many of the Marian exiles, and continued to give authoritative advice by correspondence after the exiles returned home. The great European Protestant literature was known to English theologians. Thus, the Elizabethan church did not develop in isolation from the Protestant churches of the rest of Europe, and it regarded them as 'true churches'. There was much to be found in these churches which differed from what was to be found in England. Inevitably, these differences forced some Englishmen to look critically at their own institution.[3]

The strong undercurrent of questioning, criticism and doubt about the established church might well have led to more serious consequences much earlier but for the fact that all were agreed that a government which had overthrown popery deserved well and must be given a chance to make itself secure against counter-attack. The fact that popery remained a menace for most of the reign, combined with an instinctive dislike on the part of the governing class of resisting established authority in the state, acted as a restraining influence on Elizabeth's critics.

[1] H. W. Hoare, *Our English Bible*, 1911, p. 223. Philip Hughes, *The Reformation in England*, III. 228–30.

[2] M. M. Knappen, *Tudor Puritanism*, p. 181.

[3] For a brilliant sketch of continental influence, see Professor Owen Chadwick, 'The Sixteenth Century', in *The English Church and the Continent*, edit. C. R. Dodwell, 1959.

Nevertheless, those who wanted more radical change were not content to leave well alone indefinitely. They enjoyed in these early years a considerable measure of toleration for their illegal practices, but they wanted more than that, and in 1563 they made a determined effort to get it—not, this time, through parliament but through Convocation. The Lower House of Convocation in 1559 had come out with a strong affirmation of Catholic teaching;[1] that of 1563 was strongly Protestant. Archbishop Parker had made careful preparations. Convocation was asked to consider a number of Articles of Religion defining the teaching of the Church of England and making clearer the ways in which it differed from the teaching of the Church of Rome and from that of some of the continental Protestant churches. The Thirty Nine Articles which he presented for discussion were based on the Forty Two Articles of 1553, but seven of the old ones were dropped and four new ones were added. Seventeen of the earlier Articles were considerably modified. What emerged was an English Confession of Faith which embodied a number of different religious traditions and which on a number of points could be interpreted in more than one way. The influence of the German and the Swiss reformers was clearly present, but the Articles fell far short of the wishes of zealous English Protestants. The words used in the Forty Two Articles denying 'the real and bodily presence (as they term it) of Christ's flesh and blood, in the Sacrament of the Lord's Supper' were omitted, but it was explained that 'The Body of Christ is given, taken, and eaten in the Supper, only after an heavenly and spiritual manner' and that the wicked did not receive the body of Christ. The Article on 'Predestination and Election' differed very considerably from Calvin's teaching. It dealt only with the elect who were destined for heaven and not with those predestined to damnation, and it stated that the doctrine was 'full of sweet, pleasant, and unspeakable comfort to godly persons'. The Articles no longer affirmed that the sovereign was 'Supreme head in earth, next under Christ, of the Church of England, and Ireland', but contained an elaborate explanation that the royal supremacy did not mean that the prince could minister God's word or the sacraments but only that he had the powers which God had always given to godly princes 'that they should rule all estates and degrees committed to their charge by God, whether they be Ecclesiastical or Temporal, and restrain with the

[1] See p. 8.

civil sword the stubborn and evil doers'. The authority of the Church was affirmed and it was laid down that it had 'power to decree Rites or Ceremonies, and authority in controversies of faith'. Nevertheless, as far as doctrinal beliefs were concerned, it was clearly stated that 'Holy Scripture containeth all things necessary to salvation; so that whatsoever is not read therein, nor may be proved thereby, is not to be required of any man that it should be believed as an Article of the Faith, or be thought requisite or necessary to salvation'.[1]

The Articles were stated to be agreed by the archbishops and bishops of both provinces and the whole clergy in convocation 'for the avoydyng of the diversities of opinions, and for the stablishyng of consent, touchyng true religion'.[2] Within limits, their purpose was to find formulae acceptable to people who held widely different theological views, and it is a tribute to the moderation and skilful drafting of Archbishop Parker that they were accepted by both Houses of Convocation, although there seems to have been some trouble about them in the Lower House. Theologians of different schools of thought found they could accept them with a good conscience, no doubt because they realised that what mattered was how they were interpreted. Moreover, at this stage the clergy were not required to subscribe formally to them. Later in the reign, the Articles, like the Prayer Book, were to come under fire from the Puritans.

Convocation in 1563 was prepared to follow the official lead and to approve the Articles, but in the Lower House there was a movement to secure further reforms which had not been put forward from above. One of the proposals was that Convocation should accept six articles which had what might be called, in the light of later developments, a strongly 'Puritan' flavour. All holy days were to be abolished; the minister was to read the service facing the people; the sign of the cross was to be omitted in baptism; it was to be left to the discretion of the ordinary people whether or not they should kneel to receive communion; the surplice was to be sufficient for all services but was not to be considered essential—'a comely garment or habit' would suffice; the organ was not to be used. A proposal to approve these Articles was at first carried by 43 votes to 35, but when proxy votes

[1] There is a useful short introduction to the study of the Thirty-Nine Articles in Carl S. Meyer, *Elizabeth I and the Religious Settlement of 1559*, Chapter IX.
[2] The Latin version and an English translation are printed in *Synodalia*, edit. E. Cardwell, Oxford, 1842, I. 34 ff.

were taken into account, the voting was 58 for the Articles and 59 against. It is, perhaps, going too far to call these proposals 'Puritan'. Nevertheless, they were a straw in the wind. It seems that they were in the main backed by men who had been in exile under Mary and opposed by those in positions of authority in the church.[1] They were a warning to the establishment of potential dangers from below, and steps must have been taken to ensure that in future Convocations the danger would not arise again. Presumably it was possible for the ecclesiastical authorities to exercise control over the membership, and the Puritans never again had the opportunity to use Convocation against the establishment. They were forced instead to have recourse to parliament or to find other less constitutional means of attack.

It seems clear that in the early years of the reign trouble with the 'Puritans' was avoided because the authorities were concentrating on removing the more obvious manifestations of popery and were prepared to allow Protestant deviationists a good deal of license, but sooner or later a church which was committed to uniformity would have to bring the Protestant nonconformists into line—or there would be chaos. The ways in which the ministers of the church were using their initiative and disobeying the civil and ecclesiastical authorities is admirably illustrated by a document entitled 'Varieties in the service and administration used' dated 14 February 1565.[2] This states that services and prayers were sometimes said in the chancel, sometimes in the body of the church or from the pulpit. The Book of Common Prayer was not always strictly followed. Some clergy wore a surplice and cope, some a surplice only, and some wore neither. The communion table was sometimes kept in the chancel, sometimes in the body of the church. At the communion service, some used a chalice, some a special communion cup, and some an ordinary cup. Communion was variously received, kneeling, sitting or standing. In baptism, some ministers used a font, others an ordinary basin. Some omitted the sign of the cross when administering the sacrament.

At first sight these variations do not seem to be of profound importance, and it might be asked whether there really was any need to

<hr />

[1] V. J. K. Brook, *A Life of Archbishop Parker*, p. 139.
[2] J. Strype, *Life and Acts of Matthew Parker*, Oxford 1821, I. 302; V. J. K. Brook, *A Life of Archbishop Parker*, pp. 165–6.

insist on uniformity about practices which the contestants on both sides were inclined to regard as things in themselves indifferent.[1] This diversity, however, was not due to negligence or ignorance of what had been laid down by authority. For some at least of those involved, the use of particular ritualistic practices was symbolic of theological views different from those officially prescribed. In addition, this refusal to obey lawful authority was potentially very dangerous. Those who refused to obey in matters indifferent might easily defy authority in more serious matters; they might challenge the royal supremacy. Even those who had a certain sympathy with the Protestantism of the deviationists were concerned about the resulting lack of order in the church. Disobedience might prove contagious, and authority could hardly tolerate a situation such as that described by a law-abiding Essex rector who complained that he was condemned by the neighbouring clergy because he wore the surplice.[2]

Archbishop Parker at first tried what could be done by sweet reasonableness. In 1564 he urged Thomas Sampson, dean of Christ Church, Oxford, and Laurence Humphrey, president of Magdalen College, Oxford, to agree to wear the surplice and to conform in other respects with the requirements of the church. A number of others, including William Whittingham, dean of Durham, also found themselves under pressure. Thus was sparked off what came to be known as the vestiarian controversy since it was concerned with the question of vestments and clerical dress in general. It was perhaps an unfortunate issue on which to fight, since it was not immediately clear that any great religious principle was involved, but Parker presumably felt that it was important. Those who would not conform were defying authority in a way which was plain to see. The nonconformists did not meekly give way. They argued with Parker that although the prescribed clerical dress might in itself be a thing 'indifferent', it had in fact been used by the Church of Rome and was therefore 'consecrated to idolatry'. Sampson and Humphrey questioned whether the authorities might impose on them even something which was 'indifferent'

---

[1] On 10 July 1560, Thomas Lever wrote to Henry Bullinger: 'In the injunctions, however, published by the queen, after the parliament, there are prescribed to the clergy some ornaments, such as the mass-priests formerly had and still retain . . . There are indeed but few of us, who hold such garments in the same abhorrence, as the soldier mentioned by Tertullian did the crown. But we are not ignorant what occasion the papists will take from thence, as a cause of stumbling to the weak.' *The Zurich Letters*, I. 84.

[2] Patrick Collinson, 'The Puritan Classical Movement', p. 14.

in itself unless 'there may be brought a ground out of the Scripture'.[1] Whittingham's bishop, Pilkington, who sympathised with his dean, appealed to the earl of Leicester for help to protect good men who did not want to dress like Papists.[2] There thus appeared early in the reign two features which were characteristic of Tudor Puritanism—an insistence that nothing should be prescribed which could not be supported by scriptural authority, and a readiness to seek help from sympathetic lay patrons against the ecclesiastical authorities.

When persuasion did not produce the desired conformity, the authorities decided on firmer measures. The initiative may have come from Cecil himself, for although he was prepared on many occasions to give a helping hand to Puritans, particularly after they had been harried by the ecclesiastical authorities and begged for his protection, he was nevertheless very conscious of the need to maintain order in the church as well as in the state. The queen herself had no sympathy with those who would not obey her laws. On 25 January 1565 she wrote to Parker a strongly-worded directive complaining of this 'diversity, variety, contention and vain love of singularity' which was contrary to the good orders she had established with the aim of ensuring that all might live 'without diversities of opinions or novelties of rites and manners'. She blamed the bishops for their slackness and insisted that there must be 'one manner of uniformity throughout our whole realm'. Parker was told to make a full enquiry with the other bishops and to take speedy action.[3] He put the enquiry in hand and on 8 March 1565 he informed Cecil of the action he proposed to take, asking him to get the queen's approval and authority. He laid down detailed regulations concerning clerical dress and the use of vestments. Communion was to be received kneeling and not standing or sitting. Existing licences for preachers were to be cancelled and new ones were to be obtained. Unlicensed preaching was forbidden. There was not much that was new in these regulations. The novelty lay in the fact that the ecclesiastical authorities were now going to make an effort to enforce them and to end the toleration which the nonconforming clergy had hitherto enjoyed.

From the beginning the archbishop was hampered by lack of support from the civil power. The queen did not strengthen Parker's hand

---

[1] V. J. K. Brook, *A Life of Archbishop Parker*, p. 161.
[2] M. M. Knappen, *Tudor Puritanism*, p. 190 ff.
[3] V. J. K. Brook, *A Life of Archbishop Parker*, p. 162 ff.

by giving official approval, and throughout the difficult months that followed, those in authority in the government were very careful not to associate themselves publicly with what was being done by the church. The queen's motive was probably her unwillingness to endanger her personal popularity, but a number of her advisers took no part in the business because they did not sympathise with it. Parker nevertheless went ahead. He knew what the queen wanted, and his love of order and his reluctance to allow his authority to be flouted explain why he carried on with a conflict which had been forced upon him and which he found discouraging and distasteful.

Parker took action against Sampson and Humphrey. If they conformed, their example would encourage others to do so. If they held out and were punished, that might frighten the rest.[1] When Sampson and Humphrey would not give way, Parker on 29 April 1565 ordered them to leave their places. Humphrey withdrew from Oxford for a time but later returned. He was not deprived of the Presidency of Magdalen or of his Regius Professorship. Sampson did lose his position and was for a time under some kind of house arrest.

Oxford had given the archbishop some trouble but Cambridge gave him a great deal more.[2] Early in 1565 William Fulke, a young Fellow of St. John's College and a friend of Thomas Cartwright, denounced the surplice and cap as signs of 'the popish priesthood in the Church of Antichrist'. When the Vice-Chancellor tried to insist on observing the regulations, he was rebuked by Anthony Gilby, incumbent of Ashby-de-la-Zouche, who told him that a true minister of Christ ought 'to root forth such manifest superstitions and corruptions of religion'. In the Michaelmas term of 1565 Fulke attacked the use of unleavened bread in the sacrament, kneeling at communion, and the wearing of cap and surplice. St. John's was a large college with nearly 300 members, and Fulke had a following among the Fellows and undergraduates who hissed at those who wore surplices. The conflict went on into 1566, and Parker and Cecil, the Chancellor of the Uni-

---

[1] On 20 March, the leading nonconformist clergy requested the ecclesiastical authorities to show brotherly forbearance to those who had conscientious objections. The signatories included Humphrey, Sampson, Coverdale, Whittingham and sixteen others. Thirteen of these names appear in a list of 'certain godlie learned preachers which have utterly forsaken Antichriste and al his Romishe rags' which had been presented to Robert Dudley early in the reign. Patrick Collinson, *The Elizabethan Puritan Movement*, pp. 48, 74.

[2] H. C. Porter, *Reformation and Reaction in Tudor Cambridge*, p. 114 ff.

versity, were drawn in. The upshot was that Fulke was deprived of his Fellowship, and a measure of conformity was established. Nevertheless, the tradition of dissent continued and St. John's was one of the most important seminaries for the production of Puritans—a Puritan Douay.

In March 1566 the queen again urged Parker and Grindal, bishop of London, to take action against nonconformists. After trying in vain to get public official support, they decided to call all the London clergy before them and to demand an undertaking to conform. Parker reported to Cecil, who had not answered a request to be present at the interviews, that 61 had agreed, 9 or 10 been absent and 37 refused, among them 'the best, and some preachers'. The 37 recalcitrants were suspended and given three months to obey or lose their livings.

Parker's next step was to issue a general directive for the whole church. He would have been in a much stronger position if this could have been done by Injunctions made by the queen's authority under the Act of Supremacy, but neither the queen nor the privy council had any wish to be directly involved. The document, later known as Parker's *Advertisements*, was published by the authority of Parker himself and a number of bishops and ecclesiastical commissioners.

The *Advertisements*[1] begin by pointing out that the queen knows how necessary it is for the advancement of God's glory and the establishment of Christ's pure religion that all her subjects should be joined 'in one perfect unity of doctrine . . . and one uniformity of rite and manners'. She has therefore instructed the archbishop and bishops to take action 'whereby all diversities and varieties among them of the clergy and the people . . . might be reformed and repressed, and brought to one manner of uniformity throughout the whole realm'. All preachers are to be examined 'for their conformity in unity of doctrine'. They are to encourage 'the reverent estimation' of the sacrament of Baptism and the Lord's Supper and the receiving of the Holy Communion of the Body and Blood of Christ in the form laid down in the Prayer Book. Those who preach 'any matter tending to dissension, or to the derogation of the religion and doctrine received' are to be reported to the bishop for necessary action. In cathedrals and collegiate churches the principal minister is to wear a cope in administering the sacrament and in other churches 'a comely surplice

---

[1] Printed in *Documents illustrative of English Church History*, compiled by Henry Gee and William John Hardy, London, 1910, pp. 467–75.

with sleeves'. The parish was to provide 'a decent table standing on a frame for the Communion Table' and it was to be covered with a fair linen cloth. The Ten Commandments were to be set upon the east wall 'over the said table'. All communicants were to receive the sacrament kneeling. There were regulations about baptism and about the tolling of bells. Only the official holy days were to be observed. Other articles dealt with Sunday observance, the admission of candidates to holy orders, the training of curates, the presentation by church wardens of those who would not come to church, fraudulent agreements about church property, and marriage within the prohibited degrees. There were very elaborate regulations about clerical dress. Finally, there were certain promises which had in future to be made by those admitted to ecclesiastical office. They included an undertaking 'to observe, keep and maintain such order and uniformity in all external policy, rites and ceremonies of the Church, as by the laws, good usages, and orders are already well provided and established'.

The attempt to impose uniformity met with resistance in London where some of the clergy put up a good fight. Prominent among them were Robert Crowley, vicar of St. Giles, Cripplegate; John Gough, rector of St. Peter, Cornhill; and John Philpot, rector of St. Michael, Cornhill, and of Stepney.[1] Dr. Collinson describes them as 'the ringleaders of a well organized movement of protest among the suspended London ministers'. Thomas Wood appealed to Cecil against the dismissal of '36 godly men at one instant, amongst which were divers that traveyled in preaching of the word . . . ' He referred to the disastrous consequences including 'the utter overthrow of a most frutfull and comfortable exercise named prophesying used once a week at St. Peter's where 2 or 3 hundred were assembled before th' accustomed houre on Thursday last and, seeing themselves disapointed, departed, not without abundance of teares, to the great discomfort of all godly hartes'. The lectures at St. Antholin's still continued but he feared they would not do so for long. He referred to 'The pitifull complaint of all the godly here' and to 'the wonderfull rejoysing also of the Papistes, enemyes to God and the Prince'.[2] Dr. Collinson thinks that the St. Antholin's lectures and the 'prophesyings', which seem to have been meetings at which ministers and their congregation discussed doctrine, were 'the main platform for Calvinist preaching in

---

[1] *Letters of Thomas Wood*, edit. Patrick Collinson, xii.
[2] *Ibid.*, pp. 1–2.

early Elizabethan London and the focal point of what was about to be singled out as a sectarian puritan faction'.[1]

Those who resisted were few in number, but they were determined and resourceful, and some of them were well organised. They decided to make use of the press. It had been employed with great effect by the Marian exiles against the Church of Rome, and it was now used against the authorities in the Church of England. Two tracts were produced. One of them, edited by Robert Crowley on the basis of information supplied by a number of London ministers, was *A Briefe Discourse against the Outwarde Apparell and Ministering Garmentes of the Popishe Church.* It has been described as the first published manifesto of Elizabethan Puritanism.[2]

A literary warfare ensued. The authorities put their case in *A Brief Examination for the Tyme* in which they argued the need for order and the duty of the individual to conform unless the order was against God's law.[3] A number of other writers joined in, including Anthony Gilby of Ashby-de-la-Zouche who enjoyed the protection of the Puritan-minded earl of Huntingdon. In Gilby's *A Pleasaunt Dialogue betweene a Souldior of Barwicke and an English Chaplaine*, the chaplain is a soldier turned parson and is a thoroughly discreditable character with 'but one eye and no learning'. He enjoys an easy life, and he urges the soldier to take it up himself. He can get a dispensation for his lack of learning, he need not preach, and he can enjoy himself. The honest soldier is shocked and attacks the abuses in the church, including the lordly bishops, the use of wedding rings and 'the want of true discipline'.[4]

In this early battle of the books, some of the contestants were already facing the question of how far the civil power ought to be obeyed when it ordered the Christian to do something evil. Crowley argued 'Christ onelie and not the godlie Magistrate must appoint what is necessarie for his Ministers',[5] and Gilby's soldier suggested that if the queen might lawfully prescribe one piece of popery, then logically she might prescribe the lot.[6] The royal supremacy was being called in question.

---

[1] Letters of Thomas Wood, p. xi.
[2] Patrick Collinson, 'The Puritan Classical Movement,' p. 37; M. M. Knappen, *Tudor Puritanism*, pp. 198-9.
[3] M. M. Knappen, *Tudor Puritanism*, p. 199.   [4] *Ibid.*, p. 200.
[5] Patrick Collinson, 'The Puritan Classical Movement', p. 53.
[6] M. M. Knappen, *Tudor Puritanism*, p. 202.

The stress which has been laid on the distinctively English character of the Elizabethan church settlement has led to an under-emphasis on the way in which it was affected by the European Reformation. The quarrel about ritual and dress is but one illustration of the concern of Protestant leaders abroad for what was being done in this country. What might have been 'a little local difficulty' took on a wider significance when some of those involved appealed to the leaders of 'the best reformed churches'. Some of the bishops were uneasy and apologetic about the policy which they were expected to enforce. Thus in July 1565 Horne of Winchester wrote to Rudolph Gualter explaining that the law requiring the clergy to wear square caps and surplices had been passed at the beginning of the reign without consulting the bishops who had been required to conform or resign. He said: 'We complied with this injunction, lest our enemies should take possession of the places deserted by ourselves,' and he added: 'We certainly hope to repeal this clause of the act next session, but if this cannot be effected, since the papists are forming a secret and powerful opposition, I nevertheless am of opinion that we ought to continue in the ministry, lest, if we desert and reject it upon such grounds, they insinuate themselves.'[1] In February 1566, Bishop Jewel told Henry Bullinger and Lewis Lavater that: 'The contest respecting the linen surplice . . . is not yet at rest. That matter still somewhat disturbs weak minds. And I wish that all, even the slightest vestiges of popery might be removed from our churches, and above all from our minds. But the queen at this time is unable to endure the least alteration in matters of religion.'[2]

The bishops persuaded themselves that they must not desert their posts lest worse befall, but their opponents felt that there must be no compromise with evil things. Laurence Humphrey appealed for Bullinger's support and asked whether the prescribed clerical dress did not 'savour of monkery, popery and Judaism',[3] and Thomas Sampson raised a number of fundamental issues when he asked Bullinger 'Whether the prescribing habits of this kind be consistent with ecclesiastical and christian liberty? . . . whether any new ceremonies may be instituted, or superadded to what is expressly commanded in the word? . . . whether any thing of a ceremonial nature

---

[1] *The Zurich Letters*, I. 142–3, 17 July 1565.
[2] *Ibid.*, I. 148–9, 8 February 1566.
[3] *Ibid.*, I. 152, 9 February 1566.

may be prescribed to the church by the sovereign, without the assent and free concurrence of churchmen? . . . whether a man ought thus to obey the decrees of the church or on account of non-compliance . . . be cast out of the ministry? . . . whether good pastors, of unblemished life and doctrine, may rightfully be removed from the ministry on account of their non-compliance with such ceremonies?'[1]

Bullinger made it plain that he did not approve of these 'dregs of popery', but he thought that if the bishops left their posts, they might be replaced by 'wicked and treacherous workmen' who might be 'either papists, or else Lutheran doctors and presidents, who are not very much unlike them'. He pointed out the danger of questioning the authority of kings and magistrates 'lest, by raising questions before the people respecting the extent of the magisterial authority, we should give occasion to some disorders'. He thought, however, that these things ought to be discussed in the public assembly of the realm and that the queen and the nobles ought to be reminded of their duty in private.[2]

Bullinger also wrote to Laurence Humphrey and Thomas Sampson a letter which in effect advised them to conform.[3] He urged every one of the nonconformists to consider 'whether he will not more edify the church of Christ by regarding the use of habits for the sake of order and decency, as a matter of indifference . . . than by leaving the church . . . to be occupied hereafter if not by evident wolves, at least by ill-qualified and evil ministers'.

This letter was not intended to be made public, but Bullinger sent a copy for information to Horne and others,[4] and the English bishops decided to publish it as it gave the authority of the leading European reformers to the views which they themselves were upholding.[5] The nonconformists were far from satisfied. They urged their case even more strongly to Bullinger, and they appealed to Beza and Farel in Geneva. There was a lengthy correspondence, and Percival Wiburn was sent to Europe to give first-hand information about the nonconformists' case and to seek support in Geneva and Zurich.

In the course of all this discussion, some fundamental criticisms

---

[1] *The Zurich Letters*, I. 153–5, 16 February 1566.
[2] *Ibid.*, I. 342–4. Bullinger to Horne, 3 November 1565.
[3] *Ibid.*, I. 345–55, 1 May 1566.
[4] *Ibid.*, I. 356.
[5] *The Zurich Letters*, I. 175, Grindal and Horne to Bullinger and Gualter, 6 February 1567.

were made of the established church. In July 1566, for example, Humphrey and Sampson wrote to Bullinger:[1] 'The assumption of preeminence and pride has always displeased us in the papacy, and can tyranny please us in a free church? A free synod among Christians hath heretofore untied the knots of controversy: why should everything be now referred to the pleasure of one or two individuals? Where the liberty of voting and speaking prevails, the truth is vigorous and flourishing.' They went on to say: 'We have always thought well of the bishops; we have put a candid interpretation on their display of grandeur: why cannot they endure us, who formerly bore the same cross with them? . . . Why do they cast us into prison? Why do they persecute us on account of the habits? . . . '

Men who felt like Humphrey and Sampson might, it was clear, not always 'think well of bishops', and the reference to decisions by 'a free synod' was not likely to please the Supreme Governor of the Church of England.

In order to convince Bullinger that the dispute went deeper than a mere squabble over clerical dress, Humphrey and Sampson listed 'Some blemishes which still attach to the Church of England'.[2] They found thirteen 'blemishes', some of them comparatively small but others constituting very serious defects indeed in the eyes of the godly. They thought that in the public prayers of the church there was 'a kind of popish superstition'. They objected to 'exquisite singing in parts' and to the increasing use of organs. In baptism the minister addressed the infant in whose name the sponsors answered, and he used the sign of the cross. Women were allowed to baptise in private houses, the cope and surplice were used at the Lord's Supper, popish habits were worn by the clergy out of church, women continued to wear veils at their churching. The marriage of the clergy was not allowed by the public laws and by some their children were regarded as illegitimate. Solemn betrothings still took place after the popish method with use of the ring. In the government of the church there were still retained 'many traces of the church of anti-Christ'. As formerly in Rome, so now in England, almost everything was for sale in the archbishops' courts, including licences to hold livings in plurality, licences for non-residence, for eating meat on forbidden days and in Lent, and for marriage outside the permitted seasons. Humphrey and

[1] *The Zurich Letters*, I. 161, 162, July 1566.
[2] *Ibid.* I. 163 ff.

Sampson asked the ominous question: ' . . . what shall we say respecting discipline, the sinews of religion?' and answered: 'There is none at all, neither has our church its rod, or any exercise of superintendence.' They complained that 'The free liberty of preaching is taken away from the ministers of Christ: those who are now willing to preach are forbidden to recommend any innovation with regard to rites; but all are obliged to give their assent to ceremonies by subscribing their hands.' Finally, on a point of doctrine, they said ' . . . the article composed in the time of Edward the Sixth respecting the spiritual eating, which expressly oppugned and took away the real presence in the Eucharist, and contained a most clear explanation of the truth, is now set forth among us mutilated and imperfect'.[1]

Here indeed were criticisms of the doctrine and government of the church which went far beyond minor differences of opinion about clerical dress. Beza in Geneva was very disturbed indeed and he tried to persuade Bullinger to intervene and to send a representative to England to get the queen and the bishops to put things right.[2] Although Bullinger was far from satisfied with the state of affairs in England, he and the other leaders in Zurich decided not to burn their fingers by meddling with the problem any more.[3] In February 1567 Grindal and Horne thanked Bullinger and Gualter for what they had done. They said they had themselves 'laboured with all earnestness . . . to effect what our brethren require, and what we ourselves wish . . . but since we cannot do what we would, we should do in the Lord what we can'. They were not guilty of all the faults mentioned in the list of thirteen 'blemishes' in the church, but certain things had to be tolerated 'until the Lord shall give us better times'. They said they allowed kneeling at the Lord's Supper because it was appointed by law, but they had made it plain that this was not a matter of

---

[1] See p. 11 and note 3.

[2] *The Zurich Letters*, II. 127 ff., 3 September 1566.

Beza concluded that it was not simply a quarrel about externals. He said '. . . an outward call . . . by a congregation of the brethren is the basis and foundation of an ecclesiastical ministry . . . What can be more abominable, what more extravagant, than that assumed power of the bishops, by which they admit at their pleasure parties not so called . . .' With reference to church discipline, he wrote '. . . what can it be in a country where, just the same as under the papacy, they have in place of a lawfully appointed presbytery their deans, chancellors, and archdeacons . . .' (p. 129). On 29 July 1567, Beza asked Bullinger with reference to England '. . . where did such a Babylon ever exist?' (*The Zurich Letters*, II. 153).

[3] *The Zurich Letters*, II. 154–5.

adoration unto the sacramental bread and wine 'or to any real and essential presence of Christ's natural flesh and blood there existing'[1]

The failure of the continental reformers to intervene on behalf of the Protestant nonconformists was an extremely important turning-point in the history of the Elizabethan Church. Some of the ablest and most influential of the bishops had long been uneasy about what the law required them to do and to compel others to do. If Bullinger and Gualter had come out in support of the nonconformists, bishops such as Grindal, Parkhurst, Sandys, Horne and Jewel would have had a major crisis of conscience, since they leant heavily on the advice of their friends in Zurich. Elizabeth might have been faced with the resignation of a number of her bishops and the Church of England would have been split wide open. In fact, the bishops closed their ranks, and the incipient Puritan movement had to find leaders outside the hierarchy. Grindal informed Bullinger in August 1566 that many of the more learned clergy who had seemed on the point of forsaking the ministry had now returned to a better frame of mind and that many of the laity had begun to entertain milder sentiments, now that they understood that Bullinger did not consider the ceremonies unlawful. Grindal added that the bishops did not regret their decision 'not to desert our churches for the sake of a few ceremonies'. In the Church of England 'the pure doctrine of the gospel remained in all its integrity and freedom' which otherwise would have become 'a prey to the Ecebolians, Lutherans and semi-papists'.[2]

Although only two or three of the London ministers refused to conform in the end, the Church of England did not emerge unscathed from the vestiarian controversy. There had been a hardening of views on the part of the authorities, and a number of the 'godly' must have realised that the day when 'true religion' would be established was not to be this year or the next, but possibly never—unless the godly were prepared to take action themselves. They had learnt the techniques of organisation and publicity, and they were beginning to raise fundamental issues. Few formally withdrew from the church, but it is significant that it is about this time that the word 'Puritan' first began to be used. From the mid-sixties the future leaders of Puritanism were learning their business and moving into position. It was all the easier for them to do so because uniformity was not everywhere

---

[1] *The Zurich Letters*, I. 175, 6 February 1567.
[2] *The Zurich Letters*, I. 168, 27 August 1566.

strictly enforced. The continental reformers urged the English bishops to deal gently with their brethren.[1] In the dioceses of Durham, Norwich and Worcester, the bishops tolerated illegal practices, and there was much irregularity in the University of Cambridge where so many young ministers were being trained. In many places, powerful lay patrons protected their favourite ministers and found them livings, chaplaincies and lectureships,[2] and in a number of towns where there were sympathetic corporations, the spirit of nonconformity quietly grew in the years that followed. What had seemed to a be storm in a teacup developed into something much more serious, for even a small body of determined men who believe with passionate sincerity that they are doing the Lord's work can have devastating effects on the society in which they operate.

It was not only the nonconforming ministers who gave trouble to the bishops in 1566. The parliament first elected in 1563 was recalled in that year, and there were a number of bills concerning religion. One of these was to give parliamentary confirmation to the Thirty Nine Articles. It passed the Commons and got its first reading in the Lords with the support of the bishops. Then, for reasons not absolutely clear, the queen sent order to the Lord Keeper that it was not to go any further. She summoned the archbishop and apparently told him that no bill about religion must be introduced in parliament without her consent. A little later the two archbishops and thirteen bishops asked her to allow the bill to proceed, but she refused.[3] It may seem strange that the queen refused to sanction a bill which would strengthen the attempt to impose religious unity, but her instinct was sound—sounder than the bishops. Parliament must not initiate bills about religion without her knowledge and consent. If the Commons were allowed to get the bit between their teeth, they might bolt and unseat the establishment of 1559.

[1] Thus Gualter wrote to Parkhurst, 11 September 1566: 'Some of these brethren are, I grant, somewhat hard to please, but yet their cause is not a bad one, much less a wicked one; nay, it were rather to be desired that their views might prevail' and he said '. . . it appears to us particularly hard, that the bishops should allow themselves to be the instruments of persecution . . .' *The Zurich Letters*, II. 141.

[2] On 11 September 1566 Bullinger and Gualter wrote to the earl of Bedford asking him 'not to refuse your patronage to those godly brethren, who, notwithstanding they may have erred in some respects, are yet deserving of pardon, as it is plain that they have been actuated by a fervent zeal for godliness, and that their sole object is to have the church purified from all the dross of popery'. *The Zurich Letters*, II. 137 ff.

[3] J. E. Neale, *Elizabeth I and her Parliaments*, I. 166–8.

Other bills introduced in this parliament dealt with the qualification of ministers, non-residence, simony, corrupt presentations to livings and related matters. Professor Neale describes them as 'Puritan reforms in the sense that Puritans desired them', but adds 'they were that part of the Puritan programme which might appeal to any earnest Churchman . . . ' This would seem to imply that any initiative in reforming the church must necessarily be considered 'Puritan' and to overlook the fact that the urge to end abuses was not a 'Puritan' monoply.

Most Puritans wanted to stay within the Church of England. They hoped eventually to reform it, and in the meantime they offered active or passive resistance to the authorities when they tried to impose uniformity of doctrine and worship, but there were some who thought the answer to their problem lay in separation from the church, either temporary or permanent. It is not surprising that in 1567 there should have come to light evidence of separatist tendencies. On 19 June 1567, the sheriff's officers in London discovered a meeting at Plumbers' Hall of about a hundred people who had met ostensibly to celebrate a wedding but who were in fact coming together to hear sermons and to celebrate the Lord's Supper. Some of them were arrested and brought to trial, and at the subsequent enquiry it appeared that here was an attempt to form their own congregations by people who wanted to use a different form of prayer from that officially permitted and to choose their own ministers. Bishop Grindal discovered that there had been meetings in private houses, in fields and in ships, and that the separatists had ordained their own ministers and deacons. It is probable that something like a thousand people were connected with the movement at one time or another. Grindal did not take them too seriously, since it appeared that they consisted of more women than men and that they were 'citizens of the lowest order, together with four or five ministers remarkable neither for their judgment nor learning'. They did not get support from the important Puritan leaders and in the end persuasion combined with a measure of force seems to have succeeded in suppressing this early separatism—but the danger to unity was to reappear later.[1]

* * *

In 1570 Archbishop Parker was seriously disturbed by reports of

[1] M. M. Knappen, *Tudor Puritanism*, p. 211 ff. W. Pierce, *Historical Introduction to the Marprelate Tracts*, 1908, p. 23 ff.

'. . . more massing than hath been heard of this seven years',[1] and Bishop Cox reported to Henry Bullinger that 'The schism about the habits of the clergy is still increasing, I grieve to say, among men of purer character'.[2]. The fears and complaints of these worried Elizabethan bishops appeared superficially to be exaggerated. In spite of attacks from within and without, the Church of England seemed to have come triumphantly through the crisis of its early years and to be more firmly established than anyone would have thought possible when Elizabeth made her great experiment a dozen years before. But the really serious crises were only just beginning. In 1570 two intensely committed and sincere men, one in Rome and one in Cambridge, had issued challenges to the Church of England which might undermine it and destroy it. The stern, uncompromising Dominican friar, Pius V, had issued his bull *Regnans in Excelsis* declaring Elizabeth deposed, and an earnest and devoted Fellow of Trinity College, Cambridge, Thomas Cartwright, had delivered in the university a series of lectures concerning the government of the early Christian church which were a fundamental challenge to the church established by law in 1559. For the next thirty years there was to be little peace for those who wanted religious uniformity based on the settlement of 1559. Grindal's prayer 'May God at length grant that we may all of us think the same things!'[3] was not to be answered.

[1] *Correspondence of Matthew Parker*, edit. J. Bruce and T. Perowne, Parker Society, Cambridge, 1853, p. 369.
[2] *The Zurich Letters*, I. 221, 10 July 1570.
[3] *The Zurich Letters*, I. 221, 10 July 1570.

6

The Gathering Storm in the Fifteen-Seventies: The Catholic Revival 1570–80

THE ten years which separate the papal bull of excommunication of 1570 from the arrival of the Jesuits in 1580 saw the turn of the tide in the ebbing fortunes of the Papists in England. After the coming in 1574 of the first missionary priests trained at Douay, the Papists began to grow in numbers and still more in determination. The hitherto reasonable expectations of the government that Catholicism would quietly perish as the older generation died off, and as the lack of priests made it more and more difficult for Catholics to practise their religion, were completely upset by the presence in growing numbers of zealous missionaries determined to preach their religion as widely as possible and prepared, if necessary, to die for their faith. Faced with the success of the Douay priests, the government was compelled to increase the pressure on Catholics, for it was not prepared to abandon the policy which it had consistently followed since 1559 of trying to impose religious uniformity.

The success of the missionary priests meant that at long last there was some hope of the ultimate survival of English Catholicism, but the Catholic revival was severely handicapped by the fact that in the 1570's the papal cause became increasingly identified in the English mind with the attempts to overthrow by force an extremely popular and successful queen. Government propaganda naturally made great play with the suggestion that all Catholics were potential rebels ready to welcome a foreign invasion. The fact that most English Catholics were intensely loyal to the queen could do little to counter-act this propaganda, since it was only too clear that the papacy was working hard to overthrow Elizabeth and that Philip of Spain was ready to back an invasion, provided he could do so without finding himself involved in a war on two fronts.

The Catholic revival did not appear as a serious menace until the second half of the decade. Until then the government continued the policy which it had pursued in the 1560's of keeping up the pressure on Catholics to conform, with special attention to those whose example would influence others. On occasions it intensified its efforts in particular districts and against particular individuals. The bull of excommunication was not taken too seriously, although naturally the government worked through diplomatic channels to get it withdrawn and engaged in a pamphlet campaign against the papacy. It was hardly suprising that it took drastic measures against John Felton who between two and three o'clock in the morning of 15 May 1570 had fixed to the gate of the bishop of London's palace a copy of the bull, which he had apparently obtained from the Spanish ambassador. This unwelcome incident led to a general search in London, and another copy of the bull was found in the room of a student of Lincoln's Inn who confessed that he had got it from Felton. Felton came of an old Norfolk family, his wife had been a maid of honour to Queen Mary, and he was a wealthy man living at Bermondsey Abbey, Southwark. His house was surrounded by a large force led by the Lord Mayor, the Lord Chief Justice and the two sheriffs of London. He gave himself up and admitted his responsibility. He was racked to discover whether he had accomplices, but he gave no information. He was put to death on 8 August 1570. He claimed rightly that he died for the papal supremacy and he refused to acknowledge Elizabeth as queen. His plate and jewels, valued at £33,000, were seized for the queen's use.[1]

The government can hardly be blamed for dealing drastically with Felton, but its conduct with regard to Dr. John Story was a good deal more questionable. Story had a distinguished career as a lawyer in the University of Oxford under Henry VIII, he had been in trouble for religion under Edward VI and had eventually gone to Louvain. He returned under Mary and resigned his Regius Professorship to become chancellor to Bishop Bonner whom he assisted in persecuting Protestants. Under Elizabeth he was again in trouble from time to

---

[1] Felton's son Thomas, born in 1567, later went abroad to Rheims, returned to England as a priest, and was caught and executed on 28 August 1588. John Felton was beatified by Pope Leo XIII in 1886.

time, and in 1563 he fled abroad where he entered the service of Philip II. He was employed in Antwerp as a censor of books sold in the Low Countries. In 1570 he was lured on board an English ship, kidnapped, taken to England, tortured and put on trial in 1571 on charges of being involved in the Rising of the Northern Earls and of inciting the duke of Alva to invade England. He denied the royal supremacy and he refused to plead, on the ground that he was a Spanish subject. He was executed on 1 June 1571.[1] His death seems to have been the result of personal vindictiveness rather than considered government policy.

Although Elizabeth herself was not unduly worried about the papal excommunication, the parliament of 1571 regarded the Catholic threat in a much more serious light. Bishop Sandys set the tone in a sermon in which he urged that all subjects should be compelled to hear God's Word and to receive the sacrament.[2] A bill imposing stiffer fines and requiring everyone to receive communion at least once a year was introduced in the Commons, and both Houses eventually passed a measure on these lines, but the queen vetoed it. She was a less committed Protestant than the M.P.s, the bishops and the privy councillors, and she was politically wiser. She was content to accept a minimum of conformity and she had no desire to drive men into opposition unnecessarily. She could claim with justification that her less extreme policy was producing results and that time was on her side.

Nevertheless, parliament thought that the papal challenge called for more drastic legislation than had hitherto been considered necessary. Three acts were passed to deal with the new situation. The Treasons Act of 1571[3] made it high treason to write or to signify that Elizabeth was not the lawful queen, or to publish in speech or in writing that the queen was a heretic, schismatic, tyrant, infidel or usurper.[4] This was a potential threat even to the most loyal Catholic subjects, since those who regarded her as lawful queen could hardly

---

[1] His daughter was in the Fleet as a recusant in 1570. His son John became a priest at Douay.

[2] J. E. Neale, *Elizabeth I and her Parliaments*, I. 185–6.

[3] 13 Eliz. c. 1. *Statutes of the Realm*, IV. 526–8; G. R. Elton, *The Tudor Constitution*, pp. 72–6; J. E. Neale, *op. cit.*, I. 225–34.

[4] J. E. Neale, *op. cit.*, I. 230. One speaker wanted it to be made treason to say that her Majesty was of another religion, since some 'do not spare to say that her Majesty is of another religion than is published' and that her councillors and not the queen are responsible for the doctrine of the Church.

deny that she was from the Catholic point of view a heretic and a schismatic.

Another act passed in 1571 prohibited the bringing in and putting into execution of bulls and other instruments from the see of Rome.[1] The act refers to the statute of 1563[2] abolishing the usurped power of the bishop of Rome and laying down penalties for those who maintained his jurisdiction and authority. It states that 'divers seditious and very evil disposed people . . . minding . . . very seditiously . . . to bring this realm . . . into thraldom and subjection of that foreign, usurped and unlawful jurisdiction . . . and to raise and stir up sedition and rebellion' have procured bulls and writings 'to absolve and reconcile all those that will be contented to forsake their due obedience'. These wicked persons 'in such parts of this realm where the people for want of good instruction are most weak, simple and ignorant' have reconciled people to the see of Rome, 'whereby hath grown great disobedience and boldness in many . . . to withdraw and absent themselves from all divine service now most godly set forth', and there has ensued 'most wicked and unnatural rebellion'. From 1 July 1571, anyone who uses any such bull or by colour of it reconciles any person by speech, preaching, teaching or writing, and anyone who receives such absolution, or receives from the bishop of Rome any kind of bull, writing or instrument, is guilty of high treason. Those who are 'aiders and comforters . . . after the fact' are subject to the penalties of praemunire. Anyone who does not disclose information about such matters is guilty of misprision of treason. For full measure, anyone who 'brings into this realm . . . any token or tokens, thing or things, called by the name of an *Agnus Dei*,[3] or any crosses, pictures, beads or suchlike vain and superstitious things from the bishop or see of Rome' or from his agents, anyone who delivers such things to any subject, and anyone who receives them, is subject to the penalties of praemunire.

The clauses dealing with papal bulls and instruments are understandable. The prohibition of the import of *agnus deis*, crosses and pictures from the bishop of Rome is rather more surprising. Presumably the intention was to make it dangerous to have any kind of direct and personal contact with the pope.

[1] Eliz, c. 2. *Statutes of the Realm*, IV. 528–31; G. R. Elton, *The Tudor Constitution*, pp. 418–21.

[2] See p. 55.

[3] Discs of wax with an imprint of the lamb and sometimes on the reverse the name and arms of the pope. They were blessed by the pope.

H

A third act dealt with Catholic fugitives overseas. Here the government had in mind not only the exiles like those at Louvain, whose literary efforts were regarded with alarm, but also those who had fled after the Rising of the Northern Earls. The Acte agaynst Fugytives over the sea[1] asserted that these fugitives revealed the secrets of the realm, carried away large sums of money, practised rebellion, and made fraudulent conveyance of their lands in England by which they still retained the use of them. Anyone who had gone or who should go overseas without license and who did not return within six months was to forfeit the profits of his lands and all his goods and chattels. Fraudulent conveyances were to be void, and trustees who did not report them were subject to penalties. There was, however, an interesting distinction made between the different kinds of exiles. It was enacted that 'Yf any person by reason of his blinde zeale and conscience onely, departe beyonde the Seas without Lycense' and was not in any way involved in treasonable activity, then the Lord Chancellor might make provision 'for his desolate wyef and children' to the extent of between one-third and one-quarter of his estate. Anyone who came back and who did 'fullye reconcyle hymself to the true Religion established by the order of Law', declaring this to the bishop and 'shewing the same openly by commynge to the Devyne Servyce by Order of this Realme appoynted and receavying the Holy Communion', might after a year recover his lands and profits.

The Rising of the Northern Earls in 1569 and the bull of excommunication of 1570 provided justification for those who argued that Catholics wished to overthrow the government by force. This belief was further strengthened in 1571 by the uncovering of the Ridolfi Plot. Although the traditional story of the plot can no longer be accepted, and although there is a good deal of uncertainty about the precise rôle of Ridolfi himself and of Mary Queen of Scots, and the duke of Norfolk,[2] there is no doubt that the pope gave enthusiastic support to the enterprise, which was intended to lead to a rising in England backed by Spanish troops. Ridolfi may have been in some degree a double agent and his scheme was completely unrealistic, but this does not alter the fact that the pope and the Spanish king supported the attempt to change the government of England. As Cecil and Walsingham uncovered more and more evidence in the last

[1] 13 Eliz. c. 3: *Statutes of the Realm*, IV. 531 ff.
[2] See p. 65 and note 1.

months of 1571, they found themselves in possession of a story which could be used to the full as propaganda against the Papist menace. Lord Burghley gave his version of the plot to the Lord Mayor and Aldermen of London in October 1571, and printed accounts made it known to a wider public. The duke of Norfolk had been sent to the Tower in September. He was brought to trial, condemned and eventually executed on 2 June 1572. Mary Queen of Scots was extremely lucky to escape with her life. In all this the Catholics in England were in no way implicated, but they paid the price for actions over which they had no control. The ill-advised and incompetent policy of the papacy and of Spain made it easy for the English government to treat Catholicism as a political menace. Nor was the public image of Roman Catholicism improved by the Massacre of St. Bartholomew in 1572. Archbishop Parker claimed that the Papists rejoiced at the destruction of Protestants. He admitted that those whom he saw expressed dislike of the murders, but added: ' . . . I learn by other inferiors how they triumph . . . They be full of spite and secret malice. Their imps be marvellous bold, and flock together in their talking places, as I am informed, rejoicing much at this unnatural and unprincely cruelty and murder.'[1]

It is impossible to say how numerous the Papists were in the years before the coming of the missionary priests, and, in any case, the fact that there were large numbers of Church Papists makes it difficult to say who should be counted as a Catholic. We must remember, too, that there were penalties for using any form of service other than that laid down by law and that Catholicism could only be practised in secret. The strength of Catholicism was bound to decline as the number of Catholic priests decreased with the passing of time. How many priests were still saying mass and administering the sacraments is a question about which we have little information. It may be that the number was greater than is sometimes suggested, but it is clear that there was continual loss by death or exile, and that there were very few replacements.[2] By depriving Catholics of their priests the government was achieving much more than by direct persecution.

[1] V. J. K. Brook, *A Life of Archbishop Parker*, pp. 293–4.
[2] T. F. Knox, *The First and Second Diaries of the English College, Douay*, London, 1878, lxi–lxii, suggests that large numbers of Marian priests were still at work. He produces a certain amount of evidence including that of Fr. John Peel who visited Douay in 1576 and of whom the Diary records ' . . . he had laboured for sixteen years in England at the peril of his life, reconciling to the Catholic faith those who had gone astray, and

Nevertheless, the government still acted from time to time against prominent offenders who did not come to church, and the bishops and the local authorities sometimes conducted investigations and searches which brought to light groups of Papists practising in secret. Thus, in 1571 the privy council urged the bishop of Norwich to enforce conformity in his diocese which was notorious for nonconformists, and the bishop ordered his officials to take action. Pressure was put on Mr. Townsend and his wife who had formerly come to church but who were now absenting themselves. Mr. Towsend conformed but his wife held out. The kind of pressure that could be put on a prominent country gentleman is admirably illustrated in the bishop's letter to Mr. Townsend which runs: ' . . . I hear, and thank God for it, that for your own part you come on very well, and shall by God's grace increase daily. But touching my lady, I hear she is wilfully bent, and little hope as yet of her reformation, to the displeasure of Almighty God, the breach of the queen's majesty's law, my danger and peril to suffer so long, and an evil example and encouragement to many others.' The bishop says that he had been required to certify such disobedience, and he urges them both to go to church and receive the sacraments, adding ' . . . otherwise, this is most assured, I will not fail to complain of you both to her majesty's council'.[1] We must not underestimate the effects of this kind of threat on the Catholic gentry of Elizabethan England.

Sir Thomas Cornwallis of Brome in Suffolk provides another illustration of the kind of difficulties facing a Catholic gentleman at this time. Sir Thomas had played a part of some importance under Mary when he was Treasurer of Calais and a member of the Privy Council. The accession of Elizabeth meant that he was out of office both at

---

animating others to perseverance'. Allen states that besides his own priests 'others also who were ordained in England formerly in Catholic times had by their secret administration of the sacraments and by their exhortations confirmed many in the faith and brought back some who had gone astray'. There were said to be forty or fifty Marian priests still at work as late as 1596. Dom Hugh Aveling has produced a good deal of interesting information about the situation in Yorkshire in *Post Reformation Catholicism in East Yorkshire 1588-1790*, East Yorkshire Local History Society, 1960; *The Catholic Recusants of the West Riding of Yorkshire, 1558-1790*, Leeds Philosophical and Literary Society, 1963; in his book *Northern Catholics*, 1966. See also W. R. Trimble, *The Catholic Laity in Elizabethan England*, Cambridge, Massachusetts, 1964, pp. 71, 88–9, note 103.

[1] J. Strype, *Annals of the Reformation*, Oxford, 1824, Vol. II, Part I, pp. 162–4, 1 February 1572.

national and local level. Whether he conformed and went to church is not known, but he was suspect in 1569 when he was questioned about what part he had played in the duke of Norfolk's scheme to marry Mary Stuart. He had little difficulty in clearing himself on political grounds, but the questions put to him about his religion were more difficult, and he was 'committed . . . as a Prysoner for matter of religion'. During the greater part of the time, he was in the care of Bishop Jewel, and he even went on a visitation with him. In June 1570 he was brought to London and required to engage in a religious disputation with a number of Anglican divines. He gave a very good account of himself for he was an intelligent and sincere man. Cecil, who had known him in happier days, put pressure on him to conform, and his intense loyalty to the queen, whom he had known as a child, helped persuade him to agree to go to church, but he was quite firm that he would not receive communion. He gave way with an uneasy conscience, and some time in the 1570's he once more ceased to conform. Even before that, his enemies claimed that it was notorious that 'all service tyme when others on their knees are at praiers, he will sett contemptuously reading on a boke (most likely some Lady psalter or portasse which have been found in his pue)'.[1]

Another illustration of action against Papists is found in 1572 when the bishop of London and other ecclesiastical commissioners sent the sheriff to apprehend those who were committing idolatry by hearing mass in the house of the Portuguese ambassador. The sheriff arrested four law students and put them in the Fleet prison. He reported that there were a great many Englishmen in the house intending to hear mass.[2] Again, in 1574 there was a search in London where mass was said in many places. Twenty-three people were taken at Lady Morley's house near Aldgate, including Lady Morley herself and Sir Edward Stanley. At Lady Guildford's in Trinity Lane, Queenhithe, there were taken Lady Guildford, her son and daughter, Oliver Heywood, a priest, and a number of others. At Mr. Carus' house in Limehouse, the Recorder found Thomas Carus and his wife, Lady Browne and other Catholics. It was alleged that some of the priests taken in the search said that there were 500 masses being said that day in England

---

[1] For further detail of his interesting case history, see Patrick McGrath and Joy Rowe, 'The Recusancy of Sir Thomas Cornwallis', *Proceedings of the Suffolk Institute of Archaeology*, XXVIII, Part 3, 1961.

[2] J. Strype, *Annals of the Reformation*, Vol. II, Part I, p. 315.

one-tenth of them in the diocese of Norwich.[1] The privy Council subsequently ordered those taken in the search to be released, if they paid their fines, but if they did not, they were to be kept in prison.[2]

As early as 1572 the Privy Council was concerned with the problem of Catholics who were kept scattered in various prisons and who 'as well by their craftie intelligences with other prysoners as by their practyses abrode corrupt others in stubbornes . . . ' It was thought it would be best if they were all kept in one place, and Wisbech in the Isle of Ely was suggested as suitable. They would be required to live there at their own charge. The bishop was asked to report on the fitness of the place.

The government was always very anxious to use persuasion rather than force. When Lord Stourton tried unsuccessfully to flee the realm for religious reasons, the archbishop of Canterbury was told to take steps to have him better instructed and to keep him away from all likely to hold him in his errors.[3] When the dean of St. Paul's, Alexander Nowell, petitioned on behalf of his half-brother, John Townley, who was willing to come to church but who refused to receive communion, the Privy Council suggested to the Lord President of the Council of the North and to the archbishop of York that as the prison was 'sumwhat noysum' and as by more courteous usage he would the sooner be brought to conformity, they might either banish him from Lancashire to his home in Lincoln or deal otherwise as they thought fit.[4] Nevertheless, the Council took a firm line from time to time, particularly in areas where Papists were numerous. Thus in July 1574 it thanked the Earl of Derby for his pains in dealing with popish disorders in Lancashire, a county which it described as 'the very sincke of Poperie, where more unlawfull actes have been comitted and more unlawfull persons holden secret then in any other parte of the

---

[1] J. Strype, *op. cit.*, pp. 497–8. The priests would presumably have made as generous an estimate as possible. The congregations were presumably limited because of the need for secrecy. When we consider that there were some 8,000 to 9,000 parishes in Elizabethan England, we see how little opportunity there was for Catholics to go to mass.

[2] *Acts of the Privy Council, 1571–1575*, p. 270, 17 July 1574.

[3] *Acts of the Privy Council, 1571–1575*, p. 96, 12 April 1573.

[4] *Ibid.*, p. 170, 22 December 1573. He did not conform, and in 1576 the Privy Council decided that he should be given under bond to Mr. Assheton of Chatterton who might convert him. He remained obstinate and was again imprisoned. Later he was allowed to live near London in the hope his half-brother would persuade him to submit. W. R. Trimble, *The Catholic Laity in Elizabethan England*, pp. 75–6.

realme',[1] and in November 1574 it instructed the earl of Derby and the bishop of Chester that 'they shold cause, by all meanes possible they can, suche Popishe persons to be apprehendid as are suspected to have reconciled themselfes to the Pope . . . and to procede to the ponishement thereof . . .'[2]

But although the government from time to time took vigorous action against Papists in particular areas, one gets the impression that it was on the whole satisfied with the results it was achieving by less dramatic means. The claim sometimes made that the papal excommunication had stiffened the resistance of Catholics seems difficult to substantiate.[3] Archbishop Parker might be worried about a rumour of a man who boasted that within a year Elizabeth's bones would be openly burned at Smithfield,[4] but Bishop Horne of Winchester was probably nearer the mark in 1573 when he reported to Bullinger that 'Our England, having secured tranquillity at home and peace abroad, is sailing as it were with full sails and a prosperous breeze'. He admitted that the church was vehemently agitated and not without danger, but this was 'not so much from the opposition of the papists, who are daily restrained by severe laws, as by the stumbling-blocks occasioned by false brethren . . .'[5]

The self-confidence of the government was shown in 1574 when it released from confinement a number of prominent Catholics who had long been in prison for religion. They included John Feckenham, the last abbot of Westminster; Dr. Thomas Watson, formerly bishop of Lincoln; and John and Nicholas Harpsfield.[6] The prisoners were released conditionally, usually on compassionate grounds, and they were required to give undertakings that they would not 'by speache, writing or any other meanes induce or intice any person to any opinion or act . . . contrare to the lawes established in the realme for causes of religion'.[7] Later, in 1577 when the government was a good deal less confident about its success in dealing with the Papists, a

---

[1] *Acts of the Privy Council, 1571–1575*, p. 276, 27 July 1574.
[2] *Acts of the Privy Council, 1571–1575*, p. 317, 19 November 1574.
[3] This claim is found, for example, in A. O. Meyer, *England and the Catholic Church under Queen Elizabeth*, translated by J. R. McKie, 1915, p. 131, and in J. H. Pollen, *The English Catholics in the Reign of Queen Elizabeth*, 1920, p. 156.
[4] V. J. K. Brook, *A Life of Archbishop Parker*, p. 294.
[5] *The Zurich Letters*, I. 277. Horne to Bullinger, 10 January 1573.
[6] *Acts of the Privy Council, 1571–1575*, pp. 218, 264, 269, 283; J. Strype, *Annals of the Reformation*, Vol. II, Part I, pp. 488–9.
[7] *Ibid.*, p. 264, 5 July 1574.

number of these prisoners were again put into confinement. It was alleged that 'Feckenham, Watson, and the rest, contrary to their bonds, promise, and hope conceived of their amendment, have and do daily and manifestly abuse the liberty granted unto them whereby many of her Highness' said subjects are by their secret persuasions lately fallen and withdrawn from their due obedience, refusing to come unto the church, and to perform that part of their duties which heretofore they have been dutifully contented to yield'.[1] It is possible that these aged and sick men who had suffered such long confinement for their faith did influence others when they were set at liberty, but a much more obvious and plausible explanation of the change in the government's attitude in the later seventies is that the Douay priests had begun to come to England.

When Allen established his seminary at Douay in 1568 he did not hope to get quick results. A long and thorough training was necessary for the kind of priests he needed for work in England. He later wrote an account of their training and of the means by which he tried to produce not only educated but holy men. He strove to stir up 'a zealous and just indignation against the heretics' who had done so much harm to Englishmen, but he wanted his students to realise that the evils which had come upon their land were due to the sins of Catholics. He taught that 'we should resolve to confess more frequently, communicate more devoutly and study more diligently, so as to prepare ourselves for the priesthood'. He laid great stress on the study of the Old and the New Testament, and he arranged discussions in which the arguments about disputed points were put from both sides. He emphasised the need for a Catholic English Bible.[2] He described how every Sunday 'English sermons are preached by the more advanced students on the gospel, epistle or subject proper to the day'. 'We preach in English', he wrote, 'in order to acquire greater power and grace in the use of the vulgar tongue, a thing on which the heretics plume themselves exceedingly, and by which they do great injury to the simple folks.' The pastoral work of the clergy was given great attention. Allen wrote: ' . . . since all the labourers we send are employed in administering the sacraments and above all things in hearing confessions (for the people have hardly any pastors now but

---

[1] Quoted in Philip Hughes, *The Reformation in England*, III. 415; Conyers Read, *Mr. Secretary Walsingham and the Policy of Queen Elizabeth*, Oxford, 1925, II. 280 ff.

[2] See p. 187.

them) we take care that they are most carefully instructed in the whole catechism and in pastoral matters . . . ' Cases of conscience which occurred frequently in England were discussed at Douay and the conclusions were entered in a book which priests about to go on the mission could read and even copy.

Allen's priests were not only to be technically competent, but they were to be full of confidence about the cause for which they stood. He writes ' . . . by frequent conversations we make our students thoroughly acquainted with the chief impieties, blasphemies, absurdities, cheats and trickeries of the English heretics, as well as with their ridiculous writings, sayings and doings. The result is that they not only hold the heretics in perfect detestation, but they also marvel and feel sorrow of heart that there should be any so wicked, simple and reckless of their salvation as to believe such teachers, or so cowardly and worldly-minded as to go along with such abandoned men in their schism or sect, instead of openly avowing to their face the faith of the catholic church and their own.' It was not exactly ecumenical, and there seems to be a note of arrogance about it, but Allen and his priests were certainly not arrogant, nor did they lack charity to their fellow Englishmen—even to those who tortured them and put them to death. The heresy, not the heretic, was the object of their hatred, and the long process of spiritual formation, the hearing of mass at 5 o'clock every morning after first saying the litanies for the Church and for the conversion of England, the frequent confessions and communions, the spiritual exercises and the fasting, all helped in the process of producing priests of a kind never before known in England.[1]

In 1573 the first four Douay students were ordained, and in 1574 the first Douay priests came to England. They were Lewis Barlow, Henry Shaw, Martin Nelson and Thomas Metham.[2] 7 came in 1575, 18 in 1576, 15 in 1577, 20 in 1578, 20 in 1579 and 29 in 1580.[3] The number of secular priests coming to England before the arrival of the Jesuits Parsons and Campion in 1580 was about 100. This was not very much considering the size of the problem, but the influence of the Douay priests was out of all proportion to their numbers. For English

---

[1] For these and other details, see T. F. Knox's introduction to *The First and Second Diaries of the English College, Douay*, London, 1878. The very considerable secondary literature includes A. C. F. Beales, *Education under Penalty*, 1963.

[2] Metham was not a Douay-trained priest, but he visited Douay on route for England in order to get from Allen the necessary faculties for his work there.

[3] T. F. Knox, *The First and Second Douay Diaries*, lxii and p. 24 ff.

Catholics it was the turn of the tide, and it was not very long before the English government began to realise that it was faced with a completely new situation which could not be dealt with by the old and hitherto very successful methods used in the earlier years of the reign.

Although a great deal is known about the work of many of the missionary priests, particularly those who were put to death, there has so far been no really systematic and detailed study of the priests as a group. There is need for a thorough examination of their work, based on the history of all the priests known to have been in England in this period. We need to know their distribution in the country at various times throughout the reign, the contacts they made, the people they influenced, the methods they employed, and the success or lack of success which they achieved. It is possible that concentration on the lives of some of the more brilliant and more spectacular missionaries has led to an undue neglect of the achievements of the much larger number who quietly carried on with their work and who did not fall into the hands of the authorities.[1]

It would be particularly valuable to have a study of the pioneers— the first hundred or so who came to England before the Jesuit Mission of 1580. There are indications that they achieved remarkable success. One of them, Fr. Henry Shaw, writing to Allen at the end of 1575, commented enthusiastically: 'The number of Catholics increases so abundantly on all sides that he who almost alone holds the rudder of the state[2] has privately admitted to one of his friends that for one staunch Catholic at the beginning of the reign, there were now, he knew for certain, ten.'[3] Another Douay priest, Fr. John Paine, in a letter received at Douay in July 1576, remarked that people in daily increasing numbers were being reconciled to the Church to the great astonishment of heretics. He added that 'the heretics are as much troubled at the name of the Anglo-Douay priests which is now famous throughout England, as all the catholics are consoled thereby'.[4] At the beginning of 1577 Allen said that he had been told by people coming over from England that 'the numbers of those who were daily

---

[1] Fr. Godfrey Anstruther has organised a co-operative research project into the history of seminary priests in connection with the fourth centenary of the College in 1968. The first fruits have already appeared in *The Elizabethan Seminary Priests 1558-1603*, Dominican Priory, Leicester, 1966.

[2] Lord Burghley.

[3] T. F. Knox, *The First and Second Douay Diaries*, pp. lxii and 98.

[4] *Ibid.*, pp. lxiii and 107.

restored to the Catholic church almost surpassed belief'.[1] One must take with a grain of salt enthusiastic reports of success by those who were engaged in the work. To assess satisfactorily the achievements of the early Douay priests one would need to know a great deal more about the areas in which they worked and the number and quality of those whom they reconciled to the Church of Rome. Their success may be difficult to measure, but there is no doubt that they had a great effect on morale. They gave to Catholics in England a leadership and a self-confidence which they had previously lacked. They were uncompromising in their attitude to nominal conformity which had hitherto been so widespread. They stiffened the resistance of many who had formerly been Church Papists, and they put new heart into the much smaller body which had consistently refused any sort of compromise. It seems clear that the main battle had been lost in the first dozen years of the reign, but the seminary priests came in time to fight a brilliant rearguard action and to rally the declining and wavering ranks of English Papists. They helped to destroy the Elizabethan hope of ultimate religious uniformity among all Englishmen.

The work of the Douay seminary suffered a temporary setback in 1578. The growing anti-Spanish feeling in the Low Countries had for some time made the position of the College very difficult. William of Orange made headway against the Spaniards, new magistrates came to power in Douay, and on 22 March the English were ordered to leave the town. The College was then removed to Rheims where it continued its work with great success until its return to Douay in 1593.

In 1579 the work of Douay was supplemented by the formal establishment of yet another seminary for the training of priests for England—the English College in Rome. The founding of this college was in conformity with the general policy of Pope Gregory XIII who, during his pontificate, took steps to provide priests for Germany, Switzerland, Hungary and other parts of Europe where the Reformation had triumphed. The ancient English Hospice in Rome which had since the Middle Ages made provision for English pilgrims coming to the city was gradually transformed into a college for English and Welsh students. Allen, who was closely involved in this, had from 1576 onwards been sending students there from Douay. The early days of the new College were marked by unfortunate disputes. The English

---

[1] T. F. Knox, *op. cit.*, pp. lxiii and 114.

students maintained that the first rector, Maurice Clenock, showed excessive favouritism to the Welsh, and on 1 March 1579, 33 of them left in protest and boldly put their case to the pope. The pope settled the matter by handing the direction of the college over to the Jesuits. In a bull dated 23 April 1579 he formally constituted the college and placed it under the direct care of the Holy See, assigning to it an income which enabled it to maintain between 40 and 70 students.

Official concern about the survival and spread of popery becomes a good deal more noticeable from about the mid-seventies. Indeed, one historian of the English Catholic laity takes the view that: 'From 1574 onwards the government ceased imprisoning and fining the lay Catholics haphazardly and began a consistent drive of penalization, which in intensity and severity lasted until the end of the reign.'[1] In view of what we know about the haphazard and intermittent way in which the penal laws against Catholics were enforced, this statement is a little misleading, but there was certainly growing anxiety in official circles about the Papist problem, and action against Catholics became much more common. The government collected a great deal of information about them and sent out numerous directives to the local authorities to enforce the law. Thus in 1574 the Council of the North was told to see that the laws were observed, the Inns of Court were instructed to exclude members who did not go to church, the Council of the Marches of Wales was urged to see that the Welsh bishops did their duty, and an effort was made to take a much stricter line with the very numerous Lancashire Catholics.[2] The drive continued in the following years in various parts of the country. Attempts were made to remove Catholics from the commission of the peace, and there were instructions 'that generall order be taken throughout the realme for the examininge and removinge of corrupted schoolmasters'.[3] From time to time prominent Catholics were called up for questioning and urged to conform. If they held out, they were required to confer about religion with Protestant divines, and if they still proved obstinate, they were fined, imprisoned or harassed in various ways.[4]

It would be easy to give many illustrations of the consequences of

[1] W. R. Trimble, *The Catholic Laity in Elizabethan England*, pp. 68, 69.

[2] W. R. Trimble, *op. cit.*, pp. 71, 72.

[3] *Ibid.*, pp. 71, 72, 74; F. X. Walker, 'The Implementation of the Elizabethan Statutes against Recusants, 1581–1603', unpublished London Ph. D. thesis, p. 44.

[4] W. R. Trimble, *op. cit.*, p. 76 ff.

all this for Papists, but a few examples must suffice. In June 1576 we find the Council writing to certain Hampshire Justices of the Peace to investigate one Alexander Dering in the soke of Winchester who kept in his house 'a great store of vestments, books and other massing tools to serve lewd purposes, when any so evil is disposed to have the use of them'.[1] In the same year, Richard Curtis, bishop of Chichester, reported to Walsingham that he had found in his visitation that those who were backward in religion in Sussex grew worse and worse.[2] In 1576 William Fleetwood, the Recorder of London, carried out a search of the house of the Portuguese ambassador.[3] He has left a very lively account of the proceedings. One of the sheriffs was posted at the back door to see that no mass-hearers escaped. At the front gate the porter eventually answered and said his master was not at home. He opened the gate a little and Fleetwood put in his left leg. The porter cried: 'Back, villain' and 'thrust the gate so sore about my leg, that I shall carry the grief thereof to my grave . . . And if Mr. Sheriff Kimpton had not thrust the gate from me, my leg had been utterly bruised into shivers.' The porter then took Fleetwood by the throat, but the recorder thrust him away 'for indeed he was but a testy little wretch'. The searchers then went in, and in the long gallery they found all the mass-hearers, both men and women, standing for the gospel 'and the altar-candles were lighted, as the old manner was'. They charged all the queen's subjects to come forth, and the foreigners ran towards them with daggers. However, in the end the English subjects were sent off to prison. Fleetwood adds: 'All this while the mass-sayer stood at the north end of the altar; and no man living, said a word to him, nor touched him; saving that he did give divers of our servants singing cakes; wherewith I was offended with them for receiving that idolatrous bread.'[4] Fleetwood had in fact exceeded his authority and he got into trouble, but normally the government was only too ready to approve action against the Papists. All sorts of people were caught in the net. Thus in 1577 the Lord Mayor of York, John Dyneley, who had himself taken action against popish recusants, found himself up before the Ecclesiastical Commissioners 'for that his

---

[1] J. E. Paul, 'Hampshire Recusants in the time of Elizabeth I, with special reference to Winchester', *Proceedings of the Hampshire Field Club*, vol. xxi. Part II, 1959, p. 69.

[2] W. R. Trimble, *The Catholic Laity in Elizabethan England*, p. 68 ff.

[3] For Fleetwood's activities, see P. R. Harris, 'William Fleetwood, Recorder of the City, and Catholicism in Elizabethan London', *Recusant History*, vol. 7. no. 3, 1963.

[4] J. Strype, *Annals of the Reformation*, Vol. II, Part II, pp. 26–9.

wife refuseth to come to the service, sermon and to communicate'. The archbishop evidently did not understand women; for he told him that 'he is unmete to govern a citie that cannot govern his own household'. Dyneley said his wife had been ill, but refused to give bonds for her attendance at church in the future, and the commissioners ordered him to pay a fine of 2s. for each occasion when she was absent from church.[1] Others in York who were in trouble about this time included Richard Braferton, baker, 'who was latly presented for not commying to the churche' and who 'is gone forth of this Citie, to what place we knowe not';[2] Thomas Pereson, weaver, who 'sayeth that he cometh not to the churche for his conscyens will not serve hym; bycause there lacketh the sacrament, the preist and the aultar . . . whiche Thomas is nowe in Warde';[3] Dorothy Vavasour, wife of Thomas Vavasour, doctor of physic, who 'sayeth she cometh not to the churche bycause hir conscyens will not serve hir so to doe, for she sayeth she will remayne in the feyth that she was baptised in . . . '[4] and Janet Stryckett, widow who 'sayeth that she cometh not to the churche bicause her conscyens will not serve hir; for the bread and wyne is not consecrate, as it hath bene in tyme paste . . . and as for hir goods she sayeth she hath gyven them to hir children by dede of gyfte'.[5] There were others who gave way under pressure like Janet Smythes, wife of George Smythes, butcher, 'who hath bene heretofore presoner for not comming to the church', but who 'sayeth that she now comyth to the churche'.[6]

The increase in the number of Papists raised the question of whether the existing penalties were sufficient. In 1577 John Aylmer, bishop of London, wrote to Walsingham: 'I have had conference with the Archbishop of Canterbury, and we have received from divers of our brethren, bishops of the realm, news that the Papists marvellously increase both in numbers and in obstinate withdrawal of themselves from the church and services of God.' Aylmer said that the policy of imprisonment hitherto used had been of little avail since when they were in prison they were spared the expenses of their households and grew rich. Those who had been set free in the hope that they would

[1] F. X. Walker, 'The Implementation of the Elizabethan statutes against Recusants 1581–1603', pp. 75–6.
[2] *York Civic Records* Vol. VII, edit, Angelo Raine, Yorkshire Archaeological Society, 1950, pp. 124, 131.
[3] *Ibid.*, pp. 125, 132.   [4] *Ibid.*, p. 132.
[5] *Ibid.*, p. 135.   [6] *Ibid.*, p. 133.

mend their ways 'have drawne great multitudes of their teanantes and friendes into the like maliciouse obstinacie'. He suggested that the Papists should be dealt with by 'round fynes to be imposed for *contemptuouse* refusinge of receavying the Communion . . . ' The queen was to be told that this would increase her income and she was to be 'given to understand, that it is mente hereby as well to touch the one side as the other indifferentlie, or els you can guesse what will followe . . . '[1] Aylmer urged that the queen should be persuaded to take a firm line and not to forgive the fines as a result of importunate suits made by courtiers on behalf of their friends.[2] The policy of imposing really stringent fines was not in fact adopted until 1581, but the government may have had such a policy in mind when in October 1577 it sent orders to the bishops to make a return of the recusants in their dioceses.[3]

This more drastic policy towards Papists was reflected in the treatment of Cuthbert Mayne, the first seminary priest to be put to death in England. He came from Youlston, near Barnstable. At an early age he became a Protestant minister as a result of pressure from his uncle, a conforming priest. He took his B.A. at Oxford in 1566 and his M.A. in 1570. His Catholic friends beyond the seas—Gregory Martin and Edmund Campion—urged him to come to Douay. One of their letters was intercepted by the bishop of London who sent for him. He was away from Oxford at the time and, when he was warned of what had happened, he fled from Cornwall to Douay where he was admitted in 1573. He was ordained in 1575, and in April 1576 he returned to England with another priest John Paine. He established himself at Golden, the house of Francis Tregian, five miles from Truro. Here he passed as Tregian's steward. The government had for some time been making a drive against Papists in Cornwall, and in July 1577 the sheriff, Richard Grenville, took a search party to Golden. The security

---

[1] The queen had persistently refused to allow the Papists to be required to receive communion, and she considered the Puritan nonconformists as dangerous, if not more dangerous, than the Papists.

[2] Philip Hughes, *The Reformation in England*, III, 303; Catholic Record Society, *Miscellanea XII*, vol. 22, pp. 1, 2.

[3] The returns are printed in Catholic Record Society, Vol. 22. For a discussion of them, see W. R. Trimble, *The Catholic Laity in Elizabethan England*, pp. 81 ff. By December 1577, a total of 1,562 names had been returned including 1 nobleman, 10 knights, 30 ladies, 102 esquires, 399 gentlemen, 36 priests and 984 others. It seems that about 10 per cent of these were called before the Privy Council (F. X. Walker, 'The Implementation of the Elizabethan Statutes against Recusants 1581–1603', p. 49.)

measures of Papists were sadly defective at this time. Grenville entered a room where he encountered Mayne and asked: 'What art thou?' Mayne answered: 'I am a man.' The sheriff asked if he had a coat of mail under his doublet and unbuttoned it to reveal an Agnus Dei.[1] Among Mayne's possessions was a papal bull—not the famous bull of excommunication but one issued in connection with the Jubilee of 1575 and with no relevance to England. He was lodged in Launceston gaol and treated with severity. A number of other recusants were also arrested. He was brought to trial, and there was some doubt in the minds of the jury and of one of the two judges whether he should be found guilty, but in the end he was condemned to death for bringing a papal bull into England, extolling the pope's authority, saying mass and being in possession of an agnus dei. As there was doubt about the legality of Mayne's sentence, it was referred to the Council which asked the opinion of the judges. They were divided, and in the end the Council decided to make an example. While in prison awaiting execution, Cuthbert Mayne frankly admitted that if any Catholic prince invaded England to reclaim the country for the Roman faith, he would be prepared to assist the invader, but it was not for this that he had been condemned to death. Technically he was probably guilty of treason under the act of 1571 against bringing in bulls from Rome.[2] In view of this law it is surprising that he was so careless as to be in possession of a papal bull, even though it was an old one which he had bought in Douay and forgotten about, nor was it wise of him to wear an agnus dei. Later on Catholics were to become more security-minded. They had not yet realised how seriously the government took the threat from the seminary priests, for Cuthbert Mayne was in fact the first to die under the new and more severe policy of the government. He was dragged through the streets of Launceston on a hurdle on 29 November 1577 and was hanged, cut down while still alive and quartered. One of his quarters was despatched to Barnstaple as a warning of the fate awaiting those whom the government regarded as traitors. A number of other Catholics were also indicted, and his host Francis Tregian was treated with great harshness. He remained in prison until 1601, his health was seriously affected and he suffered severely financially.[3]

[1] See p. 103 and note 3.   [2] See p. 103.
[3] A. L. Rowse, *Tudor Cornwall*, 1941, pp. 344–54, 361, 368, 372; Richard Challoner, *Memoirs of Missionary Priests*, 2 vols. 1741–2, Part I, p. 12 ff.

The second Douay priest was put to death in 1578. This was John Nelson, the son of a Yorkshire gentleman, who went to Douay in 1574 at the age of forty. He was ordained priest in June 1576 and sent to England the following November. He was taken in London on 1 December 1577 'late in the Evening, as he was saying Mattins for the next Day . . . ' He was imprisoned as a suspected Papist. He refused to take the oath of supremacy and when asked why, he said that 'he had never heard, or read, that any Lay Prince could have that Pre-eminence'. He affirmed that the head of the Church was the pope and that the religion of England was schismatical and heretical. He was asked if the queen was a schismatic, and he said he could not tell because he knew not her mind. He was pressed on this point and he said: 'If she be the setter forth and Defender of this Religion now practised in England, then she is a Schismatic and a Heretic.' This, of course, made him technically a traitor under the Treasons Act of 1571,[1] and when he gave the same answers at his trial he was found guilty. He was hanged, drawn and quartered at Tyburn on 3 February 1578. His quarters were put on four of the gates of London and his head on Tower Bridge.[2]

The third of the early victims was Thomas Sherwood, a Londoner and a layman, who had gone to Douay in 1576. He came back to London to settle his affairs, was betrayed by the son of his hostess, Lady Tregony, and was examined before a justice of the peace. He denied the royal supremacy and affirmed that the pope was head of the church. He was racked in the Tower to find out where he had heard mass and he was confined in a dark and filthy prison. He was condemned for denying the royal supremacy and was executed at Tyburn on 7 February 1578.

These executions indicated that the government was determined to strike terror into the hearts of the Papists. The men concerned had clearly not been engaged in treason in any meaningful sense of the term. Although they were technically guilty, it was their connection with Douay that was their real crime as far as the government was concerned.

The missionary priests from Douay were undoubtedly the main reason for the Catholic revival in the 1570's, but they were assisted in their work by the continuing attempt to win men to the Roman

[1] See p. 102.
[2] Richard Challoner, *Memoirs of Missionary Priests*, Part I, pp. 20–6.

I

Church by means of the printed word. The exiles produced a considerable and varied literature for English Catholics, and a certain amount was printed secretly in England itself.

Controversial works directed against the Protestants naturally played a big part in this battle for men's minds.[1] Thus, in 1570 there was published in Louvain *A Treatise of the Holy Sacrifice of the Altar, called the Masse. In the which by the word of God, and testimonies of the Apostles, and Primative Church, it is prooved, that our Saviour Jesus Christ did institute the Masse, and the Apostles did celebrate the same.* This was translated by Thomas Butler from an Italian work by a Jesuit, Antonio Possevino. In January 1574, nine copies were found in a consignment of Catholic books which were being secretly imported into England.[2]

Another controversial work was Richard Bristow's *A Briefe Treatise of diverse plaine and sure wayes to finde out the truthe in this doubtful and dangerous time of Heresie: conteyning sundry worthy Motives unto the Catholike faith.* Bristow (1538-81) had been a Fellow of Exeter College, Oxford, but joined Allen in Douay in 1569 and became one of the most influential members of Allen's College. His *Motives* sparked off a controversy with the defenders of the established church in which William Fulke played a leading rôle.

Yet another example of this kind of literature was Gregory Martin's *A Treatise of Schisme. Shewing, that al Catholikes ought in any wise to abstaine altogether from heretical Conventicles, to witt, their prayers, sermons etc.* After a distinguished career at Oxford, Gregory Martin had gone over to Douay in 1570 where he was one of the ablest scholars and lecturers.[3] His *Treatise of Schisme* was published in 1578 and it purported to be printed in Douay by John Fowler. In fact, it had been printed in England by William Carter. Carter, the son of a draper of London, had been apprenticed to the printer John Cawood for ten years in 1562. Afterwards he acted as secretary to Nicholas Harpsfield, one of the distinguished Marian clergy who had opposed the Elizabethan settlement and who had been imprisoned by the government.[4] After Harpsfield's death Carter became a printer of Catholic books, and nearly a dozen works have been attributed to his

---

[1] For a full examination of this literature, see A. C. Southern, *Elizabethan Recusant Prose*, 1950.

[2] J. Strype, *Life and Acts of Matthew Parker*, II. 392; A. C. Southern, *Elizabethan Recusant Prose*, p. 396.

[3] See p. 187.   [4] See p. 109.

press.[1] The press was discovered at the end of 1579. Bishop Aylmer wrote to Burghley on 30 December of that year: ' . . . I have founde out a presse of pryntynge with one Carter, a verye lewde fellowe who hath byn dyvers tymes before in prison for printinge of lewde pamphlets.' It seems that he distributed as well as printed Catholic books. One of the questions later put to him on the rack was 'upon what gentlemen or Catholique ladies he had bestowed or intended to bestowe certain books of prayers and spiritual exercises and meditations which he had in his custodie'.[2]

The reference to books of prayers and spiritual exercises and meditations in Carter's possession reminds us that we must not think of Catholic activity in Elizabethan England simply in terms of controversies with heretics or efforts to escape from the penalties of the law. These people were concerned with the development of their spiritual life, and a considerable amount of the literature of the period was intended to help them become good Christians. The reprinting in Antwerp in 1573 of St. Thomas More's *Dialogue of Comfort against Tribulation*, written originally in 1534, was meant to show them how to behave in time of persecution. Their spiritual formation was aided by such works as *Certaine devout and Godly petitions, commonly called the Jesus Psalter*, published in Louvain in 1575, a reprint of a late fifteenth-century book very popular with Catholics, which seems to have gone through three editions in 1575. These were produced by John Fowler (1539–79). Fowler had been born in Bristol and educated at Winchester. He was a Fellow of New College, Oxford, from 1553 to 1559, but he went abroad after Elizabeth's accession and set up as a publisher in Louvain in 1565. He has been called 'the most important person connected with the printing of early Recusant works'. Between 1565 and his death in 1579 he saw through the press over thirty English Catholic books.[3]

---

[1] See A. F. Allison and D. M. Rogers, *A Catalogue of Catholic Books in English printed abroad or secretly in England 1558–1640*, Arundel Press, Bognor, 1956, 2 Parts.

[2] He was released in 1579 but arrested in 1582. It was alleged falsely that one of the passages in Martin's *Treatise of Schisme* which he had printed was an incitement to murder Elizabeth. He confessed to printing 1,250 copies. He was executed on 11 January 1584. See A. C. Southern, *Elizabethan Recusant Prose*, pp. 351, 409.

[3] A. C. Southern, *Elizabethan Recusant Prose*, 342 ff., 411, 412; Joseph Gillow, *A Literary and Biographical Dictionary of English Catholics*, 1885, Vol. II. Fowler married Alice, daughter of John Harris, secretary to Sir Thomas More. He seems to have put Antwerp instead of Louvain on the title pages of a number of his books to make the work of government agents more difficult.

Other devotional works included *A Briefe Fourme of Confession, Instructing all Christian folke how to confesse their sinnes* (1576);[1] *A breefe Directory and playne way howe to say the Rosary of our blessed Lady* (1576);[2] *Certayne devout Meditations very necessary for Christian men devoutly to meditate upon Morninge and Eveninge, every day in the weeke: Concerning Christ his lyfe and Passion;* and *Instructions and Advertisements How to meditate the Misteries of the Rosarie of the most holy Virgin Mary* (1579), translated from the Italian of Gaspar Loarte, S.J. and published by Carter.[3]

The Catholic revival of the 1570's was the result of the efforts of men who were not concerned with politics and who strove to bring their countrymen back to the Roman Church by spiritual means. It would have been much better for English Catholics if the popes and the Catholic rulers had shared the sentiments of the man who wrote with reference to Edmund Campion's death:

> *God knowes it is not force nor might,*
> *Not warre nor warlike band,*
> *Nor shield and spear, nor dint of sword*
> *That must convert the land.*
> *It is the blood of martirs shed,*
> *It is that noble traine,*
> *That fight with word and not with sword*
> *And Christ their capitaine.*[4]

But it is hardly surprising that the popes and the Catholic princes did not see the situation in those terms and that they sought by force to bring about what it might not be possible to achieve in any other way—the return of England to the Roman Church. Throughout the 1570's the popes were doing all they could to achieve this end, and they continually urged Philip II to assist in the enterprise. If Philip was reluctant to act, it was not because he did not want to, but because he was hard-pressed in the Netherlands and elsewhere. He was concerned about the reactions of France to a possible Spanish conquest of England and about the consequences of putting Mary Stuart in Elizabeth's place.

---

[1] A. C. Southern, *op. cit.,* p. 412. Translated from the Spanish and carrying the imprint of John Fowler, Antwerp, 1576.

[2] A. C. Southern, *op. cit.,* p. 449.

[3] A. C. Southern, *op. cit.* p. 408.

[4] Quoted in A. O. Meyer, *England the Catholic Church under Queen Elizabeth,* p. 244.

We have seen how Pius V gave enthusiastic support to the hair-brained schemes of Ridolfi and how Philip II had given them sympathetic consideration.[1] When they came to nothing, both the pope and the king of Spain showed great interest in the plans of Thomas Stukeley for action in Ireland. Stukeley was the son of a Devonshire knight and he was a soldier of fortune who had for a time been in favour with Elizabeth. When he fell from grace in England, he went over to the services of Philip and proposed an invasion of Ireland. He was sent to serve with Don John of Austria against the Turks and he distinguished himself at the battle of Lepanto in 1571. On his return he was made much of in Rome, and the Cardinal Secretary of State wrote to Madrid at the beginning of December 1571 saying that the pope looked with favour on Stukeley's plans. The pope wanted Spain to carry them out, but had no objection to the enterprise being conducted in the name of the pope. However, nothing came of it during Pius V's pontificate, and he died in 1572.

His successor was Gregory XIII, a very hardworking and energetic pope who believed in fresh air and keeping fit and who continued the reforming policy of his predecessor. For a time Gregory hoped it would be possible to convert Elizabeth, but when he realised that this could not be done he showed himself eager and anxious to back military action, both directly against England and indirectly through Ireland. It was thought in 1576 and 1577 that something could be done by Don John of Austria, the governor of the Netherlands. Philip did not want open war with England and kept in the background, but the pope was ready to give his official support. There were hopes of a rising in England which would then be assisted by Don John's troops. Allen and Sir Francis Englefield[2] were summoned to Rome in 1576 to advise the pope and both urged the practicability of the scheme and the need for quick action. For various reasons Don John's Enterprise of England proved abortive, and the pope was then all the more sympathetic to plans of action in Ireland. Not only was Thomas Stukeley available and in high favour, but there was also in Rome a distinguished Irish soldier, James Fitzmaurice Fitzgerald, a relative of the earls of Desmond, who had left Ireland in 1575 to appeal for foreign intervention. The pope gave him money and promised him

---

[1] See p. 104.
[2] For Sir Francis Englefield's career, see A. J. Loomie, *The Spanish Elizabethans: The English Exiles at the Court of Philip II*, New York, 1963.

ships and arms. After many delays Stukeley sailed from Ostia in January 1578, but he put into Lisbon where he was persuaded to go off with King Sebastian on a mad crusade in North Africa. Both perished there in the battle of Alcazar in 1578.

James Fitzmaurice Fitzgerald set out in December 1577 with only one ship, but after various adventures he was compelled by shortage of provisions to put into a Spanish port in 1578. He went to Madrid where he met Nicholas Sander, whom the pope had sent as representative to Madrid in 1573 and who had long been urging direct action against Elizabeth. With some hesitation Philip II allowed Fitzmaurice and Sander to sail for Ireland, and they landed in Dingle Bay in July 1579 with a force of 80 men. In response to the appeals of Sander and Fitzmaurice, the earls of Desmond rose in arms and soon the whole of Munster was in rebellion. Fitzmaurice fell in action in August 1579. Reinforcements were slow in coming, and it was not until September 1580 that Philip allowed a force of 550 regular soldiers and 800 volunteers to go to Ireland under Bastiano San Joseppi, 'captain and general of His Holiness'. Sander died as a result of the hardships he had endured early in 1581. The fighting dragged on until the end of the year, and the whole affair achieved nothing except to show the hostility of the papacy to the English government and to provide that government with excellent propaganda material for its claim that the adherents of the pope were the enemies of England. The work of the missionary priests was severely handicapped by the papal attempts to achieve by force what they sought to achieve by persuasion. The papacy did not realise that it could not have it both ways. We must, however, remember that as the 1580's began there was no certainty that the papacy would not in fact succeed, if not by one means, then by the other, and there was always the possibility that if an invasion met with initial success, then the priests at work in England might be called upon to urge all Catholics to support the invader.

7

The Gathering Storm in the Fifteen-Seventies: The Progress of Puritanism 1570–80

THE Catholic revival of the 1570's was matched by some very significant changes among the Puritans, so that the established church was threatened from the left as well as from the right by opposition which was more formidable, more fundamental and more organised than it had been during the first twelve years of the reign.

The Puritan criticisms of the church which had been developing during the 1560's still continued and grew in intensity, but to these there was now added a new and more dangerous element—the rise of English Presbyterianism. It would be a mistake to imagine that all Puritans became Presbyterians or that they all supported the movement for fundamental changes in church government which the Presbyterians demanded. Nor must we think of the English Presbyterians as people with a clear-cut programme and party line based on the pure doctrine of Calvin and Geneva. English Presbyterianism, like the Church of England, was peculiarly English and cannot be exactly paralleled in Geneva or in Scotland or in France or in the Netherlands, although it was influenced in varying degrees by all of them. Other European reformed churches and earlier English Protestant traditions all played their part in the gradual evolution of an English Presbyterian movement whose leaders differed considerably among themselves about precisely what they wanted to put in place of the existing system of government of the church by diocesan bishops. There were many who were prepared to settle for a good deal less than a full-blooded Calvinist church on the Genevan model.

The novelty of these demands for fundamental reforms in church government and the vigour with which they were put forward by able leaders has, perhaps, resulted in their receiving more than their fair share of attention, so that English Puritanism in the 1570's and 1580's has been seen too much in terms of presbyteries, *classes* and synods. Since the Presbyterians wanted many of the reforms demanded by Puritans who were not Presbyterians, the whole Puritan movement has been tarred with the Presbyterian brush. It certainly suited those in authority in the church to suggest that all would-be reformers were supporters of a Presbyterian movement which threatened the whole basis of the established church. Nevertheless, the fully-committed Presbyterians were only a small but very vocal minority in the ranks of English Puritans.[1]

The man who more than anyone else has come to be associated with the demands for fundamental changes in church government is the very able minister and university professor, Thomas Cartwright.[2] He was born about 1535 of yeoman stock, probably at Royston in Hertforshire. He graduated at Cambridge under Mary, together with his future opponent John Whitgift. He had a distinguished academic career. He did not play much part in the vestiarian disputes of the 1560's, although he sympathised with those who got into trouble. At the end of 1565 or early in 1566 he became domestic chaplain to Adam Loftus, archbishop of Armagh. He made a great name as a preacher and was recommended to Cecil very strongly as a candidate for the archbishopric of Armagh when Loftus was translated to Dublin. In 1569 he was appointed Lady Margaret Professor of Divinity in the University of Cambridge. In 1570 he gave a series of lectures in the university on the first two chapters of the Acts of the Apostles, and in them he advanced the view which he was to develop at great length later that the Church of England differed in a number of fundamental respects from the primitive church. He did not at this stage put forward a full-blooded Presbyterian system and he was not as yet directly influenced by continental Calvinist churches, of which he had no personal experience. Nevertheless, what he proposed would have revolutionised the Church of England. The name and office of archbishop was to be abolished. There were to be bishops and deacons with the

---

[1] For a discussion of many of these points, see Patrick Collinson, 'The Puritan Classical Movement in the reign of Elizabeth I' and *The Elizabethan Puritan Movement*.

[2] See A. F. Scott Pearson, *Thomas Cartwright and Elizabethan Puritanism*, Cambridge, 1925.

functions laid down in the New Testament, that is to say, the bishop was to have a purely spiritual function and was not to govern the church, and the deacons were to look after the poor. The government of the church was not to be in the hands of bishops' chancellors and archdeacons' officials, but was to be entrusted to the minister and presbytery of each church or congregation. Each minister was to be attached to a particular congregation and was not to be put in charge until he had been chosen by the congregation.[1] The implications of this were not as yet fully worked out, but it was clear that what Cartwright wanted differed radically from what had been established by law. Here was a revolutionary challenge to the established church and the royal supremacy.

The challenge was naturally taken up by those in authority, and Cartwright was called to account. The governing body of the university was alarmed, and both Archbishop Parker and Archbishop Grindal wanted action against this dangerous man. In Cambridge the most determined and vigorous opponent of Cartwright was John Whitgift.[2] Whitgift had been born in 1530 of a Yorkshire gentry family. He had gone up to Cambridge where he took his M.A. in 1557. Like Matthew Parker, he had remained in England under Mary and had escaped the full impact of continental Protestantism. In 1570 he became Vice-Chancellor of Cambridge under a new constitution which gave the Vice-Chancellor and the Heads of Colleges much greater power than before and reduced drastically the powers of the Regent Masters of Arts, the younger teachers in the university, many of whom had Puritan sympathies. Cartwright had a considerable following in Cambridge, and there were a number of petitions in his favour to the Chancellor, William Cecil. However, the opposition to him led by Whitgift was successful and in December 1570 Cartwright was deprived of his professorship. He went abroad for a time, and in Geneva he met Beza, the great Calvinist leader, and he saw Presbyterianism in action. He still retained his Fellowship in Cambridge and in April 1572 he returned to England, apparently with Lord Burghley's approval.

Meanwhile, there had been further developments in England. Those Puritans who were not Presbyterians had made yet another attempt in

[1] For further details, see A. F. Scott Pearson, *Thomas Cartwright and Elizabethan Puritanism*, p. 26 ff.
[2] V. J. K. Brook, *Whitgift and the English Church*, 1957.

parliament to secure the changes they thought necessary in the church.[1]

The man who played a leading rôle in the Puritan drive in the parliament of 1571 was a Yorkshire gentleman, William Strickland. It is probable that he was not acting alone but with the backing of a group of radical clergy.[2] In a speech on 5 April, Strickland asked to have 'all things brought to the purity of the primitive church'. He claimed that 'although the Book of Common Prayer is (God be praised) drawn very near to the sincerity of the truth, yet there are some things inserted more superstitious or erroneous than in so high matters be tolerable'.[3] He asked for a committee to be set up to confer with the bishops about the many abuses in the church. Then Thomas Norton asked the House to consider the recently printed *Reformatio Legum*. This was a code of canon law, originally drawn up by Cranmer, which emphasised the importance of preaching, made provision for a system of parish discipline through ministers and elders and for diocesan assemblies of clergy under the presidency of the bishop. The bishop exercised his authority not only through archdeacons and rural deans but also through synods and consistories, thus enabling the ordinary clergy to have a share in governing the church.[4] There was a good deal in all this that would meet with approval from the Puritans.

On 14 April Strickland brought in a bill to reform the Book of Common Prayer and to abolish the use of surplices and copes, baptism in private houses, kneeling at communion, the ring in marriage, and other practices regarded as superstitious. The bill got a first reading and there was a good deal of support for it, but this was a clear infringement of the queen's prerogative as Supreme Governor of the Church. Strickland was called before the Privy Council and stopped

---

[1] The old grievances still remained. Thus in 1570 a minister, Mr. Axton, was up before the bishop of Lichfield and said that the surplice was 'abhominable and filthie' and 'the ragges of Antichrist'. He said that if popish practices like the use of the sign of the cross in baptism continued, the people would 'fall away from God into a seconde poperye that wilbe worse than the first'. The bishop agreed not to insist on the sign of the cross and asked Axton to wear the surplice just once, but Axton refused the peace offer, saying that the surplice was 'a polluted and a cursed marke of the Beaste'. The bishop told Axton that people like him were worse than papists 'for the papistes are afraid to stirr or saye any thinge, but you as wonderfull presumptuous and bold, feare no man, and you disquiet us and the whole state more then papists'. *The Seconde Parte of a Register*, edit A. Peel, I. 68 ff.

[2] J. Neale, *Elizabeth I and her Parliaments*, I. 195.

[3] *Ibid.*, p. 194.

[4] Patrick Collinson, 'The Puritan Classical Movement', pp. 98, 99.

from attending the House. The Commons made a great fuss about this threat to its liberties and Strickland was allowed to return, but no more was heard of his bill.[1]

The House also considered a bill to confirm the Thirty Nine Articles which Convocation had passed in 1563, but which had not yet received parliamentary approval.[2] What eventually emerged were two bills—one 'for the conservation of order and uniformity in the church', which confirmed the *doctrinal* articles in the Thirty Nine Articles and also imposed some kind of religious test on laymen, and a second bill which gave the clergy the choice of subscribing either to all the Articles or merely to those Articles which dealt with doctrine. The first bill did not get very far in view of the opposition of the queen and the bishops, but the Commons held to their point that the clergy need subscribe only to those Articles 'which only concern the confession of the true Christian faith and the doctrine of the sacraments', and the bill eventually passed in this form. Thus the parliamentary confirmation of the Thirty Nine Articles made an important concession to those Puritan ministers who could not accept them in their entirety. Nevertheless, in practice, the ecclesiastical authorities ignored the concession.[3]

A bill also passed both Commons and Lords requiring all subjects to come to church and receive communion, but this strongly anti-Catholic measure was vetoed by the queen.[4] In the Commons there were introduced again a series of bills proposing various reforms in the church which had originally appeared in the parliament of 1566, and new proposals were added to them. These reforms aimed at limiting pluralism and non-residence and providing for sermons in every parish. There was to be legislation to stop abuses in the leasing of ecclesiastical benefices and to prevent simony. The granting of licences and dispensation by the archbishop of Canterbury was to be

---

[1] J. Neale, *Elizabeth I and her Parliaments*, I. 198 ff. For some of the objections to the Prayer Book, see *The Seconde Parte of a Register*, edit. A. Peel I. 125 ff. After listing the errors, the writer goes on to say . . . if the amendment of the Booke were inconvenient, it must be said either in regard of a Protestant or a Papist. It cannot be inconveniente in regard of a Protestant, for a very great number do pray heartily unto God for it. If it were the obstinate Papist, we are not to passe (pause), for they . . . denie that we have either Church, Sacraments, Ministers or Queene in England . . .'
[2] See p. 97.
[3] For the complications of these two bills, see J. Neale, *op. cit.*, I. 203 ff. The Act did not specify which were to be considered doctrinal articles.
[4] See p. 102.

controlled and no grants were to be made which were 'contrary to the Word of God'.

Professor Neale calls all this 'the complete Puritan programme in its pre-Presbyterian phase'. He sees it as an attempt to remedy what many M.P.s considered to be deficiencies in the settlement of 1559. He writes ' . . . the Settlement of 1559 was now to be treated as an *interim* and be replaced by a final, Puritan Settlement: 1559 was to achieve fulfilment in 1571'. It must, however, be borne in mind that many of the proposed reforms were intended to remedy what many non-puritan members of the Church would consider as abuses, and that it is only by using the word 'Puritan' in a very wide sense indeed that one can talk of this as a demand for 'a final, Puritan Settlement'. It might be better to call it a demand for a final Protestant Settlement.

The attempt to reform the church through parliament was unsuccessful, and the radical reformers were bitterly disappointed. It is, however, important to realise that throughout the Elizabethan period concern for reform of abuses in the church was not a Puritan monopoly. The Convocation of 1571 approved canons which were intended to provide a better educated and more devout clergy, to ensure great seemliness in the care of churches and stricter oversight of the lives of the people. Some attempt was made to deal with pluralism and simony, and abuses in excommunication were to be checked. People were not to be excommunicated for frivolous or slight reasons, and the bishop alone, and not his officials, was to pronounce sentence.[1] It is also interesting to note that John Whitgift, whom no one would call a Puritan, was chosen prolocutor or speaker of the Lower House of Convocation in 1571 and that he, with other members, was instructed by the bishops to prepare a list of reforms needed in the church. Their report was the basis of the reforming canons of 1576.[2]

It is not surprising that in 1571 the ecclesiastical authorities began to take a firmer line with Puritans. In the summer, licences for preaching issued before May were cancelled and new ones had to be obtained. Parker began to require Puritans to subscribe to the Prayer Book and the Articles of Religion, and to wear the prescribed clerical dress. Some ministers were suspended and some deprived.[3] John

---

[1] E. Cardwell, *Synodalia*, I. 111 ff.; V. J. K. Brook, *Life of Archbishop Parker*, pp. 267–70; V. J. K. Brook, *Whitgift and the English Church*, p. 32.

[2] V. J. K. Brook, *A Life of Archbishop Parker*, p. 285.

[3] V. J. K. Brook, *Whitgift and the English Church*, p. 36; Patrick Collinson, *The Elizabethan Puritan Movement*, p. 118.

Field and some of the other Puritan leaders were called before the Court of High Commission, possibly to discover who had organised the agitation in the 1571 parliament. They were required to assent to the Book of Common Prayer, the Thirty Nine Articles and the disputed ceremonies of the church, and they offered 'a kind of agreement' to the bishop of London. Field was suspended from preaching and by early 1572 was forced to make a living by school teaching.[1]

The parliament of 1572 was very much preoccupied with the situation arising from the Ridolfi Plot and with the question of what should be done with the duke of Norfolk and with Mary Queen of Scots, but it also found time to deal with religion. The Puritans were now efficiently organised and prepared for action both in parliament and outside. Among the new leaders now coming to the top was the remarkably able young man John Field. He was probably a Londoner, born in 1545, who went up to Oxford and was ordained by Bishop Grindal in 1566. He secured influential patrons, including the earl of Warwick, Leicester's brother. He was involved in some degree in the vestiarian controversy and he eventually became a curate at St. Giles', Cripplegate. A number of the London clergy with Calvinist sympathies had, as we have seen, been meeting together from at least the mid sixties[2] and Field became a member of this London conference or 'brotherhood' which was to provide 'the nerve-centre for a presbyterian movement extending into most of the English counties south of the Trent'.[3] The main effort of this group was the publication of the *Admonition to the Parliament* which will be considered in a moment, but the conference also played a part in the attempt, made in May 1572, to get through Parliament legislation which would give a considerable measure of toleration within the Church of England to a wide range of nonconformist practices. This was a bill concerning rites and ceremonies, which has been called by Professor Neale 'an astounding piece of effrontery'.[4] It asserted that the Book of Common Prayer, though sound in substantial points of doctrine, contained 'divers orders of rites, ceremonies and observations' which had been

---

[1] Patrick Collinson, 'John Field and Elizabethan Puritanism', in *Elizabethan Government and Society*, edit. S. T. Bindoff, J. Hurstfield and C. H. Williams, 1961, pp. 132–3.
[2] See pp. 81, 90.
[3] Patrick Collinson, 'John Field and Elizabethan Puritanism', p. 131.
[4] J. Neale, *Elizabeth I and her Parliaments*, I. 297 ff. The bill is printed in *Puritan Manifestoes*, edit. W. H. Frere and C. E. Douglas, pp. 149–51.

permitted in 1559 because people were then 'blinded with superstition'. Since then the gospel had been preached by learned pastors and zealous ministers who had not precisely followed the Prayer Book but who had, with the permission of some godly bishops, introduced 'godly exercises for the better instruction and edifying of their congregations'. In this they had 'conformed themselves more neerlie to the Imitacyon of thauncyent apostolicall churche and the best reformed churches in Europe . . . ' Malicious people had prosecuted them under the Act of Uniformity and thus hindered the work of these godly ministers. It was therefore proposed in the bill that the Act of Uniformity should be in force only against those using papistical services and ceremonies, and that preachers in charge of congregations might, with the consent of the bishop, omit parts of the service or use the form of service employed 'in the righte godlie reformed Churches'. This was stated to be desirable because since 1559 'many congregationes . . . are growen to desire of atteyning to some further forme than in that book is prescribed'.

Professor Neale suggests that if this bill had been passed 'the law would have protected Puritan ministers and their lay patrons while they remorselessly destroyed the Anglican Church from within'.[1] Certainly it was the biggest threat to uniformity of religion which had so far appeared, and the Puritan leaders in the Commons tried to rush it through. It got a first reading on 17 May and a second reading two days later. It was not sent to committee, and it got its third reading the next day. A little late the government woke up to what was going on, and a committee of the House proceeded to remove from the bill some of the more offensive statements. Consent of a majority of the bishops was now required for any deviation from the Prayer Book, and this was put into a new bill which got its first reading on 21 May. The queen now intervened to say that no bills on religion were to be considered unless they had first been approved by the bishops, and she indicated that she 'very much mislikes' the bill. She was gracious about it, and the Commons did not proceed any further with the bill.[2] The affair indicates the boldness of the Puritan leaders in the House, but it also shows that the Commons as a whole were not so deeply Puritan in sympathy that they were prepared to go on with the bill at all costs. Thus the Puritan effort in the House of Commons was

[1] J. Neale, *op. cit.*, p. 298.
[2] For the full story, see J. Neale, *op. cit.*, pp. 298–303.

defeated. Dr. Collinson suggests that it was only when this relatively moderate programme failed that the more radical Puritans decided to publish the famous *Admonition to the Parliament* which they must have known would secure much less general support from Puritan sympathisers than the bill concerning rites.

An Admonition to the Parliament[1] appeared in June 1572 before the parliament had ended but too late to have much influence on it. It was printed at a secret press, it was small and easily carried about, and it went through three editions before the end of August. It consisted of two tracts—the *Admonition* itself and another pamphlet entitled *A View of Popishe Abuses yet remaining in the Englishe Church, for the which Godly Ministers have refused to subscribe*. The second tract is generally attributed to John Field, the organising genius of the militant Presbyterians, and the first to Thomas Wilcox, another very active member of the London group or brotherhood. Wilcox, like many of the Puritan leaders, built up a formidable list of important lay contacts, including Sir Francis Walsingham, the Countess of Bedford, Lady Ann Bacon, and many other influential people.[2]

The *Admonition* is a short work, but it is one of the most fascinating and most powerfully written of all the Puritan pamphlets. It attacks 'the Lordly Lordes, Archbishopps, Bishoppes . . . and the rest of that proude generation, whose kingdome must downe . . . bicause their tyrannous Lordshippe can not stande wyth Christes kingdome . . . ' It maintains that 'they have all the best reformed churches thorowoute Christendome against them'.[3] It argues that: 'Either must we have right ministerie of God, & right government of his church, according to the scriptures . . . (bothe whiche we lacke) or else there can be no right religion.' The archbishops, bishops and the rest call their opponent 'Puritanes' and set on those in authority against them, but we must all pray God 'to lighten the heart of oure moste gracious soveraigne' to help God's small flock and to overthrow their 'proude ennemies', so that 'godlinesse may by them proceede in peace . . . '

The writer then urges the parliament not only to remove 'al popish remnants' but to establish true religion. The Church of England is so far from being rightly reformed according to God's word 'that as yet

---

[1] Printed in *Puritan Manifestoes*, edit. W. H. Frere and C. E. Douglas, pp. 1–55.
[2] Patrick Collinson, 'The Puritan Classical Movement', p. 58 ff.
[3] There is an interesting parallel here with the appeals which St. Thomas More and Edmund Campion made to the belief of the universal Catholic church against the doctrines of the Church of England.

we are not come to the outwarde face of the same'. The *Admonition* asserts that: 'The outward markes whereby a true Christian church is knowne, are preaching of the word purely, ministring of the sacraments sincerely, and ecclesiastical discipline which consisteth in admonition and correction of faults severlie.' In the Church of England, ministers are not according to God's word 'proved, elected, called or ordayned'. They are not tested for their ability to instruct or for their godly behaviour, but are appointed by letters of nobles and others 'tag and rag, learned and unlearned, of the basest sorte of people'. They include popish mass-mongers, they are not learned and they are not called to their ministry 'by the common consent of the whole church'. Bishops make them in large numbers and send them into the country 'lyke masterles men'. The existing state of affairs is compared very unfavourably with the primitive church. Then, after just trial and vocation, ministers were admitted 'by the laying on of the hands of the company of the eldership onely'; now all that is required is vestments, a bishop's pastoral staff and the blasphemous saying 'receive the holy gost'. In the early church ministers were preachers, now they are readers and they may not preach without licence. They are required to wear popish garments and they are given titles and offices such as Archbishop, Lord Bishop, Dean, etc. They are compelled to use the prescribed service and Book of Common Prayer 'in which a great number of things contrary to Gods word are contained, as baptism by women, private communions, Jewish purifyings, observings of holy days etc.' The way to get rid of these deformities is to remove the bishops' authority to ordain ministers and 'to bryng in that old and true election, which was accustomed to be made by the congregation'.

As for the discipline of the church, 'Instead of an Archbishop or Lord Bishop, you must make equalitie of ministers.' Instead of chancellors, archdeacons and the rest, 'you have to plant in every congregation a lawful and godly seignorie ... And to these three jointly, that is, the Ministers, Seniors, and deacons is the whole regiment of the church to be committed.' Thus would be established a godly discipline the aim of which was 'the reforming of the disordered and to bryng them to repentance, and to bridle such as wold offend'.

There were many more trenchant criticisms and proposals packed into this masterly piece of religious dynamite which sums up with the pertinent question: 'Is a reformation good for France? And can it be evyl for England? Is discipline meete for Scotland? and is it unprofitable for this Realme?'

To this fundamental criticism of the established church there was attached for full measure *A View of Popishe abuses yet remaining in the Englishe Church*. It was essentially an appeal to parliament and to public opinion against the action of the ecclesiastical commissioners who had since the last parliament required the clergy to subscribe to statements that the Book of Common Prayer was 'not repugnante to the word of God'. It sought to explain and justify the actions of those clergy who refused to subscribe. For the sake of the peace of the church these ministers had hitherto kept quiet, but now 'We must nedes say as foloweth, that this boke is an unperfecte booke, culled & picked out of that popishe dunghil, the Masse booke, full of all abhominations. For some, & many of the contents therin, be suche as are againste the woord of God.' The writer then proceeds to note at some length the imperfections of the Prayer Book which include private communion and baptism, administration of baptism by women, observance of saints' days, kneeling at communion, the use of wafer cakes instead of ordinary bread, and the wearing of cope and surplice. He objects to the reading of services and the neglect of preaching which is by God's Word a necessity. Ministers who read and do not preach are 'emptie feeders, darcke eyes, ill workemen . . . unsavery salt, blinde guides, sleepie watchmen . . . ' Kneeling at communion was 'a shew of papisterie'; the baptismal service was 'full of childish & superstitious toyes'. The marriage service was corrupt, and use was made of a sacramental sign, the wedding ring; the burial service retained prayers for the dead; the churching of women 'smelleth of Jewishe purification'.

According to this savage and brilliant pamphlet, there was no edification in the services of the church—'they tosse the Psalmes in most places like tennice balles'. In church, people were found ' . . . some standing, some walking, some talking, some reading, some praying by themselves . . . ' The minister 'posteth it over, as fast as he can gallop. For either he hathe two places to serve, or else there are some games to be playde in the afternoone, as lying for the whetstone, heathnishe dauncing for the ring, a beare or a bull to be baited, or else Jack an apes to ride on horsebacke, or an enterlude to be plaide . . . '

The form of making bishops, ministers and deacons was 'drawne out of the Popes pontifical . . .' The bishops have titles of 'Lorde,

K

Lordes grace, Metropolitane, and so on, against the word of God; they hold civil office as well as ecclesiastical, and their officials spoile the pastor of his 'lawful jurisdiction over hys own flocke'. In cathedral churches there were many 'loytering lubbers'. There were covetous patrons of benefices, and parsons and vicars who spoiled the flock of its soul's food—'such seeke not the Lord Jesus, but theyr own bellies, clouds they are without raine, trees withoute frute, painted sepulchres full of dead bones . . . and leane locustes in all feeling, knowledge, and sinceritie'. As for the prescribed clerical dress, 'There is no order in it, but confusion: No cumlines, but deformitie. No obedience, but disobedience, both against God and the Prince.' With reference to the Thirty Nine Articles, the writer stated that the dissenting ministers accepted the substance of doctrine 'using a godlye interpretation in a point or two', but they wished their opponents would not deny the 'effect and vertue thereof'.

The *Admonition* sparked off a considerable controversy and created a good deal of alarm. In some ways its impact resembles that of Edmund Campion's *Ten Reasons* and other works which Robert Parsons issued from his secret printing press in 1580–1.[1] Field and Wilcox were arrested in July 1572, but the secret press was not discovered. Matthew Parker wrote to Burghley on 25 August 1572 ' . . . for all the Devises that we can make to the Contrarie, yet sum good fellowes still labor to printe owte the vaine admonition to the parliament. Since the first printing it hath been twise printed, and nowe with addicons . . . We wrote lettres to the Maior and sum aldermen of London to laie in waite for the Charactes, printer and Corrector, but I feare they deceave us, they are not willing to disclose this matter.'[2]

In prison the authors of the *Admonition* were unrepentant and continued to work for their cause. When he was rebuked for the fierce tone of his book, Field replied 'John calleth the Scribes and Pharisees a generation of vipers, Christ called them adders brood and an adulterous nation . . . We have used gentle words too long, and we

---

[1] See p. 171.

[2] A. F. Scott Pearson, *Thomas Cartwright and Elizabethan Puritanism*, p. 63. The printer of another pamphlet issued at this time wrote

> *Thys worke is fynyshed thankes be to God*
> *And he only wil keep us from the searchers rod . . .*

William Pierce, *An Historical Introduction to the Marprelate Tracts*, 1908, p. 42.

perceive they have done no good.' He sent collections of *Admonitions* and other pamphlets to influential ladies, with verses beginning:

> *Read and peruse this little book,*
> *With prayer to the Lord*
> *That all may yield that therein look*
> *to truth with one accord.*

From prison he sent letters to Anthony Gilby[1] urging the Puritan leaders to unite and to consider how best to defend their cause against the bishops. He suggested that ' . . . as of late there was a conference, so it might again be renewed, every one submitting their judgement to the mighty word of God'. He wanted this conference to draw up a statement of doctrine, and he asked Gilby to communicate his views to local meetings of preachers concerned with prophesyings.[2]

Field and Wilcox were sentenced in October 1572 to a year's imprisonment, but they received a good deal of sympathy from influential laymen, and the Council intervened to see that they got preferential treatment. They were obviously sincere and courageous men and even Protestants who did not agree with their views could see that their nonconformity was not in the same category as that of the Papists. The aggrieved bishop of London complained that 'the people resort to them as in popery they were wont to run on pilgrimages'.[3]

Further pamphlets appeared from the secret press in the same year, including *A Second Admonition to the Parliament*.[4] There is some doubt about who wrote the *Second Admonition* which is more wordy and not nearly so forceful as the first.[5] Its importance lay in the fact that it worked out in more detail proposals for establishing some form of Presbyterian government in the church. It attacked the abuses in the church and the wickedness of the bishops, asking: 'Why doe they not followe the examples which they sawe beyonde the seas? In which

---

[1] See pp. 81, 88, 91.

[2] Patrick Collinson, 'John Field and Elizabethan Puritanism', pp. 134–5.

[3] V. J. K. Brook, *Whitgift and the English Church*, p. 40.

[4] Printed in W. H. Frere and C. E. Douglas, *Puritan Manifestoes*, together with *An Exhortation to the Byshops to deale brotherly with theyr Brethren* and *An Exhortation to the Bishops and their Clergie to Aunswer a Little Booke that came for the Last Parliament*.

[5] It was long attributed to Thomas Cartwright, but his biographer A. F. Scott Pearson questioned this and suggested the possibility of Christopher Goodman or Anthony Gilby. D. J. McGinn, *The Admonition Controversy*, New Brunswick, 1949, argued that it was Cartwright after all.

of the reformed churches saw they a Lord Bishop allowed?' It outlined, in a somewhat confused manner, a scheme of church government based on consistories in every congregation made up of ministers and assistants chosen by the parish, conferences of ministers of convenient districts, provincial synods, and national synods, each with defined powers.

The ecclesiastical authorities were well aware of the threat presented by the two *Admonitions*. Although the number of people who wanted a Presbyterian form of church government was probably very small, and although those who wanted it were not agreed, either now or later, as to precisely what form it should take, Presbyterianism was a fundamental challenge to the Church of England. What was perhaps even more dangerous was that the *Admonitions* attacked a whole series of abuses in the Church. Their writers had the sympathy of many who did not agree with their ultimate aims.

 The man put up to reply to the attack was John Whitgift. His *Answer to the Admonition* appeared in late 1572 or early 1573. It lacked the sparkle and appeal of the *Admonition*, but it has been described as 'a devastating criticism'.[1] It questioned the alleged scriptural basis of the proposed Presbyterian form of government; it described as absurd the argument that only those ceremonies and forms of government prescribed in the scriptures could be permitted; and for full measure it attacked the Puritans as well as the Puritan arguments, alleging that they ' . . . walking in the streets, hang down their heads, look austerely, and in company sigh much and seldom or never laugh', but 'in slandering or backbiting their brethren . . . in disquieting the church and state, they have no conscience'.[2] Cartwright retaliated in his *Reply to an Answer* published in 1573 and printed by a secret press.[3] Whitgift continued the controversy in his *Defence of the Answer* published in 1574. He took the line that 'there is no one certain kind of government in the church which must of necessity be perpetually observed'. The right to ordain priests be-

---

[1] V. J. K. Brook, *Whitgift and the English Church*, p. 43.

[2] V. J. K. Brook, *Whitgift and the English Church*, p. 44.

[3] In a foreword the printer wrote: 'I neyther having wealth to furnishe the Print wyth sufficient varietie of letters, have bene compelled (as poore man doth put one instrument to divers purposes) so to use one letter for three or foure tongues . . . And being for wante of long training in thys mysterie, not so skilful to spie a faulte, so soone as it was made, have left oute, or ever I was aware, divers quotations in the margent, displaced other some, and committed some other faultes in the texte' (A. F. Scott Pearson, *Thomas Cartwright and Elizabethan Puritanism*, p. 86).

longed to bishops, but 'I do not say only to bishops'. He held that the Church of Rome was a church, although in error, and that the Protestant churches in Europe (which did not have bishops) were true churches. The government of the Church of England by bishops was justifiable. Thus Whitgift was not arguing that episcopacy was established by Christ and formed an essential characteristic of a true church. It was not a matter of principle but of expediency, and there was nothing wrong in it.[1]

Cartwright, who had fled from the country in 1573, replied in a very lengthy work which was published in two parts, the first in 1575 and the second in 1577. He maintained that he did not want separation of church and state, since they were twins who prospered or decayed together. He repudiated Whitgift's claim that Puritans were like Papists in that they opposed the Book of Common Prayer. The Papists disliked the Prayer Book because it differed too much from the mass book; the Puritans disliked it because it had too much in common with it. Cartwright defended against Whitgift his view that false teachers should be put to death, for this was laid down in God's Word. He denounced the use of homilies, the ring in marriage, the ceremony of confirmation, holy days, bowing at the name of Jesus, and prayers for the dead. He maintained that the administration of the sacraments must always be accompanied by preaching. He criticised diocesan episcopacy—the only allowable kind of bishops are presbyters, and all are equal. Christ alone is head of the Church. Presbyters or bishops must be chosen with the consent of the people. Ministers are to be tried and examined by presbyters. There are to be governing elders or seniors to help the pastor or bishop govern the church. Ministers and elders are to exercise discipline in the election of ministers, in excommunication and in all matters concerning morals.[2]

Cartwright's second reply to Whitgift did not carry the case much further. More important in the development of the Presbyterian argument was a work by Walter Travers originally published in Latin but translated into English, probably by Cartwright, under the title *Full and Plain Declaration of Ecclesiastical Discipline* which appeared in

---

[1] '... there is no suggestion that bishops, however desirable, are a necessary part of a true church, still less that apostolic succession was vital' (V. J. K. Brook, *Whitgift and the English Church*, pp. 45, 46).

[2] A. F. Scott Pearson, *Thomas Cartwright and Elizabethan Puritanism*, p. 88 ff.

1574. Travers was a Nottingham man born about 1548, who went up to Cambridge in 1560.[1] He became a Fellow of Trinity College in 1570, but his Puritan views brought him into conflict with Whitgift, and in 1570 he found it best to leave. He and Cartwright both ended up in Geneva where Travers wrote his *Ecclesiastical Discipline*. It had a preface by Cartwright and it was published in Heidelberg. The system of church government outlined by Travers differed in a number of ways from the views put forward both by Calvin and by Cartwright. The details need not concern us. What matters is that Travers provided, as it were, a textbook for English Presbyterians of which it can be said that it was 'soon generally accepted as representing the party attitude on the topic'. Although the term 'bishop' was retained to denote the pastor or leader, Mr. Knappen maintains that 'to all intents and purposes the system described was one with which modern Presbyterians are familiar, with deacons and ruling elders besides the professional clergy'.[2]

The Presbyterians thus had their own platform and presented their case with great ability. There was a danger that they might dominate the whole Puritan movement, and that those who sympathised with reform of the church might, without realising quite what they were doing, support men whose aim was not merely reform of abuses but the establishment of a Presbyterian government and a Presbyterian discipline in the church. It may be that the danger was much less than it appeared to church leaders at the time and that the ability of the Presbyterian leaders and their very effective propaganda and organisation has led historians to exaggerate their real strength.[3] C. B. Firth notes the significant fact that there are practically no ballads which testify to any popular interest in the struggle between the Puritans and the bishops, or to any sympathy with the former.[4] The danger may have been exaggerated, but it certainly existed, and it is hardly surprising that the leaders of the church reacted vigorously against the Presbyterians and against the Puritan body as a whole.

At the end of 1572 Bishop Cox of Ely expressed to Archbishop Parker the need for action against 'these godless schismatics' who threatened the realm and 'our godly and well reformed Church' and

[1] S. J. Knox, *Walter Travers: Paragon of Elizabethan Puritanism*, 1962.
[2] S. J. Knox, *Walter Travers*, p. 29 ff., M. M. Knappen, *Tudor Puritanism* pp. 247–8; V. J. K. Brook, *Whitgift and the English Church*, pp. 46–7.
[3] See Patrick Collinson, 'The Puritan Classical Movement', p. 84.
[4] *A Seconde Part of a Register*, edit. A. Peel. I. xvi.

who 'are bent against us *toto*'.[1] Bishop Sandys wrote: 'Our estimation is little, our autorite is lesse, so that we are become contemptible in the eies of the basiste sorte of people.'[2] In March the archbishop urged Burghley to take action, saying: 'The comfort that these puritans have, and their continuance, is marvellous; and therefore if her Highness with her Council . . . step not to it, I see the likelihood of a pitiful commonwealth to follow.'[3] The archbishop continued to press for action, and on 11 June 1573 a proclamation was issued against those who 'did use, of their own devices, other rites and ceremonies than were by the law of the land received and used . . . ' and requiring the surrender of the *Admonition* and similar works,[4] but Bishop Sandys reported that 'the whole city of London, where no doubt is great plenty, hath not brought one to my hands'.[5]

The difficulty about getting effective action against the Puritans was that they had powerful lay protectors.[6] Because of this, Field and Wilcox had got off comparatively lightly. An excellent illustration of the way in which a Puritan could time and again extricate himself from difficulties is to be found in the life of Edward Dering whom Dr. Collinson considers 'as a mirror in which to catch . . . some authentic reflections of the spirit and the aspiration of the Godly Elizabethan preacher who first established the English Puritan tradition'.[7] Dering came of a gentry family in Kent, and was elected Fellow of Christ's College, Cambridge, an important breeding ground for Puritans. What stirred him particularly was not the controversy about vestments but 'a limitless concern with the substance of sin' and the need to 'take hold upon Christ and his merits with a true fayth'. The preaching of the word was the ordinary and, indeed, the only means of faith. 'Without this preaching of the word, wee can never have fayth', he wrote. He made a great reputation for himself in

[1] J. Strype, *Life and Acts of Matthew Parker*, II. 193.
[2] Quoted in Patrick Collinson, *A Mirror of Elizabethan Puritanism: The Life and Letters of 'Godly Master Dering'*, 1964, p. 20.
[3] V. J. K. Brook, *Life of Archbishop Parker*, p. 304. The archbishop was trying to get the statesman to act by pointing out that Puritan ideas threatened not only the church but the whole social order.
[4] M. M. Knappen, *Tudor Puritanism*, p. 240; V. J. K. Brook, *Life of Archbishop Parker*, p. 304.
[5] M. M. Knappen, *Tudor Puritanism*, p. 240.
[6] See p. 143.
[7] See note 2 above. Although Dering can be classified as a Puritan in many respects, Dr. Collinson makes the point that 'much of what we call puritanism at this time was nothing but authentic Protestantism. . . .'

Cambridge and outside, but he had some severe criticisms to make of Archbishop Parker and of Lord Burghley, and on 25 February, 1570, in a famous sermon before the Queen and Council, he launched a fierce attack on the state of the church and the clergy. He told Elizabeth with reference to the clergy ' . . . some shake bucklers, some ruffians, some hawkers and hunters, some dicers and carders, some blind guides and can not see, some dumb dogs and will not barke . . . And yet you in the meane while that all these whordoms are committed, you at whose hands God will require it, you sit still and are carelesse, let men doe as they list. It toucheth not belike your comon wealth, and therefore you are so well contented to let all alone.'[1]

About Burghley's reactions, Dering afterwards made the masterly understatement: 'True it is hee seemed not very well pleased'.[2] Nevertheless, this outspoken sermon did not end Dering's career in the church. He had resigned his Cambridge Fellowship, but Sandys, bishop of London, was his friend, and in 1572 appointed him divinity lecturer at St. Paul's where he was very popular. He was associated with the Puritan leaders, he visited Field and Wilcox in prison, and he backed Cartwright for a chair in Cambridge. His lectures began to arouse suspicion, and Sandys told Burghley he disliked them and that Dering approved of Cartwright's reply to Whitgift. On 29 May 1573 Dering was up before the Council and was suspended from lecturing pending further investigation, but he had influential friends including Leicester, Sir Nicholas Bacon and Burghley himself. The Council lifted the ban on 28 June and Dering resumed his work of lecturing and preaching. The ecclesiastical authorities made a great fuss, and on 20 July the ban was reimposed. Eventually, before the end of the year Dering was forbidden to preach altogether. He was brought to trial and was required to subscribe to the Articles, the royal supremacy and the Prayer Book.[3]

---

[1] In 1573 a Puritan compared Elizabeth's reformation with those of Henry VIII and and Edward VI. He praised Edward VI, 'that blessed ympe', and added '. . . it is no reason that the Queenes Majesty now should maintaine those abuses that remaine, no more I thinke would he, if the Lord had given him so long a time to raigne, and such encrease of knowledge and sight to have discerned such corruptions'. (*The Seconde Part of a Register*, edit. A. Peel, I. 96.)

[2] Patrick Collinson, *A Mirror of Elizabethan Puritanism*, pp. 17, 18.

[3] V. J. K. Brook, *Life of Archbishop Parker*, p. 311, Dering was already sick with tuberculosis and he died in 1576. He had a considerable correspondence and he acted as a 'physician of the soul', writing 'godly and comfortable letters' to those with troubled

The difficulty experienced by the bishops in getting effective action against Dering illustrates the importance of lay patronage as a factor in the survival of Puritanism. It is significant that Dering was particularly critical of the rôle of the bishops in temporal affairs. The minister's job was to 'edefie the soule', and 'the lordship or civile government of a byshop' was 'utterlie unlawfull in the Churche of God'.[1] Such views were not unwelcome to Elizabethan laymen concerned to keep bishops in their place. Archbishop Parker feared the worst when he wrote to Burghley in the spring of 1573: 'If your honour knew how we be bearded and used, you would think it strange that we should be thus dealt with . . . And but that we have our whole trust in God, in her Majesty and in two or three of her Council, I see it will be no dwelling for us in England.' He warned Burghley of the threat Puritanism made to the state, and in a letter of July 1573 he wrote: 'Surely if this fond faction be applauded to, or borne with, it will fall out to a popularity, and as wise men think, it will be the overthrow of all the nobility. Both papists and precisians have one mark to shoot at, plain disobedience . . . I marvel what prudence it can be, first to hew thus at us, and certainly yourself will shortly follow.'[2]

Puritanism certainly had its uses to the laymen of the governing class, but some of them, including Burghley, realised that it had its dangers and that it must not be allowed to get out of hand. In a speech to the Judges, Burghley referred to 'a number of persons young in years, but over-young in soundness of learning and discretion' who had not only 'according to their own imaginations and conceits' altered the services but also persuaded their parishioners and hearers 'to conceive erroneous opinions, in condemning the whole government of the Church and order ecclesiastical . . . and in moving her Majesty's good subjects to think it a burden of conscience to observe the orders and rites of the Church established by law; a matter pernicious to the state of government . . . ' Burghley maintained that it would be a disaster to the ship of state if the crew turned rebellious, and he insisted that the queen's orders must be obeyed.[3]

---

minds, particularly women. Many of these were influential. They included Catherine Killigrew, sister-in-law of Burghley and Bacon. Patrick Collinson, *A Mirror of Elizabethan Puritanism*, pp. 28, 29.

[1] Patrick Collinson, *A Mirror of Elizabethan Puritanism*, pp. 25, 26.

[2] Conyers Read, *Lord Burghley and Queen Elizabeth*, pp. 116–17; *Correspondence of Matthew Parker*, edit. J. Bruce and T. Perowne, Cambridge, 1853, pp. 418, 437.

[3] Conyers Read, *Lord Burghley and Queen Elizabeth*, p. 117.

The drive against nonconformity met with a measure of success. In August 1573 Bishop Sandys reported to Burghley that he had ferreted out a Puritan printing press in the country. The printer Lacy and his confederates had been arrested while working on another edition of Cartwright's *Reply*. They had actually printed a thousand copies.[1] In October 1573 a royal proclamation complained of 'contentions, sects and disquietness . . . diversity of rites and ceremonies, disputations and contentions, schisms and divisions'. This was attributed to the negligence of the bishops and magistrates and they were ordered to enforce the Act of Uniformity. Those who did not come to church and the sacraments were to be punished, as were those who held services according to other rites. The bishops and ecclesiastical authorities were told that if they did not act they would suffer the queen's 'high displeasure' and be deprived.[2] On 7 November the Council ordered the bishops to enforce strict uniformity and appointed commissioners to take action in accordance with the royal proclamation.[3] In December orders were issued to arrest Cartwright but he fled to Germany,[4] and in the same month the London clergy were required to subscribe to certain articles and to wear the surplice. Some were deprived for refusal.[5] Action was also taken against Puritans in Northamptonshire, Norfolk and Kent.[6]

Matthew Parker continued to the end of his life to be very concerned about the Puritan menace. In 1574 there was an alleged Puritan plot to murder Burghley and Parker. One Undertree produced documents involving two Puritans, Bonham and Stonden. They were arrested, but the documents were shown to be forgeries and the men had to be released. The archbishop made a fool of himself over the affair, and clearly the Puritans were getting on his nerves. In February

[1] A. F. Scott Pearson, *Thomas Cartwright and Elizabethan Puritanism*, p. 109. See H. P. Plomer, *A Short History of English Printing 1476–1898*, 1900, p. 137, for this press, which was believed to have been worked by John Stroud and two assistants Lacy and Asplyn. Stroud was a minister who had not acted as such since 1568 when he was deprived for nonconformity (*ibid.*, p. 110).

[2] V. J. K. Brook, *Life of Archbishop Parker*, p. 309.

[3] M. M. Knappen, *Tudor Puritanism*, pp. 244; V. J. K. Brook, *Life of Archbishop Parker*, p. 310.

[4] A. F. Scott Pearson, *Thomas Cartwright*, p. 130 ff. Cartwright went to Heidelberg where the elector had in 1570 established a presbyterian system based on that of Geneva. When a new elector established Lutheranism in the Palatinate in 1576, Cartwright removed to Basel.

[5] M. M. Knappen, *Tudor Puritanism*, p. 244.

[6] *Ibid.*, p. 244.

1575 he wrote to Burghley 'the earl is unquiet and conferreth by the hate of some of the examiners to use the counsel of some precisians I fear, and purposeth to undo me'. He complained: 'I may not work against the precisians and puritans, though the laws be against them.'[1]

In spite of Parker's fears, the Puritan effort which had looked so formidable in the period 1570–4 did not achieve what the Puritans had hoped. The direct and fundamental Presbyterian assault of Cartwright, Field, Wilcox and Travers was not successfully pressed home. Cartwright and Travers had been driven into exile, Field and Wilcox were quiet for the time being.[2] Dr. Collinson suggests that the proceedings of the Council at the end of 1573 'delayed the development of English presbyterianism for ten years'.

The Presbyterian movement was not completely destroyed, however. According to Bancroft, writing in 1593, there was established in Wandsworth, near London, a Presbyterian organisation as early as 1572. Bancroft thus describes it: 'Whereupon presently after the second parliament (viz. the twentieth of November 1572) there was a Presbytery erected at Wandsworthe in Surrey (as it appeareth by a bill endorsed with Master Field's hande, thus: the order of Wandesworthe). In which order the Elder's names, eleven of them, are set downe: the manner of their election is declared; the approvers of them (one Smith of Micham and Crane of Rough Hampton) are mentioned: their offices and certaine generall rules (then given unto them to bee observed) were likewise agreed upon and described.'[3] This 'Order of Wandsworth' has aroused a good deal of interest among historians because it seems to suggest the existence of a very early Presbyterian church, but we have very little information about it, and it was not known to the authorities at the time. Mr. Brook comments: 'there is no known parallel to it at that time anywhere else. So far as we can gather, the general movement came later, subterranean, spontaneous, local, rising after the suppression of prophesyings.'[4]

With the possible exception of Wandsworth, Presbyterian

[1] It seems likely that the earl was Leicester, the great patron of Puritans (see p. 80 note 1). V. J. K. Brook, *Life of Archbishop Parker*, pp. 335–6.

[2] Wilcox was free by the end of 1573. Of Field there is no trace until he reappears in July 1575. He may have gone abroad. Patrick Collinson, 'John Field and Elizabethan Puritanism', p. 139.

[3] Richard Bancroft, *Dangerous Positions*, p. 43; V. J. K. Brook, *Life of Archbishop Parker*, pp. 290–1; A. F. Scott Pearson, *Thomas Cartwright*, pp. 74–82; Patrick Collinson, '*The Elizabethan Puritan Movement*, pp. 138–9.

[4] V. J. K. Brook, *Whitgift and the English Church*, p. 113.

organisation does not seem to have been established in any of the English parishes, but the Presbyterian movement was still in being. The London conference of the 'brethren' still continued and influenced the movement both in England and outside. It seems that Field and others encouraged Puritan ministers to seek appointment by some form of election by the congregation.[1] In 1577 the London group quarrelled with Cartwright who had by now taken up the position that it was better for a minister to conform in the matter of vestments rather than be deprived. It condemned Cartwright for setting himself 'against the Church and the brethren'.[2] It was also asked to give assistance in finding a chaplain for the Merchant Adventurers in Antwerp, and it recommended Walter Travers, who received Presbyterian ordination in the Netherlands and endeavoured to impose Presbyterianism in the Merchant Adventurers' Church.[3] In addition, Presbyterianism made great progress in the Channel Islands.[4] But although it had some measure of success, it had not really made much headway in the country as a whole. Its support was very limited, and it lost a great deal of sympathy from non-Presbyterian Puritans owing to a new policy adopted by the ecclesiastical authorities. In 1575 Matthew Parker died, and the succession of Edmund Grindal marked the beginning of an attempt by the established church to get some sort of working arrangement with its Puritan critics and to direct their enthusiasm against the menace from Rome rather than the menace from Canterbury, to 'joyne together againste the papistes, the Enemies of God and of her Majestie and not to spende themselves in Civill Warres of the churche of God'.[5]

In the 1570's those who wanted further changes in the Church of England were able to make use of, and in a number of places to get effective control of, a machinery which initially was intended primarily to raise the standards of the clergy. There had sprung up in many parts of the country meetings known as 'prophesyings'.[6] They were

[1] Patrick Collinson, 'John Field and Elizabethan Puritanism', p. 138

[2] *Ibid.*, p. 140; *The Seconde Parte of a Register*, edit, A. Peel, I. 136–143.

[3] Patrick Collinson 'John Field and Elizabethan Puritanism', p. 140. In 1580 Travers returned to become a lecturer at the Temple Church, London.

[4] A. F. Scott Pearson, *Thomas Cartwright*, p. 156 ff.

[5] Thomas Norton quoted in Patrick Collinson, 'The Puritan Classical Movement', p. 173.

[6] The word was not used in the modern sense of foretelling the future but rather of expounding the scriptures and edifying the congregation with the guidance of the Holy Spirit.

meetings of the clergy of a particular district for prayers and to hear sermons. Laymen were often allowed to take part. This was followed by a closed session at which the clergy discussed the sermon or sermons they had heard, corrected errors in doctrine and gave each other advice and reproof under the presidency of a moderator. The practice varied from one area to another, but the general aim was to train a learned and godly ministry. It was not in origin a Calvinistic procedure, it had a long history in the reformed churches of Europe, and it existed in England before the reign of Elizabeth.[1] It was not the official policy of the Elizabethan Church, but it was encouraged by a considerable number of individual bishops with the aim of raising clerical standards. Puritans did not invent 'prophesyings', but they often played a prominent part in them. In many places they took the initiative in organising them and then got the approval, enthusiastic or otherwise, of the diocesan bishop.

There are many examples of these 'exercises' and 'prophesyings' in the 1560's, including those in the diocese of Exeter begun before 1570 by Bishop Alley, who was 'a furtherer therein' and whose successor, Bishop Bradbridge, himself acted on occasions as moderator. At Coventry they were held 'almost sithence the beginning of the Queen's Majesty's reign'. They were attended by 'good and godly people' in great numbers, and Thomas Lever, the archdeacon, generally acted as moderator.[2] One of the best known of these very numerous 'prophesyings' was in Northampton. It was established by the town preacher, Percival Wiburn,[3] with the consent of the bishop and the local magistrates. The ministers of the town and countryside met every Saturday to discuss the Scriptures in the presence of laymen. They then met privately to discuss doctrine, morals and the godly life. On Sundays and holy days each parish service in the town ended at 9 a.m. and there was then a sermon in the main church which those who had had no sermon in their own church were expected to attend. After evening prayers, the young people were examined on Calvin's catechism. On Tuesdays and Thursdays there was a 'lecture of scripture' in the main church. Once a quarter every parish had a communion service. Before this took place, the ministers and churchwardens of the parishes took the names of those intending to

---

[1] Patrick Collinson, *The Elizabethan Puritan Movement*, p. 168 ff.
[2] Patrick Collinson, *The Elizabethan Puritan Movement*, p. 168 ff.
[3] See p. 93.

communicate and examined them on the state of their lives. If there were quarrels among the parishioners, those concerned were brought up before the town council, some of the Justices of the Peace and the ministers, and were reconciled, punished or excommunicated. After the communion service, those who had not attended were visited and, if necessary, disciplined. Wiburn also organised meetings of the ministers of the whole shire four times a year. After a public sermon, they had a private conference concerning the conduct of the clergy. Those who were considered unsatisfactory were exhorted to mend their ways. After three exhortations the erring minister might be reported to the bishop for disciplinary action.[1]

The very elaborate arrangements in Northampton were exceptional rather than typical, but in a greater or lesser degree these meetings of the clergy, in which the laity to some degree participated, were found in many dioceses, and as Mr. Knappen remarks, they show how much Puritanism could be introduced within the legal limits of the Anglican system if the ecclesiastical and secular authorities were prepared to co-operate.[2]

The 'prophesyings' were very popular with the laity and they enjoyed the patronage of influential men in town and country. Many of the bishops approved of them because they saw them as a means of raising the low standards of education and morals among the clergy. It was not surprising that this should be so, for we must never forget that the desire to remove abuses in the church was something which many of the bishops had in common with their Puritan critics. The official efforts to reform the church have too often been ignored or played down by historians whose sympathies are with the Puritans. There is some truth in the comment that the Northampton exercises were 'Anglicanism at its best'.[3]

There is a great deal of evidence to show how widespread these 'exercises' were by the mid 1570's and how much support they received from the civil and the ecclesiastical authorities.[4] Properly controlled, they could render invaluable service to the church. Nevertheless, they were potentially dangerous. In many of them Puritan clergy played a

---

[1] M. M. Knappen, *Tudor Puritanism*, p. 253 ff; Patrick Collinson, 'The Puritan Classical Movement', p. 191 ff. For the regulations regarding prophesyings in the diocese of Lincoln, see J. R. Tanner, *Tudor Constitutional Documents*, pp. 179–82.

[2] M. M. Knappen, *Tudor Puritanism*, p. 254.

[3] M. M. Knappen, *Tudor Puritanism*, p. 255.

[4] Patrick Collinson, 'The Puritan Classical Movement', pp. 196–8.

leading rôle and could influence their fellow clergy. The interest and support of the laity seemed all the more menacing in view of the Presbyterian challenge. Moreover, they were in some degree outside the control of the official machinery.[1] Individual diocesan bishops might approve, but they had not been authorised by Archbishop Parker or by the queen. It is possible that Elizabeth did not realise how widespread they were. In 1574, however, she ordered the archbishop to end 'those vain prophesyings'.[2] Rather surprisingly, Parker seems to have taken action only in one diocese—Norwich—where the bishop, Parkhurst, who had approved the exercises, was told by the archbishop in the queen's name to put an end to them. A few weeks later, he got a letter from the bishop of London and three Privy Councillors saying that they had heard that 'some, not well minded towards true religion' had attacked prophesyings, and they urged him to give his support to the exercises. Parkhurst was naturally very confused about what was going on, all the more so when he found on enquiry from his fellow bishops that they had not received orders to suppress them. He eventually obeyed orders, but no action seems to have been taken elsewhere.[3]

In 1575 Matthew Parker died and was succeeded at Canterbury by Edmund Grindal.[4] He had been born in Cumberland about 1519 and he had gone to Cambridge. He was chaplain to Ridley, and when in exile under Mary he had assisted John Foxe in collecting material for his famous work on the martyrs. He was one of the first bishops to be nominated by Elizabeth. He had scruples about the dress and ceremonies which he would have to accept, and he hesitated about stepping into a position of authority, but his friend Peter Martyr urged him to do so, and pointed out that if he did not, someone much less suitable might be appointed in his place. When the queen insisted in the mid 1560's on the use of the surplice and the other prescribed clerical dress, Grindal obeyed orders without any great enthusiasm

---

[1] For an examination of their significance, see Patrick Collinson, *The Elizabethan Puritan Movement*, p. 177 ff.

[2] V. J. K. Brook, *Life of Archbishop Parker*, p. 328.

[3] V. J. K. Brook, *Life of Archbishop Parker*, pp. 328, 329.

[4] For Grindal, see John Strype, *The History of the Life and Acts of the Most Reverend Father in God, Edmund Grindal*, Oxford, 1821; Patrick Collinson, *The Elizabethan Puritan Movement*, p. 159 ff. Dr. Collinson outlines the kind of church which Grindal favoured. It was very different from what Elizabeth wanted. There is great need for a modern biography of Grindal, and Dr. Collinson is writing one for Nelson's series 'Leaders of Religion in Britain'.

because he knew that good ministers were scarce, but he took a firmer line when he saw the obstinacy of the Puritans. John Strype commented that he was 'not forward to use extremities' and that because of this 'the Puritan party confided much in him; and gave out, that my Lord of London was their own, and that all he did was upon a force, and unwillingly, as they flattered themselves'.[1] In 1570 Grindal was made archbishop of York. He got on very well with the Puritan-minded Lord President—the third earl of Huntingdon.[2] In 1575 he was an obvious choice for Canterbury.[3]

Because he dealt somewhat gently with the Puritans and because, as we shall see, he got into trouble with the queen over prophesyings, he has acquired the reputation of being a Puritan himself, but it is very misleading to label him a Puritan unless the word is to be made to include anyone who wished to carry out the obviously needed reforms in the church. He was a sincere reformer, and the canons approved by Convocation in 1576 attempted to put right a number of abuses.[4] He tried hard to maintain the unity of the church and to reclaim precisians and Puritans 'who for some few ceremonies made a breach in Christian communion', but he had no sympathy with those who would not conform but who nevertheless retained their prebends and preferment in the church, as did Wiburn, Johnson and others. He argued: 'If they will do no office, let them enjoy no benefit.'[5] Since he wanted a learned and responsible clergy, he encouraged 'prophesyings', but he realised that they had their dangers and he laid down rules designed to control them.[6]

At the end of 1576 the queen told Grindal that she thought three or four preachers for each county were sufficient, and she instructed him to suppress prophesyings. Grindal replied to the queen in a famous letter dated 20 December 1576.[7] He said that he had been

---

[1] J. Strype, *Edmund Grindal*, pp. 154–5.

[2] For Huntingdon see M. Claire Cross, *The Puritan earl: the life of Henry Hastings, third earl of Huntingdon 1536–1595*, 1966; 'Noble Patronage in the Elizabethan Church', *The Historical Journal*, vol. III, no. 1, 1960. For his action against Catholics in the North, see M. Claire Cross, 'The Third Earl of Huntingdon and Trials of Catholics in the North, 1581–1595', *Recusant History* vol. 8, no. 3, 1965.

[3] He was nominated on 29 December 1575. The confirmation of the appointment was on 15 February 1576.

[4] For the Canons of 1576, see E. Cardwell, *Synodalia*, I, 132 ff.

[5] J. Strype, *Edmund Grindal*, p. 448.

[6] Patrick Collinson, *The Elizabethan Puritan Movement*, p. 195

[7] Printed in part G. Elton, *The Tudor Constitution*, pp. 441–2 and J. R. Tanner, *Tudor Constitutional Documents*, pp. 183–4, and in full in J. Strype, *Edmund Grindal*, p. 558 ff.

5 THOMAS CARTWRIGHT
The Cambridge don whose advocacy of Presbyterian forms of church government from 1570 onwards presented the Church of England with a fundamental challenge. He was brought to trial by Whitgift in 1591–2, and after suffering a term of imprisonment, settled down more or less peacefully as Master of the earl of Leicester's Hospital in Warwick.

A TEXT BOOK FOR ENGLISH PRESBYTERIANS
Originally published in Latin by Walter Travers and published at Heidelberg. An English translation, probably by Cartwright, appeared in 1574.

A full and plaine declaration of Ecclefiaſticall Diſcipline owt off the word off God/ and off the declininge off the churche off England from the ſame.

Imprinted.

M. D. LXXIIII.

7 EDMUND GRINDAL, ARCHBISHOP OF CANTERBURY 1575–158
He said of some of the Puritan ministers 'If they will do no office, let then
enjoy no benefit', but he was anxious to reclaim those 'who for some fev
ceremonies made a breach in the Christian communion'. In 1576 he refuse
to carry out the queen's order to suppress 'prophesyings' and was sequestered
In 1583 he agreed to resign but he died, old and blind, before the arrange
ments were completed.

very dismayed by the speeches the queen delivered when last he attended 'concerning the abridging the number of Preachers, and the utter suppression of all learned exercises and conferences among the Ministers of the Church, allowed by their Bishops and Ordinaries . . . ' He acknowledged his debt to the queen and said he did not intend to offend her 'unless in the cause of God, or of his Church', but that it was his duty to speak. He said he marvelled 'how this strange opinion should once enter in your mind, that it should be good for the Church to have a few preachers', for the scripture made it plain that the gospel should be plentifully preached. He piled up texts to prove the duty of preaching and argued that 'Public and continual preaching of God's Word is the ordinary mean and instrument of the salvation of mankind'. Preaching incidentally planted in the hearts of the subjects due obedience to Christian princes. The loyalty of London where there were many preachers should be compared with the rebelliousness of the north where there were few. Grindal asked whether the troubles in the north were not due to 'Papistry and ignorance of God's Word, through want of often preaching'. He said that some argued that many had been allowed to preach who were not competent to do so, but he maintained that he had done his best to see that only able preachers and good men were given licences. He said of himself and his brother bishops: 'We admit no man to the office, that either professeth Papistry or Puritanism.' Of those who criticised the preachers, some were too fussy and others disliked their sins being shown up. As for the Homilies which were read in place of sermons, they had been only a stop-gap in Edward VI's time until sermons could be provided. Unfortunately appropriations had impoverished the church 'so as at this day, in mine opinion, where one Church is able to yield sufficient living for a learned preacher, there are at least seven churches unable to do the same'.

Grindal then went to the heart of the matter. With regard to learned exercises and conferences among the clergy, he had consulted a number of his fellow bishops 'who think the same as I do, viz. a thing profitable to the Church, and therefore expedient to be continued'. The bishops in question by the law of God and the canons of the Church had authority to appoint exercises for their inferior ministers to increase their learning and knowledge of the scriptures. Meetings were held once a month or once a fortnight for two hours in the church to discuss some texts of scripture previously agreed upon. They

L

ended with a psalm and a prayer from the Book of Common Prayer. Two or three of the gravest and best learned clergy were appointed as moderators by the bishop. No man spoke unless first allowed to do so by the bishop, and no layman might speak at all. Current controversies were not discussed and personal remarks were forbidden. If anyone broke the rules he was reported to the bishop for correction. There were scriptural precedents for all this, and the exercises and conferences were in effect 'all one with the exercises of students in divinity in the Universities'. Whatever the queen might have heard, Grindal himself and the bishops of London, Winchester, Bath, Lichfield, Gloucester, Lincoln, Chichester, Exeter and St. David's would testify that as a result of these exercises ministers were more skilful in scripture and were drawn from idleness, wandering and gaming. Some who were suspect in doctrine had been brought to see the truth. The archbishop maintained that: 'Ignorant Ministers are driven to studie, if not for conscience, yet for shame and fear of discipline.' The opinion of laymen that clerics were idle was removed. Popery was beaten down when ministers grew to such good knowledge that whereas before there were not three able preachers, now there were thirty meet to preach at St. Paul's Cross, and forty or fifty men able to instruct in their own parishes. He urged that: 'Only backward men in religion, and contemners of learning in the countries abroad, do fret at it.' And he suggested that: 'The dissolution of it would breed triumph to the adversaries, and great sorrow and grief unto the favourers of religion.'

Grindal hoped that the queen would see the matter as he did, but he said frankly: 'I am forced, with all humility, and yet plainly, to profess that I cannot with safe conscience, and without the offence of the majesty of God, give my assent to the suppressing of the said exercises, much less can I send out any injunction for the utter and universal subversion of the same.' If the queen wished to remove him, he would accept it, but, he asked, 'what should I winn, if I gayned (I will not say a bushoprick but) the whole world, and lose mine own soul?' Finally, he asked the queen to refer to the bishops and divines all matters which touched religion or the doctrine and discipline of the Church, in the same way as she sent legal questions to the judges. He asked her when she dealt with faith and religion not to pronounce 'too resolutely and peremptorily' and to obey God's voice.

The very courageous stand taken by Archbishop Grindal is not evidence of his 'Puritanism' but of his desire to encourage the preaching of the gospel and to raise the standards of the clergy. It also sprang from his very understandable feeling that the bishops ought to be consulted in matters concerning religion. The practice of the Supreme Governor and other powerful laymen of riding roughshod over the ecclesiastical authorities had caused a great deal of worry to Matthew Parker and the other bishops. Grindal felt that here was a question of conscience and that he must make a stand. It was but one more illustration of the perennial problem of the relations between church and state.

Yet in many ways the conflict was not about principles but about means.[1] Grindal thought that 'prophesyings' were serving an important purpose—the spreading of the gospel—and he thought that their dangers could be kept under control. The queen saw them as forums in which the Puritan clergy could spread their views and undermine the religion established by law. They were, in her eyes, a training ground for deviationists, and she had none of Grindal's enthusiasm for a preaching clergy because she realised that many of the ablest preachers were in fact Puritans.

It may well be that the queen judged the situation better than her archbishop. She had by now had considerable experience of the determination and what she considered 'the insolence' of these committed men who threatened her ecclesiastical authority. Their supporters gave her never-ending trouble in the House of Commons. In 1576, for example, Peter Wentworth had attacked the bishops, and Mr. Pistor 'with great zeal, declared to the House the great prejudice [that] grew to the realm by the unlearnedness of the ministry, abuses of excommunication, want of discipline, dispensations, and toleration for non-residency, and such like'. The Commons had drawn up a petition to the queen which stressed the ignorance and non-residence of the clergy, the lack of discipline whereby a great number of men were admitted as ministers who lacked the gifts of their calling and who were 'infamous in their lives and conversations'. As a result 'an infinite number of your Majesty's subjects, for want of preaching of the word—the only ordinary means of salvation of souls and the only

[1] It might perhaps be argued that there was a conflict of principle in that Grindal held that preaching was 'the ordinary means and instrument of the salvation of mankind' and that by implication at least, this very much reduced the importance of the sacraments, but it must be remembered that Grindal was not discussing the relative merits of preaching and the sacraments. He was primarily arguing against an order which he thought would damage the training of preachers.

good means to teach your Majesty's subjects to know their true obedience . . . have already run headlong into destruction'. The queen graciously undertook to confer with the bishops, and the canons of 1576 were an official attempt to deal with some of the abuses.[1]

The queen was not very pleased with interference by parliament in matters of religion, but she had by now learnt that the Commons must be handled carefully. Disobedience by her own archbishop was another matter, and she was not prepared to tolerate it. She was Supreme Governor, and if the archbishop would not do what he was told, she could act directly herself. On 7 May 1577 she sent instructions to the bishops to suppress 'prophesyings'. She wrote 'we hear to our great grief, that in sundry parts of our realm there are no small numbers of persons presuming to be teachers and preachers of the Church (though neither lawfully thereunto called, nor yet fit for the same) which, contrary to our laws established for the public divine service of Almighty God . . . do daily devise, imagine, propound, and put in execution, sundry new rites and forms in the Church, as well by their unordinate preachings, readings, and ministering the Sacraments, as by procuring unlawfully of assemblies of great numbers of our people out of their ordinary parishes, and from places far distant, (and that also some of our subjects of good calling, though therein not well advised), to be hearers of their disputations, and new devised opinions, upon points of divinity, far unmeet for vulgar people: which manner of innovations they in some places term *prophecyings*, and in some other places term *exercises*'. She said that great numbers of people especially of the vulgar sort who ought to be engaged in honest labour were brought to idleness and schismatically divided 'into variety of dangerous opinions', to the breach of common order and to the offence of all her quiet subjects 'that desire to live and serve God according to the uniform orders established in the Church . . . ' The bishops were therefore ordered to see that no other rites and ceremonies were permitted except those established by law. No one was to teach or preach without a licence. Exercises were not warranted or appointed by law, and the bishops were instructed 'that you do cause the same forth with to cease . . . ' If any one continued with them, he was to be committed to prison.[2]

---

[1] J. Neale, *Queen Elizabeth I and her Parliaments*, I. 323, 349–51; S. B. Babbage, *Puritanism and Richard Bancroft*, 1962, pp. 16, 17.

[2] J. Strype, *Edmund Grindal*, p. 574 ff.

The next step was to deal with the disobedient archbishop. In June 1577 he was confined to his house and sequestered from exercising his temporal jurisdiction.[1] Those bishops who sympathised with Grindal's views about prophesyings failed to support him, and he alone paid the price for his courageous stand.

There was now another drive against the Puritans. Bishop Aylmer of London was made president of an Ecclesiastical Commission, and he and his fellow bishops did something to check the spread of non-conformity. From time to time Puritan ministers were suspended; lecturers who did not hold livings but who preached were investigated, and an effort was made to see that they used the Book of Common Prayer; illicit conventicles were suppressed, and attempts were made to deal with nonconformists in the Inns of Court and elsewhere. Bishop Aylmer, who disliked both Puritans and Papists, proposed that the leading Puritans should be banished to Lancashire, Staffordshire and Shropshire 'and such other like barbarous countries' to preach against the Papists. He also wished to appoint special investigators to attend the London churches to seek out nonconformists.[2]

The drive against the Puritans met with only limited success. It did not help matters that the archbishop of Canterbury, who might have given a lead in all this, remained sequestered.[3] As always, some of the leading Puritans enjoyed the patronage of powerful laymen, including Privy Councillors, and local magistrates in town and country often gave them strong support. It must never be forgotten that neither the queen nor the bishops had a completely free hand with the appointment and dismissal of the clergy. The rights of the laity to make presentations to livings, their control of appropriations, their powers of patronage in appointing chaplains and lecturers, and their powerful influence in local affairs meant that the efforts of the central government and the ecclesiastical authorities could often be thwarted. At Norwich, for example, the parishioners purchased the advowson and could legally choose clergy to their own liking; at Bury the congregation of the chief church claimed the right to nominate the ministers

[1] M. M. Knappen, *Tudor Puritanism*, p. 257.
[2] M. M. Knappen, *Tudor Puritanism*, pp. 257–8.
[3] Originally he had been sequestered for six months, but at the end of that period he refused to give way. There was some thought of deposing him in 1579 but it was felt that this would cause too great a scandal. Convocation petitioned for his restoration in 1580. In 1583 he accepted the queen's suggestion that he should resign, but he died, old and blind, before the arrangement was completed.

and to dismiss unsatisfactory curates. Too often the authority of the bishop was undermined by men who got some support from the Council. Thus when the bishop of Norwich tried to insist that all preachers should administer the sacraments, he was rebuked by the Council and told to leave these godly men alone.[1] The earl of Leicester, who was Chancellor of Oxford, successfully persuaded the university to license John Field as a preacher in spite of the hostility of the bishop of London.[2]

It is not at all clear how effective the attempt to suppress 'prophesyings' really was. There is evidence that both officially and unofficially meetings of the clergy continued in a number of dioceses. Thus another letter had to be sent to the bishop of Lincoln telling him again to put an end to them.[3] In 1578 the archbishop of York, Edwin Sandys, ordered 'quarterly synods' in the northern province, and in 1580 the bishop of Chester arranged meetings in his diocese three times a year.[4] There are also indications of unofficial meetings[5] and of gatherings of clergy and laity for what were known as 'Fasts'. Dr. Collinson thinks that by 1580 these Fasts, at which people met fasting to pray, hear sermons and for 'humbly waiting on grace', were very popular and that they were used to get round the orders against prophesyings.[6] Archbishop Sandys commented on them in 1581 that: 'There lurketh Matter under that pretended Pietie. The Devil is craftie: and the younge Ministers of these our Times growe madd.'[7]

It is by no means easy to assess the strength of Puritanism at the end of the 1570's. It had certainly become more formidable, and it was making much more radical criticism of the establishment than in the 1560's. The Presbyterian movement which had emerged in the early part of the decade had found able young leaders in Cartwright, Travers and Field, and it had produced a very powerful literature, but it had not been widely accepted, and the queen and the church had effectively counter-attacked. Cartwright and Travers had been driven into exile, and for a time Field's energies had been directed against the

---

[1] For other examples, see M. M. Knappen, *Tudor Puritanism*, p. 259 ff.

[2] Patrick Collinson, 'John Field and Elizabethan Puritanism', p. 143.

[3] J. Strype, *Aylmer*, p. 114.

[4] M. M. Knappen, *Tudor Puritanism*, p. 262; Patrick Collinson, *'The Elizabethan Puritan Movement*, p. 209 ff.

[5] Patrick Collinson, 'The Puritan Classical Movement', pp. 303, 323 ff.

[6] *Ibid.*, p. 325 ff., *The Elizabethan Puritan Movement*, p. 214 ff.

[7] Patrick Collinson, 'The Puritan Classical Movement', p. 329.

Church of Rome rather than against the Church of England. But although Presbyterianism had suffered a severe setback, it had not been destroyed. Moreover, other forms of Puritanism had gained in strength. Much of the impetus behind the 'prophesying' movement arose from a desire on the part of clergy and laity to remove undoubted abuses, to produce a 'godly' and preaching ministry, and to introduce into the Church of England some kind of 'discipline', not necessarily on orthodox Presbyterian lines, which would limit in various ways the powers of the diocesan bishops. This movement also had suffered a severe setback when the queen took action, but the spirit behind it had not been killed. There was plenty of inflammable material about, and attempts to establish 'true religion' were likely to get considerable sympathy. The genuine efforts of the established church to put its house in order had met with only limited success, often it might be noted, because of obstruction from those who supported the Puritans but who nevertheless had no desire to see a powerful church which might threaten their property rights in appropriations, tithes, leases of ecclesiastical lands, and the rest.

One most important factor in the spread of Puritanism was the universities, which were the main training centres for the clergy. They were producing in considerable numbers ministers who were Puritans or Puritan in sympathy, and the growing habit of the nobility and gentry of sending their children to Oxford or Cambridge meant that a considerable number of the laity were also affected. Dr. Collinson has made a rough survey of clergy and schoolmasters who have left evidence of their Puritanism in the period 1570–90. He found that at least 228 had been in residence in Cambridge at some time between 1565 and 1575. The total for Oxford was only 42, but the Oxford Puritans included some of the most radical.[1] Dr. Collinson considers that Magdalen College, Oxford, was the most remarkable Puritan seminary of either university. Cambridge, however, produced a larger number of Puritans, and St. John's College and Christ's College were particularly prominent. St. John's developed early 'a proud tradition of faction', and Mr. Knappen maintains that Dering and other Fellows at Christ's College 'began a tradition which for the decades before the foundation of Emmanuel made that college the greatest Puritan seminary of them all'.[2] In his fascinating study of Tudor Cambridge,

---

[1] Patrick Collinson, *The Elizabethan Puritan Movement*, p. 127 ff.
[2] M. M. Knappen, *Tudor Puritanism*, p. 218 ff.

Dr. Porter has shown how widespread this Puritan influence was and how radical it could be.[1] Thus, one of Cartwright's disciples preached to the university in 1572 that archbishops and bishops had been introduced into the Church by Satan and that no minister ought to have superiority over another, and two years earlier William Some claimed that 'the Queen's Majesty's laws do permit many detestable, devilish, and damnable things'.[2] When John Whitgift, the arch-enemy of the Puritans, became Vice-Chancellor of the university in 1570, he did his best to eradicate the many shocking things which he found going on there, and Giles Wigginton, Fellow of Trinity, complained that for six years he was harassed by Whitgift 'for wearing my hat instead of a square cap, and for not wearing of a surplice when I went to the chapel, for speaking against non-residents, stage plays, and popery or prelacy and such like matters'.[3]

The failure to exercise really effective control over the religion taught in the universities meant that Puritan influence was able to spread to many parts of the country. Indeed, Dr. Collinson considers that the universities were responsible for making Puritanism into a national movement. It may seem rather surprising that the establishment did not exercise more control over the teaching in such influential institutions. It is of some significance that the Chancellor of Cambridge was Lord Burghley and the Chancellor of Oxford was the earl of Leicester. Burghley was not a Puritan, but he had a good deal of sympathy with many individual Puritans, particularly when they got into trouble and asked him for help. Moreover, he showed a remarkable modesty in dealing with academic matters and was not anxious to intervene in university affairs except in the last resort. Leicester, of course, was a great patron of Puritans, and he seems to have had rather more religious conviction than used to be suggested.[4] The measure of independence enjoyed by the universities, the habit of free discussion and the relatively open and liberal atmosphere, all helped the Puritans to spread their ideas.[5]

[1] H. C. Porter, *Reformation and Reaction in Tudor Cambridge*.

[2] H. C. Porter, *op. cit.*, pp. 141, 143.

[3] *Ibid.*, pp. 171–2. Wigginton left to be vicar of Sedbergh in 1578 and was again in trouble in 1580.

[4] See H. C. Porter, *Reformation and Reaction in Tudor Cambridge*, for Burghley's work as Chancellor, and Patrick Collinson, *Life and Letters of Thomas Wood*, for Leicester's.

[5] For University Puritanism, see also M. Curtis, *Oxford and Cambridge in Transition, 1558–1642*, 1959, p. 194 ff., and V. H. H. Green, *Religion at Oxford and Cambridge*, 1964, p. 105 ff.

But if Puritan influence was spreading, the resistance of the establishment was stiffening, and this made the probability of further conflict all the greater. The main counter-attack by the establishment was not launched until after Whitgift had become archbishop of Canterbury in 1583, but Dr. Collinson points out that in the years between Grindal's disgrace and Whitgift's elevation there were big changes in the episcopate. The older generation of bishops, many of whom had been in exile under Mary and who had supported 'prophesyings' and other reforming tendencies, were dying off, and new men, less sympathetic to the 'pure milk of the gospel', were taking their place. When Bishop Parkhurst died in 1575, he was succeeded by Bishop Freke who harassed the Puritans of East Anglia and even allied with the Papists against them. Aylmer got the bishopric of London in 1576, Piers went to Rochester in the same year and was translated to Salisbury in 1578, and Young went to Rochester in 1578, a man described by Aylmer as 'fit to bridle innovators'.[1] These men had no sympathy for the Puritan cause, and when he succeeded to Canterbury Whitgift was able to find a considerable measure of support from his fellow bishops.

*   *   *

Thus in 1580 religious uniformity was seriously threatened both by the revived Roman Catholicism and the counter-reformation spirit of no compromise which the Douay priests had been spreading since 1574, and by a very active Puritanism which was being propagated in many parts of the country by ministers trained in the universities. The government was about to face even more serious challenges to its policy of imposing one form of religion on all Englishmen.[2] In the 1580's the Papists' threat came first, with the landing of the so-called Jesuit mission, but the Puritan challenge was not very long delayed. It was a pointer to the shape of things to come that the year 1580 which saw the arrival of Parsons and Campion was also the year in which the first serious separatist movement appeared and in which the

---

[1] Patrick Collinson *The Elizabethan Puritan Movement*, p. 201 ff.
[2] The peerage cannot, of course, be taken as representative of the religious views of the whole country, but it is interesting to note that in 1580, of the 66 English peers 20 were Catholic recusants, about 10 were strongly Puritan in sympathy, about 12 were supporters of the Anglican settlement, and the remaining 24 were relatively indifferent to religious issues and anxious only to back the winning side. Lawrence Stone, *The Crisis of the Aristocracy 1558–1641*, p. 741.

formidable Presbyterian leader Walter Travers returned from abroad. Significantly, Travers did not come like the Jesuits as a hunted man but with the approval of Lord Burghley, whose good offices had secured for him an appointment as Reader in Temple Church. The Church of England was threatened both by its enemies from without and by its own members from within.

8

The Crisis of the Fifteen-Eighties: The Papist Challenge from Within and from Without the Realm

Nothing in the world grieveth me more than to see her Majesty believes that this increase of Papists in her realm can be no danger to her . . . If she suffers this increase but one year more, as she hath done these two or three past, it will be too late to give or take counsel to help it.

Leicester to Walsingham, 5 September 1582[1]

THE 1580's were the most critical decade in the long reign of Elizabeth I. The régime was threatened by Papists and Puritans more seriously than it had ever been threatened before. While the Papists increased in numbers, and the Puritans pressed their case in parliament and outside, there was a growing threat of foreign invasion, culminating in 1588 in a Spanish fleet sailing up the channel with the intention of landing in England a Spanish army to overthrow the queen and restore once more the Catholic religion. It was a long drawn-out crisis, or rather series of crises, which put men's nerves on edge and which left them wondering when, and from which direction, the next blow would fall. The dangers that threatened the country were very real, but they lost nothing in the telling, and they were used with great skill by the rulers of England to win support for the government policy. In this world of complicated intrigue and brilliant propaganda, of agents and double-agents, of plots real and imaginary, it is often impossible to say where the truth lies. The country was moving towards war, and it is a commonplace that in war truth is the first casualty.

In the summer of 1580, two Jesuit priests and a Jesuit laybrother landed on English soil, an event which has often been referred to as

---

[1] Quoted in J. Neale, *Elizabeth I and her Parliaments*, II. 13.

'The Jesuit Invasion of England'.[1] The decision to allow Jesuits to participate in the work which the seminary priests had been doing since 1574 was taken reluctantly by the General of the Society of Jesus in response to urgent requests from Allen, who saw the desperate need for more priests in England and who was concerned that so many young Englishmen were being attracted to the Society although it was making no contribution to the missionary work in this country.

The Jesuits had given very careful thought to the problems which would face them. One obvious question which the Douay priests had not, it seems, raised with the pope, was whether or not the bull of excommunication was binding on English Catholics. In April 1580 the Jesuits obtained from Gregory XIII an 'explanation' of the bull which stated that although the bull was binding on heretics, the sentence 'in no way bound the Catholics, things being as they are, but then only when the public execution of the said bull can be carried out'.[2]

It is clear that there had been no fundamental change in the papal attitude towards the Elizabethan government. The papacy continued to work for the overthrow of the queen in the 1580's, as it had in the 1570's, but the missionaries could at least assure English Catholics that they were under no obligation to take any action in the present situation. Further, the Jesuits were given detailed instructions not to involve themselves in affairs of state, not to write to Rome about political matters, and not to speak, or to allow others to speak, against the queen, except, perhaps, with those whose fidelity had been long and steadfast, and even then not without strong reason.[3] The object of the mission was defined as 'the preservation and augmentation of the faith of the Catholics in England', and the missionaries were urged not to dispute with heretics and, as far as possible, to avoid them.

The Jesuits certainly understood themselves to be engaged on a mission the purpose of which was spiritual and not political. They did not come to stir up rebellion or to urge Catholics to assist in deposing Elizabeth. Campion later declared: 'My charge is, of free cost, to

---

[1] See, for example, W. H. Frere, *The English Church in the reigns of Elizabeth and James I*, 1924.

[2] A. O. Meyer, *England and the Catholic Church under Queen Elizabeth*, p. 486. For the faculties granted to the Jesuits, *ibid.*, pp. 486–8. For a general discussion of what this involved, see Philip Hughes, *Rome and the Counter-Reformation in England*, p. 257 ff., and A. O. Meyer, *op. cit.*, p. 136 ff.

[3] A. O. Meyer, *op. cit.*, pp. 142, 143, The exception was removed in 1581 and the prohibition was made absolute.

preach the gospel, to minister the sacraments, to instruct the simple, to reform sinners, to confute errors, and, in brief, to cry alarm spiritual against foul vice and proud ignorance wherewith my dear countrymen are abused. I never had mind, and am strictly forbidden by our fathers that sent me, to deal in any respect with matters of state or policy of the realm, as those things which appertain not to my vocation'.[1]

The Jesuits set out from Rome at Easter 1580 after being received in audience by the pope. The three of them formed part of a fairly large group consisting of the aged Dr. Goldwell, who had been bishop of St. Asaph's in Mary's time, Laurence Vaux of *Catechism* fame,[2] four Marian priests, two laymen and a number of young priests. The Jesuits were thus only a minority in the group. The mission might not have been seen as 'The Jesuit Mission' if the bishop of St. Asaph, who was of course the senior cleric, had not lost his nerve and decided not to attempt to come to England, nor would the arrival of Jesuit priests in England have been regarded as so tremendously significant but for the fact that the first two, Robert Parsons and Edmund Campion, were in their different ways men of quite exceptional ability who made an impact out of all proportion to their number.

Although Campion was the older man, the Jesuit General had wisely decided to put Parsons[3] in charge of the Jesuit party. Parsons is one of the most interesting, one of the most able, and, perhaps, one of the most misunderstood men of his generation. He was described in the Commons in 1581 as 'a lurking wolf', and he has become firmly fixed in English minds as the arch-intriguer, the wicked Jesuit master-plotter,

---

[1] A. O. Meyer, *op. cit.*, pp. 143, 144. Meyer comments: '*Indirectly*, of course, the mission furthered the political aims of the pope. England, once reconciled to Rome, would not endure a sovereign excommunicated by Rome. Elizabeth's overthrow would have been the inevitable result of a successful Catholic propaganda. In this sense, but in this sense alone, the mission was a political enterprise. It was neither meant to be a means of spying out the land preparatory to invasion, nor as an instrument of stirring up rebellion against the queen—especially after 1581.' This seems to be a fair comment. It is essential to remember, however, that the pope's aim was religious, the restoration of the Catholic faith in England. To achieve this he was prepared to use both political and spiritual means. The missionary priests, although not involved in politics themselves, were inevitably open to the charge that they were part of the total papal effort and that they were therefore helping in the long run in the attempts to overthrow Elizabeth.

[2] See pp. 58, 62.

[3] The late Garrett Mattingly pointed out that the form *Persons* is probably correct, but asked whether modern scholars were wise to insist on it since the *D.N.B.* and the chief libraries of the English-speaking world use the form *Parsons*. Garrett Mattingly, 'William Allen and Catholic Propaganda in England', *Travaux d'Humanisme et Renaissance*, XXVII, 1957, p. 331.

and compared unfavourably with the noble Campion, who did not meddle with politics. It is often forgotten that if after 1581 Parsons used political means, it was religion, and not politics, that mattered to him. Less than justice has been done to his remarkable educational achievements, his outstanding qualities as a writer, and his extraordinary versatility. Even with his fellow Catholics, his reputation has been under a cloud because of his political activities and because he became deeply involved in the savage dispute which shook the English Catholic body in the later years of Elizabeth. There has been no biography of him, partly because of the range of materials involved (he operated in Spain, France, the Netherlands and Italy as well as in England, and he published works in four languages), and partly because the Jesuit archives in Rome have not been thrown open, and without them any biography could be only provisional.[1]

Parsons was born in Nether Stowey in Somerset in 1546. The later story that he was illegitimate need not be taken seriously. He was not of the gentry class. He says that his parents were of humble worldly condition, although honourable and of somewhat better rank than their neighbours. With the help, financial and otherwise, of the vicar of Nether Stowey, he went to school in Stogursey and later in Taunton, and after a shaky start he did extremely well. He went up to Oxford and was elected a Fellow of Baliol in 1568. He was reluctant to take the oath of supremacy and asked Campion, who was then Proctor, to help him avoid doing so, but in the end he conformed. He was an extremely successful tutor and made many friends among the wealthy families who entrusted their sons to his care. In 1569, when things were difficult for those suspected of popish sympathy, he went down into Somerset and thought of taking up the study of law with financial help from a relative, John Stone, mayor of Bristol. However, the trouble blew over, and he continued his very successful career in Oxford until, as a result of a college row, he resigned his Fellowship and left Oxford under a cloud.[2] On the advice of Lord Buckhurst he de-

[1] Some of the material has been printed in *The Memoirs of Father Robert Persons*, edit, J. H. Pollen, Catholic Record Society, Vol. 2. 1905; Vol. 4, 1907; *Letters and Memorials of Robert Persons to 1588*, edit. L. Hicks, Catholic Record Society, Vol. 39; *Robert Persons' Annals of the English College at Seville with an account of four other foundations from 1589 to 1595*, edit. J. H. Pollen, Catholic Record Society, vol. 14, 1914.

[2] The later story that as bursar of Balliol he embezzled college funds need not be taken seriously. It seems that he aroused jealousy among his colleagues and that they ganged up on him. The fact that he was suspected of leaning to popery did not help in the crisis.

cided to go to Padua to study medicine. He was apparently quite comfortably off and he did not leave England as a religious refugee. He was probably a Catholic at heart but not deeply committed. On his way to Italy he stopped at Louvain, and there he was persuaded to make the Spiritual Exercises, which had been worked out by St. Ignatius Loyola, the founder of the Society of Jesus, and which consisted of a course of prayer, meditation and self-examination designed to help those who performed them to know and love God. Parsons was profoundly affected and would have stayed in Louvain but for the fact that he had already sent his money on to Italy. He went to Padua and settled down with two companions as a medical student. He visited Rome in 1575 for the Holy Year and commented later that he 'attended more to the profane monuments of Caesar, Cicero and other such like than to places of devotion'. He was subsequently troubled about this and thought of taking refuge in a monastery, but in the end he decided to walk from Venice to Rome as a self-imposed penance. He said 'though I was no good goer on foot and the weather was hot, yet by God's help I made all that journey without any riding, as far as I can remember'. In Rome in 1575 he entered the Jesuit novitiate and in 1578 he was ordained priest. In 1580 when the decision was made to send Jesuits to England, Parsons was put in charge.

His companion, Edmund Campion, was a Londoner by birth and also of middle-class origin.[1] He was born in 1540, the son of a bookseller. He went up to St. John's College, Oxford, and in due course he established a reputation as a brilliant tutor and orator. He was a great success during the queen's visit to the university in 1566, and he gained the patronage of both Cecil and Leicester who were always on the lookout for able scholars likely to be of service to church and state. He was made a deacon in 1568 by his friend Bishop Cheney of Gloucester. He had taken the oath of supremacy, but he had doubts about the Church of England and he was reluctant to proceed to ordination. His position in Oxford became difficult, and in 1569 he went to Ireland as a tutor to the family of some friends. Here he wrote part of a *History of Ireland* which he dedicated to Leicester. When things became uncomfortable for those of Papist sympathy, he returned to England in disguise and he was present at the trial of

---

[1] The standard biography is Richard Simpson, *Edmund Campion*, 1896. For a short and stimulating study, see Evelyn Waugh, *Edmund Campion*, 1935.

Dr. Story in 1571.[1] He decided to go abroad, but his boat was stopped and he was brought back to Dover. He bribed the captain and was allowed to go free. Eventually he succeeded in reaching Douay where he spent the next two years. Then in 1573 he left on foot for Rome to join the Society of Jesus. He was sent to Prague where he came Professor of Rhetoric in 1574. In 1579 he was recalled to Rome to go on the mission to England.

The companion of Parsons and Campion was a Jesuit laybrother, Ralph Emerson, who was described as 'a very little man in build, but in endurance and sturdiness of spirit he was as great as you could wish anybody to be'.[2]

The party which included the three Jesuits made its way slowly towards England in the summer of 1580. While they were on the way, they learnt with dismay of the papal intervention in Ireland which they realised would make it appear that they were coming to England to stir up rebellion.

In France the party broke up and the members made their separate arrangements to get into the country. Parsons went ahead and landed at Dover disguised as a soldier on 17 June 1580. He had arranged for Campion to follow him disguised as a merchant in precious stones. With characteristic resource, Parsons made friends with the Customer at Dover and asked him to look out for his friend who would be coming over shortly. He procured a horse to take him to Gravesend and then hitch-hiked a lift on a boat taking a party of gentlemen and musicians to London. Early in the morning before the rest were awake he got himself put ashore in Southwark. He landed about four in the morning, he had nowhere to go and no friends, and the inns were reluctant to take in strangers. It seems surprising that six years after the first landing of the Douay priests, the Catholics had not worked out some kind of system to facilitate the entry of priests into the country and to distribute them in the places where they could work most effectively.[3] Parsons walked about in the streets for some hours and

[1] See pp. 101–102.

[2] *John Gerard the Autobiography of an Elizabethan*, edit. Philip Caraman, 1956 edition, pp. 78–9. After Campion's capture, Emerson escaped abroad and joined Parsons. He went to Scotland with the Jesuit Fr. Holt, and in 1584 he came to England again with the Jesuit William Weston. He was taken while arranging for the distribution of smuggled books and he spent many years in prison before he was at length released.

[3] Parsons and Garnet were later to do a great deal to organise the work of the priests, but there were many difficulties. They had no authority over the secular clergy and could work only on a voluntary basis. As the overwhelming majority of the priests in Eng-

8 HENRY GARNETT S.J.

He came to England in 1586 with Robert Southwell and was Superior of the Jesuits for nearly twenty years until his capture and execution at the time of the Gunpowder Plot. He made a major contribution to the organisation of the Catholic 'underground'.

FR. ROBERT PARSONS, S.J.

This remarkably able and versatile Somerset man joined the Society of Jesus, and from his landing in England in 1580 until his death in 1610 exercised tremendous influence for good and ill on the fortunes of English Catholicism.

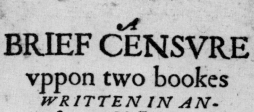

A BRIEF CENSVRE

vppon two bookes

WRITTEN IN AN-
fwere to M. Edmonde
Campions offer of
diſputation.

Deuter. capit. 5. ver. 5.
Yow feared the fyre , and therfore you
aſcended not vp the mountayne.

Imprinted at Doway by Iohn Lyon.
1581.
WITH PRIVILEGE.

---

10 THE TITLE PAGE OF ROBERT PARSONS' *BRIEF CENSURE*
This was written in reply to attacks on Campion's *Brag*. It purports to be
printed at Douay but it was in fact printed at Parsons' secret press in England.

then went to the Marshalsea prison where he enquired for Mr. Thomas Pounde, a well-known Catholic recusant gentleman who had been in prison on and off since 1574.[1] Pounde was delighted to see Parsons and told him that he had known for some time that he was coming to England.[2] He introduced him to a visiting Catholic gentleman who found him lodgings and he then met a number of other Catholics, including George Gilbert who had organised a group of young men in London drawn from Catholic families such as the Vaux, the Throckmortons, the Fitzherberts, the Tichbournes. Gilbert and his companions were to be of immense help to the priests, acting as guides and arranging for their movement about the country.[3] Parsons then left London for a time after making arrangements for the coming of Campion and Emerson.

Campion and Emerson crossed to England on the night of 25 June, but they ran into trouble. There was a security scare, and Campion was arrested at Dover. For some reason (possibly because Parsons had spoken to the Customer about him) he was released. He made his way to London where he was met and looked after. While waiting for Parsons to return to London, he spent his time contacting Catholics. On one occasion he preached to a large group in a hall of Lord Norrey's house, which was hired for the occasion by Lord Paget. (It must be remembered that the passion for hearing sermons was not confined to Puritans. Campion and Parsons were continually being asked to preach.)

When Parsons returned, there was an informal meeting of the

---

land were seculars, there was clearly a need for a master planner with proper authority to organise and control them. Many difficulties would have been avoided if the papacy had appointed a bishop or bishops to work in England. See p. 284 ff.

[1] He was a Hampshire gentleman whose mother was sister to the earl of Southampton. He became a Catholic in 1571, and from 1574 to 1603 he spent most of his time in prison. He was admitted into the Society of Jesus in 1594, but never became a priest. Philip Caraman, *Henry Garnet 1556–1606 and the Gunpowder Plot*, 1964, p. 290; A. C. Southern, *Elizabethan Recusant Prose*, pp. 54–5, 149–51; Henry Foley, *Records of the English Province of the Society of Jesus* 1877–83, vol. III.

[2] There seems to have been an effective 'grape vine' among the Catholic prisoners by which information was spread. The government, of course, had known well in advance about the mission for it had an excellent intelligence service at home and abroad.

[3] George Gilbert was a Suffolk gentleman, who was educated at Cambridge and became a Puritan under the influence of Edward Dering. While in Paris he had been converted to Catholicism. He wet to Rome and placed himself under the direction of Parsons. He returned to England to organise a Catholic centre in London. Philip Hughes *The Reformation in England*, III. 309; Catholic Record Society, II. 201.

M

Jesuits and a number of secular priests and laymen. At this 'Synod of Southwark' in the second week of July, Parsons read out his instructions. He made it clear that he was forbidden to take part in politics and that he had known nothing of Sander's mission to Ireland until he reached Rheims. At this meeting the Jesuits affirmed that it was the official policy of the Church that English Catholics might not for any reason at all attend the services of the Church of England.

The risk in holding such a meeting was great, for the government was very anxious to capture the Jesuits. One of the priests had actually been arrested on the way to the meeting. As the hunt in London was so hot, Parsons and Campion then decided to leave for a time and carry on their work in other parts of the country. They were asked by Pounde, who had temporarily got out of prison, to leave statements with him of their reasons for coming to England. These were to be used in the event of their capture, to counteract any official propaganda that might be put out. Both did so, and Campion's statement, which was not intended for publication, was circulated by Thomas Pounde, and a number of manuscript copies were made. This document was taken very seriously by the government, and two men were put up to reply to it—the Puritan William Charke, who wrote in December 1580 *An Answere to a Seditious Pamphlet lately cast abroade by a Jesuite with a Discoverie of that Blasphemous Sect*, and a more orthodox member of the Church of England, Meredith Hanmer, who published early in January 1581 *The Great Bragge and Challenge of M. Champion a Jesuite* which reproduced Campion's letter to which it was a reply.[1]

One of the disturbing things about Campion's *Bragge* from the government's point of view was its note of confidence and challenge. Campion not only asserted with great conviction that he was engaged in a purely spiritual enterprise but also demanded the right to dispute publicly before the Council and before learned men of universities.[2] He undertook to maintain 'the fayth of our Catholike church, by proofes invincible, scriptures, councells, fathers, hystories, naturall and moral reasons . . . ' At the end there is the confident assertion ' . . . touching our Societie, be it known to you that we have made a

[1] The Elizabethan controversialists on a number of occasions reproduced their opponent's works in order to confute them, thereby making them known to a larger public than would otherwise have been able to read them.

[2] It must be remembered that he intended this challenge to be made public in event of his being captured.

league . . . cheerfully to carry the cross you shall lay upon us, and never to despair of your recovery, while we have a man left to enjoy your Tyburn, or to be racked with your torments, or consumed with your prisons. The expense is reckoned, the enterprise is begun; it is of God, it cannot be withstood. So the faith was planted, so it must be restored . . . '[1]

This bold and challenging note, reminiscent of Jewel's *Challenge Sermon* much earlier in the reign when the Church of England was first struggling to establish itself,[2] was not at all to the liking of a government which had hoped that Catholicism would gradually wither away. It might, as Charke said, stir 'inconstant mindes to the mislike of religion, and desire of Poperie'.[3] Protestants were also troubled, as John Keltridge, a London preacher, pointed out, 'because that the Papistes and Jesuites, with other the riffe raffe and scumme of this Realme are nowe seen to appeare, who before this tyme have beene hidden in the dytches and channelles of England'.[4]

The two Jesuits then went off on a tour of many parts of England. Parsons described how 'we passed through the most parts of the shires of England, preaching and administering the sacraments in almost every gentleman's and nobleman's house that we passed by, whether he was a Catholic or not, provided he had any Catholic in his house to hear us . . . '[5] They met again at Uxbridge after three months, and then Parsons sent Campion north to Lancashire, asking him if possible to write a work in Latin for publication. Like the government, the missionaries aimed primarily at winning the governing class and the intellectuals. They could not in any case go around preaching publicly to the ordinary people.

Parsons remained in and around London. Among his many activities was the organisation of a secret printing press. This was not, of course, the first Catholic press,[6] but it proved one of the most important. It is known as the Greenstreet House Press, for it was originally set up between five and seven miles from London in a 'large and fair house . . . near a place they call Greenstreet'.[7] Stephen

---

[1] Helen C. White, *Tudor Books of Saints and Martyrs*, Wisconsin, 1963, p. 207 ff.; A. C. Southern, *Elizabethan Recusant Prose*, p. 148 ff.; Evelyn Waugh, *Edmund Campion*, p. 124 ff.

[2] See p. 50.

[3] Helen C. White, *op. cit.*, p. 207.

[4] *Ibid.*, p. 209.

[5] Evelyn Waugh, *Edmund Campion*, pp. 133, 134.

[6] See p. 120.

[7] A. C. Southern, *Elizabethan Recusant Prose*, p. 353 ff.

Brinkley was in charge with seven workmen. Apparently the press was dismantled after one book had been printed and was set up again in a house provided by Francis Browne, brother of Lord Montague. Work went on here until March 1581 when things became too hot and the press was moved to Stonor Park near Henley. It was tracked down and seized there on 8 August 1581. Parsons had a narrow escape, Brinkley and four assistants were imprisoned.[1]

It seems that Brinkley printed six books at this press. One of them was an important work by Parsons entitled *A Brief Discours contayning certayne reasons why Catholiques refuse to goe to Church*.[2] This was necessary because from the very beginning large numbers of Catholics had conformed outwardly to avoid the penalties of the law, and recently there had been circulating a manuscript written by a Catholic priest justifying such conduct. Some prominent Catholics, including Lord Paget, had acted on the advice it gave.[3] Two other works by Parsons were *A Brief Censure uppon two bookes written in answere to M. Edmonde Campions offer of a disputation* and *A Discoverie of I. Nicholas, minister, misreported a Iesuite, latelye recanted in the Tower of London*. The first was a reply to Charke and Hanmer, and the second dealt with a man who had recently been given much publicity by the government. John Nichols was a minister in the Church of England, with a discreditable career, who had gone overseas and become a Catholic. After an even more unsatisfactory career abroad, he returned to England and, while in prison, repudiated his Catholicism. He was made much of by the authorities who magnified his importance as a Catholic and helped him to publish *A declaration of the recantation of Iohn Nichols (for the space almost of two yeeres the Popes Scholar in the English Seminarie or Colledge at Rome) which desireth to be reconciled, and received as a member into the true Church of Christ in England*. Parsons, with the help of information from Allen, was able to discredit Nichols and cut down to size this man whom the authorities were trying to present as a distinguished convert.[4]

Of the three other books attributed to this press one was Cam-

---

[1] He was in the Tower for two years until friends got him released on bail. He went overseas and continued there his work of printing Catholic books.

[2] A. C. Southern, *Elizabethan Recusant Prose*, p. 460 ff.

[3] A. C. Southern, *op. cit.*, p. 461; W. R. Trimble, *The Catholic Laity under Elizabeth I*, pp. 102, 103.

[4] A. C. Southern, *Elizabethan Recusant Prose*, p. 160 ff., 465 ff.

pion's *Decem Rationes*—a Latin work of some 20,000 words giving 'Ten reasons, for the confidence with which Edmund Campion offered his adversaries to dispute on behalf of the Faith, set before the famous men of our universities'. Campion argued that the Protestants realised that they were in an intellectually desperate position and because of this they used force instead of argument: 'Ye wey neyther Crosse, nor racke, nor torment, nor prison, nor pikes, nor tyburne . . . ' He outlined the reasons why they were in despair, putting the case against them from the scriptures, from history, from the Councils of the Church and from the Fathers. The book was intended to appeal to the learned, and copies were placed on the benches in St. Mary's Church, Oxford, on a formal academic occasion on 27 June 1581.[1] It aroused great excitement, and there was a spate of answers to it, including some from William Whitaker, the Regius Professor of Theology in Cambridge.

Campion had come south to see his book through the press and he spent some time in and around London. On 11 July 1581 he said goodbye to Parsons, intending to go first to Lancashire and then to Norfolk. With him went Brother Ralph Emerson whom Parsons put in charge of the expedition. Campion and Parsons exchanged hats. Parsons gave Campion permission to accept a long-standing invitation to visit Lyford Grange in Berkshire. The owner, Mr. Yate, was in prison for religion, but his mother lived in the house with some nuns and two priests. The visit went off quietly and Campion and Emerson proceeded on their way. When it was known that Campion had been at Lyford a number of Catholics who had not met him persuaded Mrs. Yate to send Fr. Ford after him to persuade him to return. Fr. Ford found him at an inn near Oxford, and Ralph Emerson was persuaded to give permission for Campion to return while he himself went on to finish the business they had in Lancashire. Campion returned to Lyford and for a few days all went well. Then there came to the house a priest-hunter, George Eliot, a man who had worked in various Catholic houses, who had been in prison for rape

---

[1] Helen C. White, *Tudor Books of Saints and Martyrs*, p. 209 ff. The man responsible was William Hartley, a young Derbyshire priest of 23, who had been ordained in Rheims in February 1580. He came to England in the same year and went to work in Oxford. He was arrested with Brinkley in August 1581 and eventually condemned to death for conspiring against the queen. In 1585, however, he was deported. Later he returned to England and was put to death in 1588. Philip Hughes, *The Reformation in England*, III. 308, note 2.

and homicide and who had got out of his difficulties by offering his services to the government to hunt down priests. The cook at Lyford knew Eliot, and believing him to be a Catholic, invited him to go up to where Catholics were assembled. Eliot found about forty people there. Fr. Ford was just finishing his mass. Then Campion said mass and preached for nearly an hour on the text 'Jerusalem, Jerusalem, thou that killest the prophets'. Eliot waited quietly until the end and then went off to get a magistrate and a large search party. The house was surrounded, but there were a number of hiding holes. The three priests went into a secret place which opened out of a room near the top of the house. There were provisions and just enough space for them to lie side by side.

The search party found nothing and was actually going away, but Eliot insisted on a more thorough search and they came back. They found several hiding holes and sent for more help. Some of them remained in the house all night, intending to continue their work in the morning. In the night Campion came out and said words of encouragement to a number of Catholics who had come to the room where Mrs. Yate had put her bed. The searchers were disturbed by the noise, but Campion managed to get back safely. The search continued next day. Nothing was found and they were giving up when one of them saw a chink of light in a well over the staircase. With a crowbar they opened up the back of the hiding-place where the three priests were lying with food for three or four days.

And so Campion was taken with two priests and a number of laymen who were in the house. He was brought before Elizabeth and Leicester who had known him in the old days. He explained that he had come only to save souls and that he acknowledged Elizabeth as his queen. When he was asked if he thought the pope had the power to depose the queen, he said it was a matter to be debated in the schools and was not one with which he was concerned. He must have convinced the queen that he was not a traitor in the usual sense of the term, and he was offered preferment in the Church of England if he would conform. He refused the offer. He was severely tortured to get information about those who had helped him, and some details were rung from him but nothing, apparently, of any great significance. A series of disputations were arranged between him and Protestant theologians, but although he was under tremendous disadvantages he acquitted himself well and the discussions were broken off. He was tortured again in an attempt to get evidence of treasonable activity. The government then staged a mass trial of Campion and seventeen others on charges of conspiring in Rome and in Rheims to murder Elizabeth, of encouraging foreigners to invade England, and of coming to the country to stir up rebellion. It is clear that Campion and his companions were innocent of the particular charges brought against them, that there had been no such conspiracy, that the witnesses were giving false testimony, and that the accused were not traitors in any meaningful sense of the word. Most of those concerned must have known that the case was not proven in law and that this was 'judicial murder'.[1]

When Campion was asked if there was any reason why sentence should not be passed on him he replied: ' . . . The only thing that we have now to say is, that if our religion do make us traitors, we are worthy to be condemned; but otherwise are, and have been, as good subjects as ever the queen had. In condemning us you condemn all your own ancestors—all the ancient priests, bishops and kings—all that was once the glory of England, the island of saints, and the most devoted child of the see of Peter. For what have we taught, however you may qualify it with the odious name of treason, that they did not uniformly teach? To be condemned with these old lights—not of England only, but of the whole world—by their degenerate descendants, is both gladness and glory to us. God lives: posterity will live: their judgment is not so liable to corruption as that of those who are now going to sentence us to death.' Of the batch of prisoners condemned for the alleged conspiracy, Campion and two Douay priests, Ralph Sherwin and Alexander Briant, were selected as the first to die. They were hanged, drawn and quartered on 1 December 1581.

Robert Parsons, too, was condemned to death—*in absentia*. He had had a narrow escape when his secret press was discovered at Stonor in August. He then went into Sussex, and there he was offered a chance of crossing with a party going to France. He had to make an agonising decision. There were good reasons why he should leave England for a time, but there was the danger that he would appear to be deserting his post. There can be no doubt about his courage. After spending the night in prayer he decided to go, and his decision was almost certainly the right one, although it would have been better for

---

[1] For a discussion of the trial under the Treason Statute of 1352 see Philip Hughes, *The Reformation in England*, III, 357 ff.

his reputation if he had died with Campion. He crossed to France in the autumn of 1581, and as it turned out, he was never again given the opportunity of returning.

It is not easy to assess the achievements of Parsons and Campion during their remarkable year in England. We do not know how many people they brought into the Church of Rome or how many Catholics had their faith strengthened as a result of their work. One cannot weigh their success against that of less publicised missionary priests who worked for much longer periods in England. Nor must we forget that they built on foundations laid by the Douay priests, who had been coming over since 1574. But taking all this into account, it is nevertheless clear that they made a quite exceptional impact on the Catholic community and that they greatly strengthened its morale. They were in different ways men of genius, and in combination they were one of the most formidable pair of adversaries that the government ever had to face. The government's efforts to capture them and to discredit them bear witness to their effectiveness.[1]

The realisation that Catholicism was not dying out, the papal aggression in Ireland, and the coming of the Jesuits produced fresh legislation against Papists. In the Parliament of 1581 Sir Walter Mildmay, speaking for the government on 25 January, stated the official attitude. He praised the queen who 'even at her first entry, did loosen us from the yoke of Rome', and restored the pure and holy religion of the gospel. This had aroused the 'implacable malice' of the pope and his confederates, who had made many attempts against the queen, including the Northern Rising and the recent invasion of Ireland, which showed the pope, 'turning thus the venom of his curses and the pens of his malicious parasites into men of war and weapons to win that by force which otherwise he could not do'. By his secret practices he was 'emboldening many undutiful subjects to stand fast in their disobedience to her Majesty and her laws . . . ' He went on: 'The obstinate and stiff-necked Papist is so far from being reformed

---

[1] It was particularly important to discredit Campion since he obviously did not fit in with the conception of a false-hearted traitor. George Eliot who had betrayed him and whom he had forgiven was encouraged to produce *A Very True Report of the Apprehension and Taking of that Arche Papist Edmund Campion*. Thomas Alfied, who was later executed himself, published in 1583 *A True Report of the Death and Martyrdome of M. Campion Jesuite and Preist, and M. Sherwin, and M. Bryan Preistes, at Tiborne the First of December 1581*. There were a considerable number of other works about him. Helen C. White, *Tudor Books of Saints and Martyrs*, p. 212 ff.

as he hath gotten stomach to go backwards and to show his disobedience, not only in arrogant words but also in contemptuous deeds. . . . You see how late he hath sent hither a sort of hypocrites, naming themselves Jesuits, a rabble of vagrant friars newly sprung up and coming through the world to trouble the Church of God; whose principal errand is, by creeping into the houses and familiarities of men of behaviour and reputation, not only to corrupt the realm by false doctrine, but also, under that pretence, to stir sedition.' As a result very many who had previously conformed now refused to come to church. Gentle means had done no good, and now ' . . . it is time for us to look more narrowly and straitly to them, lest . . . they prove dangerous members . . . in the entrails of our Commonwealth'.[1]

Both Lords and Commons considered the matter, and after conferring they jointly produced a very severe bill which, among other things, made the saying of mass a felony punishable with death, imposed on Catholic recusants who refused to come to church a fine of £20 for the first offence, £40 for the second, £100 for the third, and the penalties of praemunire (forfeiture of all goods and imprisonment during the queen's pleasure) for the fourth. There were special penalties for lawyers and schoolmasters.

Professor Neale thinks that these proposals appear to indicate that 'Burghley was in favour of a measure to eradicate Catholicism from England by making life intolerable even for its peaceful and loyal adherents'.[2] It was probably as a result of intervention from the queen that what eventually emerged was less drastic than parliament had intended. This was an Act to retain the Queen's Majesty's subjects in their due obedience.[5] It stated that since the passing of the act against bringing in bulls from Rome, evilly affected persons had used other means to withdraw the subjects from their natural obedience and to 'persuade great numbers to withdraw their due obedience to her Majesty's law established for the due service of Almighty God'. To prevent this, it was enacted that any one who shall 'absolve, persuade or withdraw any of the Queen's Majesty's subjects . . . from their natural obedience to her Majesty, or . . . withdraw them for that intent from the religion now by her Highness' authority established

[1] J. Neale, *Elizabeth I and her Parliaments*, I. 382 ff.

[2] J. Neale, *Elizabeth I and her Parliaments*, I. 391. See p. 385 ff. for examination of the history of this bill.

[3] 23 Eliz. c. 1. *Statutes of the Realm*, IV. 657–8. G. R. Elton, *The Tudor Constitution*, pp. 422–4.

... to the Romish religion, or ... move them or any of them to promise any obedience to any pretended authority of the see of Rome shall be to all intents adjudged to be traitors'. Anyone after this session of parliament who is willingly absolved or withdrawn as aforesaid ... or shall promise any obedience to any such pretended authority ... shall suffer as in cases of high treason. Anyone who aids or abets such persons or conceals knowledge of them is guilty of misprision of treason. Anyone who says or sings mass shall be liable to a fine of 200 marks and one year's imprisonment, and anyone who hears mass shall be liable for a fine of 100 marks and a year's imprisonment. Anyone over 16 years of age who does not go to church shall forfeit for every month £20. Anyone who is absent from church for 12 months shall be bound with two sureties in the sum of £200 at least to good behaviour until such time as they conform and come to church.

It has been argued that this Act made it treason to convert anyone to the Church of Rome (or to be converted) *only* if this was done with the intention of withdrawing the convert from his natural obedience to the queen. Meyer, for example, writes 'the law refrains from plainly defining conversion to catholicism as treason, it was rather conversion accompanied by withdrawal of allegiance, which was condemned',[1] and Professor Neale, endorsing Meyer's view, argues 'Those significant words, *for that intent*, made the approach political and secular'.[2] If one reads the preamble and the act as a whole, it seems very doubtful whether it does in fact make the distinction which modern historians have found in it. The law does seem to treat as treason *in itself* the act of reconciling or of being reconciled to the pope's authority. According to Fr. Hughes, this was how the statute was interpreted in the courts. He argues that 'in practice, this reservation was mere words' and that 'all reconciliation was treated as, by the fact, a withdrawal of allegiance and an adherence to the queen's enemy'.[3]

Another bill brought into the parliament of 1581 was directed 'against seditious words and rumours uttered against the Queen's most excellent Majesty'. It was a government bill probably aimed primarily at Papists. It extended an earlier act of 1554, and it imposed,

[1] A. O. Meyer, *England and the Catholic Church under Queen Elizabeth*, p. 148.
[2] J. Neale, *Elizabeth I and her Parliaments*, I, 388.
[3] Philip Hughes, *The Reformation in England*, III, 343 and note 3.

much more severe penalties. A second offence could be treated as felony punishable with death. The Commons made objections and amended the bill, which they were quick to realise could also be used against the Puritans. They would have liked to make the penalties much more severe for Catholic recusants than for others. They failed to achieve this, but they did scale down the punishments. Nevertheless, the death penalty for a second offence was still retained.[1]

The year 1581 was marked by the beginning of a much more severe policy towards the priests and their lay helpers than had been adopted hitherto. There were four executions in 1581, eleven in 1582, and four in 1583.[2] Although this might not seem an excessively large number, the government evidently felt the need to justify what it was doing in the eyes of Englishmen, and, still more, in the eyes of foreigners. At the end of 1583 there appeared an unsigned pamphlet entitled *The Execution of Justice in England*.[3] It was the work of William Cecil, and its purpose was to show that the priests and their helpers were traitors who were being punished for treason, not for religion. The rising of the Northern Earls in 1569 and the trouble in Ireland in 1579 had been instigated by the pope, who had declared Elizabeth excommunicated and absolved her subjects from obedience. The missionary priests trained by Allen and led by Parsons and Campion had come to England to ensure that all Catholics knew that they were absolved from their allegiance and that they were under an obligation to rebel when the opportunity came. The priests were being treated with great leniency and they were not being punished for religion. They were unable to give direct answers to the questions whether they thought all Catholics should obey the bull and rebel against the queen, whether they considered Elizabeth was in fact their lawful queen, whether the pope could lawfully authorise the earls of Northumber-

---

[1] For the history of this Act, see J. Neale, *Queen Elizabeth I and her Parliaments*, I. 393.

[2] The figures for 1581–90 are as follows: 1581, 4 priests; 1582, 11 priests; 1583, 2 priests, 2 lay people; 1584, 6 priests and 3 lay people; 1585, 2 priests, 2 lay people; 1586, 12 priests, 3 laymen; 1587, 6 priests; 1588, 21 priests, 10 lay people; 1589, 5 priests, 3 lay people; 1590, 9 priests, 2 lay people.

[3] See *The Execution of Justice in England by William Cecil and A True Sincere and Modest Defense of English Catholics by William Allen*, edit. Robert M. Kingdon, Cornell University Press, 1965. Cecil's pamphlet first appeared in December 1583. A second edition, including *A declaration of the Favourable Dealings of Her Majesty's Commissioners*, appeared in January 1584. Latin, French and Dutch translations appeared in the same year. There was an Italian version in 1589.

land and Westmorland and Dr. Sander to take up arms against the queen, whether the pope might discharge subjects of a Christian prince from their obedience, whether Dr. Sander and Bristow wrote truly or falsely in approving the bull, and what part they would take if the pope, or anyone approved by him, invaded the realm.[1]

Cecil argued that the refusal of the priests to answer these questions directly might justly convict them of treason, but he maintained they were not in fact condemned on these grounds. They were condemned because, being long conversant with traitors beyond the seas, they came hither by stealth in time of war and rebellion by command of the pope to contact those who would be ready to rebel and to poison the senses of the subjects, pouring into their hearts malicious and pestilent opinions against the queen and the laws of the realm, and to kindle the flames of rebellion. He maintained that: 'These kinds of seditious actions for the service of the Pope and the traitors and rebels abroad have made them traitors, not their books, nor their beads, no, nor their cakes of wax which they call *Agnus Dei*, nor other their relics; no, nor yet their opinions for the ceremonies or rites of the Church of Rome.' Thus, 'these did justly deserve their capital punishment as traitors, though they were not apprehended with open armor or weapon'.

The questions to which Burghley referred were the famous 'Bloody Questions' which, in one form or another, were asked of priests and others whom the government was considering putting on trial for treason. The point of putting the questions was that if the prisoner stated that he did not think the pope had the power to depose Elizabeth and declared that he would not assist any attempt by a foreign power to enforce the bull, then his attachment to the papacy would be in some measure weakened, since the papacy asserted that it had this power and was in fact continually trying to use it. If the man asserted that the pope had the deposing power and that he would co-operate if the pope tried to use it, then there would be a presumption that he was a traitor, or, at the least, a potential traitor. If he refused to answer or answered evasively, then there would be a widespread belief that the man was prepared to dabble in treason.

[1] Robert N. Kingdon, *op. cit.*, pp. 38, 39. For the questions and the government's summary of the answers given by Campion and his companions, see *Dodd's Church History of England with Notes, Additions and a Continuation* by M. A. Tierney, 5 vols., 1843, III. Appendix, no. III.

Fr. Hughes has pointed out that after the execution of Campion, Sherwin and Briant in December 1581 these questions were regularly put to suspects.[1] He suggests that this was done because the trial of Campion and his companions was so notoriously unjust that there had been a storm of disapproval and because their protestations of loyalty on the gallows were believed. Before executing the others found guilty in the mass trial of 1581, the government put the questions to the condemned men and published their replies.[2] Since the priests had already been tried and found guilty along with Campion and his companions, the point of putting the questions was not to establish whether they were traitors but to convince public opinion that they were, before they were actually executed. Fr. Hughes also makes the general point that the men and women put to death under Elizabeth were not in fact condemned because they gave unsatisfactory answers to the Bloody Questions. They were tried and found guilty under particular statutes which made certain offences treason.[3] The Bloody Questions had nothing to do with establishing their legal guilt but were put in the hope their answers would deprive them of any sympathy.[4]

There is no doubt that a number of those to whom the Bloody Questions were put were unable or unwilling to say without ambiguity whether they considered the pope had the power to depose Elizabeth and whether they would in any circumstances support attempts to enforce her deposition. A few said they would resist the invaders; a small number seem to have replied frankly that if the pope declared the bull to be in force, they would accept his ruling. Many of them evaded the questions. Campion said that the pope's deposing

[1] Philip Hughes, *The Reformation in England*, III. 359.

[2] *Ibid.*, p. 359. The government's publication was *A particular Declaration or Testimony, of the undutifull and traiterous affections borne against her Majestie by Edmond Campion, jesuite and other condemned priestes, witnessed by their owne confessions: in reproofe of those slanderous bookes and libels delivered out to the contrary by suche as are malitiously affected towards her Majestie and the State*. Published by authoritie. Printed by Christopher Barker, 1582.

[3] See Philip Hughes, *Rome and the Counter Reformation in England*, p. 246 ff. for an examination of the numbers condemned under particular statutes: Act of 1352, 20; Act of Supremacy of 1559, 11; Act against Papal Bulls 1571, 3; Act of 1571 (13 Eliz. c. 2) 2; Act of 1581 to retain the Queen's subjects in due obedience, 18; Act of 1581 against seditious words and rumours, 4; Act of 1585 against Jesuits and Seminary priests, 123.

[4] See Philip Hughes, *The Reformation in England*, III. 351 ff. for a discussion of this matter and for criticism of the views of A. O. Meyer, J. B. Black and other modern historians.

power was a subject for discussion, that he was not concerned with it, and that he accepted Elizabeth as his queen. Others said that in the hypothetical circumstances of an invasion, they would try to act as good Catholics and as good subjects of the queen.[1] All of them, of course, could accept Elizabeth as their *de facto* queen, since the pope had declared that the bull was not binding on Catholics as things then stood.

The reputation of the accused was seriously damaged, as the government intended it to be, by the difficulty they found in answering the questions. Their problem was that the papacy vigorously affirmed its right to depose an heretical sovereign and it was certainly very anxious to secure the deposition of Elizabeth. Catholics did not hold that rulers had an absolute divine right and that it was never permissible to depose them or rebel against them. The missionary priests had been sent to England with definite instructions not to concern themselves with politics and they had obeyed their instructions, but there was always a possibility that at some future date the instructions might be changed and that they might be called upon to cooperate in plans to overthrow Elizabeth.[2] They were not traitors in the ordinary meaning of the word and the government was dishonest in treating them as though they were, but they could hardly expect the government to dismiss the possibility of invasion as purely hypothetical. Their reluctance to give unambiguous answers to the Bloody Questions meant that they were in the government's eyes potential traitors.

The dishonesty of Burghley's pamphlet lay in the fact that it deliberately identified the work of the missionaries with the attempts that were being made to overthrow the government by force, that it claimed that the efforts were of a piece with the rebellion of 1569 and Sander's expedition to Ireland in 1579. In fact, the missionary priests were not engaged in such schemes, and Burghley was unable to show that they were. If he had merely claimed that they were potentially dangerous and must be restrained, he would have had quite a good case, but in fact he asserted that they were engaged in treasonable activities and were trying to stir up rebellion. Campion and his companions in the mass trial were indicted for their part in an alleged plot against the queen. The case against them was obviously fabri-

[1] There is need for a detailed analysis of all the answers which have been preserved.
[2] See pp. 200, 201.

cated. Later it was unnecessary for the government to manufacture evidence in this way, for in 1581 the definition of treason was extended to include reconciling or being reconciled to the Church of Rome, and from 1585 any priest ordained by the pope's authority since 1559 and being in England was by that very fact guilty of treason.[1]

But although the government was not honest in treating the missionary priests as though they were traitors in the ordinary sense of the term, it is surely unreasonable to expect it to behave as though the activities of the priests could be considered in isolation and without reference to the general political situation. The queen's ministers must have become increasingly aware as they examined the priests that there was little or no evidence that they were engaged in political activity, but they also knew that the papacy was so engaged and that a number of Catholics abroad, and a handful of Catholics in England, were involved in plots and enterprises against the queen.

In the 1580's the success of the missionary priests and the revival of Catholicism were in themselves very alarming to the government, but they were all the more so because the international situation became more and more critical. The scare about papal and Spanish intervention in Ireland in 1579–80 was followed from 1581 to 1583 by very serious danger from Scotland. James VI put his trust in a Catholic favourite, Esmé Stuart, a relative of the duke of Guise. There was a possibility that James might become a Catholic, and there were various plans for the duke of Guise, backed by the papacy, to land in Scotland, convert James and proceed with an invasion of England. When Esmé Stuart fell from power in 1583, there were plans on the part of Guise to invade England direct. In all this, Parsons and Allen, the Jesuits Crichton and Holt, and a number of Catholic exiles in France were deeply involved. The plans did not mature, but the danger was serious. Then in 1583 there was another scare when an apparently half-witted Warwickshire squire, John Somerville, set out for London 'to shoot the queen with a dag (pistol)'.[2]

It was also in 1583 that Walsingham arrested a young Catholic gentleman, Francis Throckmorton, and got from him under torture many details about the invasion plans of the duke of Guise. Then in

---

[1] See pp. 192.

[2] He was arrested along with his father-in-law Edward Arden, a number of other relatives and a priest Hugh Hall who saved his life by going into Walsingham's service. Somerville was found strangled in his cell, Arden was hanged, drawn and quartered. Philip Hughes, *The Reformation in England*, III. 376 and note 6.

the next year William of Orange was assassinated. Fear that Elizabeth would suffer the same fate, and determination that the Catholic Mary Stuart should not succeed her, led to the drawing up of the Bond of Association aimed at the Catholic heir presumptive. The signatories swore to pursue to the death anyone who should attempt anything to the queen's harm.[1]

In such a situation the government could hardly be expected to accept Allen's argument that the work of the missionary priests was purely spiritual, even though in fact it was. The government saw the efforts of the missionaries as an attempt to make as many Englishmen as possible Catholics, and it considered that this was not done simply for the good of their souls but so that they would, when the time came, support an invasion designed to restore Catholicism. The missionary priests were not in the least interested in invasion or rebellion, but Allen certainly was, and we know that if the Spaniards had gained a beachhead in 1588 he would have called upon the Catholics of England to support the invaders for the sake of restoring the Catholic faith.[2]

It is quite true, then, to say that the motives of the government in putting the priests to death were partly political. The priests were treated as agents of the pope and of the Catholic princes who intended to overthrow Elizabeth. Their own actions were not political, but they were killed because the government maintained that what they did—converting Englishmen to Roman Catholicism—would have political consequences. They were the victims of policies in which they themselves had no part.

Although the motives of the government in putting the priests to death were, to a considerable degree, political, it is wrong to see the matter simply in terms of saving the state from attack by invaders and rebels. Ever since 1559 the Elizabethan government had shown quite clearly that it had no intention of allowing more than one religion to flourish in England. If there had been no threats of invasion and no plots at home, the government would still have reacted vigorously against the revival of Catholicsm, for it was determined to insist on religious uniformity. If the international situation had been less serious, the government's reactions might have been less violent and

---

[1] For the Bond and its subsequent history, see J. Neale, *Elizabeth I and her Parliaments* II, Chapters II and III, 'The Queen's Safety'.

[2] See pp. 200–201.

there might have been fewer executions, but drastic action of some kind was inevitable in the face of the Catholic revival.

It is also important to remember that many of those who helped to make Elizabethan religious policy were determined to destroy Catholicism, not merely because they considered it politically dangerous, but because they thought that it was an evil and abominable religion. Not everyone was prepared to go as far as Cartwright who firmly believed that those who corrupted the people by teaching falsehood ought to be put to death, but the fierce hostility to Catholic teaching found among many politicians, churchmen, Members of Parliament and country gentlemen is not purely political in origin. For many of them Rome stood for anti-Christ. Roman Catholicism must be stamped out since it led men to damnation. Its priests must be driven from the country, or put to death if they persisted in staying, and the practice of it must be made difficult or impossible for the laity. Only thus could true religion flourish in England. The fierce Protestantism which was found in many places, not least in parliament itself, was not absent even from the minds of statesmen who were guided primarily by political consideration. The queen might not be unduly concerned about the theological issues, but many of her ministers saw the Papists not simply as politically dangerous but as a threat to men's chances of eternal salvation.

Granted that those responsible for policy were convinced that the Papists were dangerous for political or for religious reasons, or for both, what course should they have followed? This is a question of morality, and the answer to it is conditioned by the moral standards of the person making the judgment. If the end never justifies the means, if the safety of the state may not be accepted as a reason for putting to death innocent people, if it is never permissible to slander and libel one's opponents, then it is impossible to justify many of the actions of the Elizabethan government towards the Papists. In particular, it is impossible to justify the consistent attempts to make it appear that the victims of the persecution were traitors, since they were clearly not so in intention or in any meaningful sense of the word.

Yet it would have been asking too much of the Elizabethan government to expect it to allow the missionary priests to operate freely and to continue unchecked their work of making England a Catholic country. In so far as the government considered the priests a potential

N

danger politically, it could legitimately have placed them under restraint and prevented them spreading religious views which might well lead to political danger for the country. In so far as it saw them teaching religious error, it might with equal justice have tried to prevent them doing so. As it was, it persecuted them both for political and for religious reasons and it executed nearly two hundred of them, but for propaganda reasons at home and abroad it deliberately represented the victims as traitors and claimed that it put them to death not for their religion but for their politics. A number of modern historians have excused the executions on the grounds that those who could not give satisfactory answers to the Bloody Questions were at the very least the stuff of which traitors can be made, but Burghley cut the ground from under his own feet when he asserted that these people were not executed for the treason they might do, but for the treason they had actually done.

Burghley's *Execution of Justice* was answered in 1584 by William Allen in his *True, Sincere, and Modest Defense of English Catholics . . . Wherein is declared how unjustly the Protestants do charge Catholics with treason.* Allen argued that many priests and other Catholics in England had been persecuted, tortured, condemned and executed for mere matter of religion, under the new statutes which made matters of conscience treason, as, for example, denying that the queen was head of the church. He had no difficulty in showing that Campion and others had been condemned on false evidence for an alleged conspiracy in Rome and Rheims. He maintained that priests and Catholic laymen had in fact behaved with all due reverence and respect to the queen, notwithstanding the bull of excommunication. He admitted that Dr. Sander and Dr. Bristow had spoken against her, but, he said, many Catholics regretted this and wished the matter had not been touched upon but left to higher powers, and especially to God's judgment. He claimed 'We never procured our Queen's excommunication; we have sought the mitigation thereof; we have done our allegiance notwithstanding; we have answered, when we were forced unto it, with such humility and respect to Her Majesty and council, as you see, no man can charge us of any attempt against the realm or the prince's person'.[1]

Allen's argument was that Catholics had behaved loyally and that

[1] *The Execution of Justice in England and A True, Sincere, and Modest Defense of English Catholics*, edit. Robert M. Kingdon, p. 127

they were not traitors by the old treason laws, but only by the new laws which had been passed since 1558 to make their religion treason. In this he was right. Only 20 of those put to death were indicted under the treason law of 1352. The rest were executed under various laws passed since 1558.

In the second part of his work Allen went on to argue what he believed to be true—that the pope had in certain circumstances the right to depose an heretical sovereign. In so doing, he was being honest and straightforward, for the popes had for centuries claimed this right and exercised it, and the Middle Ages had not, on the whole, accepted the view that kings might never be deposed.[1] Allen was at some pains to show that the papal deposing power did not worry the Catholic princes, to whom it also applied, but he did not take into account in his argument the fact that the pope had in 1570 actually declared Elizabeth deposed. His opponents could claim that he was providing in advance the arguments that would justify the actions of the missionary priests and their supporters if at some future date they were called upon to help enforce the papal bull of deposition.

Although it was very frank in this respect, Allen's *Defense* did not convey the whole truth about the Catholic position. It insisted on the loyalty of English Catholics to the queen and it played down the importance of the bull of excommunication. It implied that they had not wanted it, and it insisted that they had done nothing to implement it. The *Defense* seems to suggest that the question of what would happen if the pope decided to declare the bull in force was a purely hypothetical one, and that the government need not worry itself about the possibility of it becoming a live issue. And yet Allen was himself deeply involved in plans for the overthrow of government by force, and there can be no doubt that if England had been invaded by a foreign army seeking to restore Catholicism, he would have called upon English Catholics to assist the invader. Further, it has been convincingly argued that although Allen very consciously kept separate for the time his two main activities—the training of the priests for a spiritual mission in England, and co-operation in plans for over-

[1] Sixteenth-century rulers, Catholic and Protestant alike, were anxious to discourage such views and to spread the belief that even wicked rulers might not be actively resisted by the subject. But Calvin had taught a qualified right of rebellion and the Calvinists in the Netherlands and in France had gone a good deal further than Calvin. For a discussion of the position of English Catholics, see T. Clancy, 'English Catholics and the Papal Deposing Power' *Recusant History*, vol. 6, nos. 3 and 5, vol. 7, no. 1 (1962–3).

throwing Elizabeth by force—nevertheless he intended in the long run to bring these two activities together and to use the priests to support an invasion when the time came.[1]

The whole question is thus very complicated, and one cannot answer it simply by saying that the reasons for the persecution were political (as Burghley did) or by saying that they were religious (as Allen did). There is justification in Professor Kingdon's comment that the arguments of both were advanced 'with a certain lack of frankness'.[2] The missionary priests, carefully avoiding politics and ministering to Catholics at the risk of their lives, were caught between a murderous crossfire from a papacy prepared to use temporal as well as spiritual means for religious ends, and a government determined to conceal its mixed political and religious aims by smearing its victims with what Campion called 'the odious name' of traitor.[3]

The main weight of government's attack in the 1580's fell on the priests and those who assisted them. Every priest put to death, imprisoned or exiled meant that fewer English Catholics would have the opportunity of practising their religion and that there would be fewer converts. It was cheaper and easier to destroy English Catholicism at its source—the priests—than to try to deal with the whole Catholic community. In addition, the drive against Catholic recusants was intensified. The government reacted to the danger 'by resolving to destroy the Catholic priesthood through execution, exile, and imprisonment; by repressing Catholic religious activities through stricter laws; by continuing control of the lay Catholics through fine and imprisonment'.[4] The statute of 1581 had made things much more difficult for lay Catholics. It was a punishable offence to assist a seminary priest or to hear mass. The fine of £20 a month was not generally enforced, but it was there as a threat, and selected victims could be

---

[1] Garrett Mattingly, 'William Allen and Catholic Propaganda in England', *Travaux d'Humanisme et Renaissance*, XXVIII, 1957. See also pp. 200, 201.

[2] *The Execution of Justice*, etc., edit. Robert M. Kingdon, p. xxx. Professor Kingdon adds: 'In fact, if one wanted to be brutal, one could accuse both authors of dishonesty.'

[3] There is a short but valuable discussion of the problem in E. I. Watkin, *Roman Catholicism in England from the Reformation to 1950*, 1957.

[4] W. R. Trimble, *The Catholic Laity in Elizabethan England*, p. 107. There do not seem to be any satisfactory figures of Catholics in prison for religion at different periods during the reign. The London prison lists were printed by Fr. H. Pollen in Catholic Record Society, vols. I and II (1905, 1906). Philip Hughes, *The Reformation in England*, III, p. 364, gives the following statistics of prisoners in the London returns: 1583, 103; 1584, 100; 1586, 95; 1588, 73.

made to suffer as a warning to others.[1] The Privy Council was very active, the numbers in prison appear to have increased, and pressure was kept up on local authorities to take action against offenders. Thus in October 1583 the Council instructed the ecclesiastical authorities to tell ministers to warn parishioners on the first Sunday of every month of the duty of attending the parish church. The names of recusants were to be reported so that they might be charged, and those who managed to escape indictment were to be excommunicated.[2] Although laymen were not generally put to death unless they were directly involved in assisting the seminary priests and the Jesuits, life could be made very difficult and unpleasant for them, particularly if they were men of some importance in their district. Under this pressure, a number inevitably conformed.

The battle of words and of ideas continued throughout the 1580's. In 1582 the government tracked down another secret printing press— that of Richard Verstegan, who had printed Thomas Alfield's *A True Report of the death and martyrdom of M. Campion.* The Recorder of London, Fleetwood, wrote to Burghley describing how 'it fell owt that in the first wike of lent there was a booke cast abroad in commendinge of Campian and of his fellows, and of theire deathe. I pursued the matter so nere that I found the presse, the letteres, the figures and a nosmber of the bookes . . . '[3] This ended for a time the printing of Catholic books in England, but the work went on abroad and there was a brisk import trade.

Two works published in 1582 were of particular importance. Allen had been very much concerned with scriptural studies, and he had put in hand in 1578 the production of the first Catholic version in English of the Bible. The man principally responsible for the translation was Gregory Martin, a young man born in Sussex about 1540. He had gone to St. John's College, Oxford, but in 1570 he left England for religious reasons. He was ordained priest at Douay in 1573. He was a very capable Greek and Hebrew scholar, but his translation was made from the Latin Vulgate. It was copiously annotated and to that extent it was controversial—so much so that it provoked a number of

---

[1] See pp. 198–199.
[2] W. R. Trimble, *op. cit.,* p. 114.
[3] A. C. Southern, *Elizabethan Recusant Prose,* pp. 358, 359. For Verstegan, see p. 189 below. The man captured was Stephen Vallenger. He was sentenced to life imprisonment and a fine of £200 as well as to the pillory and the loss of an ear. A. C. Southern, *op. cit.,* pp. 279–82.

Protestant commentaries. Gregory Martin had translated the whole Bible, but Allen's resources were so limited that he could afford to finance only the New Testament, and the rest was not published till 1609. Gregory Martin's work was one of the most remarkable achievements of the Elizabethan Catholic exiles, and it has been claimed as the 'crowning glory' of Elizabethan recusant prose.[1]

The year 1582 also saw the publication of Parsons' *The First Booke of the Christian Exercise, appertayning to resolution. Wherein are layed downe the causes and reasons that should move a man to resolve hym selfe to the service of God.* This was the book which later came to be known as *The Christian Directory.* It used to be thought that Parsons had merely translated and edited a work of a Spanish Jesuit on the christian life, but it has now been shown that this was an original work of Parsons, and not merely a translation or edited version of someone else's book. It is a tribute to Parsons' remarkable ability that his *Christian Directory* became one of the most widely read books on the spiritual life not only in Catholic but also in Protestant countries. In 1584 Edmund Bunny, Calvinist vicar of Bolton Percy, produced in England a pirated version which removed from Parsons' work its 'Catholic errors and corruptions'. Parsons himself produced an expanded second edition in 1585, and before his death in 1610 there were 4 Catholic and at least 15 Protestant editions.[2] It is characteristic of his immense energy and resource that in order to continue the printing of Catholic books in English he made use of the services of a comparatively unknown printer in Rouen, George L'Oyselet, who worked for him between 1582 and 1585 and who became, in Dr. Southern's opinion, 'by far the most important printer of Recusant works on the Continent during the decade 1580–1590'.[3]

The Catholic writing of the 1580's naturally laid increasing stress on the martyrs. We have seen that Campion's death produced a considerable literature both for and against him. In 1582, for example, Allen published *A briefe historie of the Glorious martyrdom of XII reverend priests,* and Parsons sought to appeal to a learned and a Euro-

---

[1] A. C. Southern, *Elizabethan Recusant Prose,* p. 231 ff.

[2] J. P. Driscoll, 'The Supposed Sources of Persons' Christian Directory', *Recusant History,* vol. 5. No. 6, 1960; *Letters and Memorials of Fr. Robert Persons, S. J.,* edit. L. Hicks, Catholic Record Society, vol. 39, 1942; A. C. Southern, *Elizabethan Recusant Prose,* p. 182 ff. Southern states that there were 9 editions of Bunny's version between 1584 and 1600.

[3] A. C. Southern, *op. cit.,* p. 360.

pean audience with his *De Persecutione anglicana libellus*. Another important contributor to the growing literature on the martyrs was Richard Verstegan, whom we have already seen in connection with secret printing in England.[1] After his flight from England, he turned his attention to publishing Catholic books and to illustrating them with his own engravings. In 1584 he brought out *Descriptiones quaedam illius inhumanae et multiplicis persecutionis* and in 1587 *Theatrum Crudelitatum Haereticorum Nostri Temporis*, an illustrated account of the cruelties of the heretics in England, France and the Netherlands.[2]

Another remarkable work produced in the late 1580's, and printed at a secret press in England, was the Jesuit Robert Southwell's *An Epistle of Comfort* addressed 'to the Reverend Priests, and to the Honourable, Worshipful, and other of the Lay sort, restrained in durance for the Catholic Faith'. It was based on letters which Southwell wrote to Philip Howard, earl of Arundel, the son of the duke of Norfolk executed in 1572. Philip Howard had been restored to his earldom and had been in favour with Elizabeth, but after leading the life of a courtier, he became a Catholic and in 1585 he attempted to cross the seas. He was put in the Tower where he died under mysterious circumstances ten years later. Southwell was urged to publish the substance of the letters as they would be of great help to all who were suffering for their faith, and he elaborated eleven reasons why they should take comfort in their suffering.[3] He ends with a warning: 'When you persecute us, you do but sow seeds that will spring with a more plentiful harvest. You think it is the seminary priest that enlargeth the Catholic faith, whereas you yourselves make the chief seminary, in which Catholics do grow . . . '

There was in the 1580's no shortage of Catholic books of all kinds, but the government tried very hard to stop them circulating.[4] Its agents abroad reported on what was being published and sometimes

[1] See p. 187.

[2] Anthony G. R. Petti: 'A Study of the Life and Writings of Richard Verstegan', London M.A. thesis, 1957; *The Letters and Despatches of Richard Verstegan (c. 1550–1640)*, Catholic Record Society, vol. 52, 1959; 'A Bibliography of the writings of Richard Verstegan', *Recusant History*, vol. 7, No. 2, 1963.

[3] *An Epistle of Comfort*, edit. Margaret Waugh, 1966. Fr. Caraman comments on its 'tone of exultant confidence from the first page to the last' which recalls Campion's challenge and gave new heart to the resistance.

[4] See A. C. Southern, *Elizabethan Recusant Prose*, pp. 33–43, for an examination of the way in which the books were distributed.

managed to secure copies in advance of publication. Its officials tried to intercept smuggled books at the ports, and it kept a check on what was being sold by the booksellers. From time to time it carried out searches of Catholic houses and seized the prohibited literature. Nevertheless, books were smuggled in by priests, merchants and Catholic agents. Parsons, writing in 1584 about his work of getting priests into England, commented: 'Others take charge of the preparation and introduction into England of books written in English on spiritual and devotional subjects and on matters of controversy.' He adds: 'They sometimes send money back, but it is done with great uncertainty and much loss and danger.' Thomas Alfield, a priest, and Thomas Webley, a Gloucester dyer, were arrested in 1585 for dispersing slanderous books and were executed as felons at Tyburn.[1] Alfield admitted at his trial that he had brought in between 500 and 600 copies of Allen's *True, Sincere and Modest Defense*. Others engaged in the work included William Bray, described in 1588 as 'a common conveyer of priests and recusants and of naughty books over seas.' Peter Lowson, when he was arrested in 1583, had in his possession a number of packs of books listed as follows: 'In primis in the fyrste packe 1111er C (400) Catechisms. Item in another pack oon C (100) Catechisms and certen other books and XXXti (30) lattyn premers. Item in a nother packe XV (15) latten testaments and XIV (45) Medytacions.' Richard Lacey of Brodishe in Norfolk confessed 'thatt one Mr Godshale and one Mr Moore and one Marshm(an) are common cariers of papisticall bookes and letters from one papist to an other'.[2] Dr. Southern believes that in spite of the danger and the high cost, these books were read in all parts of the kingdom and were in constant demand.[3] He puts very special emphasis on the devotional literature about which he comments: 'The popularity of these

---

[1] Thomas Alfield was born in Gloucester in 1552 and was educated at Eton and King's College, Cambridge. He became a Catholic at Cambridge and crossed to Douay in 1576. He returned to England for a time and then went back to Douay where he was ordained in 1581. He was sent to work in England, and was present at Campion's execution. His account was printed by Verstegan's secret press. He was arrested in 1582 and eventually he agreed to go to church. He was released and returned to Rheims where he was reconciled. He came back to work in the Gloucestershire area. He was apparently involved in a network of people circulating Catholic books. See J. N. Langston, 'Robert Alfield, schoolmaster of Gloucester, and his Sons', *Transactions of the Bristol and Gloucestershire Archaeological Society*, vol. 56, 1934.

[2] See A. C. Southern, *op. cit.*, pp. 36–8.

[3] *Ibid.*, pp. 38–9. He gives lists of books seized in the houses of a number of Catholics.

works in England in the sixteenth and seventeenth centuries can only be described as exceptional . . . '[1]

All the time, in spite of the increasing dangers, priests from Rheims and from the English College in Rome continued to find their way into the country. In 1580, the number of new arrivals was 29; in 1581, 31; and in 1583, 36. There were 18 in 1584 and the same number in 1585, making a total of 179 in five years.[2]

The Parliament which assembled at the end of 1584 met at a time of increasing tension at home and abroad. The assassination of William of Orange, the Bond of Association reminding men that Elizabeth might be assassinated and replaced by a Catholic, the continued propaganda alleging that the missionary priests were preparing the way for invasion and rebellion, all contributed to the fear in the minds of the legislators. Sir Walter Mildmay, one of the official speakers, set the tone of the meeting.[3] 'You see', he said, 'that we enjoy freely the preaching of the Gospel, delivered from the superstitions and tyranny of Rome . . . ' Under a virtuous and wise queen the country had enjoyed peace for twenty-six years, but the pope was 'knitting together all the Popish princes and states to the overthrow of the Gospel in all places, but especially in this kingdom'. His 'malicious and secret practisers', in particular the Jesuits and seminary priests, 'creep . . . into sundry parts of the realm and are occupied to stir sedition . . . under pretence of reforming men's consciences'. Campion and his fellows were prosecuted 'not for the superstitious ceremonies of Rome' but for 'most high and capital offences and conspiracies'. When asked whether the queen was rightful queen, they had answered: 'It is a question of divinity; we pray you demand no such thing of us.' Allen had recently maintained the pope's deposing power and Parsons had exaggerated the persecution of Catholics 'as though we lived here in England under Nero, Domitian, Caligula, and such other tyrants . . . ' In Rome and in Rheims there were maintained notable and false traitors such as Parsons and Allen. In England 'home Papists' refused to come to church, harboured Jesuits and priests, brought up their children in popery and uttered violent threats

---

[1] A. C. Southern, *Elizabethan Recusant Prose*, p. 43.
[2] *Records of the English Province of the Society of Jesus*, edit. H. Foley, III. 44 ff. for the names of the priests. Philip Hughes, *The Reformation in England*, III, 347, note 2, says that by 1585 the total sent from Douay (Rheims) was 229 and from Rome 33. Of these 23 had been put to death and 70 were in prison.
[3] For his speech, see J. Neale, *Elizabeth I and her Parliaments*, II. 28.

to the régime. Rebels and fugitives were 'ready at the Pope's beck to trouble the State . . . ' Invasion was planned and the result would be 'devastation of whole countries, sacking, spoiling and burning of cities and towns and villages, murdering of all kinds of people without respect of person, age or sex, and so the ruin, subversion and conquest of this noble realm, the utter rooting out of the whole nobility and people . . . and the placing in of strangers'. The moral was that they should provide for the queen's safety against all malicious enemies[1] and take action against Jesuits and seminary priests.

What eventually emerged was An Act against Jesuits, seminary priests and other such like disobedient persons.[2] The preamble stated that Jesuits, seminary priests and other priests ordained beyond the seas had of late years been sent into the realm 'of purpose (as hath appeared as well by sundry of their own examinations and confessions as by divers other manifest means and proofs) . . . to withdraw the subjects from their due obedience' and 'to stir up and moue sedition, rebellion and open hostility within her Highness' realms'. It was therefore enacted that all Jesuits, seminary priests, other priests, deacons and religious persons ordained out of the realm or within it by authority from the see of Rome since Feast of the Nativity of St. John the Baptist in the first year of the queen's reign must within forty days after the end of the present session of Parliament depart from the realm. Any priest so ordained who remained in the country or who came to it in future was guilty of high treason. Anyone who should 'willingly and wittingly receive, relieve, comfort or maintain' any such priests or religious person was guilty of felony and might be sentenced to death. Any subject of the queen not in the above categories, brought up in any college of Jesuits or seminaries, who did not within six months after proclamation made to that effect return to England and take the oath of supremacy was to be judged a traitor. Anyone who conveyed money or other relief to the colleges or those in them could be sentenced to the penalties of praemunire (loss of all goods and imprisonment at the queen's pleasure). Anyone who sent children beyond the seas without special licence (except merchants sending them on business or as mariners) could be fined for every offence £100. Anyone

---

[1] For the steps taken to ensure that Mary Stuart did not benefit from the assassination of Elizabeth, see J. Neale, *Elizabeth I and her Parliaments*, II. Chapters II and III.

[2] 27 Eliz. I. c. 2. *Statutes of the Realm*, IV. 706–8; G. Elton, *The Tudor Constitution* pp. 424–7.

who knew the whereabouts of such priests and who did not give information within twelve days could be fined and imprisoned at the queen's pleasure. Any official given such information who failed to inform the Council within twenty-eight days could be fined 200 marks for each offence.

Some had wanted to make the Act even more drastic and to declare 'that whosoever should teach the Romish religion should be a traitor'.[1] There was also a proposal that a second offence of sending relief to the seminaries should be treated as treason, but neither suggestion was accepted. On the other hand, one member thought 'that it might seem a very hard case to make it treason for a man to come into the realm without doing of any other thing', and Dr. William Parry spoke against the bill in violent terms as tending to 'blood, danger, despair and terror to the English subjects of this realm . . . ' He hoped that when the bill came into the queen's 'most merciful hands' it would stay there. The House arrested Parry and demanded an explanation. He said he would reserve his explanation for the queen. Elizabeth and Burghley intervened, and the House was told that she was partly satisfied with his explanation. He submitted to the House and was released from confinement.

Under this act, if it could be shown that a man had been ordained by the pope's authority since 1559, no further proof was required in law that he was a traitor. The prosecution might for propaganda reasons try to show that he had engaged in the treasonable activities or had given unsatisfactory answers to the Bloody Questions, but this was irrelevant in law once it was proved that he was a priest ordained since 1559. Fr. Hughes stresses the fact that of the 146 people put to death between the passing of the Act and the death of the queen in 1603, 123 were indicted under the Act of 1585 and not under the Treason Statute of 1352 or the earlier Elizabethan acts of 1559, 1571 and 1581.[2]

Professor Neale considers that this Act has been unwarrantably maligned. He argues that it was 'a humane and reasonable attempt to resolve the dilemma of a state, exposed by ideological warfare to insidious and deadly peril. If a society has the right to defend its existence, the individual can hardly claim a conflicting right to remain within the community while acknowledging an external allegiance

[1] J. Neale, *Queen Elizabeth I and her Parliaments*, II. 37 ff.
[2] Philip Hughes, *Rome and the Counter Reformation in England*, pp. 246–7.

that threatens to destroy it. English Catholic priests were at liberty to retain their religion, provided they lived abroad . . . '[1] The difficulty as far as the priests were concerned was that they felt they had a duty to God which required them to minister to the Catholics in England and to reclaim from heresy and schism those whose souls were in deadly peril. They were not, with exceptions that can be counted on one hand, involved in any attempts to overthrow the state, even though the action of the papacy and the Catholic exiles exposed them to the charge that they were. The Act of 1585 made it unnecessary for the government to produce any proof beyond the fact that they were priests.[2]

The public image of Roman Catholicism was further damaged in 1585 by strange revelations concerning Dr. Parry who had spoken against the Act of 1585. He was a doctor of law with a disreputable career.[3] He had acted as a spy for the government among the Catholic exiles, including Thomas Morgan and Charles Paget who worked for, and very probably double-crossed, Mary Stuart.[4] While abroad, Parry seems to have expressed his willingness to assassinate Elizabeth. He obtained from the papal Secretary of State absolution in case he died while carrying out the task he had in hand, but it is not absolutely clear that this was understood in Rome to be the assassination of the queen. Quite what he was up to is uncertain. As Professor Neale puts it: 'Whether he was an *agent provocateur*, or was double-crossing Elizabeth and Burghley, or was just drifting about in perilous seas, irresolute, exalted by conceit, a little mad: these are questions that later events pose.'[5] In 1585, after his surprising attack on the bill against Jesuits and seminary priests, he was accused of being involved in a plan, backed by the papacy, to murder Elizabeth. Parry maintained that he had played the part of an *agent provocateur* to get in-

---

[1] J. Neale, *Elizabeth I and her Parliaments*, II. 37.

[2] It is quite true that the government did not put to death a considerable number of the priests it captured but merely kept them in prison or deported them. It did not want a blood-bath and it also had to keep an eye on public opinion. Walsingham remarked: 'The execution of them, as experience showeth, in respect of their constancy, or rather obstinacy, moveth men to compassion and draweth some to affect their religion, upon conceipt that such an extraordinary contempt of death cannot but proceed from above, whereby many have fallen away.' Conyers Read, *Mr. Secretary Walsingham*, II. 312.

[3] J. Neale, *Elizabeth I and her Parliaments*, II. 39–41, 48–51; L. Hicks, 'The Strange Case of Dr. William Parry—the Career of an Agent-Provocateur', *Studies*, Dublin, 1948.

[4] L. Hicks, *An Elizabethan Problem*, 1964.

[5] J. Neale, *Elizabeth I and her Parliaments*, II. 40, 41.

formation from the enemy, but he was found guilty and put to death.[1]

The fear that Elizabeth would be assassinated was greater than ever and the government made very effective use of the Parry Plot for propaganda purposes. Whether the papacy approved of what Parry was alleged to be trying to do is not absolutely clear, but the evidence indicates that in the early 1580's it would not have regarded anyone who killed Elizabeth for religious reasons as acting sinfully. On the 12 December 1580 the Cardinal Secretary of State in answer to an enquiry had written: 'There can be no doubt that while that guilty woman of England holds the two noble Christian Kingdoms she has usurped, and while she is the cause of such great harm to the Catholic faith and of the loss of so many millions of souls, whoever moves her from this life with the due end of God's service, not only would not sin, but would even be doing a meritorious deed, especially as the sentence still stands which Pius V of holy memory pronounced upon her.'[2] The Elizabethan government did not know of this letter, but it believed, almost certainly correctly, that if a Catholic did kill Elizabeth, Gregory XIII would not have disapproved.[3]

The next year there was yet another alarm—this time over a conspiracy planned in England. As in most of these plots, there are endless complications and doubts about what exactly was going on. Anthony Babington, a young man who had been one of the pages to Mary Queen of Scots, listened to the proposal of John Ballard to assassinate Elizabeth and put Mary on the throne. Ballard had been ordained as a Catholic priest, but had ceased to act as one. A number of young men from the Catholic gentry families were involved. They

[1] Philip Hughes, *The Reformation in England*, III. 376, argues that the government had known for a considerable time about Parry's alleged assassination plot but did not use the information to charge Parry until he spoke against the Act of 1585. It then used it to finish off Parry 'the spy who knew so much and who could no longer be trusted'. The plot was also useful as showing how necessary the Act was.

[2] The Italian version is in A. O. Meyer, *England and the Catholic Church under Elizabeth*, pp. 490–1. There is a translation in Philip Hughes, *Rome and the Counter Reformation in England*, p. 214. For a discussion of the moral issues, see A. O. Meyer, *op. cit.*, pp. 266–74; Philip Hughes, *op. cit.*, 210–26. Fr. Hughes argues that the papacy was not giving general approval to assassination as a political weapon but merely saying that someone duly sentenced by lawful authority might be killed in order to save the state. The assassin is not acting on his private judgment but as an agent of lawful authority against the declared enemy of the state.

[3] Gregory XIII (or perhaps it would be more correct to say Gregory's Secretary of State, presumably expressing the official view) seems to have been the only pope who took this line with regard to Elizabeth. His successor, Sixtus V, would not listen to the proposals of those who offered to assassinate her.

may not have known about the plans to kill Elizabeth and may have thought only that this was a scheme to free Mary from her long imprisonment. Walsingham was aware from an early date of the development of the plot, and it has been suggested that Ballard may have been, like Parry, an *agent provocateur*,[1] nursing a scheme the purpose of which was to get Mary Stuart so involved that Elizabeth would be compelled to agree to her execution. After trying unsuccessfully to get Babington to betray the whereabouts of the Jesuits, Southwell and Garnet, who had arrived in England in 1586, Walsingham had Babington arrested along with a number of others who were involved. Under torture Babington and Anthony Tyrell, a priest, gave away a lot of information. Tyrell saved himself by conforming and agreeing to act as a spy, but Babington and twelve others were put to death. None of the missionary priests was involved, but inevitably the suggestion that all priests were traitors gained even wider currency.[2] A dozen priests and three lay people were executed in this year, including Margaret Clitherow who was accused of aiding priests. When she refused to plead to her indictment, she was pressed to death at York.

The disastrous consequences of the Babington Plot were offset to a considerable degree by the work of the two remarkable Jesuits, Henry Garnet and Robert Southwell. Like Campion and Parsons, they made in different ways outstanding contributions to their fellow Papists. Garnet was a Derbyshire man, born in 1555, the son of a schoolmaster who conformed to the Elizabethan settlement, but who sent his son to Winchester College where Catholic influence was considerable in the early years of the reign.[3] After leaving school he seems to have been reconciled to the Roman Church. For three years he worked for Richard Totell, a distinguished legal printer, as 'corrector for the press', an experience which came in useful later when he had his own secret press. It was probably early in 1575 that he decided to become a Jesuit and went to Rome via Portugal and Santiago de Compostella. He entered the Jesuit novitiate at the age of twenty-one

[1] L. Hicks, *An Elizabethan Problem*, p. 147 note. Ballard had been sent to England by Morgan and Paget against whose integrity Fr. Hicks has made a very strong case.

[2] Robert Southwell wrote on 21 December 1586 of 'that wicked and ill-fated conspiracy which did to the Catholic cause so great mischief, that even our enemies, had they the choice, could never have chosen aught more mischievous to us or more to their mind.' *English Martyrs 1584–1603*, edit. J. H. Pollen, Catholic Record Society, 1908, vol. 5, p. 314.

[3] See Philip Caraman's biography *Henry Garnet 1555–1606 and the Gunpowder Plot*, 1964.

and was joined in the same year by another man who was to make his mark as a Jesuit in England, William Weston.[1] Parsons was a novice of three months' standing when Garnet joined the Society. Garnet seems to have been ordained priest in 1582, and on 8 May 1586 he left Rome for England in company with another Jesuit, Robert Southwell, who was six years his junior. Robert Parsons rode out from the city to say goodbye to them. He asked them to do what they could to help his old mother who was still in England.

Robert Southwell came of a Norfolk gentry family. He was born in 1561. On his mother's side he was connected with the Cecils and the Bacons, and it is not quite clear why in 1576 he decided to go overseas to Douay.[2] He joined the Jesuit novitiate two years later. His poetical and imaginative temperament was an excellent complement to that of Garnet whose particular interests were mathematics and music. The two made their way to England by different routes and met in one of the London prisons. Garnet had been accompanied by Brother Ralph Emerson who was captured while arranging for the distribution of a consignment of smuggled books. They arrived at a bad time, for the Babington affair was about to come to a head and a number of Catholic families were to find themselves in serious trouble. They contacted William Weston who sent Garnet to work in the houses of the Vaux family in Northamptonshire and Leicestershire and stationed Southwell near London. Then Weston was caught, and Garnet found himself after less than three weeks in the country Superior of the Jesuits in England. At the time he had three Jesuits under him, and two of them—Weston and Emerson—were in prison. He remained Superior of the Jesuits for nearly twenty years till he was caught after the Gunpowder Plot, and he proved one of the most resourceful and capable of leaders for the English Catholics.

The two Jesuits during their first year in England also appear to have established what Fr. Caraman calls 'a sorting office' for incoming priests in order to make arrangements for posting them

---

[1] William Weston had come to England in 1584 and was superior of the Jesuits. He was captured in 1586 and he was not released till after the queen's death. He was a very influential man even in prison, and a central figure in the 'Wisbech stirs' (see p. 197 ff.). His remarkable autobiography has been edited by Fr. Philip Caraman (*William Weston The Autobiography of an Elizabethan*, 1955).

[2] See Christopher Devlin, *The Life of Robert Southwell*, 1956. He has, of course, attracted a great deal of interest as a poet and as a writer. See Pierre Janelle, *Robert Southwell the writer*, 1935.

quickly to the places where they were needed. The work developed always on a voluntary basis and much later Garnet described it as follows: 'When the priests first arrive from the seminaries, we give them every help we can. The greater part of them, as opportunity offers, we place in fixed residences. This is done in a very large number of families through our offices. The result now is that many persons, who saw a seminary priest hardly once a year, now have one all the time and most eagerly welcome any others no matter where they come from'.[1] A great deal was also done to help Catholic prisoners.[2]

When parliament met in October 1586 action was taken to remedy defects in the statute of 1581 which imposed a fine of £20 a month on Catholics who did not come to church. The statute had not been systematically enforced. A report in 1586 pointed out 'some recusants escape indicting through the corruptness of juries, some being indicted are wincked at by justices in respect of kindred or friendship; some goe untouched throughe the fault of the custos rotulorum, clerke of the assises and sherif, whoe doe not their duties in orderly sending out processe, or in forbearing to apprehend the offender, when they maye, or in comitting some error or other whereby the execution of the lawe is deferred, and by meanes thereof many are incouraged to offend and to make small accompt of the paynes sett down agaynst them'.[3] It would seem that the gentry and local officers did not always share the fierce anti-Catholic feeling displayed in parliament. Dr. Walker estimates that the number fined under the 1581 statute was only 69, and the total amount received only £8,938.1.11d.[4] The new statute[5] tightened up the law. Once a Catholic had been convicted and paid the £20 fine, there was no need for another indictment. He was required to pay the amount due into the Exchequer twice a year. If he failed to do so, the crown could bring an action against him to take all his goods and two-thirds of his landed property. As a result, the amount received in recusancy fines from 1587 to 1592 increased to £36,332.9.0d.[6] But Dr. Walker points out that there was only a small

---

[1] Philip Caraman, *Henry Garnet*, p. 45 ff.   [2] *Ibid.*, p. 46.

[3] F. X. Walker, 'The Implementation of the Elizabethan Statutes against Recusants, 1581–1603', p. 222.

[4] *Ibid.*, p. 266.

[5] 28 and 29 Eliz. c. 6. 1587. There is an extremely valuable study of the history and working of the law in Dom Hugh Bowler's Introduction to *Recusant Roll No. 2. 1593–1594*, Catholic Record Society, vol. 57, 1965.

[6] F. X. Walker, *op. cit.*

11 POPE SIXTUS V
The quick-tempered and vivacious pope who was doubtful whether the Armada would succeed but who agreed with Philip II to provide one million gold ducats if the Spaniards secured a bridgehead in England.

12 ELIZABETH I
'She knows—and thinks you know—she is Supreme Governor of this Church, next under God . . . she will receive no motion of innovation, nor alter or change any law whereby the religion or Church of England standeth established at this day. . . .' (The Speaker to the Commons, 1585).

number of new names in the list, and he thinks the total number of those paying the fines in the period 1581 to 1593 was considerably less than 200.[1] The increase in receipts between 1587 and 1592 was the result of levying large fines on a small number of people. Thus, 16 people paid over £26,000 in these years. Michael Hare in Suffolk, for example, paid £1,946; John Gage in Sussex, £2,160; Ferdinando Paris in Norfolk, £2,273.1s.8d; Thomas Tresham in Norfolk, £1,773.6s.8d; William Tirwight in Lincolnshire, £2,440.0s.0d; John Townley in Lancashire, £1,700, and Thomas Throckmorton in Buckinghamshire, £1,120.[2] Very many Catholic gentry escaped altogether, but the fate of these victims served as an awful warning of what might happen.

Meanwhile, the international situation deteriorated rapidly and events moved towards a major crisis. In 1585, in view of the success of the duke of Parma in reconquering the Spanish Netherlands and because of the growing danger from Spain, England intervened openly in the Netherlands and sent a force there under Leicester. The cold war was turning into a shooting war. In 1587 Mary Stuart was executed. Ponderously Philip II was making up his mind to launch a direct attack on England. Gregory XIII had been succeeded in 1585 by Sixtus V, a quick-tempered and vivacious Franciscan Friar who was no admirer of Spain and who was not at all optimistic about the chances of an attack succeeding.[3] Nevertheless, in 1587 under pressure from Spain he made William Allen a cardinal and signed an agreement with Philip about the invasion.[4] The pope was to provide one million gold ducats, half to be paid as soon as the Spanish landed and the remainder in instalments. If England was conquered, the Spaniards were to set up a good Catholic sovereign approved of by the Holy See, and he was to receive investiture from the pope. The church property and rights alienated since the time of Henry VIII were to be restored, and the agreement was to be ratified by the future king of England.

The Enterprise of England had the enthusiastic support of William

---

[1] F. X. Walker, *op. cit.*   [2] *Ibid.*, p. 275

[3] When he appointed Allen a cardinal at Philip II's request, Sixtus V wrote to Philip telling him his expedition against England could only succeed if he reconciled himself with God and stopped usurping the rights of the Church. L. von Pastor *The History of the Popes*, XXI. 270.

[4] Printed in A. O. Meyer *England and the Catholic Church under Elizabeth* pp. 520–3. See L. von Pastor, *The History of the Popes*, XXI. 51.

O

Allen, the Cardinal of England. He assured Philip II in March 1587 that the English Catholics were longing for his coming, remembering the time when he had been king and his zeal for the faith. He wrote: 'I think there can be very few indeed who love their country and religion who do not from their hearts desire to be once more subject to your most clement rule.'[1] In fact the English Catholics had no such enthusiasm. The leading laymen protested their loyalty to the queen and their anxiety to fight against the invaders. If the Spaniards had landed, they would have received little or no support from English Catholics. Nevertheless, the government understandably took no chances and placed the important recusants under restraint during the time of crisis.[2]

As part of his preparations for the invasion of England Philip II asked the pope to make plain that the Armada was putting into effect the papal bull of excommunication.[3] There was drawn up, probably by Allen, what Meyer calls 'a half papal, half Spanish broadside' renewing Elizabeth's excommunication and announcing her impending deposition in accordance with sentence passed by Pius V and Gregory XIII.[4] The *Declaration*, printed under Allen's name, stated that since there seemed to be no other way, the pope had asked the king of Spain to take action. The pope released all the queen's subjects from obedience to her and asked them 'unite to themselves to the Catholike army'. Catholics were promised protection against pillage, and heretics would not be punished 'till by conference with lerned men and better consideration, they may be informed of the truth . . . ' Rewards were offered to any who captured 'the said usurper, or any of her complices' and there was a plenary indulgence to those 'being duely penitent' who assisted in 'the deposition and punishment of the above named persons'. The existing laws and customs were not to be changed except by agreement between the pope, the king of Spain and 'the states of the lande' (Parliament).[5]

[1] Latin version in *Letters and Memorials of Cardinal Allen* edit. T. F. Knox, 1882, p. 272 ff. For a study of the relations of the Catholic exiles with Philip II, see A. J. Loomie, *The Spanish Elizabethans*, New York, 1963.

[2] W. R. Trimble, *The Catholic Laity in Elizabethan England*, p. 131 ff.

[3] A. O. Meyer *England and the Catholic Church under Elizabeth*, p. 322 ff. Meyer suggests that Sixtus V was not at all sure that the invasion would succeed and that he did not want the papacy to look foolish in the eyes of the world if it failed.

[4] In 1583 Gregory XIII had prepared a draft bull renewing the excommunication, but it had not in fact been issued.

[5] Printed in M. A. Tierney, *Dodd's Church History of England*, 5 vols. 1839–1842. III. Appendix XII; Philip Hughes, *The Reformation in England*, III. 38.

Allen also signed *An Admonition to the Nobility and People of England* which made a savage personal attack on the queen. She was 'an incestuous bastard, begotten and borne in sinne of an infamous courtesan'. Her kingdom was 'a place of refuge and sanctuarie of all Atheystes, Anabaptistes, heretikes, and rebellious of all nations'. The Catholic king had undertaken the sacred and glorious task of driving her from the throne for the honour of God, the welfare of Christendom, and for 'your deliverie (my good brethren) from the yoke of heresie and thraldom of your enemies'. The Catholics of England must now show whether they will endure 'an infamous, depraved, accursed, excommunicate heretike the very shame of her sexe, and princely name; the chief spectacle of sinne and abomination in this our age; And the onely poison calametie and destruction of our noble Church and Countrie'. Allen urged his fellow countrymen, 'Feight not, for Gods love, feight not, in that quarrel, in which if you die, you are sure to be damned: feight not against all your auncestors soules, and faith, nor against the salvation of all your deerest, wives, children, and what so ever you wolde wel to, ether now or in the time to cum. Matche not yourselves against the highest: this is the daie no doubte of her fall, this is the hower of Gods wrathe towardes her and all her partakers: Forsake her therefore betime, that you be not inwrapped in her sinnes, punishment and damnation.'[1]

This *Admonition* was intended for distribution in England if the invaders succeeded in landing. It was printed but not actually published. A copy of it was in Burghley's hands on the 12th June 1588. He wrote to Walsingham that 'Good consideration would be had now both to suppress it from being public here and to have some answer made to the reproof and remedy ... For answer I could wish some expert learned man would feign an answer as from a number of Catholics that notwithstanding their evil contentment ... should profess their obedience and service with their lives and power against all strange forces offering to land in this realm, and to advertise the Cardinal that he is deceived in his opinion to think that any nobleman in this land or any gentleman of possessions will favour the invasion of the realm'.[2]

It is surprising that Burghley did not publish a suitably annotated edition of Allen's *Admonition*, for it would have been very damaging

[1] A. O. Meyer, *England and the Catholic Church under Elizabeth*, p. 327.
[2] Conyers Reed, *Lord Burghley and Queen Elizabeth*, p. 426.

to the image of English Catholicism.[1] The *Admonition* must never-theless have helped to convince Burghley and others in the govern-ment that Papists were potential traitors, since the man who had de-fended their loyalty so plausibly in 1584 was prepared to call on them to help an invader when the time came. The argument that Allen kept the missionary effort distinct from his political activity loses much of its significance when we read the *Admonition*. He was certainly pre-pared in 1588 to bring the two together as part of a total effort to overthrow the queen.[2]

Instead of publishing the *Admonition*, Burghley put out an in-genious (and dishonest) propaganda pamphlet purporting to be *The Copy of a letter sent out of England to Don Bernardino de Mendoza . . . declaring the State of England*. It was alleged to have been found among the papers of Richard Leigh, a seminary priest executed at Tyburn on 30th August. It was a lament for the failure of the Armada and an assertion of the great strength of England. It pointed out that the Catholics had been loyal to the queen and were prepared to defend her. It complained that the priests being sent to England were very young and of light behaviour and that they preached treason. It asked for 'discreet, holy and learned men' who would not meddle in affairs of state, and it suggested that the pope might allow recusants to attend church occasionally to avoid the fines.[3]

On 31st May 1588 the Spanish Armada had at long last set sail. By the end of July the crisis had passed and the damaged fleet was in the North Sea, trying laboriously to make its way back to Spain. The Spanish threat was over for the time being, but the war still went on. The passing of the immediate danger did not mean that the govern-ment relaxed its drive against the Papists. In 1587 only 6 priests had been put to death, but in 1588 there were 31 executions, including

---

[1] Philip Hughes, *The Reformation in England*, III. 381, suggests that he did not do so because 'England was not yet so wholeheartedly Elizabethan that such a hostile blast could have no other effect than to bind the nation still more closely to the queen'. The implication of this might be that there were a large number of Englishmen whose loyalty was in doubt, but there is no evidence of this.

[2] Allen's reputation with English historians has, surprisingly, stood much higher than that of Robert Parsons, in spite of the fact that Allen was, as Fr. Hughes points out, wholeheartedly pro-Spanish, much more so than Parsons who 'has only one care, that England shall have a Catholic sovereign. Spaniard or Scot or Englishman is all one to him as a ruler, if only the faith be safe . . .'. Philip Hughes, *Rome and the Counter-Refor-mation in England*, p. 232.

[3] Conyers Read, *Lord Burghley and Queen Elizabeth*, p. 431 ff.

10 laypeople. They were all executed in the second half of the year, four of them while the Armada was still in the Channel and the rest from 28th August onwards, after it had failed. Eight were hanged, drawn and quartered on the 28th August and six on the 30th August. Meyer suggests that 'the intense excitement of those weeks and the increased dread of assassination' explains the holocaust of August, He thinks that England's consciousness of her military weakness, added to the passion excited by war, helps to account for the fact that 'after 1588 English Catholics were watched and oppressed with the same severity as before or even with greater'.[1]

The new Lord Chancellor, Sir Christopher Hatton, at the meeting of parliament early in 1589, delivered a tremendous oration against the papacy. He reminded his hearers, 'What a raging bull did that monster Pius V bring forth' and how Gregory XIII had attempted an invasion of Ireland. They had arranged 'that the litter of seminary priests, from nine days old and upward[2] tag and rag, should be sent hither, pell mell, thick and threefold, under pretence of planting of Popery to increase this number and to reconcile such again to his Holiness as had neglected their duties in not assisting of the foresaid rebellions.' In addition, sundry enchantments had been used, Somerville[3] had made his attempt against the queen's life with his dag (pistol), Parry had been set on by the cardinal of Como with the pope's consent to kill the queen with a dagger, and other traitors had attempted the like. Then Sixtus V, 'exceeding all others that went before him in tyranny and cruelty . . . will needs have a bridge of wood made over our seas'. He had renewed the excommunication and taken it upon himself to dispose the crown as he thought best. The Pope (that wolfish blood sucker) and the Spaniard (that insatiable tyrant) had never bent themselves with such might against the Turk as they had against a Virgin Queen and a country which 'embraceth without corruption in doctrine the true and sincere religion of Christ'. He made a fierce attack on 'that shameless atheist and bloody Cardinal Allen' and on 'those vile wretches, those bloody priests and false traitors, here in our bosoms, but beyond the seas especially' who 'will not cease to practise both at home and abroad'. The pope would give his soul to the devil rather than the invasion should not go forward, and the king of Spain would do whatever he could to invade us. He

[1] A. O. Meyer, *England and the Catholic Church under Elizabeth*, p. 346.
[2] After their ordination.   [3] See p. 181.

warned his hearers: 'An enemy is never so much to be feared as when he is contemned . . . we have lopped off some of his boughs; but they will sooner grow again than we think of . . . ' And so we must look to our defence.[1]

In view of this attitude there was justification for Robert Southwell's summary of the situation in January 1590: 'The condition of Catholics is unchanged, full of fears and perils.' They had to soldier on as best they could in spite of the executions of the 1580's, the weakening of the ranks of Catholic gentry under the pressure from the government, and the intolerable stigma of belonging to a religion which inevitably appeared as anti-national and pro-Spanish.

There were gains as well as losses. The priests from Rheims and the English College in Rome continued to come in, and in 1588 the Jesuits Garnet and Southwell were reinforced by John Gerard and Edward Oldcorne. Both of them were to work in England until the time of the Gunpowder Plot in 1605 when Oldcorne was captured and executed and Gerard managed to escape from the country. Both of them were to achieve a great deal in strengthening the Catholic body in the country, and Gerard's fascinating account of his work provides a vivid inside story of what it was like to be a hunted priest in Elizabethan England.[2]

A further source of strength to late Elizabethan Catholicism was the foundation of a third seminary for the training of priests to work in England. This was part of the remarkable achievements in Spain of Robert Parsons. He had been sent there in 1589 to settle difficulties in connection with the Spanish Jesuits, and he conceived the idea of establishing a seminary at Valladolid. He got Allen to send him some students to begin the work, he raised money to buy a house, and he set up in the face of formidable difficulties the English College of St. Alban. Within three years it had 75 students, and within a year of its foundation it had sent 12 men to England.[3]

[1] J. Neale, *Elizabeth I and her Parliaments*, II. 195 ff.

[2] *John Gerard: The Autobiography of an Elizabethan*, edit. Philip Caraman, second edition, 1956. Gerard's account of how he got out of the Tower of London is, of course, one of the greatest escape stories of all time.

[3] A. C. F. Beales, *Education under Penalty*, p. 46.

9

The Crisis of the Fifteen-Eighties: The Puritan Onslaught

(The queen is) most fully and firmly settled in her conscience, by the word of God, that the estate and government of this Church of England, as now it standeth in this reformation, may be justly compared to any church which hath been established in any Christian Kingdom since the Apostles' times; that both in form and doctrine it is agreeable with the scriptures, with the most ancient general Councils, with the practice of the primitive church, and with the judgments of all the old and learned fathers.

The Lord Chancellor's speech at the opening of Parliament, 1588[1]

In the 1580's the powerful and organised opposition which threatened the established church appeared at times to be so formidable that it seems remarkable that the church managed to emerge fundamentally unchanged at the end of the decade and to be in a position to launch a vigorous counter-offensive against those who sought to change it. There were many very influential people in the 1580's who were prepared to answer 'yes' to the question asked in a Puritan petition of 1588—'whether the desire of a further and better reformation in the Church of England, in dutiful manner, be not warranted by the word of God and law of England?'[2]

But the fierce onslaughts were repelled, mainly, it seems, because the queen resolutely and skilfully resisted any attempts to alter a church which in her view might 'justly be compared to any church which hath been established in any Christian Kingdom since the

[1] J. Neale, *Elizabeth I and her Parliaments*, II. 198
[2] *Ibid.*, II. 224.

Apostles' time'. In addition, the assailants were not united. There were many who wanted reform of *some* kind, but they were not agreed about what they wanted or about how it should be obtained. The Protestant reformers certainly won a number of battles, but in the end they lost the campaign. The outcome of the struggle might easily have been different. Although it seems most unlikely that the Church of England would have become Presbyterian, it might well have become a good deal more 'Protestant'.

One of the queen's greatest difficulties was that in her religious policy she could not count on the unqualified support even of her closest advisers. Indeed, there are times when one almost gets the impression that among the policy-makers she was if not the only, at least one of the very few, 'Anglicans', surrounded by people who were in different degrees 'Protestants'. It did not, for example, augur well for the ultimate success of her conception of the church that Lord Burghley not only approved of the return to England of the Presbyterian leader Walter Travers, but made him a chaplain in his own household and secured for him in 1581 an appointment as Reader in the Temple Church, London, a very influential position which Travers did his best to exploit.[1] Nor did it assist the cause of the establishment that the formidable John Field in 1580 was once more preaching in London and became in 1581 parish lecturer in St. Mary Aldermary, helped by the earl of Leicester to whom Field wrote 'not only I but the whole Church do owe thankfulness unto you as the instrument both of my peace and liberty and of the poor blessing it enjoyeth by my preaching'.[2] Travers had not even been ordained according to the rites of the Church of England, and Field, joint author of the *Admonition to the Parliament*,[3] was to show that he was by no means a reformed character. There were plenty of other occasions in the 1580's when Elizabeth was, if not exactly stabbed in the back by her councillors, at least pushed none too gently along the path of godliness.

The Puritans had high hopes of achieving some or all of their objectives by carefully organised publicity and propaganda in the country, leading to direct action in parliament. At the opening of the 1581 parliament, the Lord Chancellor gave 'a special admonition unto

[1] S. J. Knox, *Walter Travers*, p. 54 ff. Travers ran into difficulties, some of which were of his own making.
[2] Patrick Collinson, 'John Field and Elizabethan Puritanism,' p. 143.
[3] See p. 133 ff.

this House not to deal with matters touching her Majesty's person or estate, or touching religion'.[1] The queen had warned the members off the field, but Paul Wentworth nevertheless moved for a public fast 'to the end that it might please God to bless us in our actions better than we had been heretofore, and for a sermon to be heard every morning'. This looked like simple piety, but public fasts had of recent years taken on a special significance. They were one of the means by which Puritans circumvented the prohibition against prophesyings. Professor Neale wonders whether Wentworth's proposal was part of the concerted action of a group of Puritans intending to launch an attack 'in the aura of daily revivalist excitement'.[2] It was in any case an assertion of the Commons' claim to deal with matters of religion in spite of the queen's prohibition. A proposal for a public as against a private fast, 'everybody for himself', was carried by 115 votes to 100. The queen promptly informed the Commons that 'No public fast could be appointed but by her' and that they were impeaching her jurisdiction. She explained that she 'liked well of fasting, prayer and sermons' and that she attributed their mistake to zeal and not to malice.[3] She objected to the manner in which it was done, 'tending to innovation, presuming to indict a form of public fast without order and without her Majesty's privity, intruding upon her Highness's authority ecclesiastical'.[4]

The Commons were temporarily thrown off balance, and in any case they had urgent business concerning the Catholics to occupy their immediate attention,[5] but in March 1581 they turned to reform in religion. Some of the Privy Councillors pointed out that the queen had already commanded certain councillors to confer with the bishops about the necessary reforms. The House decided that these councillors should be asked to consult the bishops again in the name of the House. The councillors subsequently reported to the M.P.s that they had conferred with the bishops about a number of abuses, including unsatisfactory ministers, excommunication for small matters, and pluralism. They had asked the bishops to join with them in a petition to the queen. 'Some of the bishops' admitted that the abuses existed, and were willing to do so. A petition went forward and the queen answered graciously that she had at the last meeting of parliament

---

[1] J. Neale, *Elizabeth I and her Parliaments*, I. 377.
[2] *Ibid.*, I. 379. [3] *Ibid.*, I. 380.
[4] *Ibid.*, I. 382. [5] See p. 174 ff.

entrusted consideration of these things to some of the clergy. They had not performed their task and she would now entrust it to others who would quickly carry it out.

At the end of this parliament the speaker reminded the queen about a request made in 1576 'for redress . . . of certain enormities in the Church . . . ' Through the Lord Chancellor, the queen said she would deal effectively with the bishops, and if they were unsuccessful, she would use her supreme authority.

Evidence of the kind of reform a Puritan group in the Commons hoped to achieve is provided by a series of articles drawn up 'by some of the Lower House' which the queen sent to the archbishops of York and some of his colleagues for their comments. The articles requested that no one should be admitted a minister unless there was available for him a vacant benefice in the diocese in which he was to be ordained. The people were to have some chance of expressing their views about a minister whom it was proposed to appoint as their pastor. There was to be no obligation on Cambridge Fellows to be ordained.[1] The bishops made some pointed criticisms of these and other proposals and expressed the view that some of them were based on the false principles of Thomas Cartwright.

The proposals may have been drawn up by Puritans in the Lower House of Convocation[2] or by Puritan clergy and sympathetic M.P.s. There is at least the possibility that the Puritans had intended to press for these reforms in parliament. If this was the plan of campaign, it was not put into operation.[3] From the point of view of those who wanted radical reform, the parliament of 1580–1 was remarkably unfruitful. It is true that the queen told Sandys to get on with reforms so that negligence would not again be complained of in parliament,[4] but the Puritans were not likely to get what they wanted in that way.

---

[1] Cartwright had been deprived of his Fellowship because he had not taken orders as he was required to do by the statutes.

[2] In 1581 John Nashe from the Marshalsea prison petitioned Convocation against 'reading service and tossinge of psalmes from syde to syde in the quyer, and turning their arses and backs to the people etc., where Chrystes ministers do all to edifye both in prayers and preachinge, and prophesying and ministring, and in Psalmes syngune together with the whole church, etc., and not service readynge and psalmes in partes songe'. Otherwise the unlearned 'shall never come to see nor knowe the lighte of lyffe, but thorow blynde leaders and dombe dogges and unpreaching ministers, bee still blynde and so loose their salvation etc.' A. Peel, *The Seconde Parte of a Register*, I. 51 ff.

[3] J. Neale, *Elizabeth I and her Parliaments*, I. 401.

[4] J. Neale, *op. cit.*, I. 403.

Parliament did not meet again until November 1584 and in the meantime a good deal had happened which explains the much more determined Puritan drive which was then made.

The most significant and, from the queen's point of view, the most dangerous development was that the Puritans, and in particular the Presbyterians, became much more organised. One very important aspect of this development is what has come to be known as 'the classical movement'. This has been defined by Dr. Collinson as 'an association of puritan clergy of the Elizabethan Church in an organisation of ministerial conferences in some sort resembling, and for a period actually styled as, the *classes* and synods of the presbyterian church polity which its members hoped to establish in the Church of England'.[1] We must not think of the movement as resulting from a piece of careful planning from above, leading to the formation of *classes* all of which conformed to a definite pattern and obeyed the same regulations. What seems to have happened was that there came into existence a number of conferences and assemblies of various kinds arising more or less spontaneously. Attempts were then made to weld these bodies into some kind of unity and to spread the movement by establishing still more *classes*. The London group and its secretary, John Field, played a leading rôle in these efforts to unify the movement, and a number of provincial and national synods tried to formulate an agreed policy. Nevertheless, taking the country as a whole, what emerged was a loose federation rather than a centrally directed and united organisation. In many parts of the country there is no evidence of *classes*, and even where conferences of some sort did exist, they often seem to have played little or no part in the national movement. There is very little evidence that lay 'elders' participated in *classes* or synods, although in a number of parishes attempts were made to associate 'elders' with the ministers in various unofficial 'presbyteries'.[2]

[1] Patrick Collinson, 'The Puritan Classical Movement', p. v. The *classis* was a regional group fitting into a pyramid of authority based on presbyteries in the individual churches and going up through the *classes* to provincial and national synods. At each stage there should ideally have been laymen or 'elders' as well as ministers. See Patrick Collinson, *The Elizabethan Puritan Movement*, p. 350 ff., and V. J. K. Brook, *Whitgift and the English Church*, 117 ff. for further discussion.

[2] Dr. Collinson's immensely detailed and valuable study of the movement has thrown a great deal of new light on the subject, but these various assemblies were naturally careful not to make their activities too public and we have little or no information about many of them. Much of our material comes from a hostile witness, Richard Bancroft, who

The beginning of this large-scale organisation seems to have been at Cockfield in Suffolk where in May 1582 some 60 ministers met to discuss the Prayer Book and to work out a common policy. Information about this comes from a letter which Oliver Pig, minister of Rougham, near Bury St. Edmunds, sent to John Field in London, and it seems not unlikely that Field and the London group were involved in this regional conference. Cockfield was the parish of another prominent Puritan minister, John Knewstub. Not much is known about the conference, but a meeting of this size was clearly important. There were further conferences in 1582 in Cambridge and in Wethersfield in Essex.[1]

On a much smaller scale and of a different nature from these regional assemblies was the conference which on 22 October 1582 began to meet at Dedham in Essex and which drew up rules for regular monthly meetings. These went on until June 1589, and the Dedham conference or 'classis' has aroused special interest because the Minutes of its meetings have been preserved.[2] From these Minutes we get a picture of some 20 ministers meeting regularly and secretly in private houses for prayer, discussion of the scriptures and consideration of problems of common interest. It seems that less than half the members were beneficed clergy. The rest held lectureships or positions as readers.[3] There were no lay 'elders' present and this was not a 'typical' example of Presbyterian organisation.[4] The conference exercised a very limited 'discipline' over its members and from time

published in 1593 *Dangerous Positions and Proceedings* (partly reprinted in R. G. Usher, *The Presbyterian Movement in the Reign of Queen Elizabeth*, 1905) and *A Survey of the Pretended Holy Discipline*. See pp. 314–315.

[1] Of the Cockfield meeting, Dr. Collinson writes: 'we cannot tell whether it marked the beginning of a new advance in presbyterian action or whether there had been other conventions like this in the past'. Patrick Collinson, *The Elizabethan Puritan Movement* p. 218 ff.

[2] *The Presbyterian Movement in the Reign of Queen Elizabeth as Illustrated by the Minute Book of the Dedham Classis, 1582–1589*, edit. R. G. Usher, Camden Society, Third Series, VIII. Dr. Collinson, 'Puritan Classical Movement', p. 350 ff. points out that three of the leading members had been associated with the Norwich 'prophesyings' in the mid 1570's. The Dedham 'classis' may in origin have been simply another 'prophesying'.

[3] Patrick Collinson, 'The Puritan Classical Movement', p. 357–60; *The Elizabethan Puritan Movement*, p. 225 ff.

[4] See a petition to the queen from Norwich in 1583 asking her to remove the government of Antichrist 'with all his archprelates ... by planting that holie Eldership ... which is so plainlie described and so waightilie authorised in God's word ...' *The Seconde Parte of a Register*, edit A. Peel. I. 158.

to time gave them advice about what course of action they should take. It decided, for example, that the surplice should not be worn, and that the members should not subscribe their names to the articles which Whitgift required them to accept, but on a number of burning issues the conference refrained from giving definite instructions. Not all the members were uncompromising Presbyterians and some of them were prepared to come to terms with the episcopal system. They were in touch with the 'brethren' in other parts of the country, but they were not always prepared to accept the decision of the national synods which met from time to time in the 'eighties.[1]

We do not know to what extent the Dedham conference had parallels in other parts of the country in the early 1580's.[2] Dr. Collinson thinks that there is little doubt that in West Suffolk the ministers led by Knewstub were organised in a similar way, and certainly in London there was a powerful Presbyterian group in which John Field played the leading part. It seems probable that in areas where there were like-minded ministers they would get together from time to time to discuss common problems, even though they may not have been as well organised as those who met regularly at Dedham. Such meetings were not necessarily illegal, but if the ministers discussed the controversial issues of the day they obviously would not seek publicity. It is only through the accidental survival of the Minutes that we have detailed knowledge about the Dedham Conference.

Field and his London group were well organised and in touch with what was going on in many parts of the country by means of personal contact and a voluminous correspondence. Field had not himself called the Cockfield meeting in 1582, but he suggested a follow-up meeting in Cambridge.[3] The Suffolk group replied that this could 'easily be brought to pass, if you at London shall so think well of it, and we here may understand your mind'. The London group was also in touch with sympathisers in Scotland and the Netherlands. Thus in the early 1580's Field and his friends were in a position to start fashioning a national Presbyterian movement building on various existing local assemblies like Dedham.[4] It was not strict Presbyterianism

---

[1] For a discussion of its disciplinary and advisory functions, see Patrick Collinson, *The Elizabethan Puritan Movement*, p. 226 ff.
[2] Patrick Collinson, *op. cit.* p. 231 ff.
[3] Patrick Collinson, 'John Field and Elizabethan Puritanism', p. 149.
[4] Patrick Collinson, 'The Puritan Classical Movement', p. 381; 'John Field and Elizabethan Puritanism', p. 149; *The Elizabethan Puritan Movement*, p. 233 ff.

and it was very much on an *ad hoc* basis. The number of fully committed Presbyterians was small, and in the various groups there were probably many who were fellow-travellers rather than party members. The committed Presbyterians were able to exploit the discontent arising from the determined drive against all Puritan nonconformity which was inaugurated by Whitgift when he became archbishop of Canterbury in 1583.

The leaders of the movement seem to have been thinking in the early stages of infiltration rather than of a take-over bid, and one of the early conferences held either in London or in Cambridge about 1583 put forward a scheme by which no one was to seek the ministry unless 'called' by a particular church. If his 'call' was approved by the local conference or classis, he was to be sent to the bishop for ordination. When a living was vacant, the local 'classis' was to urge the patron to present a suitable candidate. Churchwardens and collectors for the poor were to be transformed into 'elders' and 'deacons'. There were to be county, provincial and national synods. Thus there came into being what Fuller later called 'the embryo of the Presbyterian Discipline lying as yet (as it were) in the wombe of Episcopacy'.[1] Field's London group constituted an unofficial central executive of a loosely knit organisation which did not fit into the official machinery of the established church and which could be used to press for further reform. It had the appearance of being, potentially at least, a church within a church, a 'shadow' organisation which might one day be in a position to transform the establishment.

Some progress was being made in the early 1580's, but it was more limited than is sometimes suggested. In June 1583 a correspondent abroad congratulated Field on what he had done to establish Presbyterian assemblies, but added: 'I will tell you that which is true: you have begun this course too late.'[2] Field himself admitted to the Dedham Conference that he had been 'strongly drawn of late not to be so careful, diligent and zealous in God's causes as I was wont . . .'[3] Possibly he was disappointed at the amount of support he was receiving. As Dr. Collinson points out, 'it took Whitgift's general assault on nonconformity to stir this embryonic organism fully into life'.[4] Whitgift's policy drove into opposition a considerable number of

---

[1] V. J. K. Brook, *Whitgift and the English Church*, pp. 113–14.
[2] Patrick Collinson, 'John Field and Elizabethan Puritanism,' p. 149.
[3] *Ibid.*, p. 149.   [4] *Ibid.*, p. 149.

people of many different shades of opinion, and the Presbyterian leaders were able to use this opposition in the way that militant Communists are sometimes able to exploit the grievances of those who are not themselves Communists.

The appointment of John Whitgift to Canterbury in August 1583 has been called the most important event in the history of the Elizabethan Church since the settlement of 1559.[1] In a sermon at Paul's Cross the new archbishop described the Puritans as being 'in yoke with Papistes, Anabaptistes and Rebelles'.[2] After consulting the bishops and getting the support of the queen, he issued on 19 October 1583 a series of articles directed against both Puritans and Papists, but which endeavoured at the same time to reform some of the admitted abuses which made the church so vulnerable. The laws against recusancy were to be enforced and action was to be taken against offenders in the civil and in the ecclesiastical courts. Private and family meetings for 'preaching, reading, catechising, and other such exercises' were prohibited if outsiders were allowed to attend. No one was to preach, read or catechise in church unless he said the service and administered the sacrament according to the Book of Common Prayer at least four times a year.[3] All ministers were to wear the clerical dress prescribed in Parker's *Advertisements*. No one was to preach or perform any ecclesiastical function unless he put his signature to three articles by which he (1) acknowledged the royal supremacy, (2) agreed that the Book of Common Prayer and the Form of Ordination of bishops, priests and deacons contained nothing contrary to the Word of God, and undertook to use it in public prayers and in administration of the sacrament, and (3) agreed that the Thirty Nine Articles and everything contained in them was agreeable to the Word of God.

The Articles of 1583 attempted to deal with some of the very serious problems of the Church by laying down that except in the universities no one should be ordained unless there was a definite cure or living available for him. Candidates for ordination must produce evidence

[1] Patrick Collinson, 'The Puritan Classical Movement', p. 389. Sir John Neale calls it 'one of the decisive events of the reign' and he adds that 'It was none too soon'. J. Neale, *Elizabeth I and her Parliaments*, II. 20.

[2] Patrick Collinson, *op. cit.*, p. 389.

[3] This was aimed at preachers, lecturers and readers who had conscientious objections to using the Book of Common Prayer, but who were prepared to preach and catechise.

of good character and moderate learning. Bishops who offended by ordaining unsuitable applicants were to lose the right of ordination for two years. They were to be given protection against legal action if they refused to institute in benefices unsuitable men presented to them by patrons of livings. Ecclesiastical penances imposed by church courts were not to be commuted for money payments except on rare occasions and for good reason. The regulations about marriage by licence and without calling the banns were made more strict. Finally, information was to be sent to the archbishop from all dioceses concerning the clergy and the extent to which they were conforming to the law.[1]

To help enforce his policy of uniformity, Whitgift, at the end of 1583, got a new High Commission set up under his own presidency and he proceeded to take action against those who would not conform. A considerable number of ministers found themselves in difficulty when faced with the agonising question of whether they could with a good conscience put their signatures to Whitgift's three articles. As in the earlier vestiarian controversy, the ministers had to decide whether they should make a stand against evil things, cost what it might, or obey the authorities rather than desert their flock. What they were required to agree to this time was much less easy for the conscientious Puritan to accept than the wearing of vestments, which, it could be argued, were in themselves 'things indifferent'.

In November and December 1583 the ministers in the diocese of Chichester were required to subscribe to the articles. Most of them did so, but 24 would subscribe only with qualifications. They were suspended, and some of them came to see Whitgift to put their case. He was willing to accept a modified subscription.[2] In January 1584, about 60 ministers in Suffolk and about the same number in Norfolk were suspended. In Lincolnshire there were 22 suspensions, and there was trouble in Kent where a number of those in difficulty appealed to the Privy Council. Dr. Collinson estimates that in the country as a whole more than 300 ministers, and perhaps nearer 400, refused to subscribe.[3]

There was very considerable discussion in Puritan circles about

---

[1] V. J. K. Brook, *Whitgift and the English Church*, pp. 81–2.

[2] Patrick Collinson, *The Elizabethan Puritan Movement*, p. 249 ff.

[3] *Ibid.*, p. 253. The figures do not include Liecestershire where there was general delay in subscribing (p. 252).

JOHN WHITGIFT, ARCHBISHOP OF CANTERBURY 1583–1604
Sir John Neale calls his appointment to Canterbury 'one of the decisive events
of the reign' and adds 'It was none too soon.' He led a successful counter-
attack against Puritanism and John Field remarked that 'the peace of the
Church is at an end if he be not curbed'.

Hay any worke for Cooper:

**Or a briefe Pistle directed by waye of an
publication to the reverende Byshopps / counselling
them / if they will needs be barrelled vp / for feare of smelling
in the nostrels of her Maiestie & the State / that they would
vse the aduise of reuerend Martin / for the prouiding of their
Cooper. Because the reuerend T. C. (by which misticall
letters / is vnderstood / eyther the bounsing Parson of Eastmeane, or Tom Coalies his
Chaplaine) to bee an vnskilfull and a beceptfull
tubtrimmer.**

**Wherein worthy Martin quits himselfe like a man
I warrant you / in the modest defence of his selfe and his
learned Pistles / and makes the Coopers hoopes
to flye off / and the Bishops Tubs to
leake out of all crye.**

Penned and compiled by Martin the Metropolitane.

**Printed in Europe / not farre from some
of the Bounsing Priestes.**

14 HAY ANY WORKE FOR COOPER

This was the fourth of the Martin Marprelate tracts and was printed by Rob
Waldegrave in March 1589 at his secret press which was at that time locate
Coventry. Thomas Cooper, bishop of Winchester, had attacked Martin wh
his reply made use of the familiar London street-cry.

whether the articles could be accepted with qualification, and a number of efforts were made by Puritans to find a formula which would allow them to subscribe without violating their consciences. Since even modified subscription would split the ranks of Whitgift's opponents, John Field resolutely opposed any compromise. He prepared a statement, which was probably circulated, against subscription of any kind and he condemned conditional subscription as 'vain and frivolous'.[1]

The campaign for uniformity in 1583 and 1584 caused a great deal of concern to some of the nobility and gentry as well as to members of the Privy Council. There were a number of different reasons for the opposition to the archbishop's policy, and one or more of them might influence individual opponents. For some the religious motive was predominant—they were fundamentally in agreement with those ministers who could not in conscience give unconditional approval to the Book of Common Prayer and the Thirty Nine Articles. In addition, the nobleman or gentleman who had given his patronage to a 'godly' preacher was reluctant to see his protégé dragged before an ecclesiastical court. It was damaging to the patron's prestige as well as outrageous from the point of view of his religious sympathies. Others who were in the habit of having meetings for private and family prayers for their households, including their servants and their guests, must have resented the prohibition of such meetings to outsiders. This was an interference by the central government with the gentleman's right to run his household in the way that seemed best to him.[2] Others were very disturbed at the weakening of national and religious unity at a time when the country was threatened from abroad and when the Papists seemed to be increasing dangerously at home. Thus in June 1584 Knollys expressed his concern at seeing 'the course of Poopyshe treason to be neglected and to see the zealous preachers of the ghospell, sownd in doctryne (who are the most dylygent barkers agaynst the popyshe wolfe to save the folde and flocke of Chryste) to be persequted and put to silence'.[3] The twenty-five gentlemen from Kent who protested to the archbishop about the suspension of their ministers alleged that they would be without preachers, and they

---

[1] Patrick Collinson, 'John Field and Elizabethan Puritanism,' pp. 150–3.

[2] John Bossy has examined this aspect of Elizabethan life, with reference to the Papists, and what he has to say is also relevant to the Puritan nobility and gentry. See John Bossy, 'The Character of Elizabethan Catholicism, *Past and Present*, vol. 21.

[3] Patrick Collinson, 'The Puritan Classical Movement,' p. 405.

P

pointed out that the ministers in question did in fact use the Prayer Book. Whitgift replied that they did not use it fully and that they selected what they chose.[1]

The Puritans knew that they had sympathisers in high places. There were complaints to the Council from Kent and Suffolk, and the Council asked Whitgift to appear before it. He firmly declined to do so,[2] but the fact that the Council had tried to make him answer to it is evidence of another factor in the resistance to his policy—resentment of the laity against an ecclesiastic who was determined to use his authority. Anticlericalism reinforced religious sympathies in the Council. Robert Beale, the clerk to the Council, sympathised with the views of the dissenting ministers, and Whitgift accused him of encouraging the resistance.[3] In September 1584, eight Privy Councillors, including Burghley, protested to Whitgift and the bishop of London about the deprivation of certain Essex ministers who had appealed to the Council. They contrasted the immunity of 'lewd, evil, unprofitable and corrupt' clergy with the treatment of the Puritans, and they asked most earnestly 'that the people of the realm might not be deprived of their pastors, being diligent, learned and zealous, though in some points of ceremonial they might seem doubtful, only in conscience and not of wilfulness'.[4]

Whitgift was also open to attack because of the way in which he used High Commission against some of the offenders. He had drawn up in May 1584 a series of twenty-four questions to be put to suspects. They were designed to find out in great detail whether the man under examination accepted the teaching and practice of the established church. The suspect had to say, for example, whether he used the Book of Common Prayer without alteration, whether he wore the prescribed dress, whether he attended conventicles,[5] whether he criticised the Prayer Book, whether he omitted the sign of the cross in baptism, and so on. The Court used what was known as the *ex officio* oath by which the person being examined was required to swear to answer questions truthfully before he knew what the questions were. The procedure caused a great deal of concern to common lawyers since it was not a common law procedure. The lawyers were in any case unwilling to see

[1] V. J. K. Brook, *Whitgift and the English Church*, pp. 85, 86.
[2] *Ibid.*, pp. 84–5.
[3] Patrick Collinson, 'The Puritan Classical Movement', p. 446.
[4] J. Neale, *Elizabeth I and her Parliaments*, II. 22.
[5] Unauthorised religious meetings not held in the church.

any growth in power of ecclesiastical courts which rivalled common law courts. Burghley, whose concern for justice was less marked when it was a matter of putting the Bloody Questions to Papists, was disturbed at these detailed enquiries into the orthodoxy of the Puritans and wrote to Whitgift telling him that the questions were 'rather a device to seek for offenders than to reform any' and that he thought the Spanish Inquisition 'use not so many questions to comprehend and to trap their preys'.[1]

In the face of this determined opposition, Whitgift did not give way, but he showed himself willing to accept a modified form of subscription to his three articles. Most of those who had originally refused submitted to the extent of signing some form of consent to the articles. Although the number of those who stood out is not known, Dr. Collinson thinks that it was very few.[2] The reluctant signatories were, of course, anxious to get the demand withdrawn as soon as possible, and they looked to the next parliament to take action, but by compromising they had weakened their position. Dr. Collinson comments: 'There is no knowing what the outcome for the Church of England might have been had parliament met in the early months of 1584, with hundreds of pulpits silent, the radical Protestant gentry in an uproar, and everyone at court, with the exception of Sir Christopher Hatton and the Queen herself, opposed to Whitgift's policy.'[3] Like the Papists in the 1560's, the Puritans in the 1580's had made a dangerous mistake. They had failed to make a stand.

Field had played the rôle of William Allen in urging a policy of no compromise.[4] Like him he must have been bitterly disappointed that

[1] For Burghley's letter see John Strype, *Life and Acts of John Whitgift*, Oxford, 1822. III. 104–7; V. J. K. Brook, *Whitgift and the English Church*, p. 88. For a detailed examination of the working of the church courts, see R. B. Marchant, *The Puritans and the Church Courts in the Diocese of York 1560–1642*. Burghley's reference to the Spanish Inquisition was lifted from a letter which had just received from Robert Beale (Patrick Collinson, *The Elizabethan Puritan Movement*, p. 270).
[2] Patrick Collinson, *The Elizabethan Puritan Movement*, p. 263.
[3] Patrick Collinson, 'John Field and Elizabethan Puritanism', p. 153.
[4] See, for example, his letter circulating among the ministers of Lincolnshire urging them to 'stand stoutly to the cause, affirming the same not to be theirs but the Lord's' (Patrick Collinson, 'John Field and Elizabethan Puritanism', p. 152), and his advice to the Dedham classis early in 1584 concerning Whitgift's articles—'The peace of the Church is at an end if he be not curbed. You are wise to consider by advice and by joining together how to strengthen your hands in this work. The Lord direct both you and us that we may fight a good fight and finish with joy. Amen'. J. Neale, *Elizabeth I and her Parliaments*, II. 21.

so many were prepared to conform. Nevertheless, there were plenty of grievances which could be exploited, and there was always the hope that the Presbyterians would gain some of their objectives if they played a leading rôle in urging reforms which were demanded by those who were not themselves Presbyterians. Judging from what happened when parliament met at the end of 1584, there had been tremendous activity in the country in the months which preceded it, and this included the preparation in a number of places of 'Surveys of the Ministry' in which the deficiencies of individual clerics were reported on in order to show from detailed evidence how unsatisfactory was the state of the church.[1]

The Presbyterian movement in England was also influenced and strengthened in 1584 by a number of Scottish Presbyterian ministers who had temporarily been driven out of their own country. Some of them came to London[2] and others to Oxford or Cambridge. Two of them, James Melville and John Davidson, were in London during the meeting of the parliament in 1584–5 and they certainly conferred with John Field.[3]

In order to get suitable men returned to the parliament of 1584–5 the Puritans did what they could to influence the elections. The Dedham Conference, for example, urged Field and the London group to do their best to secure the return of godly members—'Confer among yourselves how it may best be compassed. You are placed in the highest place of the Church and land to that end.'[4] A conference was called to meet in London at the same time as the parliament. The Dedham Conference decided on 2 November 'so far as we could procure it' to arrange 'in every country . . . that some of best credit and most forward for the Gospel should go up to London to solicit the cause of the Church'.[5] Unfortunately we know comparatively little about who attended the Conference, what precisely they did, which M.P.s they lobbied and consulted, and what exactly they hoped to achieve. It would be unwise to assume that all the members were committed Presbyterians. Some were, no doubt, 'fellow travellers' and radical reformers of varying shades of opinion. What does seem clear

---

[1] See pp. 19–20, 227.
[2] Patrick Collinson, 'John Field and the Puritan Movement', p. 155.
[3] *Ibid.*, p. 156; *The Elizabethan Puritan Movement*, p. 275 ff.
[4] Patrick Collinson, 'John Field and the Puritan Movement', p. 154; *The Presbyterian Movement in the Reign of Queen Elizabeth*, edit. R. G. Usher, p. 58.
[5] J. Neale, *Elizabeth I and her Parliaments*, II. 60.

is that they were active propagandists who tried hard to influence the course of events. It was said that their representatives 'were all day at the door of Parliament House and some part of the night in the chambers of Parliament-men, effectively soliciting their business with them'.[1]

Parliament assembled at the end of November 1584. The Lord Chancellor gave the queen's consent to the Speaker's usual request concerning freedom of speech, but added 'only she restrained the cause of religion to be spoken of among them'.[2] Elizabeth must have thought there was no harm in trying.

The first bill of the session was one for 'the better and more reverend observing of the Sabbath Day'. It was not a Puritan bill. We must remember that although Puritans in the sixteenth and seventeenth centuries were particularly interested in the stricter keeping of the sabbath,[3] they had no monopoly in this matter. There were others, Catholics as well as Protestants, who thought the Sabbath was not properly kept. This bill after various alterations went through both Houses, but the queen vetoed it. Presumably she did so because she objected to parliament interfering with religion. It may also have been, as Professor Neale suggests, that 'she preferred a Merry to a Puritan England'.[4]

It seems that the Puritan plan of attack in this parliament was to show the unsatisfactory state of the church, to present complaints against Whitgift's methods and to use the material collected in the surveys of the ministry to drive home the need for a reform in church government. In all this the Presbyterians could hope to get considerable support from a large group of M.P.s, and the opportunity might arise to suggest 'a godly discipline' as an alternative to rule of the church by archbishops and bishops.

On 14 December 1584 Sir Thomas Lucy, M.P. for Warwickshire, Sir Edward Dymock, M.P. for Lincolnshire, and Mr. Geoffrey Gates, M.P. for Essex, nephew of Walsingham and stepson of Peter Wentworth, presented to the House petitions from their counties with signatures of 'very many . . . of the gentlemen of greatest worship in the same shires' complaining of the state of the church and the

---

[1] J. Neale, *Elizabeth I and her Parliaments*, II, 60; *The Presbyterian Movement in the Reign of Queen Elizabeth*, edit. R. G. Usher, pp. 40–1.

[2] J. Neale, *op. cit.*, II. 26.

[3] M. M. Knappen, *Tudor Puritanism*, Chapter XXIV, p. 442 ff. 'Sabbatarianism'.

[4] J. Neale, *op. cit.* II. 60.

restraint of so many worthy preachers. They asked the House to petition the queen for a reform of abuses.[1] In spite of the queen's order
not to meddle with religion, the House heard the petitions. Then, no
doubt feeling that the atmosphere was sympathetic, a Presbyterian
member, Dr. Peter Turner,[2] made a bid to get Presbyterian proposals
considered by the M.P.s. He asked leave to bring in 'a bill and a book'
which he had apparently already given to the Speaker or to his clerk.
Dr. Turner said that these had been 'digested and framed by certain
godly and learned ministers', and he asked that they might be read to
the House.[3] The proposal apparently was to replace the Book of
Common Prayer with a new book which seems to have been the
Genevan *Forme of Prayer* recently revised and printed by the Puritan
printer, Robert Waldegrave.[4] The book provided forms of prayer
only for a single congregation, but Field and his friends had apparently pasted into it a scheme of Presbyterian church government
arranging for conferences and synods.[5] It does not seem to be absolutely certain what was in Turner's bill, but Professor Neale gives
reasons for believing that it not only provided for a new Calvinist
Prayer Book, but also made arrangements for setting up a system of
church government by ministers and elders, without actually abolishing the existing system of government by archbishops and bishops.[6]

We do not know much about what lay behind this interesting take-
over bid by the Presbyterians or whether they seriously expected to
get the bill approved. Possibly what they wanted was an opportunity
to get their views discussed in the hope that they would make converts. It may be that their original plan was to introduce this alternative form of church government only after the deficiencies of the
existing system had been examined by the House when it considered
the various petitions from the counties. In either case their efforts
failed, for the House refused to give leave to read Dr. Turner's bill.[7]

Although it was not prepared to listen to Presbyterian schemes, the

---

[1] J. Neale, *op. cit.* II. 61.

[2] M. M. Knappen, *Tudor Puritanism*, p. 277, describes him as the son of the botanist
and a celebrated physician in his own right. He was M.P. for Bridport, Dorset.

[3] J. Neale, *op. cit.* II. 62.

[4] Patrick Collinson, *The Elizabethan Puritan Movement*, p. 296 ff.

[5] Patrick Collinson, 'John Field and Elizabethan Puritanism', p. 156.

[6] J. Neale, *op. cit.*, II. 62. Professor Neale assumes that it was the same as the un-
dated bill printed in *The Seconde Parte of a Register*, edit., A. Peel, II. 215–18.

[7] For a discussion of Turner's bill see Patrick Collinson, *The Elizabethan Puritan
Movement*, p. 286 ff.

House was very ready to consider the complaints against the church presented to it in the petitions from Warwickshire, Lincolnshire and Essex. It appointed a committee to examine the petitions and to consult with the Lords.[1] This committee drew up a moderate petition asking for the removal of unqualified and unlearned ministers and requesting that steps be taken to prevent such appointments in future. The parishioners were to have some share in choosing their ministers. No oaths were to be required of the clergy other than those laid down in the statutes.[2] No one was to be proceeded against for making minor omissions from the Book of Common Prayer or rites of the Church of England. The suspended ministers were to be restored and the *ex officio* oath was not to be administered. Provision was to be made against abuses in excommunication and against pluralism and non-residence.[3] These were relatively moderate requests many of which could be supported by M.P.s who were in no sense Puritans.

The next step was to take the petition to the Lords. A delegation led by Sir Francis Knollys delivered it to a committee of 5 spiritual and 12 temporal lords. Mildmay was spokesman for the Commons. The Lords were at first disinclined to take action on complaints coming from only three counties, but they were assured that these were 'the grief of the whole realm'. They then said they would like to consult the queen through their members who were Privy Counsellors. While the Commons were awaiting the reply of the Lords, the Puritans got their machinery to work, and similar complaints were brought in from Leicester, East Sussex and Folkestone. These were read to the House.[4]

On 22 February 1585 Burghley told a deputation from the Commons that the queen had been shown the petition and that she had discussed it with Whitgift and the bishops. Some of the proposed reforms were under consideration, some she would deal with by her supreme authority, and others were not fit to be granted 'as requiring innovation and impugning the Book of Common Prayer'. The queen wanted complaints to be dealt with in the first instance in the dioceses. Only if that failed to produce results would they be dealt with

[1] J. Neale, *Elizabeth I and her Parliaments*, II. 63.
[2] In 1571 the clergy had been required to accept only the doctrinal articles in the Thirty Nine Articles. Whitgift had been requiring the clergy to approve all the articles. See pp. 129, 213.
[3] *Ibid.*, p. 63; M. M. Knappen, *Tudor Puritanism*, p. 277 ff.
[4] J. Neale, *Elizabeth I and her Parliaments*, II. 64.

at a higher level. Whitgift also spoke. He defended what had been done and suggested that the proposals smelt of popular election. He claimed that objections to the *ex officio* oath came from Jesuits and seminary priests and others 'that mislike government and would bring the Church to an anarchy'.[1]

The committee reported back and 'the House was nothing satisfied'. Robert Beale, the clerk to the Council, said bitterly: 'The lamentable face of the Church at this day is not unknown to you all . . . how the shires and boroughs whence you come . . . are served with unlearned and insufficient ministers, and how that many of the learneder sort, for a refusal to a certain subscription, have been called up from far parts' and examined on oath. Some had been silenced, some imprisoned without bail, and some suspended, all contrary to God's word, the canon law and the laws of England. Beale said he had no complaint about anything the High Commission did to Papists, but, he argued, 'no spiritual person has the authority to imprison free men, except in cases specially granted to them by the law or their commission ecclesiastical . . . ' Their authority did not extend against 'honest and godly ministers'. The bishops, he maintained, 'will never reform anything'. They were guilty of praemunire and the House should ask the queen to pardon them for a 'favourable and easy fine and ransom'.[2]

The Commons' next step was to reinforce its committee and to require it to prepare a detailed answer to the points made by Whitgift and others in the Lords. Knollys and Mildmay were on the committee which drew up a statement. It stressed the fact that the *ex officio* oath was not recognised by statute or by common law, and that the ministers had not been lawfully deprived. This statement was completed by 27 February 1585, but was never discussed by the Commons because the queen intervened. On that day, in the presence of some of the Privy Council, she received Whitgift, three bishops and representatives of the Lower House of Convocation who came to tell her of a grant made by the clergy. She made a pointed comment on the fact that the clergy gave freely whereas the laity had to be entreated to give. She told the bishops that some in the Commons had made 'divers reproachful speeches' against them and that she understood these men had been countenanced by some of the Council 'which we

---

[1] J. Neale, *Elizabeth and her Parliaments*, II. 65–6.
[2] *Ibid.*, II. 66 ff.

will redress or else uncouncil some of them'.[1] Although some of the
Commons were rash and intemperate, she thought there were also
wise and discrete men among them who found just cause of grievance
against the bishops. She rebuked the bishops for not taking sufficient
care in choosing ministers. She went on: 'Again you suffer many
ministers to preach what they list and to minister the sacraments
according to their own fancies, some one way, some another, to the
breach of unity . . . ' She warned them: 'I wish such men to be
brought to conformity and unity: that they minister the sacraments
according to the order of this Realm and preach all one truth . . . '

The queen told the bishops not to show favour to those who would
not conform, out of pity or because of letters in their favour sent by
noblemen and gentlemen 'for they will be hanged before they will be
reformed'. She went on 'as for these curious and busy fellows, their
preaching tendeth only to popularity'. She told the bishops to look
to private conventicles, and she referred with sharpness to the bishop
of London 'who looketh no better unto the City, where every merchant must have his schoolmaster and nightly conventicle, expounding scriptures and catechizing their servants and maids: insomuch,
that I have heard how some of their maids have not sticked to control
(contradict) learned preachers and say that such a man taught otherwise in our house'.[2]

Elizabeth's attitude was thus as firm as it had ever been, and she
made it clear that she was behind Whitgift's policy of imposing uniformity. The speaker of the Commons was evidently given very definite instructions, for he reported to the House 'She knows—and
thinks you know—she is Supreme Governor of this Church, next
under God' with power in her own right as queen and by statutes to
reform disorders. She believed that some matters needed reform, but
parliament had been instructed not to meddle with them and they
must stop any further proceedings. The House was told 'she will receive no motion of innovation, nor alter or change any law whereby
the religion of Church of England standeth established at this day . . .'
She would deal with grievances, but complaints must be made in the
proper way—first to the bishop, then to the archbishop, then to the
Council, and finally, if no redress had been obtained, to the queen
herself.[3]

[1] J. Neale, *Elizabeth I and her Parliaments*, II. 69.   [2] *Ibid.*, II. 70–1.
[3] *Ibid*, II. 74, 75.

The Commons were thus confronted with the firm opposition of the queen. There was some discussion about whether they should defy her orders. They were in fact dealing at the time with three bills concerning religion—one requiring archbishops and bishops to take an oath of due obedience to the queen, another controlling fees in ecclesiastical courts and instructing bishops to make visitations in person and only 'upon just causes complained of', and a third permitting marriages to be celebrated at times when the canon law forbade it. On 1 March 1585 the queen instructed the Speaker not to allow any further readings of the bills.

The Commons did not make a grand gesture of defiance, as they might have done, by continuing to discuss the petitions about religious grievances or by going on with the three bills, but they did make a gesture of another kind in order to save their faces. They had 'the effrontery', as Professor Neale puts it, to bring in a bill for the better execution of a statute of the thirteenth year of Elizabeth regulating admission to the ministry. Since this concerned religion, they were in fact disobeying the queen's orders, but it could be argued that they were merely strengthening an existing law. The Speaker tried to hold up the measure, but parliamentary privilege was involved and the Commons insisted on passing the bill. The queen must have decided that it was not worth fighting on this particular issue. The bill was quietly killed in the Lords.

Thus Puritan propaganda and organisation had in fact achieved very little in the parliament of 1584–5. The Commons' actual demands had indeed been very moderate and they had not pressed them home in the face of the queen's determined opposition. What had been achieved was to draw the queen's attention very firmly to the fact that her Church was open to criticism on a number of matters—criticism which had the support of non-Puritans as well as of Puritans. In her closing speech she commented: 'Thus much I must say, that some faults and negligences may grow and be, as in all other great charges it happeneth . . . All which, if you, my Lords of the clergy, do not amend, I mean to depose you: look ye therefore well to your charges.'[1] Although she was willing to take action about genuine abuses, her basic policy was unchanged. She told them she minded not 'to animate Romanists . . . nor tolerate new fangledness'.

The Puritan opposition nevertheless battled on and continued, as

[1] J. Neale, *Elizabeth I and her Parliaments*, II. 99, 100.

always, to make effective use of the printing press, both legally and illegally. There was a brisk paper warfare. A small pamphlet, *The Unlawful Practises of Prelates*, published soon after Whitgift had become archbishop, stressed the view, which was not confined to Puritans, that the ecclesiastical authorities were in a number of ways acting illegally.[1] In 1584 Robert Waldegrave printed *A Briefe and Plaine Declaration concerning the desires of all those faithfull Ministers that have and do seeke for the Discipline and reformation of the Churche of Englande*. It attacked pluralism, non-residence, ignorant ministers and the lack of godly ministers, and it proposed that the government of the church should be in the hands of elders chosen by the people.[2] This had been written by William Fulke over ten years earlier but had not been published. Fulke had since changed his views, but his manuscript had fallen into Field's hands, and Field published it without the author's consent.[3] There also appeared from a printing press in Cambridge a reprint of Walter Travers' *Explicatio* in an English translation made in 1574 by Thomas Cartwright. Whitgift had it seized and burnt so that no copies now survive.[4]

It was of great help to the Puritan cause in the 1580's that it was able to make use of the service of Robert Waldegrave, a very courageous printer who was willing to take risks for the cause. In 1584 he also printed an anonymous *Dialogue concerning the Strife of Our Church* attacking the establishment,[5] and in 1585 he was imprisoned for nearly three months for printing *A Lamentable Complainte of the Commonalty* and other Puritan works.[6] In addition to illicit printing at home, Puritans, like Papists, were also able to get a good deal of literature published overseas.[7]

---

[1] William Pierce, *An Historical Introduction to the Marprelate* Tracts, 1908, p. 92; M. M. Knappen, *Tudor Puritanism*, chapter on 'The Alliance with the Lawyers 1583–85'. p. 265 ff.

[2] William Pierce, *op. cit.*, p. 135 ff.

[3] Patrick Collinson, 'John Field and Elizabethan Puritanism', p. 145.

[4] S. J. Knox, *Walter Travers*, p. 65. For the *Explicatio*, see p. 140.

[5] M. M. Knappen, *Tudor Puritanism*, p. 289.

[6] Patrick Collinson, *The Elizabethan Puritan Movement*, pp. 273–4. For Waldegrave, see W. J. Couper, *Robert Waldegrave King's Printer for Scotland*, Scottish Typographical Journal, Glasgow, 1916; William Pierce, *An Historical Introduction to the Marprelate Tracts*, p. 151 ff., and *infra*, p. 247 ff.

[7] See J. Dover Wilson, 'Richard Schilders and the English Puritans', *Transactions of the Bibliographical Society*, XI, 1909–11, pp. 65–134. Schilders was in London in 1567, probably as a religious refugee, and became a member of the Stationers' Company in 1568. He worked in England for some years but by 1580 he was settled in Middleburg.

The need to exercise more effective control over the printing presses must have become more and more obvious to the ecclesiastical authorities. The Privy Council's order against seditious books, issued in 1566,[1] was now supplemented by a much more rigorous Star Chamber decree of 23 June 1586.[2] It referred to the 'great enormities and abuses' which had of late 'more than in times past' been practised by printers and booksellers. The queen had therefore charged the archbishop of Canterbury and others of the Privy Council to take the necessary action. All existing and all future printing presses were to be registered with the Stationers' Company. Unregistered presses were to be rendered unserviceable. Printing presses were to be allowed only in London and the suburbs, apart from one in Cambridge and one in Oxford. They were not to be set up 'in any secret or obscure corner or place', and the wardens of the Stationers' company were to have ready access to them. No printer who had set up business in the last six months was to be allowed to continue, and no new printers were to be licensed 'till the excessive multitude of printers . . . be abated' and 'brought to so small a number of masters . . . being of ability and good behaviour as the archbishop of Canterbury and bishop of London . . . shall think . . . requisite and convenient . . . ' Provision was made for the selection of new printers in future by the Stationers' Company with the approval of the archbishop of Canterbury and the bishop of London. No book was to be printed unless it had first been examined by them. There were to be penalties for booksellers who sold unauthorised books. The number of apprentices and journeymen in the trade was limited. The Stationers' Company was to enforce the regulations and to destroy illegal presses.

Although the new regulations did not prevent illegal printing, they made more difficult and more dangerous the publication and distribution of unauthorised works and they put considerable powers into the hands of an archbishop who was a determined opponent of the Puritans. It is rather surprising that more drastic action had not been taken sooner. Possibly no one in the government was enthusiastic about regulations which would primarily affect Puritans.

Meanwhile, the critics of the establishment continued their work of collecting information designed to show the very unsatisfactory state of the clergy. As we have seen, they used some of their evidence

[1] G. E. Elton, *The Tudor Constitution*, p. 105.
[2] G. E. Elton, *op. cit.*, 179 ff.

in the parliament of 1584–5.[1] The advantage of this kind of activity was that it seriously damaged the reputation of the establishment, it received the support of 'godly ministers' of all shades of opinion, and it won sympathy from those laymen, both among the country gentry and in the towns, who took their religion seriously and who were active in appointing to livings and to lectureships educated preaching ministers.

A mass of evidence was thus collected in the 1580's from many parts of the country.[2] There does not seem to be much information about the number of people engaged in making these surveys or about who they were and how they set about their task. One feels that they were not impartial, that they were looking for evidence to support a case, and that they did not err on the side of charity. The surveys were presumably intended to shock the Elizabethans, and they make entertaining reading.[3] Thus, the Cornish Survey of 1586 reports on Mr. Fletcher of Mangan and Martin parish that he is 'a preacher sometimes', that he has another benefice, and that he is 'A man carelesse of his callinge and suspected of whoredome',[4] and of Mr. John Raulph of Wendon and Helston that 'He keepeth two leud readers in his charge, himself an Idle Ruffian'.[5] The Norfolk Survey reported of Mr. Smith of Redham that he was 'scarse able to read', of Mr. Jurdan of Old Buckenham that he was 'taken in adulterie, he was a bankrupt Baylie', and of Mr. Rust of Slowlie and Westwick that 'he was a worstead weaver, then a masse priest'.[6]

Although there was, no doubt, a good deal of prejudice and self-righteousness in the makers of the Surveys, many of their comments must have seemed very much to the point to contemporaries. Lord Burghley himself, in a memorandum written in 1584, had suggested the need for a general survey of the church, from the bishops downwards, in order to remove those who 'either for their manifest insufficiency or their corrupt and covetous conversation were out of credit with the

---

[1] See pp. 219–221.

[2] Patrick Collinson, 'The Puritan Classical Movement', p. 509 ff., states that we have the surveys, or parts of them, from Berkshire, Buckinghamshire, Cornwall, Essex, Lincolnshire, London, Middlesex, Oxfordshire, Surrey, Warwickshire and parts of Norfolk and Suffolk, and that there are references to them in Devon, Cambridgeshire, the Isle of Ely, Hertfordshire, Northamptonshire and probably Leicestershire.

[3] Some of the material is calendered in *The Seconde Parte of a Register*, edit. A. Peel, 1915, 2 vols.

[4] *The Seconde Parte of a Register*, II. 98.

[5] *Ibid.*, II. 98.   [6] *Ibid.*, II. 147, 149, 152.

people under their charge'. He thought that if conditions in the parishes were not reformed 'the people must needs be without knowledge of God' and 'easily led into errors or popery by any that will secretly resort to teach them'.[1] Standards were still very low in many parishes, and the income of the clergy was often so small that their calling could not attract able men. It is true that things were getting better in Elizabeth's reign and that the universities were producing educated and devout ministers, but a good many of the young men going from the universities to the parishes had been influenced to a greater or lesser degree by university Puritanism and were critics, not defenders, of the establishment. The colleges where Puritan influence was strong had been supplemented in 1584 as a result of the foundation by Sir Walter Mildmay of Emmanuel College, Cambridge, with the purpose of rendering 'as many as possible fit for the administration of the Divine Word and Sacraments; and that from this seed ground the English Church might have those she can summon to instruct the people and undertake the office of pastors, which is a thing necessary above all others'.[2]

The man primarily responsible for organising the collection of material for propaganda purposes was John Field. He had early in his career been an assistant to John Foxe the martyrologist, and Dr. Collinson suggests that he may have had in mind publishing a Puritan 'Book of Martyrs' based on a 'register of all acts and proceedings in his day'.[3] The work which he seems to have begun in his capacity of correspondent with sympathisers in many parts of the country received, as it were, official approval when a Puritan assembly in the winter of 1586 gave instructions that cases of oppression by the bishops and their officers should be 'registered and gathered'.[4] Bancroft said of him that he 'was a great and chiefe man among the brethren of London, and one to whome the managing of the discipline (for the outward practise of it) was especially (by the rest) committed. So as all the letters that were directed from the brethren of other places to have this or that referred to the London assemblies, were for the most part directed unto him.'[5]

[1] Conyers Read, *Lord Burghley and Queen Elizabeth*, pp. 293, 294.
[2] H. C. Porter, *Reformation and Reaction in Tudor Cambridge*, 238 ff.
[3] Patrick Collinson, 'John Field and Elizabethan Puritanism', pp. 146, 147.
[4] *Ibid.*, p. 146; R. G. Usher, *The Presbyterian Movement in the Reign of Queen Elizabeth*, p. 93.
[5] Richard Bancroft, *A Survey of the Pretended Holy Discipline* 1593, p. 369.

The task of gathering Puritan grievances was supplemented by an attempt to get an agreed programme among the Presbyterians. In this a very important part was played by Walter Travers, urged on by John Field. When the Master of the Temple died in August 1584, Travers made a determined effort to get appointed to this very influential position. Burghley supported him, but Whitgift was not prepared to approve unless Travers would subscribe to the articles and prove that he had been ordained according to the rites of the Church of England.[1] Travers maintained that his ordination was valid, and he was not willing to be re-ordained. In the end the appointment went in March 1585 to Richard Hooker. There followed a famous controversy between Hooker and Travers, who still retained his Readership in the Temple. As Fuller put it later, 'the pulpit spake pure Canterbury in the morning and Geneva in the afternoon'. Travers even tried to persuade Hooker not to preach his first sermon until Travers had given notice of him to the congregation 'so that their allowance might seal my calling'.[2] The purpose of this was to indicate that the minister had to be 'called' by the congregation. In a series of sermons Hooker and Travers joined issue on a number of important theological questions, including the meaning of predestination and the rôle of reason in determining man's religious beliefs and practises. Later they both published their views. In March 1568 Whitgift deprived Travers of his licence to preach, and when Travers tried to get it back, Whitgift insisted on the need for him to be ordained according to the rites of the Church of England.[3]

While he was still at the Temple, Travers was being pressed to prepare an agreed Presbyterian programme. From 1585 he was able to count on the help and advice of Thomas Cartwright who returned to England in April after an absence of eleven years.[4] Cartwright was imprisoned for a few days, but owing to Burghley's influence he was soon set free.[5] Leicester wrote to Whitgift in July 1585 asking him to licence Cartwright to preach, but Whitgift refused to do so 'until he might be better persuaded of his conformity'.[6] Cartwright was

---

[1] Travers had been 'called to the ministry' according to Genevan rites in Antwerp in 1578.
[2] S. J. Knox, *Walter Travers*, p. 72.
[3] S. J. Knox, *op. cit.*, p. 81.
[4] A. F. Scott Pearson, *Thomas Cartwright*, p. 229.
[5] *Ibid.*, p. 233.
[6] V. J. K. Brook, *Whitgift and the English Church*, pp. 103, 104.

appointed Master of the new hospital which the earl of Leicester had established at Warwick.[1]

Travers' biographer maintains that 'From 1585, onwards, Cartwright and Travers appear as the two chief leaders of the [Presbyterian] movement, the latter being engaged on its literary side of the work, while the former acted as organiser from his headquarters in Warwick . . . '[2] This is rather misleading since it does less than justice to John Field, the most active and most able leader of the three, and it does not take into account the anxiety of Cartwright not to fall foul of the authorities in the Church. Moreover, Travers seems to have proceeded very slowly in the urgent task of drawing up an agreed Presbyterian programme.

The basis of the work was possibly 'the book' which Dr. Turner had presented to parliament in 1584.[3] The Puritan conference which had met in London during the session of parliament had considered a 'Book of Discipline' and found some imperfections in it. It seems likely that it had asked Travers to prepare a revised work.[4] In July 1585 Field told Travers that he wanted it 'read over with as much speed as could be', so that instructions could be given to local conferences to put it into practice.[5] In September 1585 Gellibrand, the secretary of the Oxford group, wrote to Travers: 'I pray you haste the forme of Discipline and send it',[6] but in January 1586 it was still not ready, and Gellibrand was still asking Field to send him the Discipline 'which Master Travers promised to make perfect, when it is finished'. He added: 'We will put it in practice and try men's minds therein as we may'.[7]

The intention of the Presbyterians at this stage was to get an agreed programme and to begin to put it into practice where they were able to do so without waiting for parliamentary authority. As Dr. Collinson puts it, their aim was 'To "erect discipline" that is, to set up pres-

[1] Cartwright's controversy with the separatist, Robert Browne, had made him a good deal more conservative. He was now stressing his loyalty to the established church. He was still a Presbyterian but he hoped to reform the church by gradual and constitutional means, and he was not anxious to go on his travels again. See A. F. Scott Pearson, *Thomas Cartwright*, pp. 222, 231.

[2] S. J. Knox, *Walter Travers*, p. 98.

[3] Patrick Collinson, 'John Field and Elizabethan Puritanism', p. 156. See p. 220.

[4] S. J. Knox, *Walter Travers*, p. 96.

[5] *Ibid.*, p. 99; Patrick Collinson, 'John Field and Elizabethan Puritanism', p. 156.

[6] S. J. Knox, *Walter Travers*, pp. 99–100.

[7] Patrick Collinson, 'John Field and Elizabethan Puritanism', p. 157.

byterian church government secretly, within the Church of England'.[1] Cartwright supported this policy and wrote: 'That if the Cyvill maiestrate . . . shall refuse to admytt of the desired discypline that then the mynisters may allure the people unto ytt and for their owne partes not only may putt the same in practise as they maye themselves but likewyse use all other meanes of the better acceptance or establishinge of ytt'.[2]

In fact, Travers' eagerly awaited revision of the Book of Discipline was not ready until early in 1587, although draft versions were circulating for discussion and comment some time before then.[3]

Meanwhile, Whitgift was making an effort to counteract the general criticism of the church by removing some of the causes of complaint. Articles passed by Convocation in 1585 and confirmed by the queen on 31 March provided for stricter standards for candidates for ordination. Bishops who did not keep to them were to lose the right to ordain for two years. The Articles attempted to prevent abuses in excommunication and in marriages by licence. Ministers might hold more than one living only if the livings were not more than thirty miles apart and if a suitable curate was provided. The fees in church courts were not to exceed what they had been in 1559. As soon as possible, and not later than one year after the issue of these articles, bishops were to report on the morals and learning of the clergy in their dioceses. An attempt was also made to make the clergy study the Bible and to improve their educational standards by writing essays under supervision. A genuine effort was being made, as Mr. Brook points out, to meet the Puritan complaints.[4]

Whitgift also seems to have been relaxing a little his drive against nonconformists and to have been concentrating only on 'really tiresome puritan ministers'.[5] It may be that he now felt strong enough to adopt a more lenient policy towards minor offenders. There is also a possibility that he had realised the danger of taking on too much at

---

[1] Patrick Collinson, *op. cit.* p. 155. Dr. Collinson has shown that a great deal could be done by ministers, patrons and others to assist in the growth of Presbyterian practices in places where they had influence. See Patrick Collinson, *The Elizabethan Puritan Movement*, p. 333 ff. 'Presbytery in Episcopacy'.

[2] S. J. Knox, *Walter Travers*, p. 98.

[3] M. M. Knappen, *Tudor Puritanism*, p. 285. For the authorship of the Book of Discipline see Patrick Collinson, *The Elizabethan Puritan Movement*, p. 294 ff.

[4] Edward Cardwell, *Synodalia* I. 139 ff; J. Strype, *Life and Acts of John Whitgift* III. 145; V. J. K. Brook, *John Whitgift and the English Church*, p. 99.

[5] V. J. K. Brook, *John Whitgift and the English Church*, p. 103.

Q

once and that he saw the advisability of attacking only the ring-leaders. Mr. Brook thinks that in spite of the violent charges of his opponents, he was really a man of peace not anxious to drive the Puritans to extremes by unnecessary provocation and that there was no vindictiveness in him.[1] Whatever his motives may have been, he agreed, at a date which cannot be definitely fixed, to a conference with the Puritans. It seems to have taken place some time between 1584 and 1586. The suggestion came from the earl of Leicester and the conference was held at Lambeth in the presence of Leicester himself, Lord Grey and Sir Francis Walsingham. Burghley was also present part of the time. Whitgift and the bishop of Winchester argued their case against two Puritan ministers, Walter Travers and Dr. Thomas Sparke, on the question of 'things needful to be reformed in the Book of Common Prayer'.[2] Although no agreement was reached, Whitgift in 1585 accepted Walsingham's advice not to suspend or deprive existing incumbents of benefices if they gave a written undertaking to use the Book of Common Prayer according to the usage and laws of the Church. Subscription to the articles was to be required only of those enterings into livings for the first time.[3] It was presumably as a result of adopting this policy that in his visitation articles for the diocese of Chichester in 1585 Whitgift did not enquire whether ministers had subscribed to the three articles of 1583, and asked instead whether they used the Prayer Book services and whether they had spoken against the book or against the Thirty Nine Articles.[4]

At the end of 1586 parliament met again, and once more the Puritans made a determined effort to achieve some of their objectives. They now had ready evidence about the state of the ministry from at least thirteen counties, and summaries of the evidence had been prepared and attached to a great 'General Supplication'.[5] The Puritans did what they could to influence the elections and they prepared petitions concerning suspended or deprived ministers. It seems probable that a general conference met in London in November 1586 at

[1] V. J. K. Brook, *op. cit.*, p. 103.
[2] S. J. Knox, *Walter Travers*, p. 64; V. J. K. Brook, *John Whitgift and the English Church*, p. 104; M. M. Knappen, *Tudor Puritanism*, pp. 279, 280.
[3] J. Strype, *The Life and Acts of John Whitgift*, I. 430–3; M. M. Knappen, *Tudor Puritanism*, p. 280.
[4] V. J. K. Brook, *John Whitgift and the English Church*, p. 105; J. Strype, *Life and Acts of John Whitgift*, I. 462 ff.
[5] Patrick Collinson, 'John Field and Elizabethan Puritanism', p. 158.

the time of the parliament, and there was certainly a meeting in February 1587 when 'many of our godly brethren and fellow labourers' were assembled in the capital.[1]

It seems that under cover of this general barrage of complaints the Presbyterian leaders hoped to bring their Genevan 'Form of Prayer' once more before Parliament as an alternative to the Book of Common Prayer, and that the conference of 'godly brethren' was in contact, probably through Field, with a small group of M.P.s, including Peter Wentworth, Cope and Lewkenor who met together 'before the Parliament'.[2]

The official attitude to all this agitation was made plain from the start by the Speaker who told the House: 'Specially you are commanded by her Majestie to take heed, that none care be given or time afforded the werysome sollicitation of those that commonly be called Puritans, wherewithall the late Parliaments have been exceedingly importuned: which sort of men, whilest (in the gyddinesse of their spirits) they labour and strive to advance a new Eldership, they do nothing else but disturbe the good people of the Church and Common Wealth; which is as well grounded for the body of Religion it selfe, and as well guided for the Discipline as any Realme that professeth the Truth.'[3]

The House was initially very much preoccupied with dealing with Mary Queen of Scots, but on 27 February 1587 Anthony Cope offered to the members 'a bill and a book'. The bill had a preamble which surveyed the whole history of the English Reformation. Henry VIII had done well, and Edward VI had worked worthily. Elizabeth had been compelled at first simply to revive the reforms of her father and brother, but now the light of the gospel had increased and had revealed the imperfections of the Prayer Book. The Church of England was contrasted with the perfect Presbyterian church 'approved by the general judgment and practice of all the best-reformed Churches'. The bill proposed the use of the annexed book, which was a revised Genevan Prayer Book incorporating a scheme of Presbyterian government of the church, and it made utterly void all existing laws, customs, statutes, ordinances and constitutions concerning the Church.[4]

[1] J. Neale, *Elizabeth I and her Parliaments*, II. 147–8; Patrick Collinson, 'John Field and Elizabethan Puritanism', p. 158.
[2] J. Neale, *op. cit.* II. 148; Patrick Collinson, 'The Puritan Classical Movement', p. 569.
[3] Patrick Collinson, 'The Puritan Classical Movement', p. 561.
[4] J. Neale, *Elizabeth I and her Parliaments*, II. 148, 149.

It is difficult to believe that Cope and the little group which supported him seriously expected to carry through a bill which completely destroyed the established church. It seems more likely that what they aimed at was maximum publicity for their views. The Speaker tried right away to kill the proposal, but Cope, no doubt by previous arrangement, was supported by a little group of M.P.s who called for the bill to be read in spite of some opposition. Job Throckmorton made a tremendous speech in support of the proposal to read the bill. He said bitterly, 'To bewail the distresses of God's children, it is puritanism. To banish an adulterer out of the house, it is puritanism. To make humble suit to her Majesty and the High Court of Parliament for a learned ministry, it is puritanism ... I fear me we shall come shortly to this, that to do God and her Majesty good service shall be counted puritanism ... ' He urged members to open their ears to the lamentable cries of poor distressed souls, adding: 'And it may be some of them stand now at your door, thirsting for relief.'[1] The House listened to the speeches, but as it was by now very late it agreed that the bill should be read the next day. The queen acted at once. She sent for the bill and the book, and also for the bill and book which Dr. Turner had tried to introduce in 1585. The Speaker informed the House of what had happened, but, unabashed, the M.P.s proceeded to debate the state of the church, and the member for Carmarthen presented a petition on behalf of Wales written by a young Welsh preacher John Penry. Richard Topcliffe[2] asked that everyone should hand in a note on the disorders of the church in his own district, and Peter Wentworth made a famous speech on the right of the House to discuss and act in matters of religion.[3] As Professor Neale puts it, 'through the plottings of the godly brotherhood and their organised group of Parliamentary agents, Queen Elizabeth was menaced with revolution in Church and State'.[4] Once again, she took action. Cope, Wentworth, Lewkenor and two others were sent to the Tower. This did not deter Sir John Higham, a keen Puritan, from speaking on 4 March about the sad state of religion in his own county and asking the House to petition the queen for the release of the imprisoned members.[5]

[1] J. Neale, *Elizabeth I and her Parliaments*, II. 151.
[2] Topcliffe is, of course, best remembered for his sadistic persecution of Papists. He was a cruel, lustful and greedy man, but in addition he may have had in full measure the Puritan's intense and genuine hatred of popery.
[3] J. Neale, *Elizabeth I and her Parliaments*, II. 153 ff.
[4] J. Neale, *op. cit.* II. 156.   [5] J. Neale, *op. cit.*, II. 158 ff.

An official counter-attack was now launched by a number of government spokesmen, including Mildmay, Egerton and Hatton. Hatton showed the M.P.s the real nature of the bill which they had so readily agreed to have read. He put to them the stark question: 'Will you alter the whole form and order of your church service?' Did they really wish to replace it with something in which 'all or the most part is left for the minister's spirit?' The proposed bill would affect their financial interests in church livings and 'toucheth us all in our inheritance'. Every parish would have to support at least a pastor, a doctor and two deacons. Where was the money to come from? Bishops' lands and cathedral churches would be despoiled, but it would not stop there—'... we are bound to surrender ... our Abbey lands and such other possessions as have at any time belonged to the Church'. He concluded: 'Out of my heart, I think the honest zealous gentleman of this House (Cope) hath been slily led into this action.'[1] Mildmay and Egerton underlined Hatton's scathing denunciation of the bill, and at the end there must surely have been a good many members who felt that they had been 'slily led into this action'. There must have been many, also, who were concerned about the financial implications, for Puritan laymen, anxious for higher standards of education in the clergy and the end of pluralism, showed on a number of occasions during Elizabeth's reign that they were not ready to pay the price if it had to come out of the wealth which they had taken from the church.

The queen's determined attitude, the reasoned case put against the bill and, possibly, the realisation that they had been led by the nose by a small group of members, no doubt help to explain the feeble reactions of the House. Dr. Turner courageously moved that the House request the queen to free the imprisoned members. Sir John Higham moved for alterations in some of the things to which the clergy were required to swear, and for steps to be taken to provide a learned ministry. A committee was set up and it is possible that a petition of some sort was presented, but nothing came of all this, and the whole business quietly fizzled out.[2]

The sheer courage and effrontery of the Presbyterian group, combined with the propaganda put out by Puritans with very different

---

[1] J. Neale, *op. cit.* II. 158 ff. For Bancroft's part in preparing Hatton's case, see Patrick Collinson, *The Elizabethan Puritan Movement*, p. 313 ff.

[2] J. Neale, *op. cit.*, II. 162–3.

objectives from the Presbyterians, have possibly led to undue stress being placed on what was attempted in the parliament of 1586–7. The House had, it is true, given leave for Cope's bill and book to be read, but it seems to have done so without knowing much about their contents. Dr. Collinson, commenting on the queen's action in confiscating the bill and book and imprisoning the M.P.s, remarks: 'These events proved once and for all that, so long as Elizabeth lived, the most masterly tactics which Field and his parliamentary friends could devise would not achieve the establishment of presbyterianism by public authority',[1] but it was not merely the opposition of the queen that defeated these efforts. It was also the fact that the M.P.s who were ready to listen to general Puritan grievances had no enthusiasm for Presbyterianism.

It was possibly about the time of this second parliamentary defeat that Field told a wavering brother: 'Tush, Mr. Edmunds, hold your peace. Seeing we cannot compass these things by suit nor dispute, it is the multitude and people that must bring the discipline to pass which we desire.' If Presbyterianism could not be imposed by law, it could to some extent by practised in secret by its adherents.[2] An agreed programme was more than ever necessary.

Travers had been slow in producing the Book of Discipline which was intended to be the new textbook of English Presbyterians.[3] The long-awaited work was entitled *Disciplina Ecclesiae Sacra ex Dei Verbo Descripta*. It was not printed at the time, and only five manuscript copies have survived.[4] Presumably a large number of copies were made, for they were sent to the *classes* for examination, discussion and subscription. The Dedham *classis* received a copy on 8 March 1587.

The *Disciplina Ecclesiae* was in two parts. The first affirmed that Christ had fixed the form of church government for all time and that this was to be found in the Bible. All ministers were of equal status. After being 'called' by a particular congregation, they were to be ordained to the Ministry of the Word. In each congregation there were to be four officers—minister, teacher or doctor, elder and deacon. Ministers were to preach and administer the sacraments,

---

[1] Patrick Collinson, 'John Field and Elizabethan Puritanism', p. 159.

[2] *Ibid.*, p. 159.

[3] The reasons for the delay are examined in Patrick Collinson, *The Elizabethan Puritan Movement*, p. 296 ff.

[4] S. J. Knox, *Walter Travers*, p. 101; Patrick Collinson, p. 297 ff. *op. cit.*

teachers were to deal with doctrine, elders were to help govern the church, and deacons were to care for the poor. Each church was to have its presbytery, consisting of ministers, teachers and those chosen as elders. They governed the church and could excommunicate members with the approval of the congregation. All this was alleged to be based on the authority of scripture. In addition, in the second part of the work there was outlined a scheme of conferences, provincial synods and national synods. This did not claim to be scriptural but was said to be based on 'the use of the churches'. There were directions about the constitution and powers of these various assemblies, including the *classis*; the provincial synod, which was to have 2 ministers and 2 elders from each of its 24 constituent *classes;* and national synods which were to be called when required. No individual church had power over another, but all should obey the sentence of the majority on any point if it was agreeable to the Word of God.[1]

The scheme which Travers and others had so laboriously worked out was not strict Presbyterianism of the type found in Geneva or in Scotland. It was an English adaptation drawn from a number of sources. It has been described as 'frankly congregational',[2] but it was also strongly tinged with Presbyterianism. The hope was that it would receive approval from the various assemblies and conference throughout the country. They were asked to accept it 'as agreeable to God's Word', to work for its establishment by petitions to the queen and parliament, to advance it 'by other lawful and convenient means', and to practise it in so far as the law of the land and the peace of the Church allowed. Ministers were to observe the discipline, to meet every six weeks in local *classes* of not more than 10 members each, to hold half-yearly provincial synods, and to attend national assemblies in parliament time and on other necessary occasions.[3]

Here then was a programme of action. Its implementation would depend on whether it could command general support and on how strong and widespread the Presbyterian classical movement was in England at this time.[4]

---

[1] S. J. Knox, *Walter Travers*, p. 101; V. J. K. Brook, *John Whitgift and the English Church*, pp. 115, 116.

[2] V. J. K. Brook, *op. cit.*, p. 115.

[3] Patrick Collinson, 'John Field and Elizabethan Puritanism', p. 157.

[4] See Patrick Collinson, 'The Puritan Classical Movement', p. 610 ff., for an examination of the evidence. The summary given here is largely based on his detailed investigation.

One point which emerges from Dr. Collinson's very thorough examination is that there were considerable areas of the country for which no evidence has yet been produced that Puritanism existed on a sufficient scale to imply organisation. This appears to be true of Wales, much of the northern province, Berkshire, Derbyshire, Dorset, Gloucestershire, Hampshire, Stafforshire, Wiltshire and Worcestershire.

A second point which Dr. Collinson stresses is that even in those counties which are traditionally associated with Puritanism, the Puritan ministers were often concentrated in pockets within the county and were not spread evenly over the whole area. Thus, in Northamptonshire, Leicestershire, Warwickshire and Oxfordshire there were a number of concentrations, as for example, on the eastern borders of Warwickshire, the western borders of Northamptonshire and the northern borders of Oxfordshire. In East Anglia, there were pockets in south-west Suffolk and in north-east and south-east Essex, whereas east Suffolk and west Essex were on the whole not Puritan.

A third point is that the organisations found in a number of places were very loose organisations and may well have been meetings for 'exercises' and prayers rather than self-conscious Presbyterian *classes*. The synods which met in London in 1586–7 and in Cambridge in 1587 tried to impose organisation and to mould into shape a mixed collection of existing groups of ministers.[1] It is difficult to say how far they succeeded. For a great many of these 'conferences' or 'classes' we have little or no evidence about how they were organised or what exactly they did.

There is evidence of 'classical' organisation in Northamptonshire which was apparently divided into three groups, one around Northampton, one around Daventry, and a third around Kettering. In Warwickshire there were synods, but little is known about them. In Essex there was the famous Dedham *classis*. Another existed at Braintree, and there were probably *classes* at Colchester and Maldon. There is a possibility that there were two more in other parts of the county. Suffolk probably had three. Dr. Collinson thinks that they almost certainly existed in the west country, where the earl of Bedford used his influence to protect Puritans, and where there is evidence of Puritan strength on the Devon–Cornwall border. He points out, how-

---

[1] In 1587 general conferences seem to have been held in London, in Oxford and in Cambridge. Patrick Collinson, *The Elizabethan Puritan Movement*, p. 320 ff.

ever, that Norfolk and Leicestershire are conspicuously absent from the national conferences and from Field's letters. Only the groups in London, Oxford, Cambridge, Essex, Suffolk, Northamptonshire and Warwickshire were regularly active in the national movement.[1]

Dr. Collinson's detailed investigation seems to reduce considerably the importance of the Presbyterian classical movement as a nation-wide organisation of conferences pursuing a definite and uniform programme. The strength and the numbers of the Presbyterian groups appear to have been exaggerated, but nevertheless they existed to an extent that justifies us in regarding them as a 'shadow church' within the Church of England working to obtain legal sanctions for a 'take-over'. When they failed to get parliamentary support, they tried to put some of their ideas into practice quietly and without formal authorisation in those places where they were strong enough to do so.

There was always the danger that they might form a break-away movement. Dr. Collinson points out that Bancroft in his *Dangerous Positions*[2] produced impressive evidence that the Puritans of the Classical movement regarded themselves as a distinct fellowship, a 'gathered church' of the godly, divided from the rest of the Church of England.[3] He believes that an important General Meeting held in Cambridge in September 1587 'came within a hair's breadth of advocating separatism, when it decided to refer to the conferences and to other reformed churches overseas the motions that the brethren should cease to communicate with unlearned ministers, should withhold recognition from the bishops and repudiate the unlawful episcopal discipline, and should base their ministries on the true presbyterian discipline'.[4] A synod in Warwickshire in 1588 ruled that the faithful should not communicate with unlearned ministers, that the godly should not be ordained by them or accept deprivation by them unless compelled to do so by force, that 'men of better understanding' should be persuaded to accept the discipline and practise it 'so far as they shall be well able, with the peace of the Church'.[5]

The danger of a large-scale separatist movement was in fact much less than might appear. Some of the Presbyterians toyed with the idea of separating from the Church of England and in some degree they

[1] Patrick Collinson, 'The Puritan Classical Movement', pp. 634–5. [2] See pp. 314–315.
[3] Patrick Collinson, 'The Puritan Classical Movement', p. 606.
[4] Patrick Collinson, 'John Field and Elizabethan Puritanism', pp. 159, 160; J. Strype, *Annals of the Reformation*, III. Part III. 4777–9.
[5] Patrick Collinson, 'John Field and Elizabethan Puritanism', p. 160.

were separatist in practice, but they were not in the last resort prepared to break away from the establishment which they hoped to reform.[1]

Moreover, the attempt to get the conferences to accept and subscribe to the *Book of Discipline* made it plain that there were serious divisions about objects and methods. There were differences of opinion about whether the Book was in fact in harmony with the teaching of scripture and, still more, there was concern as to whether it could be used without endangering 'the peace of the church'.[2] At a meeting of 17 delegates at Cambridge in September 1587 when Field, Cartwright and other prominent leaders were present, doubts were expressed about parts of the Book, and as a number of conferences had not replied to an enquiry whether they would subscribe, the matter was referred to the next meeting.[3] The Dedham *classis* showed continual reluctance to commit itself.[4] At a provincial synod at Coventry in April 1588, Cartwright and eleven others subscribed, but on the understanding that the only parts to be put into practice were those concerned with preaching and meetings conformable to the peace of the church and the laws of the realm.[5] Even in London there were doubts about whether the Discipline could be put into practice.[6] Revision was still going on at assemblies which met in London and in Cambridge in 1589.[7] The Book was not printed, although the Cambridge assembly of 1587 had decided that it should be.

John Field died in March 1588. The national movement to which he had given such brilliant and forceful leadership had already failed. Walter Travers who succeeded him as the London corresponding secretary was not the kind of man to rally the failing ranks of the

---

[1] There were, of course, genuine separatists in the 1580's who decided they could no longer remain in the Church. They included Robert Browne and Robert Harrison, John Greenwood and Henry Barrow. Although they are of great interest, their numbers were small and they were outside the main stream of Elizabethan Puritanism. These separatists can more conveniently be considered later. See p. 304 ff.

[2] M. M. Knappen; *Tudor Puritanism*, p. 293–4; J. Strype, *Annals of the Reformation*, III. 692.

[3] Patrick Collinson, 'John Field and Elizabethan Puritanism', pp. 157–8; S. J. Knox, *Walter Travers*, pp. 111, 112.

[4] R. G. Usher, *The Presbyterian Movement in the Reign of Queen Elizabeth*, pp. 63, 65, 66; Patrick Collinson, *The Elizabethan Puritan Movement*, p. 318 ff.

[5] S. J. Knox, *Walter Travers*, p. 113.

[6] *Ibid.*, pp. 113, 114.

[7] Patrick Collinson, 'John Field and Elizabethan Puritanism', p. 158.

Presbyterians. The last synod met in September 1589, but characteristically it could not agree about the Book of Discipline.[1]

John Field has been described as 'one of the most brilliant revolutionaries in an age of revolution',[2] but it seems clear that there could not have been a Presbyterian revolution in Elizabethan England for there were too few Presbyterians and most of them were not revolutionaries.[3] What made the movement appear so formidable in the 1580's was its effective organisation, and, still more, the fact that it was able to exploit for its own purposes the undoubted weaknesses in the Church, so that it secured the sympathy of a considerable number of people who were not Presbyterians but who wanted reform.

Although the organised Presbyterian movement failed, there were plenty of opportunities for ministers and laymen with Presbyterian sympathies to indulge in various practices associated with Presbyterianism, to make arrangements for a minister to be 'called' by the parishioners even though he had to be ordained by a bishop, to impose some sort of 'discipline' in their parishes, to consult the local 'classis' in the matter of appointments, to establish in some towns 'promising small Genevas' in which Puritan lecturers and town councillors worked together to maintain godliness. It was possible in a few places to introduce elders under the guise of churchwardens and to use forms of worship which were considerably influenced by Calvinist and Presbyterian ideas.[4] Here the rôle of the lay patron, the nobleman, the gentleman and the town councillor, was of considerable importance, and the existence of this powerful lay support means that English Presbyterianism cannot be dismissed simply as a clerical movement. Nevertheless, in spite of lay support the movement failed in its major objective of establishing by open or secret means an alternative form of church government to that of diocesan episcopacy.

The Puritan effort in the last parliament of the 1580's was on a much more modest scale than in the earlier parliaments. The heart seemed to have gone out of the movement. Parliament had been called for 12 November 1588, but it was prorogued until 4 February

---

[1] S. J. Knox, *op. cit.*, p. 117.

[2] Patrick Collinson, 'John Field and Elizabethan Puritanism', p. 162.

[3] See Patrick Collinson, 'The Puritan Classical Movement', p. 698 ff., for an examination of the weaknesses inherent in English Presbyterianism.

[4] See Patrick Collinson, *The Elizabethan Puritan Movement*, Part 7, 'Presbytery in Episcopacy', pp. 333–82, for an examination of the ways in which Presbyterian and semi-presbyterian practices were introduced into the establishment.

1589. The Lord Chancellor's opening speech dealt primarily with the Papists,[1] but in the course of it he switched his attention for a time to the Puritans. He said that the queen expected the Papists to rage and rail but that she was very grieved 'that there are divers, of latter days risen up, even among her friends, who, being men of a very intemperate humour, do greatly deprave the present estate and reformation of religion, so hardly attained to, and with such her danger continued and preserved; whereby her loving subjects are greatly disquieted, her enemies are encouraged, religion is slandered, piety is hindered, schisms are maintained, and the peace of the Church is altogether rent in sunder and violated'. The queen knew that their platforms and devices were absurd, that they tended to intolerable innovation, that they aimed at an intolerable tyranny and that they were dangerous to all good Christian government. The M.P.s were told that the queen asked them, and as their Prince did 'most straitly charge and command you, upon your allegiance' not to meddle with religion unless it be 'to bridle all those, whether Papists or Puritans, which are therewithal discontented'. She assured them that when better opportunity and occasion required, order would be taken for reformation.[2]

The Puritan sympathisers in this Parliament must have been well aware that they must proceed cautiously. Since October 1588 the Martin Marprelate tracts had been appearing and causing a sensation.[3] Bancroft in a celebrated sermon on 9 February 1589 had already launched a counter-attack on Puritanism as a subversive and revolutionary movement.[4] The Puritan sympathisers were not anxious to play with fire too much. The shadow of earlier defeats lay over them, and they had lost by death their ablest leader, John Field, and their greatest patron, the earl of Leicester. They fought now on a much more limited front, concentrating, under the guidance of the lawyers, on the legal weaknesses in the conduct of the church leaders.[5] Thus on 25 February 1589 a young lawyer, Humphrey Davenport, asked for an examination of the methods being used by the ecclesiastical authorities.[6] The government spokesmen intervened quickly to

---

[1] See p. 203. [2] J. Neale, *Elizabeth I and her Parliaments*, II. 198–9.
[3] *Infra*, p. 244. [4] *Infra*, p. 250 ff.
[5] It seems that the Midland Puritans wanted to adopt a militant policy but that Travers and the London group were much more cautious. Patrick Collinson, *The Elizabethan Puritan Movement*, p. 397 ff.
[6] J. Neale, *Elizabeth I and her Parliaments*, II. 222.

remind the House that the queen had prohibited discussion of religious matters. Davenport then produced a document asking, it seems, for a conference of the Lords and Commons in the presence of the bishops and the judges to examine the abuses committed by the bishops and the ecclesiastical commissioners against the Word of God and the liberties of England.[1] The alleged abuses included the *ex officio* oath, the silencing of ministers who would not subscribe to Whitgift's articles, and imprisonment for trivial offences. The document asked for a measure of toleration for Puritan nonconformist practises. Although at one point it raised the question 'whether the desire of a further and better reformation in the Church of England, in dutiful manner, be not warranted by the word of God and law of England', it was in the main a fairly moderate constitutional approach concentrating on the legal issues. The matter was not pressed in the Commons, and although those sponsoring the document had a meeting with Whitgift, they got no help from him.[2]

In spite of the queen's prohibition another young lawyer, Henry Apsley, raised on 27 February 1589 the question of pluralities and non-residence. He offered a bill to remedy the abuses. The Commons took up the idea, and a bill was passed rapidly through all its stages and was sent to the Lords. It laid down the principle of one man, one benefice (with some exceptions), and in general it made residence obligatory. Burghley supported the first reading in the Lords, but Whitgift pointed out the difficulties, alleging that there were 9,000 benefices of which 10 per cent were insufficient in themselves to maintain even 'a mean person' and that less than 5 per cent were worth more than £30 a year clear of all charges. The bill got no further, and it seems that it was stopped by the queen.[3]

There was more trouble in the Commons on 3 March when, we are told, 'Divers articles are preferred unto the Nether House for reformation of the Book of Common Prayer and such like matters; but the Speaker dare not read them'.[4] In the last days of the session there was apparently a proposal to petition the queen about the bishops' proceedings against Puritan ministers and to request that 'by a preaching ministry all the people of your kingdom may be taught to obey and serve your Highness'. The queen was to be asked to allow 'a Christian and peaceable toleration, not contrary to the law' and it

---

[1] J. Neale, *op. cit.*, II. 222–3.
[2] *Ibid.*, II. 224 ff.
[3] J. Neale, *op. cit.*, II. 224 ff.
[4] *Ibid.*, II. 231.

was argued that the bishops had agreed 'that the disagreement between them and many good and learned ministers is not in any substance of doctrine, but only in some ceremonies and indifferent things,
whereto the Apostle teacheth that every man's conscience is not to be
forced . . . '[1]

It is not clear whether the petition was actually presented, and Professor Neale thinks that it was possibly embodied by the Speaker in
his closing speech at the end of the session.[2] The official attitude was
made plain in the Lord Chancellor's closing speech on 29 March 1589
in which 'For the service of God and preservation of His holy religion
among us, his Lordship did with great zeal reprehend the fanatical
humour of the Precisian and the Puritan, most impure' and informed the parliament of 'her Majesty's benign inclination, in love
of the peace of Christs Church, to suppress them, and her clemency
not to persecute them . . . '[3] The Puritans might feel that this was a
distinction without a difference.

While the members of the Commons were making their cautious
and limited criticism of abuses in the Church, a much more vigorous
assault was being delivered in the Martin Marprelate tracts. The
violent tone of these pamphlets, their vigorous and often crude
humour at the expense of the bishops, the mystery of who wrote them
and the fascinating circumstances concerning their production by
secret presses have combined to make them appear more important
than they really were in relation to the total Puritan effort of the
1580's.

The first of the Marprelate tracts appeared about October 1588. It
is known as the *Epistle* and it was dedicated to 'the right puisante and
terrible Priests my cleargie masters of the Confocation-house whether
sickers generall worshipfull Paltripolitans or any other of the holy
league of subscription . . . '[4] It was stated to have been written by
Martin Marprelate gentleman and to have been printed oversea in
Europe within two furlongs of a Bounsing Priest.

The pamphlet was in part a comment on an officially inspired work
of some 1,400 pages by Dr. John Bridges, Dean of Sarum, entitled

---

[1] J. Neale, *op. cit.*, II. 237.   [2] *Ibid.*, II. 236–7.   [3] *Ibid.* II. 238.
[4] For the Marprelate literature, see William Pierce, *An Historical Introduction to the
Marprelate Tracts*, 1908; Edward Arber, *An Introductory Sketch to the Martin Marpre-
late Controversy*, 1879. A number of the tracts were reprinted in London 1843–5. *The
Epistle* was reprinted by Edward Arber in 1880 (The English Scholar's Library, No. 11).
In 1911 an annotated edition was produced by William Pierce.

A Defence of the Government Established in the Church of Englande for Ecclesiasticall Matters. It attacked the bishops for exercising authority not granted by God's ordinance. It asserted that ' . . . our L(ord) bishopps . . . as Iohn of Canterburie, Thomas of Winchester (I will spare Iohn of London for this time, for it may be he is at boules, and it is a pitie to trouble my good brother, lest he should sweare to bold) my reverend prelate of Litchfielde, with the rest of that swinish rabble, are pettie Antichrists, pettie popes, proud prelates, intollerable withstanders of reformation, enemies of the gospell, and most covetous wretched priests'. The authority which the bishops claimed was accounted anti-Christian by most of the churches in the world such as those in Switzerland, Scotland, France, Bohemia, the Low Countries, Denmark, the Palatinate, Saxony and Suabia. The writer demanded of the bishops that they should 'let the gospell have a free course, and restore unto their former libertie in preaching all the preachers that you have put to silence . . . '

Commenting on a sermon by the bishop of Gloucester to the effect that 'there had not been since the Apostles time, such a flourishing estate of a Church, as we have now in England', Martin asks: 'Is it any marvaile that we have so many swine, dumbe dogs, non residents, with their iournemen the hedge priests, so many lewd livers, as theeves, murtherers, adulters, drunkards, cormorants, raschals, so many ignorant and atheistical dolts, so many covetous popish B(isho)ps in our ministery: and so many monstrous corruptious in our Church, and yet likely to have no redresse: Seeing our impudent, shamelesse and wainscote faced bishops, like beasts . . . dare in the eares of her Maiestie, affirme all to be well, where there is nothing but sores and blisters, yea where the grief is even deadly at the heart.'

Martin laid down as conditions of peace with the bishops that they should labour to promote the preaching of the word, should admit to the ministry only godly and learned men and put an end to nonresidence, that they should not suspend anyone for speaking against the corruption in the church, for refusing to wear the surplice, cap and tippet, or for omitting the corruptions in the Book of Common Prayer, such as the churching of women, the use of the ring in marriage or the sign of the cross in baptism. No one was to be molested in connection with this book, for not kneeling at communion, or for not going to church on the sabbath if there was no preacher to preach the word and administer the sacraments. Bishops were not to excommunicate privately or for trivial reasons, nor were they to forbid public fasts. They were not to slander the cause of reformation by calling it anabaptism or schism and labelling its advocates Puritans and enemies of the state.

If the bishops would not agree to these terms, Martin threatened to publish all their secret faults and to keep continual watch over them. He wrote: 'To this purpose I will place a young Martin in everie dioces, which may take notice of your practizes . . . I hope in time they shalbe as worthie Martins as their father is, every one of them able to mar a prelate.' He intended to publish 'al the books that I have in store already' concerning their misconduct, and to make his own visitation 'among my cleargie men'. He will note 'all their memorable pranckes' and he thinks he will need 'many Scribes and many reames of paper for this purpose'.

The second tract, generally known by its short title of *The Epitome*, appeared at the end of November 1588. The writer commented on the success of his earlier pamphlet—'I have bene entertayned at the Court everye man talkes of my worship. Manye would gladly receive my bookes, if they coulde tell where to finde them.' The Puritan preachers, however, were angry, 'Because I am to open. Because I iest.' He complains: 'I did thinke that Martin shoulde not have beene blamed of the puritans, for telling the trueth openly' and he asks ' . . . may I not say, that Iohn of Canterbury is a pettie pope, seeing he is so . . . I am plaine, I must needs call a Spade a Spade, a Pope a Pope.'

In addition to the usual knock-out comedy at the expense of individual ecclesiastics, Martin dealt in *The Epitome* with some of the arguments of Dr. Bridges in defence of the establishment. He now committed himself definitely against the institution of episcopacy and he affirmed that Christ had ordained that the church should be controlled by pastors or doctors, elders and deacons. He tells the bishops that he would like to make 1588 a wonderful year 'by remooving you all out of England'.

Meanwhile Thomas Cooper, bishop of Winchester, had been put up to answer Martin, and his *Admonition to the People of England* appeared in January 1589.[1] Cooper laments that 'even now, when the views of the mightie Navie of the *Spaniards* is scant passed out of our sight: when the terrible sound of their shot ringeth, as it were, yet in our eares . . . Wee should see in mens handes and bosomes, com-

[1] Edited by Edward Arber in The English Scholar's Library, No. 15. 1882.

monly slaunderous Pamphlets fresh from the Presse, against the best of the Church of Englande, and that we shoulde heare at every table, and in Sermons and Lectures, at private conventicles, the voyces of many not giving prayse to God, but scoffing, mocking, rayling and depraving the lives and doings of Bishoppes, and other of the Ministerie, and contemptuously defacing the state of Government of this Churche . . . ' He proceeded to give a defence of individual bishops and of the episcopal system of church government.

Martin continued his attack in *Certain Mineral and Metaphysical Schoolpoints* in February 1589 and *Hay any worke for Cooper* in March 1589.[1] He asked the bishop of Winchester 'doe you thinke our Churche governement, to be good and lawfull, because hir Maiestie and the state, who maintaine the reformed religion alloweth the same?' and he asserts ' . . . the Lorde doth not allow it, therefore it cannot be lawfull'. He hopes the offices of archbishops and bishops may be lawfully abolished out of the church by her Majesty and the state, and that deans, archdeacons and chancellors 'wilbe so kind unto my Lords grace, as not to stay, if his worship and the rest of the noble clergie Lords weare turned out to grasse'.

The man responsible for printing the first four Marprelate tracts was Robert Waldegrave.[2] His press had been raided in April 1588 when he was engaged in printing a pamphlet for the Puritan minister John Udall of Kingston-on-Thames, but he had escaped with some of the type. He later got hold of another press and probably set it up at Kingston, where he printed a work for John Penry. When the search by the Stationers' Company got too hot, he moved to the house of widow Crane at East Molesey.[3] Here, probably in July and August 1588, he printed for Udall and Penry. He managed to get hold of some black-letter type and early in October he used this to produce the first Marprelate tract. When the hunt was hot, he got permission through the help of Penry to use the house of Sir Richard Knightley of Fawsley, Northamptonshire, and the second pamphlet was printed there.

Penry clearly played a very important part in organising the work, and there were a number of distributors, including Humfry Newman,

---

[1] It was good journalism to use the words of the common London street cry for his reply to Thomas Cooper, bishop of Winchester.

[2] See p. 225.

[3] She was the widow of Nicholas Crane, a Puritan minister who had died while in prison in Newgate.

R

a cobbler. The authorities redoubled their efforts to find the press. In February 1589 there was a proclamation against those who secretly printed 'Schismatical and seditious bookes, diffamatorie libels and other fantasticall writings . . . against the godly reformation of Religion and Government Ecclesiasticall established by lawe . . . ' and who attacked the persons of the bishops 'in raylinge sorte and beyond the boundes of all good humanitie'. Mrs. Crane's servants at East Moseley were arrested, and as stories were getting about concerning unusual goings-on at Fawsley House, the press was moved to a farm north of Daventry, where it was unused for several weeks. Then it was shifted to Coventry where the *Minerals* and *Hay any Work for Cooper* were printed in February and March 1589.

Waldegrave, who must have been under tremendous strain, was not prepared to continue, but he and Penry approached Job Throckmorton of Haseley Manor, near Warwick, and Humfry Newman was commissioned to find another printer. He contacted in London John Hogkins who was not a member of the Stationers' Company, but who had probably learnt the trade of printing abroad. Hogkins engaged two assistants who were licensed printers, and they set off for Haseley Manor. Hogkins met Penry and Throckmorton, and was told that the press had now been moved from Coventry to Wolston Priory, the residence of Roger Wigston, six miles east of Coventry. On the way there Hogkins found at a pre-arranged spot the manuscript of another pamphlet—*Theses Martinianae* usually called *Martin Junior*. In July 1589 he printed at Wolston both this pamphlet and another one called *Martin Senior*. Unlike the first four pamphlets, these were printed in Roman and not in black-letter type.

Hogkins then decided to move the press again and they set off for Warrington in Lancashire with part of the manuscript of a pamphlet entitled *More Work for the Cooper*. While they were unloading their cart at Warrington, some of the goods fell out, a crowd gathered and some of the spectators must have got hold of part of the type. Hogkins found a suitable house a mile from Manchester and they were printing the first sheets of *More Work for the Cooper* when they were arrested.

As a last gesture of defiance Throckmorton summoned Penry to Haseley and they managed to bring out the final pamphlet *The Protestatyon of Martin Marprelat*.

The printers and other suspects were examined under torture.

Hogkins gave very little away, but a good deal of information was obtained from other prisoners. Sir Richard Knightley was eventually fined £2,000; Roger Wigston, 500 marks; and Mrs. Wigston £1,000 and imprisonment during the queen's pleasure. Penry escaped to Scotland. Job Throckmorton was convicted at the Warwickshire assizes, but seems to have escaped punishment, possibly through the influence of his cousin, Bess Throckmorton, who was maid of honour to the queen.

There has been a great deal of speculation about who wrote the pamphlets. Suggestions include John Udall, Thomas Cartwright, Job Throckmorton and John Penry. Mr. A. L. Rowse thinks that the pamphlets are 'far too secular and amusing to have been written by the earnest Penrys of this world' and suggests that they were written by someone who was in a position to know everybody who was anybody and who was so safely ensconsed at Court that he was confident he would never be brought to book. The author might, he thinks, have been Michael Hicks, Burghley's secretary, who had 'a merry facetious pen'.[1]

It has often been suggested that the importance of the Marprelate tracts was that their savage attack on the bishops did much to discredit the Puritan and Presbyterian cause in the eyes of moderate men who had hitherto been sympathetic. There is a measure of truth in this, although we must bear in mind that the cause had already suffered a number of major set-backs before the pamphlets ever appeared. It is certainly true that Cartwright, Travers and other leaders were anxious to dissociate themselves from Marprelate. A Puritan sympathiser, the earl of Hertford, commented on one of the later works that 'he liked not that course . . . that as they shoote at Bishopps now, soe they will doe at the Nobilitie also, if they be suffred'.[2] The pamphlets are not as scandalous or shocking as is often alleged, and they had little to add to the current arguments against the establishment. Although sober men might be shocked, many must have delighted in their satire, and it has been said that they made 'an immediate and wide appeal to readers less strait-laced who loved a joke even if—and perhaps because—it was broad or scandalous'.[3] They may have damaged the reputation of individual bishops,

---

[1] A. L. Rowse, *The England of Elizabeth*, p. 476, footnote.
[2] William Pierce, *An Historical Introduction to the Marprelate Tracts*, p. 182.
[3] V. J. K. Brook, *John Whitgift and the English Church*, p. 124.

but their main importance perhaps lay in the fact that they spread alarm in official circles which are never happy about underground activities and secret printing presses. Conyers Read thinks it very likely that they finally convinced Burghley that something must be done about the Puritans, and he comments on a new note in Burghley's hitherto sympathetic attitude. In 1590 the Lord Treasurer wrote: 'Care is to be taken to suppress all the turbulent Precisians who do violently seek to change the external government of the church.'[1] They probably strengthened Whitgift's hand in the fight which he had for a number of years been waging against nonconformist elements.

A man who played an important rôle in the counter-attack against Martin Marprelate in particular and against nonconformity in general was Richard Bancroft, a Lancashire man and a product of Christ's College, Cambridge, the training ground of many Puritans.[2] Bancroft had been ordained in 1574 and steadily carved out a career for himself in the church. He had been appointed a member of the High Commission in 1587 and was able to continue the task, which he had begun earlier, of making himself an expert on the subject of Puritanism. He was prominent in ferreting out those who had been associated with the Marprelate tracts.

On 9 February 1589 Bancroft preached at Paul's Cross a famous sermon on the text: 'Believe not every spirit, but try the spirits whether they be of God; for many false prophets are gone out into the world'.[3] It was in part a savage personal attack on the arrogance, ignorance and greed of the Puritans. He said: 'I am fully of this Opinion that the Hope which many men have conceived of the Spoil of Bishops Livings, of the Subversion of Cathedral Churches, and of a Havock to be made of all the Churches' Revenues, is the chiefest and most principal cause of the greatest schisms that we have at this day in our Church . . .'[4] 'The clergy factious', he said, 'do contend that all the Livings which now appertain to the Church, ought of right to be employed for the maintenance of their Presbyteries . . . The

[1] Conyers Read, *Lord Burghley and Queen Elizabeth*, pp. 470, 490.

[2] For Bancroft, see R. G. Usher, *The Reconstruction of the English Church*, 2 vols., 1910; S. B. Babbage, *Puritanism and Richard Bancroft*, 1962. For an examination of Bancroft's rôle in unearthing the Marprelate Press, see Owen Dugmore, 'Richard Bancroft's Submission', *Journal of Ecclesiastical History*, iii; Patrick Collinson, *The Elizabethan Puritan Movement*, p. 404.

[3] This very lengthy sermon was printed by George Hickes in *Bibliotheca Scriptorum Ecclesiae Anglicanae*, 1709.

[4] R. G. Usher, *op. cit.*, I. 53.

lay factious . . . that our preachers ought to conform themselves to the Example of Christ and his Apostles . . . to the Intent that they may obtain the prey which they look for.'[1] It was a neat, if not entirely just, delineation of the Two Faces of English Puritanism.

Bancroft examined the question of authority for religious beliefs. He attacked 'The prattling old woman, the doting old man, the babbling sophister' and others who presume they can interpret the scriptures correctly and that they know more than the ancient fathers.[2] Against these private judgments he set the authority of the Church 'which maintaineth without error the faith of Christ . . . which holdeth up the true doctrine of the gospel in matters necessary to Salvation and preacheth the same'; and against the interpretation of individuals, he set 'the decrees of our learned fathers in their lawful assemblies'. He made powerful and new claims on behalf of episcopacy—'There is no man living, as I suppose, able to show where there was any church planted ever since the apostles' time, but there bishops had authority over the rest of the ministry.' Although he did not explicitly say that episcopacy was commanded by Christ as the only form of church government, he was getting very near that position.[3]

Bancroft also strove in this sermon to identify Puritanism with sedition. The Martinists had challenged ecclesiastical authority and would seek to challenge the authority of the queen herself, just as in Scotland 'under the pretence of their presbyteries they trod upon the sceptre'.[4]

Bancroft's sermon did not mark the beginning of the counter-attack by the Church of England, for that had begun some years earlier. Nevertheless, it was an indication that there was going to be renewed vigour in dealing with nonconformity. The hunt for the

[1] R. G. Usher, *op. cit.*, I. 53.

[2] V. J. K. Brook, *John Whitgift and the English Church.* p. 127.

[3] See Philip Hughes, *The Reformation in England*, III. 211, for some interesting comments on this important sermon. See also A. Peel, *Tracts ascribed to Richard Bancroft*, Cambridge, 1953, p. 133. Burghley was clearly very worried about Bancroft's claims on behalf of episcopacy and consulted Dr. Hammond, Chancellor of London, who said he did not think that bishops could claim any authority other than that given them by statute. He expressed the opinion that if it had pleased the queen to establish a church without bishops, we could not justly complain of any defect in it. Sir Francis Knollys asked the opinion of Dr. John Reynolds of Oxford who said that Bancroft seemed to hold that the authority of the bishops over the clergy was God's own ordinance. Reynolds expressed his disagreement with this view.

[4] V. J. K. Brook, *Whitgift and the English Church*, p. 128; Norman Sykes, *Old Priest and New Presbyter*, pp. 25–6.

secret press went on and achieved success in August 1589. There was a thorough investigation of those involved or thought to be involved. John Udall was summoned before the Privy Council at the end of the year, and in 1590 Penry's books and papers were seized. At the beginning of the 1590's the outlook for the Puritans seemed very gloomy. The Presbyterian organisation, which in the 1580's had given such able leadership, had to all intents and purposes been destroyed.[1] Both physically and intellectually the establishment was engaged in a vigorous counter-attack. The Puritans, like the Papists, were not again to enjoy the successes which had been so marked a feature of their history in the 1580's.

[1] In September 1589 a provincial conference was held at Cambridge, and this seems to have been the last of such conferences if we except *ad hoc* meetings in London in 1590 in connection with the case against Cartwright. The Cambridge conference failed to agree on the vital question of whether non-preaching clergy were genuine ministers and whether communion might be received at their hands. Patrick Collinson, *The Elizabethan Puritan Movement*, pp. 400–2.

10

The Triumph of the Establishment 1590–1603: The Difficulties and Divisions of the Papists

DURING the last dozen years of Elizabeth's reign the established church under the leadership of John Whitgift, archbishop of Canterbury, and of his very able lieutenant Richard Bancroft,[1] made strenuous efforts to put its own house in order and to suppress and divide its opponents. The reorganisation of the church made it more formidable and less vulnerable to criticism than it had been earlier on.[2] During these years, too, there were appearing in England the first signs of the general European reaction against Calvinism,[3] and in 1593 Richard Hooker published the first four books of his great work *Of the Laws of Ecclesiastical Polity*.[4] Slowly a new 'Anglicanism' was coming to birth, and although Hooker's main influence was post-Elizabethan rather than Elizabethan, his book was an important landmark in the history of a church which sought to be neither Papist nor Puritan. Thus the Church of England was able to face the problems of the last years of Elizabeth with better organisation and greater self-confidence than it had known in earlier years, while its enemies and its critics were increasingly divided and harassed.

Looking back on the history of the reign, we tend to see the defeat of the Spanish Armada in 1588 as the end of the serious menace from Spain, but we must not forget that in the 1590's there was still no certainty in men's minds that the Elizabethan government would

---

[1] Bancroft became bishop of London in 1597.
[2] For an examination of this reorganisation, see R. G. Usher, *The Reconstruction of the English Church*, vol. 1, 1910.
[3] For a general sketch of this reaction, see Owen Chadwick, *The Reformation*, p. 211 ff. 'The Assault upon Calvinism'; H. C. Porter, *Reformation and Reaction in Tudor Cambridge*.
[4] For further discussion of Hooker, see p. 315 ff.

survive intact the assaults of its enemies abroad and its opponents at home. The triumph of 1588 naturally increased tremendously the self-confidence of the governing classes and intensified that English nationalism which had come into conflict with the cause of Roman Catholicism, but the international situation still remained very threatening. Spain did not accept 1588 as final, and for the rest of the reign she remained at war with England. The civil war in France after 1589 led to both English and Spanish intervention, and there was a danger that Spain might obtain naval bases in Brittany or in Picardy which could be used against England. In 1596 Philip II sent out a second Armada of 100 ships and 16,000 men. It was dispersed by gales, but in the following year he sent 136 ships and 9,000 men with the intention of establishing a bridgehead at Falmouth. This, too, was driven back by adverse weather, but a few ships actually reached England and landed Spanish troops on English soil.[1]

Ireland also presented a serious problem.[2] Hugh Roe O'Donnell and Hugh O'Neill, earl of Tyrone, entered into negotiation for Spanish help, and papal agents such as James O'Hely, bishop of Tuam, gave support and encouragement to the rebels. Eventually in 1598 almost the whole of Ireland rose in a national rebellion, and Philip III sent a fleet to assist Tyrone. Professor Black comments: 'Had this expedition reached its destination, it is hard to believe that English sovereignty in Ireland would have survived the onslaught.'[3] In 1601, 3,000 Spanish troops were landed at Kinsale, and although they were forced to evacuate in the following year, the rebellion had not been crushed.

There was, moreover, a great uncertainty in men's minds about what would happen when Elizabeth died, and fears were all the greater because the queen explicitly forbade the question to be discussed. When Peter Wentworth tried to raise it in the Commons in 1593, he was sent to the Tower and died in prison.[4] We know now that when Elizabeth died in 1603, James VI of Scotland succeeded without a struggle, but events might well have taken a different turn, and at one time even Robert Cecil was conducting secret negotiations with Spain over the Spanish claim to the throne.

[1] For a summary of the international problems of the later years of Elizabeth, see, J. B. Black, *The Reign of Elizabeth 1558–1603*, second edition, 1959, p. 406 ff.
[2] *Ibid.*, p. 461 ff. Chapter XII, *The Irish Problem*.
[3] *Ibid.*, p. 486.
[4] J. Neale, *Elizabeth I and her Parliaments*, p. 251 ff.

It was hardly surprising therefore that Spain and the papacy should continue to be seen as major threats to English Protestantism. It is true that Clement VIII, who held the papacy from 1592 to 1605, was not a crusader and was prepared to give only cautious moral support to the Irish rebels[1] and that in the later years of Elizabeth's reign the Roman curia was dimly beginning to see that the Protestant régime in England had come to stay.[2] Nevertheless, both the king of Spain and the pope wanted for their own reasons to see the end of the Elizabethan government, and those who defended it naturally regarded them as enemies. In the parliament of 1601 there must have been many who agreed with the Speaker when he attacked Spain and Rome who, he said, called 'their rapines and murders the war of God' and who 'have tossed and turned themselves into all colours, only white excepted'.[3]

Professor Black maintains that 'it is difficult to believe that the international problems confronting Elizabeth in the later years of her reign were appreciably less grave than at any previous period'.[4] It may well be that it was because of this continuing atmosphere of crisis that the government maintained against Papists and Puritans alike a determined policy of repression in spite of the fact that they seemed in many ways to constitute less serious threats to the establishment than they had done in the 1580's.

The hunting, imprisoning, exiling and executing of seminary priests and Jesuits still went on vigorously, for the priests were the main means by which the Catholic religion was kept alive. Laymen who assisted the priests and who rendered notable service to the Catholic cause also received special attention. Between the beginning of 1590 and the death of Elizabeth in March 1603, there were 88 executions

---

[1] A. O. Meyer, *England and the Catholic Church under Elizabeth*, p. 364.

[2] 'The papacy itself formed a new estimate of its foe and abandoned forthwith the use of the medieval weapons it had hitherto employed. Pius V, with the holy zeal of a crusader, stands at the opening of the period ... Clement VIII, gentle, cautious, reserved stands at its close—the forerunner of that subtle, diplomatic man of the world, Urban VIII, who was lavish with his compliments to Charles I.' Commenting on the negotiations between the pope and the appellant priests in 1602, Fr. Hughes remarks, '... the pope was to be brought, for a moment, to the point that the actual possibility of a *modus vivendi* between the Catholic Church and Elizabeth was actually suggested to him', and again, '... it was no longer unthinkable that the pope and the heretical government might, some day, come to the point of negotiating'. *The Reformation in England*. III. 385, 389.

[3] J. Neale, *Elizabeth I and her Parliaments*, II. 424.

[4] J. B. Black, *The Reign of Elizabeth*, p. 408.

for religion. 53 of those put to death were priests and 35 were lay-people.[1] The priests included the two remarkable Jesuits, Robert Southwell and Henry Walpole, and four others who were received into the Society of Jesus when they were in prison awaiting trial and execution. Most of the priests were condemned under the act of 1585 against Jesuits and Seminary Priests, and most of the laypeople, including one woman, Anne Line, were found guilty of treason because they had helped the priests. There were, however, some executions for other offences, including denying the royal supremacy, being reconciled to the pope, persuading others to be reconciled, and distributing seditious books.[2]

The government's continuing concern with the activities of the priests and their helpers was shown in a proclamation it issued towards the end of 1591.[3] It was headed: 'A declaration of great troubles pretended against the Realme by a number of Seminaries Priests and Jesuits, sent, and very secretly dispersed in the same, to worke great Treason under a false pretence of Religion . . . ' It stated that the king of Spain was waging an unjust war against the French king,[4] that he had seduced the pope into invading France, and that England was thereby threatened. By colour of the pope's authority he had practised with seditious Englishmen to gather 'a multitude of dissolute yong men, who have partly for lacke of living, partly for crimes committed, become Fugitives, Rebelles and Traitors'. For these there were in Rome, Spain and other places 'certaine receptacles made to live in, and there to be instructed in Schoole pointes of sedition, and from thence to be secretly and by stealth conveyed into our

[1] The figures for each year are as follows: 1590, 9 priests, 2 laymen; 1591, 7 priests, 8 laymen; 1592, 4 priests, 2 laymen; 1593, 3 priests; 1594, 5 priests, 5 laymen; 1595, 4 priests; 1596, 3 laymen; 1597, 2 priests, 3 laymen; 1598, 3 priests, 4 laymen; 1599, none; 1600, 6 priests, 3 laymen; 1601, 5 priests, 2 laymen, 1 woman; 1602, 4 priests, 2 laymen; 1603, 1 priest.

[2] A chronological list of *Martyrs of England and Wales 1535–1680* has been prepared by Philip Caraman and James Walsh, Catholic Truth Society, 1960. The very considerable literature about the martyrs includes Richard Challoner's *Memoirs of Missionary Priests 1577–1584*, edit. J. H. Pollen, 1924; J. Morris, *The Troubles of our Catholic Forefathers*, 3 vols., 1872–7; H. Foley, *Records of the English Province of the Society of Jesus*, 8 vols., 1877–83, and various volumes in the Catholic Record Society.

[3] Dated 18 October 1591, but not published till later. The Proclamation is printed as an appendix in *An Humble Supplication to Her Majestie by Robert Southwell*, edit. R. C. Bald, Cambridge, 1953.

[4] The Huguenot Henry of Navarre had succeeded to the throne after the assassination of Henry III, but the Catholic party in France was resisting him and Spain had sent an army against him.

Dominions, with ample authorities from Rome, to moove, stirre up, and perswade as many of our subiects, as they dare to deale withall to renounce their naturall allegeance . . . and upon hope by a Spanish Invasion to be enriched and endowed with the possessions and dignities of our other good subiects . . . ' These traitors have been impeached 'for meere treasons, and not for any poynts of religion'. The proclamation asserted that no one in England suffered death for matter of religion and that a number of men of wealth professing a religion contrary to the established religion were not impeached for it but merely had to pay a pecuniary sum for not coming to church.

The Proclamation goes on to say that the heads of the seminaries, and in particular Allen and Parsons, have assured the king of Spain that he will have many thousands supporting him if he invades, and have provided him with lists of names of those who will, they allege, help him. They have given an assurance 'that these their Seedmen named Seminaries, Priests, & Jesuites are in the sundry parts of the Realme secretly harbored . . . and shall be ready to continue their reconciled people in their lewde constancie to serve their purpose both with their forces, and with other trayterous enterprises when the Spanish power shall be ready to land . . . ' In view of all this and in view also of the intention of the king of Spain to employ all the forces he can by sea next year, the English government must take counter-action. The queen therefore requires the ecclesiastical authorities to see that 'the like diligence be used by the godly Ministers of the Church, by their diligent teaching and example of life, to retaine our people stedfastly in the profession of the Gospell . . . ' All subjects must look to the defence of the realm. To provide against the Seminaries, Jesuits and traitors, commissioners are to be appointed in every shire and city to enquire into suspects.

The Proclamation states that the traitors are known to come into the realm 'by secret Creekes, and landing places, disguised, both in their names and persons. Some in apparell, as Souldiers, Mariners, or Merchants, pretending that they have bene heretofore taken prisoners, and put into Gallies, and delivered. Some come in as gentlemen with contrary names, in comely apparell, as though they had travailed into Forreine countreys, for knowledge . . . and many of them in their behaviour as Ruffians, farre off to be thought, or suspected to be Friers, Priests, Iesuits, or Popish schollers. And of these many doe attempt to resort into the Universities and houses of Lawe . . . many into service of Noblemen, Ladies and gentlemen, with such like fraudulent devises to cover themselves from all apprehension, or suspicion: and yet in processe of time, they do at length so insinuate themselves to get themselves credite with hypocrisies, as they infect both the Masters and Families, and consequently adventure also yea secretly to use their office of priesthood and reconcilements.' To prevent all this, all heads of households and lodgings are required to make full enquiry into all who resorted to their residences in the last year, or who shall do so in future. They are to find out full particulars about them, including whether they go to church. All this is to be recorded and suspicious persons are to be examined by the commissioners.

The proclamation of 1591 is in a way a tribute to the effectiveness of the Catholic 'underground' arrangements by which in the eighties and the nineties priests were brought into the country and enabled to work with considerable success in spite of the government's elaborate counter-measures. The Catholic 'underground' is a subject in itself, and only few of its features can be noted here.

There was no master-planner or central planning organisation in charge of the whole business of training priests, arranging for their transport to England and seeing to their distribution and maintenance when they got into the country. This was in many ways a weakness since it led to a good deal of inefficiency and often left individual priests to sink or swim on their own. The Papists were at a disadvantage in this respect compared with their opponents who were able, through the Privy Council and through individual members of the government like Burghley and Walsingham, to exercise a considerable degree of central control over the security measures against the Papists.[1] Through ambassadors and numerous agents abroad, including spies in the seminaries themselves, the government was able to obtain in advance a great deal of information about the priests long before they reached England, and at home it was able to co-ordinate and direct the efforts of local authorities and the ecclesiastical authorities to capture the priests and prevent the practice of Catholicism.

Although there was no overall planning on the Catholic side, there was some brilliant and effective organisation from time to time in parts of this underground work. We have already seen the masterly

[1] The Cecil Papers published by the Historical Manuscripts Commission, the State Papers Domestic published by the Public Record Office, and the Acts of the Privy Council contain a mass of material illustrating this point.

improvisation of Parsons and Campion during their first year in England.[1] After he had left England, Parsons not only organised the printing abroad of books in English but also helped arrange the movement of priests into the country. In 1584, for example, he wrote: 'During these last days there had been a most violent and searching persecution, and the English ports have been guarded so carefully that there was no way open either to enter or to leave the country. And so it seemed necessary for someone to be in this place near the coast and to imploy industry and money in devising new ways whereby members of our Society and other Catholics may pass to and fro. ... And so we have shared the business between us, he (Allen) sending me priests from the seminaries, I arranging to the best of my powers for safe transport to England. To do this ... I am obliged to maintain a modest establishment at Rouen which is the most convenient city on account of its nearness to the sea, so that from there someone can make trips to the coast to arrange for boats to convey people across (for they cannot use either the public boats or the ordinary ports) ... others take charge of the preparation and introduction into the country of books written in English both on spiritual and devotional subjects and on matters of controversy and in answer to the calumnies ... Then too there are the holy oils, chalices, vestments and bibles to be sent over.'[2]

Other illustrations of *ad hoc* organisation can be seen in the group of young Catholic gentlemen associated with George Gilbert who helped Parsons and Campion while they were working in England, and in the arrangements for the posting and maintenance of priests made on a voluntary basis by Henry Garnet, the Jesuit Superior, during his work in England from 1586 to 1605.[3] Indeed, part of the strength of the very small number of Jesuits at work in England during this period was that they were centrally controlled by their superior and that they met together at more or less regular intervals for spiritual formation and for discussion of their work and its problems. They did not have that intense feeling of isolation which must have troubled many of the secular clergy.

The routes taken by the priests and the methods by which they got

[1] See p. 166 ff.
[2] *Letters and Memorials of Fr. Robert Persons, S.J.*, edit. L. Hicks, Catholic Record Society, vol. 39, p. lxvi ff.
[3] Philip Caraman, *Henry Garnet and the Gunpowder Plot, passim.*

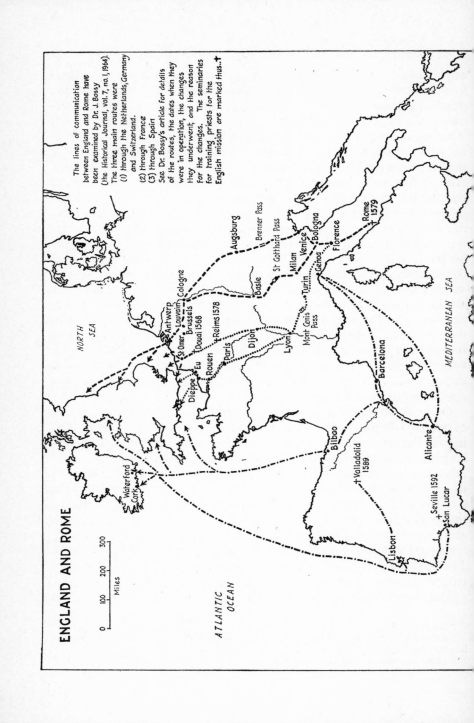

ENGLAND AND ROME

The lines of communication
between England and Rome have
been examined by Dr. J. Bossy
(the Historical Journal, vol.7, no.1, 1964).
The three main routes were
(1) through the Netherlands, Germany
and Switzerland.
(2) through France
(3) through Spain

See Dr. Bossy's article for details
of the routes, the dates when they
were in operation, the changes
they underwent, and the reason
for the changes. The seminaries
for training priests for the
English mission are marked thus.✝

NORTH SEA

ATLANTIC OCEAN

MEDITERRANEAN SEA

Miles
0 100 200 300

Augsburg
Brenner Pass
St Gotthard Pass
Basle
Cologne
Antwerp
Louvain
Brussels 1568
St Omer
Douai 1578
Reims 1578
Eu
Dieppe
Rouen
Paris
Dijon
Lyon
Mont Cenis Pass
Turin
Milan
Venice
Bologna
Genoa
Florence
Rome 1579 ✝

Waterford
Cork

Bilbao
Barcelona
Valladolid 1589 ✝
Seville 1592 ✝
San Lucar
Lisbon
Alicante

into the country have been examined in some detail by Dr. David Mathew and Dr. Bossy.[1] Dr. Bossy discusses the three main lines of communication between England and the seminaries in Rome and elsewhere—the Imperial route, the French route, and the route from Spain. He shows how the international situation led from time to time to the blocking of one or other of the roads to England, and suggests that the vitality of English Catholicism owed a good deal to the need to show initiative in organising new methods of approach.

This was an enterprise in which many different kinds of individuals were involved—the priests themselves, merchants, sea captains, fishermen, innkeepers and others without whose help the priests would never have got into the country. In 1602 for example, a government agent reported: 'This Hermooke has, as a French merchant, the means of many "passenges" to Calais, Bullen, &c, and these . . . most secret, by fishermen and small "catches" which usually run from coast to coast unsuspected or questioned . . . By these small boats the Jesuits commonly pass in and out . . . with all speed and safety . . . They also use much the help of one Gibels, resident in Calais, who with a few hours warning can provide at any time a "schife" or fisherboat for a sudden passage, landing at some odd creek either upon the coast or in the river of Thames in the night.'[2] The very long English coastline, the willingness of foreign and English seamen to carry dubious passengers for religious or financial reasons, the impossibility of maintaining day and night a priest-observer corps on the coasts, the unreliability of local officials, and assistance given by Catholic sympathisers in the maritime counties, all helped the entry of priests, and it was comparatively rare for them to be intercepted on or immediately after landing.

Once he was in England, the priest was faced by much more serious dangers, for the whole machinery of central and local government, as well as that of the ecclesiastical authorities, was directed against him. Naturally the priests established themselves more often than not in the households of Catholic gentry in the guise of friends or servants of the master. In the rambling Elizabethan mansions, with their crowds of servants and visitors, they stood a chance of escaping

---

[1] David Mathew, 'The Celtic Peoples and Renaissance Europe', 1933, Chapter XVI, 'The Landing of the Priests'; John Bossy, 'Rome and the Elizabethan Catholics: A question of Geography', *The Historical Journal*, 1964, vol. 7, no. 1.

[2] Hist. MSS. Com.: Marquis of Salisbury, Part xii, p. 231.

detection and of exercising their influence on the governing class. Some of them took houses of their own, and this was often more satisfactory since they did not then endanger the lives of their hosts and they were not at the mercy of inquisitive or suspicious servants.

A very detailed account of the various means by which the priests managed to operate is given in John Gerard's autobiography.[1] Both Gerard and his superior, Henry Garnet, survived in England for nearly twenty years, although they were in constant danger and had many narrow escapes. Usually, however, the effective life of a missionary priest was very much shorter. Professional and amateur priest-hunters acting sometimes for religious reasons and often in hope of reward cut short many of their careers. Richard Topcliffe, the 'Queen's pursuivant', who achieved such a great reputation as a torturer as well as a priest-hunter seems to have had very mixed motives for his savage brutality.[2]

The open enemies of the priests were easier to guard against than 'false brethren'. Renegades, both priests and laymen, were a really serious menace at every stage from the seminaries onwards.[3] John Gerard describes the difficulties he had with one of his fellow prisoners, the priest William Atkinson, who was excessively curious about him. Another priest, Anthony Tyrell, who was arrested at the time of the Babington Plot frequently changed sides and was a great problem to his fellow Catholics; Campion was betrayed by George Eliot who had attended his mass at Lyford Grange; and Robert Southwell fell into the hands of Topcliffe as a result of information given by Anne Bellamy whom Topcliffe had seduced while she was in prison.

In addition, a remarkably large amount of information was obtained from prisoners examined under torture. The rack is the best known of the instruments employed, but a number of different methods were used and the practice of breaking a man down by treating him alternately with brutality and kindness was well known to the Elizabethan experts. Edward Rishton who was himself a prisoner gives the following account: 'Of the means or instruments of torture employed in the Tower, there are seven different kinds. The first is the Pit, —a subterraneous cave, twenty feet deep, and entirely without light.

[1] *John Gerard: The Autobiography of an Elizabethan*, edit. Philip Caraman.
[2] J. Neale, *Elizabeth I and her Parliaments*, II. pp. 153, 176, 313 ff.
[3] For spies in the seminaries, see L. Hicks, 'An Elizabethan Propagandist: The Career of Soloman Aldred', *The Month*, May–June, 1945, and Anthony Munday, *The English Roman Life*, Harleian Miscellany, 1746, VII, 137–40.

'The second is a cell, or dungeon, so small as to be incapable of admitting a person in erect posture: from its effect on its inmates it has received the name of "*Little Ease*".

'The third is the rack, on which, by means of wooden rollers and other machinery, the limbs of the sufferer are drawn in opposite directions.

'The fourth, I believe from the inventor, is called "*The Scavenger's Daughter*". It consists of an iron ring, which brings the head, feet, and hands together, until they form a circle.

'The fifth is the iron gauntlet, which encloses the hand with the most excruciating pain.

'The sixth consists of chains, or manacles, attached to the arms: and

'The seventh, of fetters, by which the feet are confined.'[1]

There were a number of other forms of torture in addition to these. As Mr. Grahame Green pointed out, some people are torturable and some are not, and not all had that tremendous power of resistance shown by John Gerard whose detailed account of what it felt like to be hung up by the arms for hours on end is recorded so vividly in his autobiography.[2] Robert Southwell in *An Humble Supplication* gives a harrowing account of what went on—'Some are whipped naked soe long and with such excesse, that our enemies . . . sayd, that noe man without the help of the Divell could with such undauntedness suffer soe much. Some, besides their tortures, have bene forced to lie continually booted and Cloathed many weekes together, pined in their diett, consumed with verymyne, and almost stifeled with stench. Some have bene watched and kept from sleepe, till they were past the use of reason, and then examined upon the advantage, when they could scarcely give account of their owne names. Some have been tortured in such parts, as is almost a torture to Christian eares to hear it . . . Some with Instruments have bene rowled up together like a ball, and soe Crushed, that the bloud sprowted out at divers parts of their bodies . . . '[3]

The fact that the priests managed to survive at all is partly explained by the construction in many Catholic houses of hiding holes

[1] This is from Edward Rishton's account printed in *Dodd's Church History* edit. M. A. Tierney, 1840, III. 148 ff.

[2] *John Gerard The Autobiography of an Elizabethan*, edit. Philip Caraman, p. 104 ff: 'The Tower and Torture'.

[3] *An Humble Supplication to her Maiestie by Robert Southwell*, edit. R. C. Bald, Cambridge, 1953, pp. 33, 34.

S

which often enabled them to escape even very prolonged and careful searches.[1] The best known and the most skilful maker of hiding holes was Nicholas Owen, the son of an Oxford carpenter. Two of Nicholas's brothers became priests and another ran a secret printing press in Northamptonshire from 1595 to 1601. Nicholas may have acted as a servant to Edmund Campion, and from 1586 he attached himself to Henry Garnet. He was a small man affectionately known as Little John, and he was remarkably discreet. He constructed a very large number of hiding-places, often working secretly at night after he had done the tasks on which he was ostensibly engaged. He was not, of course, the first to undertake such work, and many Catholic families must have gone in for 'do-it-yourself' schemes with the help of trusted servants and local craftsmen, but Owen's hides seem to have been constructed with extraordinary cleverness. Whenever possible, he made a hide within a hide with an escape route if the hide was discovered. He also tried to arrange some system by which those inside could communicate if necessary with their friends in the house and receive provisions (through a tube or by some other means) if the search went on for long.[2] He apparently taught his craft to others. He was captured with John Gerard in 1594 and tortured to get information, but his rôle in the Catholic underground was not then known to the authorities and eventually his friends managed to get him released. He helped Gerard in his famous escape from the Tower. He was captured along with Garnet and others after the Gunpowder Plot, coming out of his hiding hole partly to avoid starvation and partly to draw the attention of the search party away from the two priests who were also concealed in the house. This time the authorities knew who he was and tortured him so violently to get him to talk that he died as a result. The government did its best to blacken his name and an inquest returned a verdict of suicide—the equivalent of the formula 'shot while trying to escape' used by modern totalitarian states. John Gerard comments: 'How many Priests then may we think

[1] The subject of hiding holes is a considerable one which cannot be fully explored here. The standard work is still Granville Squiers, *Secret hiding-places*, 1934, but in the light of work done by Mr. Michael Hodgetts and others since then, a new edition is very necessary. Mr. Hodgetts work includes 'Priests' Hiding Holes', *The Venerabile*, XIX no. 3, November 1959; 'Nicholas Owen in East Anglia', *The Month*, New Series, vol. 26 1962; and articles in *Country Life*, 22 March 1962; and in *Transactions of the Worcester shire Archaeological Society*, vol. XXXIX, 1962.

[2] Provisions presented a difficulty in the days before canned foods, and there were also serious problems of heating and sanitation.

this man did save by his endeavours in the space of seventeen years, having laboured in all shires and in the chiefest Catholic Houses in England.'[1]

Occasionally we catch glimpses of others who were engaged in this dangerous business. Thus it was reported in February 1595 that 'At Little Ogle, viii miles distance from Rowell in Northamptonshire, lieth Mr. Bentley, who hathe a prieste in his howse continually, and commonly a Seminary Prieste, whom his wife calleth her chicken. The said Bentley had an old man named Green, a carpenter and mason, who maketh all the beades that lie in little boxes (rosaries). He made a secret place in Mr. Bentley's house at Lea (Derby) with a doore of free stone that no man could ever judge there was any such place, and he makes all the secrett places in recusants' houses in that country.'[2] The makers of hiding-places did not publicise their work and a number of hiding holes remained undiscovered until modern times.[3]

John Gerard gives accounts of a number of searches, and one of them will serve to illustrate the hazards and the tensions facing the priests and those who helped them. Gerard was staying for a time at Mrs. Wiseman's house at Braddocks in Essex when there suddenly arrived a search party acting on information received from a traitor, John Franks, whose treachery was still unsuspected. Gerard relates how 'On Easter Monday we rose earlier than usual for Mass, for we felt there was danger about. As we were preparing everything for Mass before daybreak we heard, suddenly, a great noise of galloping hooves . . . We barred the doors: the altar was stripped, the hiding places opened and all my books and papers thrown in.' Gerard wanted to use a hiding-place near the dining-room which was furthest away from the chapel and had a supply of provisions—'a bottle of wine and some light sustaining biscuits and other food that would keep', but the mistress of the house insisted on his using another one. The searchers were very thorough, 'even lifting up the tiles of the roof to examine underneath them . . . They measured the walls with long

---

[1] There is a short account of him in Margaret Waugh's pamphlet, *Blessed Nicholas Owen*, Catholic Truth Society. He was received into the Society of Jesus as a lay brother by Henry Garnet.

[2] H. Foley, *Records of the English Province of the Society of Jesus*, V. 470.

[3] The full story can never be told because many of the houses have been pulled down or altered. In addition to the substantial hiding-places, which are with few exceptions in the houses of gentry, there must have been many make-shift and temporary arrangements to hide for a short time priests on the run.

rods and if the measurements did not tally they pulled down the section that they could not account for.' They searched without success for two days and then removed temporarily the mistress of the house and the Catholic servants. Before she was taken, Mrs. Wiseman, who was afraid that Gerard would die of starvation (he had only a biscuit or two and a little quince jelly which she had thrust into his hands as he went into the hiding-place) instructed John Franks to go to a certain room and call for Gerard when all was clear. Franks reported this to the magistrate and an even more thorough search was then made. Gerard was all this time in a hiding-place which he had entered by raising part of the floor under the grate of a fireplace on which wood was kept as though it were meant for a fire. In the night the men on guard lit the fire and the floor partially subsided, so that Gerard had to move to one side to prevent the hot embers falling on his head. The guards noted that there was something odd about the fireplace and expressed an intention of investigating it next day, but they apparently forgot all about it.

The searchers did in fact discover the other hiding-place in which Gerard had originally intended to go, but although they ripped off a good deal of plaster and got very near where he was concealed, they eventually gave up after a search lasting four days. Gerard relates how he was 'very wasted and weak with hunger and lack of sleep. All that time I had been squatting in a very confined space.' The mistress of the house, who had been allowed to return, went without food all this time 'partly because she wanted to share my discomfort and find out by testing herself how long I could live without food, but chiefly to draw down God's mercy upon me and upon herself and her whole family by fasting and prayer'. He says that when he came out: 'I found her face so changed that she looked a different person; and had it not been for her voice and her dress I doubt whether I would have recognised her.'[1]

The government's Proclamation of 1591 was another public reiteration of its policy of treating the priests as traitors and of its determination that they should not be allowed to gain sympathy at home or abroad on the grounds that they were being put to death for their religion. It provoked a number of replies from leading Catholics including Richard Verstegan,[2] Thomas Stapleton,[3] Robert Parsons

---

[1] *Autobiography of John Gerard*, edit. Philip Caraman, p. 58 ff.
[2] See pp. 187, 189.   [3] See pp. 60, 61.

and Robert Southwell. After his flight from England Verstegan had been busily engaged in editing and publishing Catholic books and in acting as an 'intelligencer' collecting information about conditions in England.[1] In his *A Declaration of the True Causes of the Great Troubles*, published in 1592, he made a fierce attack on Burghley and on his policy, based partly on a long letter from Southwell describing the persecution in England.[2] The now aged Thomas Stapleton produced in the same year *Apologia pro Rege Catholico Philippo II* which made 'stinging accusations against the queen as a persecutor, a woman of light morals and questionable antecedents, and the responsible party in an alleged collapse of morality and religion in England'.[3] Meanwhile in Spain Robert Parsons, who was adding to his remarkable achievements by establishing a centre for Catholic students and travellers at San Lucar in 1591 and yet another seminary for the training of priests for England at Seville in 1592,[4] rushed into the controversy with a Latin work *Elizabethae Angliae Reginae haeresim Calvinianam propugnantis saevissimum in catholicos sui regni edictum . . . promulgatum Londini, 29 Nov. 1591*.[5] It was a passionate defence of the missionary priests addressed to a European audience and published in Italy, Germany, the Netherlands and France, warning the queen in a manner reminiscent of the famous sermon of the Puritan Dering many years earlier.[6] Elizabeth was told that she had forsaken the commandments of the Lord—'This is the true cause, from this, believe me, spring all the confusion, all the misfortune of thy country, Elizabeth, forasmuch as thou hast forsaken the Lord and gone astray from the royal road of the Christian and catholic religion . . . Learn this, Elizabeth, that God is, and that He is the same who has chastised other Kings, queens, monarchs, and emperors before thee and far more powerful than thou art.' If England had been spared by God at the time of the Armada, it was because it was like a barren fig-tree which the husbandman allows to continue for one more year to see if it will bring forth fruit.[7] There is a moving plea

---

[1] See *The Letters and Despatches of Richard Verstegan (c. 1550–1640)*, edit. A. G. Petti, 1959.
[2] A. G. Petti, *op. cit.*, xli. Southwell's letter is printed by Mr. Petti, pp. 1–33.
[3] Marvin R. O'Connell, *Thomas Stapleton and the Counter-Reformation*, p. 48, note 3.
[4] See A. C. F. Beales, *Education under Penalty*, p. 47.
[5] Written under the pseudonym Andrew Philopater. See A. O. Meyer, *England and the Catholic Church under Queen Elizabeth*, p. 351 ff.
[6] See pp. 141, 142.   [7] A. O. Meyer, *op. cit.*, p. 352.

for the missionary priests, 'youths nobly born and wealthy for the most part, who could live quietly and comfortably at home, and who solely from zeal for the faith have left parents and friends, and all that is dear to them in this life in order to go into voluntary exile, with such greatness of soul and steadfastness that they fear neither spies nor prisons, neither executioner nor instruments of torture for the sake of religion and salvation of souls'.[1] Replying to the accusation in the 1591 proclamation that they were 'a multitude of dissolute young men', Parsons, who seems to have been rather sensitive on the question of noble birth, asserts 'They are not descended from the dregs of mankind like your ministers of the Word, but frequently from noble families and wealthy parents, and I venture to say that in the three English seminaries of Rome, Rheims and Valladolid, there are more flowers of nobility than among all your clergy at home.'[2] For full measure he attacks the 'well-nigh crazy' Walsingham and the wicked Burghley, and he compares the cruelty of Elizabeth to that of Diocletian and Domitian.[3]

These violent attacks were not at all to the liking of a number of English Catholics who pointed out that they had to take the consequences for what was done by their co-religionists abroad. Sir Thomas Cornwallis complained rather bitterly: 'I am very sorry and so (I am sure) be all good Catholics of those lewd libels. It will but exasperate matters. In nos cudetur faba. They be out of the way themselves and therefore do not regard what we endure.'[4]

Much more in accord with English Catholic sentiment was an answer to the Proclamation written by a priest actually at work in England, the Jesuit Robert Southwell. It took the form of An Humble Supplication to her Maiestie[5] and it was written in the period between the issue of the Proclamation and Southwell's capture in June 1592. It demolished very effectively the official propaganda that no one in England was persecuted for religion. Southwell repudiated with great emphasis the accusation that the priests were disloyal—'protesting upon our soules and salvations, and calling Allmighty God and his Angells for witnesses, that as we hope to have any benefitt by the most pretious wounds and death of our Lord Jesus Christ, the whole and

---

[1] Ibid., p. 352–3.   [2] Ibid., p. 353.   [3] Ibid., p. 353.
[4] Patrick McGrath and Joy Rowe, 'The Recusancy of Sir Thomas Cornwallis', Proceedings of the Suffolk Institute of Archaeology, vol. xxviii Part 3, 1961, p. 257.
[5] An Humble Supplication to Her Maiestie by Robert Southwell, edit. R. C. Bald, Cambridge, 1953.

only intent of our coming into this Realme, is noe other, but to labour for the salvation of soules, and in peaceable and quiet sort to confirme them in the auntient Catholique Faith in which their Forefathers lived and died these 1400 years, and out of which we undoubtedly believe it is impossible that any soule should be saved'.[1] He told the queen 'we doe assure your Maiestie that what Army soever should come against you, we will rather yeald our brests to be broached by our Cuntrie swords, then use our swords to theffusion of our cuntries bloud'.[2]

When parliament met in February 1593 the government prepared to take further action against those who would not conform. What eventually emerged was two Acts, one aimed specifically at popish recusants, the other against seditious sectaries. The history of these laws and the extraordinary changes they underwent in the Lords and in the Commons has been examined in detail by Professor Neale.[3] It seems clear that by now both Lords and Commons were much less violently anti-Catholic than they had been earlier, and two government bills, which aimed at taking very severe measures indeed against Papists, were in their passage through parliament drastically modified. The original government bill in the Commons, for example, had proposed to increase very severely the fines on recusants, as well as imposing a £10 a month fine on anyone keeping a recusant guest or servant. It would have made husbands with recusant wives liable for their fines, it would have excluded Catholics from all offices and from the learned professions, and it would have taken children away from recusant parents at the age of seven and had them brought up at their parents' expense by Protestants.[4] Commenting on this and on another government bill which was introduced in the Lords, Professor

[1] *Ibid.*, p. 11.
[2] Dr. Bald points out that Southwell was here anticipating in some measure the views of John Bishop in 1598 (see p. 287). Southwell is not saying he will fight the invader but he is saying he will not support him, even, one must assume, if he came with papal backing. Dr. Bald suggests that Southwell realised 'the vital necessity, if English Catholicism was to survive, of reconciling loyalty to Church and State'. The Supplication circulated in MS and was not published till 1600 when it was issued, in an edited form, by an appellant priest, John Boswell, and printed at a secret press in Staffordshire. It was being used by the secular priests who opposed the Jesuits, and Garnet got the archpriest Blackwell to try to suppress it (R. C. Bald, *op. cit.*, xii ff.)
[3] J. Neale, *Elizabeth I and her Parliaments*, II. 280 ff.
[4] It was possibly in order to anticipate this danger that Parsons established a new school for Catholic English boys at St. Omer. He had in 1582 set up a school at Eu which lasted for ten years. It never had more than 30 boys at one time. St. Omer by the end of

Neale remarks: 'Catholics were to be treated as an alien pest in society; immobilized, rendered impotent by virtual expropriation and exclusion from all influential vocations, and eradicated in a single generation.'[1]

On this occasion it was parliament and not the queen which exercised a moderating influence on anti-Catholic legislation. What had originally been a drastic bill affecting Papists much more than other recusants emerged in the end as an Act against Seditious Sectaries. This can be more conveniently examined when we discuss the Puritans.[2] The Act against Popish recusants[3] was severe enough, but much less drastic than the government had intended. It refers to 'sundry wicked and seditious persons, who terming themselves Catholics and being indeed spies and intelligencers, not only for her Majesty's foreign enemies but also for rebellious and traitorous subjects . . . hiding their most detestable and devilish purposes under a false pretext of religion and conscience do secretly wander and shift from place to place within this realm to corrupt and seduce her Majesty's subjects and to stir them to sedition and rebellion'. It enacts that everyone over the age of sixteen who is a Popish recusant, and who before the end of Parliament has been convicted for not going to church, must within twenty days after the end of the session go to his usual dwelling-place and not depart more than five miles from it. This also applies to those convicted of recusancy in future. Those without a certain dwelling-place must go to the place where they were born or where their father or mother is living. They are to notify their names in writing to the authorities, and these are to be recorded. In order to rid the realm of multitudes of such seditious people who are unable to support themselves and who 'being committed to prison . . . do live for the most part in better care there than they could . . . at their liberty', it is enacted that those who do not

---

its first year had 50 and by 1600 there were 100. This is the ancestor of the modern Stonyhurst. A. C. F. Beales, *Education under Penalty*, pp. 64–8. For Catholic schoolmasters in Elizabethan England, see A. C. F. Beales, 'A Biographical Catalogue of Catholic Schoolmasters in England', Part I, 1558–1603, *Recusant History*, vol. 7, no. 6. 1964.

[1] J. Neale, *Elizabeth I and the Parliaments*, II., 281. It is true he points out that 'Tudor laws were often intended to be held *in terrorem* over offenders, and were neither expected to be, nor cabable of being, rigidly enforced'.

[2] See p. 313.

[3] 35 Eliz. c. 2. *Statutes of the Realm*, IV. 843; J. R. Tanner, *Tudor Constitutional Documents*, p. 159 ff.

reach a certain property qualification and who break these regulations may be required to abjure the realm and to depart from it. If they refuse to do so or if they subsequently return, they are to be adjudged felons. Further, any person suspected to be a Jesuit, seminary or massing priest who refuses to answer whether he is one, shall be committed to prison without bail and remain there until he does answer. Licences might be issued for travelling beyond the five mile limit. Offenders under the act might before conviction escape the penalties of the act by coming to church.

In 1594 the cause of English Catholicism suffered a severe blow by the death of Cardinal William Allen who had long been the unofficial head of the English Catholics and whose death removed the one man who might have been able to minimise, even though he could not have removed, the causes of division which were becoming increasingly serious. Allen had rendered inestimable service to the cause by establishing and fostering the seminary movement, but he had also done it serious harm, as things turned out, by his political activities and by his attachment to Spain, whose armies, he hoped, would restore the faith which alone mattered to him. His long exile from England blinded him, as it blinded Robert Parsons, to the fact that English Catholics were deeply affected by nationalism and would rather put up as best they could with persecution than see Catholicism restored by Spanish soldiers. Allen, like the popes who relied so much on his advice in English affairs, failed to see that he could not have it both ways and that he was placing the missionary priests in an impossible situation when he sent them to work for the Catholic cause by spiritual means while at the same time he was supporting attempts to overthrow the Protestant régime by force. In his later years he was increasingly detached from politics and his remarkable and attractive personality has enabled him to escape from much of the criticism directed against Parsons, even though Parsons was much less deeply attached to Spain than Allen; nor was Allen involved in the fierce divisions over the archpriest which have done so much damage to Parsons' reputation.

It was a serious misunderstanding of the reactions of English Catholics that led the Allen–Parsons group to make yet another most unfortunate blunder in 1595. In that year there appeared in Europe a book entitled *A conference about the next succession to the crowne of Ingland . . . Where unto is also added a new and perfect genealogie of the discents of all the Kinges and princes of Ingland.* It was dated 1594 and it bore the name of R. Doleman.[1] It was widely attributed to Robert Parsons and he played a major part in writing it, but several others, including Allen, Sir Francis Englefield and Richard Verstegan, had a hand in it, and it appears to have been, as it were, a manifesto from the Allen–Parsons group.

In the first part of the *Conference* there is a discussion about the nature of government. Monarchy is chosen as the best form, but it is argued that the kingly power is not absolute. The decision about who is to be king depends partly on succession by birth and partly on election by the commonwealth. The obedience which the people give to their ruler is conditional on his ruling according to the laws of the land and the advice of his councillors. The prince is bound by his coronation oath to protect the Church and true religion, and a prince who adheres to a false religion should not be accepted. The point of this argument, which derived much from the views that the Catholic Leaguers were putting out against Henry of Navarre,[2] was that the succession to the crown was not inevitably determined by who was next in blood to the previous ruler, and that in certain circumstances the commonwealth might choose someone else.

The second part of the *Conference* examines in detail the nine principal candidates for the English succession after Elizabeth's death, tracing their descent from Edward III and discussing the case for and against each of them. There are four on the Lancastrian side—Philip II, his daughter the Infanta, the duke of Braganza, and the duke of Parma; and there are five on the Yorkist side, James VI; Arabella Stuart; Edward Seymour, Lord Beauchamp; Henry Stanley, earl of Derby; and Henry Hastings, earl of Huntingdon.[3] Doleman is inclined to back a Spanish claimant, but he does not give unqualified support to a Spaniard. The essential point is that the successor should be of the true religion, that is a Papist. He thinks that of the nine possible candidates the three 'most lykest to prevail' are the Infanta,

---

[1] Essential reading on this book is L. Hicks, 'Father Robert Persons S.J. and the Book of Succession', *Recusant History*, 1957, vol. 4, no. 3, and T. H. Clancy, *Papist Pamphleteers*, p. 62 ff.

[2] Thomas Clancy, *Papist Pamphleteers*, p. 57 ff. In particular the argument owed a good deal to the thought of another Englishman, William Rainold, who had written in support of the Guise against the claims of Henry of Navarre. See also J. H. M. Salmon, *The French Religious Wars in English Political Thought*, Oxford, 1959.

[3] *Ibid.*, pp. 69, 70.

Edward Seymour and Henry Stanley, earl of Derby, and they will attract the support respectively of the Papists, the Protestants and the Puritans.[1]

It was certainly unwise of Doleman to raise in this public fashion the question of Elizabeth's successor. It was a matter which Englishmen had been forbidden to discuss, and Peter Wentworth had been sent to the Tower in 1593 for daring to do so. The fact that it was a forbidden subject made it impossible for government propagandists to deal with Doleman, and Fr. Leo Hicks maintains that the book did not in fact cause as much fury in England as has often been suggested.[2] Nevertheless, it must surely have contributed to the feeling among a number of English Catholics that their future was being calmly decided for them by a group abroad over which they had no control, that Parsons and others were trying to shape the destiny of England and to hand the country over to a Spaniard. If they had known of the plans that were forming in Parsons' mind for the future of the country once the Catholic succession had been established, they would have been even more disturbed.[3]

Meanwhile, the Catholic laity carried on as best they could, avoiding publicity and often trying merely to escape notice from the authorities. For the limited number who were prepared to risk everything by giving active encouragement and support to the missionary work of the priests, there must have been many who were content as long as they could avoid recusancy fines and have mass said by priests living quietly in their houses and not creating trouble by trying to proselytise outside. The government kept up a continual pressure on the Catholic gentry throughout the last decade of the reign, and although there were fluctuations in the extent of the persecution, the Catholic gentry can never have felt really secure.[4] Orders to local officials to draw up schedules of recusants, instructions to search Catholic houses for armour and weapons, attempts to remove from the Commission of the Peace recusants and conformists with recusant wives and

---

[1] Thomas Clancy, *Papist Pamphleteers*, p. 70.

[2] L. Hicks, 'Father Robert Persons S.J. and the Book of Succession', *Recusant History*, 1957, vol. 4, no. 3.

[3] Parsons drew up in 1596 a kind of blue-print showing what would have to be done. This interesting document is discussed by T. H. Clancy in 'Notes on Persons' *Memorial for the Reformation of England* (1596)', *Recusant History*, vol. 5, no. 1, January 1959.

[4] See W. R. Trimble, *The Catholic Laity in Elizabethan England*, p. 140 ff. for many illustrations of the pressures on the laity.

children, efforts by the Exchequer to put the records of recusancy in order and to devise new methods of collecting recusancy fines,[1] all added to the difficulties and worries of life for the Catholic gentleman.[2] In his study of the Catholic laity, Mr. Trimble expresses the opinion that by 1600 'The limitations hindering an active Catholic spiritual life and the interferences preventing close relations with revitalized Catholic institutions on the Continent were now rendering conformity less onerous in conscience'.[3] He thinks that Catholic resistance was being worn down 'by raids by pursuivants which could jeopardise property and even personal safety, the refusal to recognise both the validity of marriages not celebrated by the Anglican rites and the legitimacy of births not registered in a parish of the Establishment, difficulties in educating children in surroundings not inimical to Catholicism, social and political advantages in being a Protestant, and the ever-present fear of imprisonment'.[4] It may be that Mr. Trimble is painting too gloomy a picture, for there was gain as well as loss. The Jesuit Richard Blount wrote to Robert Parsons on 22 October 1600: 'We are all well and follow our accustomed trade with good gain, for our customers (thanks be to God) do daily increase, which is perceivable even to our enemies and hath caused the Chief Justice to complain very bitterly to her Majesty now of late of the great multitude of Catholics in this land.'[5] It is not easy to say whether the tide had turned against the Papists before the reign was over, but it is clear that the Papist cause was very seriously damaged by the fierce internal disputes which manifested themselves openly from 1595 onwards.

Divisions within the ranks of English Catholics were not, of course, new. We have seen earlier the difference of opinion on the question of whether Papists could in good faith attend the services of the Church of England in order to escape the penalties of the law.[6]

---

[1] The Exchequer began a separate Recusant Roll in 1592. For a detailed discussion of the operation of the Recusancy laws and their relationship to the Recusancy Roll, see *Recusant Roll No. 2.* (1593–4), edit. Hugh Bowler, Catholic Record Society, vol. 57, 1965.

[2] Two interesting studies of particular Catholic families are Augustus Jessopp, *One Generation of a Norfolk House*, second edition, 1879, and Godfrey Anstruther, *Vaux of Harrowden*, Newport, 1953.

[3] W. R. Trimble, *op. cit.*, p. 172.

[4] W. R. Trimble, *op. cit.*, p. 172.

[5] Quoted in Philip Caraman, *The Other Face; Catholic Life under Elizabeth I*, 1960, p. 284.

[6] See pp. 58, 170.

There was, too, a fundamental divergence between most English Catholics and the various groups of exiles abroad on the question of whether Elizabeth ought to be disposed of by force. There had been no enthusiasm among English Papists for the various invasion schemes of the eighties and the nineties. Although the Allen–Parsons group took it upon itself 'to offer (to the papacy) in the name of the Catholics of England, their lives, their property and all their powers for the service of God and of his Holiness in this expedition',[1] they had no authority to do so. Later on, when the group was backing the Spanish invasion plans, it must have had some doubt about the reception that would be given to Philip's armies, for it insisted on the need to stress religion as the main reason for the attack. Philip's claim to the throne was to be played down, and only after the victory was it to be put forward in a book which could be secretly prepared in advance and published and distributed immediately the Spanish armies were victorious.[2] There were, too, very serious differences between the pro-Spanish group of exiles and the Morgan–Paget group in France which was ostensibly working for Mary Queen of Scots. It is possible that Morgan and Paget were double-agents and that they deliberately sabotaged the invasion plans of their rivals in the early 1580's.[3]

Allen was well aware of the danger of division within the ranks when he wrote in 1577 that the Catholic Church in England 'hath no forme of externall common wealth, no one that governeth the rest, no discipline or censures neyther to dryve the preists nor people into order, no man subject to his fellowe, no way to call disorders to accompt, no common conference, no soveraignty nor subjection; but every one living severally and secretly by himself, and often farre from any

---

[1] *Letters and Memorials of Father Robert Persons, S.J.*, vol. 1, edit. L. Hicks, Catholic Record Society, vol. 39, 1942, p. 146 ff.

[2] *Ibid.*, p. 292 ff. 'Considerations indicating that it would be in no wise advisable that the special interest of His Majesty in the English succession should be made known to His Holiness in advance of the enterprise'; p. 299 ff. Memorandum of Persons and Allen on the succession, 1587; p. 303 ff. another Memorandum of *c.* June 1587. These memoranda seem to show that the pro-Spanish group was deliberately concealing the truth from those whom it hoped would support the invaders.

[3] The pro-Spanish group has been studied by A. J. Loomie in *The Spanish Elizabethans*, New York, 1963 which examines its activities by means of biographical studies of Sir Francis Englefield, Hugh Owen, Lady Jane Dormer, Sir William Stanley, and Joseph Creswell, S.J. For the 'French Elizabethans', see John Bossy, 'Elizabethan Catholicism: the Link with France', Cambridge Ph.D. Thesis, 1961; John Bossy, 'Henry IV, the Appellants and the Jesuits', *Recusant History*, vol. 8, no. 2, 1965; L. Hicks, *An Elizabethan Problem*.

fellowes, is ruled onley by his own skill and conscience; which even amonge the apostles had bredd disturbance, yf by sundry meetyngs, counsels, and conferences yt had not bene looked into'.[1]

Yet another warning that trouble might come was given by what happened in the English College in Rome. In 1579 there had been serious conflict when the English students complained that the Welsh rector was giving preferential treatment to the Welsh students, and a group of English students had left the College. They were given an opportunity of putting their case to the pope in person and they were granted their request that the management of the College be entrusted to the Jesuits. The new arrangement had not been satisfactory, and in the 1580's there were serious disputes within the College. The malcontents objected to the system of discipline through 'Guardian Angels' whom they regarded as spies for the authorities, and they maintained that special favour was shown to those who toadied to the Jesuits and joined their 'Sodality'. In 1588 matters were so serious that pope had been forced to send Cardinal Sega to make a special visitation. The authority of the Jesuits was upheld, a number of malcontents were sent elsewhere, and some concessions were made to the complainants,[2] but the difficulties were not finally solved and there was to be more trouble later.[3]

The establishment of the Jesuits in England in the 1580's did not in itself create conflict within the Catholic body, but it added yet another element which might be dangerous, for there was a long history of trouble between the religious orders and the secular clergy. Moreover, the Jesuits had their own organisation and their own loyalties, and the most important English Jesuit abroad was after 1581 increasingly committed to a policy of restoring Catholicism by force.

The English Catholics showed plainly at the time of the Armada that they had no desire to support a foreign invasion. A paper written by a priest Wright after the Armada provided a theoretical justification for their conduct. In answer to the question 'Whether catholics in England might take up arms to defend the queen and country against the Spaniards?', he maintained that it was lawful for them to do so, since the Spaniards had taken up arms not for the Faith but for

---

[1] *Letters and Memorials of Cardinal Allen*, edit. T. F. Knox, 1882, p. 378.
[2] A. O. Meyer, *The Catholic Church under Elizabeth*, p. 105 ff.
[3] See p. 280.

their own selfish reasons.[1] He did not repudiate the papal deposing power, but he argued that in this particular case Catholics were not bound to obey the pope. To what extent his work was read by his fellow Catholics we do not know, but their behaviour suggests that they agreed with his views.

The unfortunate *Conference about the next succession*[2] did nothing to endear the Allen–Parsons party to their fellow English Catholics since it tended to identify Papists in the eyes of the government with views about a highly controversial and dangerous topic on which discussion was forbidden. Although the purpose of the book may, as Fr. Leo Hicks suggests, have been simply to ensure that there was discussion and to insist that nearness in blood was not the only ground for a claim to the throne, those English Catholics who knew what was going on must have felt that policy was being shaped by exiles who had no right to make decisions for them and who were prepared in certain circumstances to hand the country over to the national enemy.

Divisions among Papists first became public in the affair known as 'the Wisbech Stirs'.[3] Wisbech Castle near the Isle of Ely had been used as a prison for important Papist prisoners since 1580. At the time of the trouble there were 33 prisoners there, all of them priests with the exception of Thomas Pounde.[4] Treatment of the prisoners had fluctuated considerably in its severity over the years, and what had originally been intended as a concentration camp in which potentially dangerous men were isolated from the outside world seems to have become a Catholic centre in which the prisoners enjoyed a good deal of freedom and considerable contact with people outside. The internees were held in high respect by their fellow Papists and what they did was consequently of great importance. They had included among their number Bishop Watson who, at his death in 1584, was the last surviving Catholic bishop in England, and John Feckenham, the last abbot of Westminster, who died there in 1585.

[1] *An licitum sit catholicis in Anglia arma sumere et aliis modis reginam et regnum defendere contra Hispanos'*. Written after 1590. Translated in J. Strype, *Annals of the Reformation*, 1824, III. ii. 583–97. See A. O. Meyer, *The Catholic Church under Elizabeth*, pp. 161, 355 ff. His views should be compared with those of the Jesuit, Robert Southwell. See p. 269 note 2. It is interesting to note that Doleman in his *Conference about the next succession* does not mention the papal deposing power.

[2] See pp. 271–72.

[3] See P. Renold, *The Wisbech Stirs 1595–1598*, Catholic Record Society, Vol. 51, 1958.

[4] See pp. 167, 168.

Some of the priests had been in prison for a very long time. Thomas Metham,[1] for example, who was one of the first four seminary priests to land in England, had been arrested and imprisoned in the year of his arrival. He survived at Wisbech till 1592 and he seems to have exercised considerable influence over his fellow prisoners.[2] Another man of importance was Thomas Bluet who had been a prisoner since shortly after his arrival in 1578. At Wisbech he acted as keeper of the common purse, and he played an important part in the disputes from 1595 onwards.[3]

In 1588 there arrived at Wisbech two men who were in different ways very difficult characters. One of them was William Weston, the Superior of the English Jesuits, who had been captured in 1586 and who was now transferred from London to Wisbech.[4] Weston was a very interesting and remarkable man of unquestioned holiness, but he cannot have been altogether easy to get on with, and it is not surprising that he fell foul of some of his fellow prisoners who differed temperamentally from him. One of these was the secular priest Dr. Christopher Bagshaw who arrived in Wisbech in the same year as Weston. Bagshaw had been Principal of Gloucester Hall, Oxford. He had played a part earlier on in securing the resignation of Robert Parsons from his Balliol Fellowship. Later, in 1582, Bagshaw became a Catholic, went to Rheims and was ordained priest in 1583. He had played a part in the troubles of the English College in Rome and had been sent away after the papal visitation of 1585. After picking up a doctorate at Padua in rather dubious circumstances, he had come to England and had been captured soon afterwards. He had strong feelings against the Jesuits, and in view of his difficult character it was likely that sooner or later there would be trouble at Wisbech.

There had been earlier difficulties among the prisoners as one might expect among people forced to live in each other's company under unpleasant conditions with little prospect of ever getting away.[5] No doubt nervous tension built up after long years of imprisonment.

---

[1] See p. 111 and note 2.   [2] P. Renold, *op. cit.*, p. xii.
[3] Bluet had been a Protestant minister, but went to Douay in 1577, was ordained priest and returned to England in 1578. He was arrested in the same year and was a prisoner in Wisbech from 1580 to 1601. See P. Renold, *op. cit.*, p. 31.
[4] See *William Weston: The Autobiography of an Elizabethan*, edit. Philip Caraman, 1955.
[5] One wonders why they did not go in for escaping. John Gerard had even managed to get out of the Tower.

Fr. Weston disapproved of the behaviour of his fellow prisoners and towards the end of 1594 he was no longer prepared to eat at the common table. What then happened was a split between the prisoners. A group of 19, including 18 priests and the one layman, Thomas Pounde, drew up a set of rules for themselves and placed themselves under the spiritual authority of William Weston. Fr. Garnet, the Superior of the Jesuits in England, was drawn in because he was asked to approve the rules and Weston's spiritual authority over the group. The other group, led by Bagshaw and Bluet, resented what had been done, and a considerable amount of unpleasant wrangling followed. Accusations were thrown about freely and apparently without too great a regard for the truth. The group under Weston felt, probably with some justification, that the way of life in the prison had been far from satisfactory, and the Bagshaw party resented what appeared to be a 'holier than thou' attitude on the part of the followers of Weston.[1] Weston reported to Garnet on the endless quarrelling, the excessive drinking, and shiftiness in distributing alms collected for the prisoners,[2] and there were suggestions of 'whoredome, drunkennes, and dicing'.[3] Bagshaw later described savagely how Weston 'lifted up his countenance, as if a new spirit had bin put into him, and tooke upon him to controll, and finde fault with this and that: (as the comming into the Hall of a Hobby-horse in Christmas) affirming that he would no longer tolerate these and those so grosse abuses, but would have them reformed'.[4] It is extremely difficult if not impossible to get a true picture of the situation because as time went on the protagonists on both sides wrote with increasing venom in order to substantiate their case and demolish the characters of their opponents.

The troubles at Wisbech might possibly have remained simply a little local difficulty if they had not come increasingly to the attention of the public and if they had not become part of wider disputes that were going on elsewhere.

When the 'stirs' became known to a number of English Catholics,

---

[1] See P. Renold, *op. cit.*, for some of the documents in the case; T. G. Law, *A Historical Sketch of the Conflicts between Jesuits and seculars*, 1889; T. G. Law, *The Archpriest Controversy*, Vol. I, Camden Society, 1896.

[2] Philip Hughes, *Rome and the Counter-Reformation in England*, p. 279.

[3] T. G. Law, *A Historical Sketch*, p. 21.

[4] Bagshaw's highly partial account *A True relation of the faction begun at Wisbech, by Fr. Edmonds, alias Weston, a Iesuite . . .*, printed in 1601, is reprinted in T. G. Law, *A Historical Sketch*.

T

there were attempts to arbitrate between the parties. Eventually at Garnet's request two prominent secular priests, John Mush and Richard Dudley, carried out lengthy negotiations which led to the signing of a peace treaty on 6 November 1596. Both sides agreed to abide by a new set of rules and there were moving reconciliations. Unfortunately the peace was not lasting.

The Wisbech 'stirs' were linked directly with anti-Jesuit groups in Europe by the visit to England from September 1596 to the summer of 1597 of a young student Robert Fisher who came as the representative of a number of students engaged in disputes with the Jesuit authorities in the English College in Rome.[1] Fisher also had contact with two anti-Jesuit groups centring around Charles Paget and Dr. William Gifford, Dean of Lille, in Flanders, and Hugh Griffin, Provost of Cambrai, Nicholas Fitzherbert and others in Rome.[2]

The renewed trouble in the English College in Rome seems to have been to a considerable extent due to the same causes which had led to conflict in the 1580's, resentment by the English against a system of discipline which they regarded as spying and a belief that special favours were shown to those who ingratiated themselves with the Jesuit superiors. The malcontents among the students also charged the Jesuits with aiming at supremacy over the whole of the English mission and with monopolising the education of the English missionary priests. They claimed that the Jesuits were more welcome than the seculars in the houses of the leading Catholics in England because they were given special powers to dispense the holders of church property from the censures of the church and that the payments they made were used by the Jesuits for their own purposes.[3] The nature of these complaints certainly seems to suggest a link between the students and a number of secular priests in England who resented the rôle of the Jesuits in the English mission.

During his stay in England Robert Fisher not only contacted Bagshaw in Wisbech but also travelled about the country, with the help of the funds provided by Bagshaw, Bluet, Mush, Dudley and other sympathisers. Mr. Rainold thinks that by the time he returned to Flanders in the summer of 1597 'the anti-Jesuit group in England had, in spite of internal arguments, achieved a certain measure of co-

---

[1] P. Renold, *op. cit.*, p. xvi.
[2] *Ibid.*
[3] A. O. Meyer, *England and the Catholic Church under Elizabeth*, p. 391 ff.

hesion'.[1] Parsons became increasingly of the opinion that there was a conspiracy against the Jesuits centred in the Netherlands,[2] but also involving people in Rome and in England. In the savage controversies that ensued, men on both sides were only too ready to see their opponents as wicked conspirators and to put the worst possible interpretation on all they said and did.

Meanwhile, the trouble in the English College in Rome continued and to the other causes of dispute was added outraged national feelings on the part of young men who resented the pro-Spanish policy of the Jesuits. Dr. Barrett wrote to Parsons in April 1596 that the scholars had such an indignation and aversion to the Society 'as though the fathers were enemies to them, to their cause, and their country . . . ',[3] and the Rector Alphonso Agazzari reported to Parsons that the rebellious students 'speak frequently and cuttingly against the book on the succession to the English throne and against its author, that is to say Father Persons, as they think, and they can hardly endure to hear his name mentioned. All openly rejoice over the Spanish reverses . . . and grieve over their successes . . . I know not whether they hate the Society (of Jesus) more on account of the Spaniards, or the Spaniards on account of the Society . . . '[4]

In 1596 the papacy arranged for another visitation of the college by Cardinal Sega who gave his support to the Jesuit authorities, but the problems were not solved. In July 1596 the Rector commented: 'We have gained nothing here so far beyond a certain outward show of peace and quiet in avoiding scandals', and at the end of August he told Parsons in Madrid: 'They have such a hatred against the Society that I fear they would be ready to join hands with the heretics in order to be delivered from them . . . '[5]

It was largely because this trouble had such serious repercussions that in 1597 Parsons was brought back from Spain in order to deal with it. Meyer thinks that he did not come back merely to deal with a students' rebellion and that the reputation of the Jesuits was at stake.[6] Parsons enjoyed a great personal triumph. He was conciliatory, he made concessions in the matter of discipline which the

[1] P. Renold, *op. cit.*, p. xvi.
[2] A. O. Meyer, *op. cit.*, p. 393; T. G. Law, *The Archpriest Controversy*, I. 28.
[3] *Dodd's Church History of England*, edit. M. A. Tierney, III, Appendix XV, p. lxxiii.
[4] A. O. Meyer, *op. cit.*, p. 395; *Dodd's Church History*, edit. M. A. Tierney, III, Appendix XV, p. lxxv.
[5] A. O. Meyer, *op. cit.*, p. 396.   [6] *Ibid.*, p. 397.

English students had found intolerable, and he made friends with those who had looked forward with dread to his coming. He also enhanced his reputation in Rome and he was appointed Rector of the College, a post which he held until his death in 1610.

Thus there was building up in England and abroad a party of English Papists which was critical of the Jesuits for a large number of reasons.[1] The motives and conduct of some members of the party were highly suspect and many of the charges they were to bring against the Jesuits in the course of the controversy were unjust and absurd, but not all their complaints can be summarily dismissed as the work of a tiny minority of jealous malcontents among the secular clergy. There was, inevitably, a feeling that the well-organised and highly trained Jesuits were getting more than their fair share of the credit for the work in England than was justified by their small numbers, and that the secular clergy were being regarded as inferior second-line troops. The self-confidence and self-assurance of the Jesuits and their intense pride in their Society aroused jealousy and dislike. The secular priest John Mush put the position with moderation and restraint in the early days of the conflict when he wrote: 'The Jesuits helpe well and doe much good; they also that are wholly guided by them doe well: but in truth the greatest weight and burthen of the worke, the chiefe maintenaunce, upholdinge, and progresse of the cause, within this realm is principally be (by) the secular priests, and the people guided by them.' He went on to plead for understanding on both sides—'Both sorts spend their lives, and yield their blood with equall courage and constancy for one and the same cause. Let not then theire children contend emulously for the preferringe or more credit of either, but reverence, love and honour all.'[2]

Mush's counsels of moderation were not followed, and there was a great deal of bitterness, some of it due to jealousy, some of it going much deeper. Just as Parsons was ready to see everywhere signs of a great conspiracy against the Jesuits, so a number of secular priests saw a conspiracy on the part of the Jesuits to seize control of English Catholicism and to manipulate it in the interests of an anti-national, pro-Spanish policy. Although the Jesuits in England were few in num-

---

[1] For a long list of complaints against the Jesuits, see an Abstract of the Memorial and of sundry letters against the Jesuits sent by certain Englishmen in the Low Countries to Clement VIII in September 1597, printed in T. G. Law, *The Archpriest Controversy*, I. 7 ff.

[2] T. G. Law, *The Archpriest Controversy*, pp. 59, 61.

bers, their Society was very powerful abroad, they controlled the
education of the secular clergy in the seminaries, and Robert Parsons
had the ear of the pope. Resentment against the Jesuits produced
savage comment such as this: 'So holie, so godly, so religious would
they seeme to be, as nothing is holie that they have not sanctified, no
doctrine catholick and sound that commeth not from them, no dispensation available that is not granted by them, and, which is worse,
they have beaten into the heads of the most, that the masse is not
rightly and orderly celebrated of any but a Jesuite.'[1] The secular
priest, Watson, was one of the most violent opponents of the Jesuits.
Commenting on the establishment of an archpriest, which we shall
examine in a moment, he said: 'That it was foysted in by Parsons
procurement onely upon a pointe of extremity to colour his impietie
and to stop the discovery of his treacherous minde towards his
countrey . . . for it came in . . . at that time when bothe in Spaine
Italie and the lowe countreis his dealings began to be odious for his
tyrany against all priests and lay persons that consented not to his
Jappon Kingdome,[2] and in England his bookes and all his dealings
being by catholics generally disliked and by Sem(inary priests) condemned and reiected as full of ambition, bloodshed, infamy and
crime intended to our whole countrey.' It was inevitable in such an
atmosphere that not only the fanatics among the secular clergy but
also more moderate men, clerical and lay, should begin to toy with the
idea that it might be as well if the Jesuits were withdrawn from England
and deprived of their control over the seminaries. The suggestion
was also made that if the Jesuits were no longer in England the Papists
might be able to come to some kind of terms with the government. As
we shall see, the English government for its own purposes went to
remarkable lengths to encourage this idea.[3]

It would be wrong to see the whole Catholic priesthood in England
in the later years of Elizabeth as divided into a tiny group of Jesuits
and their supporters in conflict with the large secular majority. A
great many of the secular clergy were, as far as we know, not directly
involved at all and were busy getting on with their work as priests.
As far as the small Jesuit group was concerned, a number enjoyed

---

[1] A. O. Meyer, *England and the Catholic Church under Elizabeth*, p. 404, quoting
from *Brevis declaratio miserrimi status catholicorum in Anglia degentium*, 1597.

[2] T. G. Law, *The Archpriest Controversy*, I. 91–2. The Japanese imperial government
was used to represent the extreme of tyranny.

[3] See p. 291.

very happy relations with the seculars, and Garnet, the Jesuit Superior, although inevitably involved, generally speaking did his best to avoid conflict and keep the temperature down. Nevertheless, there was a potentially explosive situation. Unfortunately for the Papists, the Roman Curia handled it with such remarkable ineptitude that what might have been a comparatively minor dispute assumed formidable proportions.

After the death of Allen it had become increasingly clear that it was desirable to give some kind of effective ecclesiastical government to the English Catholic body, which had been without bishops since 1559, and whose needs could not be adequately served by a Cardinal Protector resident abroad.

The most sensible scheme was that put forward by Robert Parsons in 1597 when he petitioned the pope for the appointment of two English bishops, each with a staff of archpriests, one of them resident in England and the other in the Low Countries.[1] This scheme was not adopted, nor did Rome pay any attention to proposals put forward by the English secular clergy to form an association to elect one of their number as bishop and to introduce some very necessary organisation and discipline into the government of English Catholics.[2] What happened then was that Parsons put forward an alternative plan, and as a result on 7 March 1598 George Blackwell, a secular priest, was appointed archpriest, with limited authority over the secular clergy working in England and Scotland.[3]

The Brief appointing the archpriest did not come direct from the pope but from the Cardinal Protector of England.[4] The archpriest was given limited disciplinary powers over the seminary-trained priests working in England. He had no jurisdiction over the laity or over the Jesuits. He was to be helped in his work by twelve assistants, six of whom were named in the brief and six of whom were to be appointed by Blackwell himself. His powers, then, were small. He

---

[1] A. O. Meyer, *English Catholics under Elizabeth*, p. 409; Philip Hughes, *Rome and the Counter-Reformation in England*, p. 295.

[2] A. O. Meyer, *op. cit.*, p. 410–11; L. von Pastor, *History of the Popes*, xxiv, 21.

[3] A. O. Meyer, *op. cit.*, p. 412 ff.

[4] The Brief and a number of other documents in the case are printed in *Dodd's Church History*, edit. M. A. Tierney, III. cxix ff. See also T. G. Law, *The Archpriest Controversy*, 2 vols.; T. G. Law *A Historical Sketch of the Conflicts between Jesuits and Seculars*, 1889; J. H. Pollen, *The Institution of the Archpriest Blackwell*, 1916; Philip Hughes, *Rome and the Counter-Reformation in England* and *The Reformation in England*, vol. III. For Garnet's relations with Blackwell, see Philip Caraman, *Henry Garnet*.

could not ordain priests nor administer the sacrament of confirmation and he was in no sense an adequate substitute for a bishop.

The scheme was in itself inept and of its very nature likely to lead to trouble. The whole conception of government of the church in England by an archpriest was novel and was bound to arouse surprise and opposition. The office of archpriest was, as Parsons asserted, an ancient dignity in the church, but duties of archpriests in earlier times were entirely different from those now assigned to Blackwell, and Parsons' opponents had a good deal of justification when they later told him: 'It is a mockery that you call it *an ancient dignity in Christ's Church*, who knoweth it not? The question is not of the ancientness of the dignity but of this new and never-before-heard-of jurisdiction and authority.'[1]

But if the scheme was in itself unsatisfactory, its chances of being accepted without trouble were completely sabotaged by the way in which it was put into operation. The secular clergy in England had not been properly consulted, it was known that Parsons was the man behind the scheme, and inevitably the charge would be made that this was part of a Jesuit plot to get control of the Church in England. The authority behind the Brief appointing Blackwell was not the pope himself but the Cardinal Protector of England. Opponents of the scheme were thus given an opportunity of questioning whether Rome was fully informed and whether it had in fact given its backing to the Cardinal's scheme.[2] The Brief, moreover, went out of its way very tactlessly to give special praise to the work of the Jesuits who had striven so hard for the cause of England by founding seminaries, instructing the young, engaging in works of charity, and even shedding their blood, and it ignored the fact that at the time there were only 14 Jesuits in England, 4 of them in prison, as compared with some 400 secular priests.[3] As for the shedding of blood, the number of Jesuit martyrs up to that time was 6 as compared with 154 secular clergy and laypeople.

The man appointed as the first archpriest was George Blackwell. Although he had a very satisfactory record up to this time, he was not outstanding among the secular clergy. He was, however, known to be

[1] T. G. Law, *A Historical Sketch*, p. lxvii; Philip Hughes, *Rome and the Counter Reformation in England*, p. 298 ff.

[2] T. G. Law, *op. cit.*, p. lxiii ff.

[3] Philip Hughes, *Rome and the Counter-Reformation in England*, p. 288; Henry Foley, *Records of the English Province of the Society of Jesus*, VII. lxvi ff.

very closely attached to the Jesuits and it was inevitable that he would be seen by his opponents as a tool of Parsons and of the Society. This seemed to be borne out by the fact that he was given instructions to consult the Jesuit Superior in England in all matters of importance.[1] The dispute had not yet led to the intense bitterness of later years, but the arrangements gave some substance to the charge subsequently made by William Watson, one of the most savage opponents of the Jesuits, that 'All Catholics must hereafter depend upon Blackwell, and he upon Garnet and Garnet upon Persons, and Persons upon the Devil, who is the author of all rebellions, treasons, murders, disobedience, and all such designments as this wicked Jesuit hath hitherto designed against her majesty, her safety, her crown, and her life'.[2]

Blackwell's actions made certain that there would be trouble. He was, it is true, in an extremely difficult position, but power seems to have gone to his head. He was determined to assert his novel jurisdiction and he encountered resistance, partly through his own fault. In August 1598 he petitioned the pope for confirmation of his appointment so that he might defend it against a small number of ambitious priests who envied the Jesuits. He asked that no hearing should be given to the trouble makers, 'only few in numbers compared with the large number of the good' who had, he said, joyfully approved of what had been done.

Blackwell's opponents in the late summer of 1598 sent two priests, William Bishop and Robert Charnock, to appeal on their behalf to the pope. The two representatives were to request the appointment of a bishop chosen by the secular clergy and to ask that the seculars should be allowed to form themselves into a 'sodality' of their own. The government of the English College in Rome was to be taken out of the hands of the Jesuits, and that order was to be forbidden to publish books against the queen unless they had been approved by ecclesiastical superiors, since such books did no good. The appointment of Blackwell was questioned on the ground that he had not been

[1] Philip Hughes, *Rome and the Counter-Reformation*, p. 297; T. G. Law, *op. cit.*, lxv. A. O. Meyer, *England and the Catholic Church under Elizabeth*, p. 415, quotes a letter of Blackwell, of 10 December 1597, in which he said of the opponents of the Jesuits 'There is no greater perversity than to be the enemy of the best'.

[2] Quoted in Philip Hughes, *Rome and the Counter-Reformation in England*, p. 298, from Watson's *A sparing discoverie of our English Iesuits and of Fa. Parson's proceedings under pretence of promoting the Catholick faith in England.* (1601.)

appointed in a regular fashion by the pope but only in a letter from the Cardinal Protector of England.[1]

Meyer argues that behind all this agitation lay the idea that the Catholic Church in England ought to have a measure of independence of the central authority in Rome, that the principle of national independence was coming in conflict with centralising policies in the Church, and that there is a parallel here with the 'Gallican liberties' of the Church in France.[2] He finds this tendency present, for example, in a work written by John Bishop and published in 1598, not in connection with the archpriest controversy. In his *A Courteous Conference with the English Catholickes Romane* Bishop argued that the pope had no earthly sovereignty and that he could not depose princes or release their subjects from obedience.[3]

Meyer's view of the significance of the dispute is, however, questionable. It is not clear that objections to the archpriest, or even a questioning of the papal deposing power, amounts to a claim for 'Gallican liberties' for the Church in England.

How much support the petition against the archpriest had among the secular clergy is very difficult to estimate. The petition had thirty-one signatures, but they included a number of highly respectable priests, some of whom had been in prison for very many years. It was certainly not, as Garnet alleged, the opposition of 'a few turbulent youths'.[4] We must bear in mind the difficulty of communication between priests who were liable to the death penalty if they were caught and the natural reluctance of many of them to involve themselves in so momentous a step as an appeal to Rome against the archpriest and the Cardinal Protector who had put him in authority over the secular clergy. In these circumstances the fact that some 30 priests were willing to back the appeal is significant. Fr. Hughes comments that 'the most of those who so resisted were by no means scallawags nor trouble makers (seditiosi) either by nature or by habit . . . '[5] It is also significant that a petition in support of the archpriest had less than sixty signatures.[6]

While the two representatives of the dissatisfied secular clergy were

---

[1] A. O. Meyer, *op. cit.*, p. 421.
[2] A. O. Meyer, *op. cit.*, p. 419 ff.
[3] *Ibid.* p. 420.
[4] *Dodd's Church History*, edit. M. A. Tierney III. pp. 48, 49, note 2.
[5] Philip Hughes, *The Reformation in England*, III. 386
[6] *Dodd's Church History*, edit. M. A. Tierney, III. 48, 49, note 2.

on their way to Rome, Garnet sent to the pope a letter signed by himself and the nineteen other Jesuits in England (four of whom were in prison) praising the pope's attempt to put an end by means of the archpriest to 'the disturbances caused by certain of our countrymen in Rome and Flanders'. He asserted that the appointment had given great satisfaction to Catholics in general and that Blackwell was the most worthy man to be entrusted with such jurisdiction. He maintained that the few priests of unquiet disposition who opposed the archpriest seemed to be moved by no other purpose than a desire for faction and contention. He thought the remedy was for the pope to confirm and extend Blackwell's jurisdiction and 'that those two priests who, after first trying to win support here, went to Rome, should be treated with some severity by your Holiness or should be prevented from returning unless they change their temper of mind'.[1]

The story of ineptitude continued when the two priests reached Rome in December 1598. The pope was away from Rome at the time and they lodged at the English College of which Parsons was Rector. On 29 December 1598 they were placed under house arrest in the charge of Parsons and were treated with considerable contempt. They were then subjected to a form of trial and had no opportunity of presenting their case to the pope. Judgment was given against them in April 1599. They were ordered to leave Rome without seeing the pope and they were not to communicate with each other. Bishop was sent to Paris and Charnock to Lorraine.[2] On 6 April 1599 a papal letter confirmed the action of the Cardinal Protector in appointing the archpriest and stated that it had been done by orders of the pope.[3]

Whatever the rights and wrongs of the case, and whatever the motives of the two secular priests, it was an extraordinarily unjust way of proceeding. The pope had undoubtedly been very seriously misinformed and misled by Parsons and others. The secular priest, John Mush, bitterly commented on this refusal by Rome to hear the appeal 'Our statute of *premunire* may well be repealed now, Father Parsons, a Jesuite, hath laid a plot sufficient enoughe to hinder

---

[1] Philip Caraman, *Henry Garnet*, pp. 247, 248. It is no doubt true, as Fr. Caraman remarks, that Garnet realised that it was most urgent that the Catholic body should be united, but it is also true that Garnet, like Parsons, was trying to prevent his opponents getting a fair hearing.

[2] A. O. Meyer, *op. cit.*, 424; T. G. Law, *Conflicts of Jesuits and Seculars*, p. lxx ff.

[3] *Dodd's Church History*, edit. M. A. Tierney, III. cxxviii–cxxix; Philip Hughes, *The Reformation in England*, III. 387.

appellation (appeal) or accesse to the See of Rome',[1] and Dr. Humphry Ely, a distinguished canon lawyer who had been one of those who came to England with Campion and Parsons in 1580, later wrote to Parsons ' . . . Cloak and disguise it so well as you can now, posterity hereafter will wonder to hear or read that two catholic priests coming as appellants to Rome out of an heretical country, in which they maintained constantly, with danger to their lives, the honour and preservation of that See, and one of them had suffered some years' imprisonment, with banishment afterwards, for the article of St. Peter or his successors' supremacy over all other princes and prelates, that these priests (I say) should, before they were heard what they had to say, be cast into prison, yea and imprisoned in the house and under the custody of their adversaries. Never was there heard of such injustice since good S. Peter sat in the chair.'[2]

It is not easy to understand the conduct of Parsons and others concerned in this extraordinary affair. It is a mistake to see them as wicked men deliberately acting in an evil or unscrupulous manner. They did what they thought was best for the good of the Church in England. It is only too clear that justice was not done and that those in authority made the mistake, which those in authority so often make, of assuming that their opponents must necessarily be seditious and factious and that such people must be suppressed and not given a fair hearing.

The papal decision backing the archpriest led to the submission of nearly all who had hitherto resisted him,[3] and peace seemed to have been restored—at the cost of some injustice. It might have been preserved in spite of all that had happened if Blackwell had acted with common sense. While the appeal to Rome was still pending, he had suspended two of his opponents John Mush and John Colleton. When the decision arrived, they submitted to his authority. He removed the suspension, but he demanded that they make satisfaction for the sin of schism in challenging his authority in the first place.[4] They refused

---

[1] John Mush to Parsons, 13 November 1600, quoted by A. O. Meyer, *op. cit.*, p. 424. See also *ibid.*, p. 430, Mush to Parsons, 'The trouble and scandall you have wrought in our church these late years . . . doo quite cancel all your former deserts . . .'
[2] Quoted in T. G. Law, *A Historical Sketch of the Conflicts between Jesuits and Seculars*, p. 87, note 1.
[3] A. O. Meyer, *England and the Catholic Church under Elizabeth*, pp. 424–6.
[4] Philip Hughes, *Rome and the Counter Reformation in England*, p. 301; T. G. Law, *The Archpriest Controversy*, I. xviii, xix.

to admit they had been guilty, and they too demanded satisfaction for the false charges brought against them. They were angered among other reasons by a pamphlet written by one of the English Jesuits, Thomas Lister, entitled *Adversus Factiosos in Ecclesia* which accused the dissidents of schism and argued that they were *ipso facto* excommunicated. Both Blackwell and Garnet had expressed their approval of the work and refused to condemn it.

And so the dispute went on and a major factor in it was whether or not the dissidents had been guilty of schism. In 1600 Blackwell heard of the intention of the accused priests to publish an explanation of their conduct and he forbade them to do so under threat of ecclesiastical penalties.[1] Early this year John Colleton referred the question of schism to the University of Paris, and in May the Faculty of Theology gave a judgment that there was no question of schism. In the same month Blackwell condemned the university's decision as prejudicial to the dignity of the Apostolic See and forbade anyone to defend it by word or in writing. On 17 October he suspended Mush and Colleton. Thereupon a formal appeal to Rome against Blackwell's misgovernment and against certain Jesuits said to be his advisers was drawn up at Wisbech on 17 November 1600. It was signed by 33 priests and was forwarded to Rome through the archpriest.[2] It charged Blackwell and Garnet with supporting those who accused the petitioners of being schismatics, with showing partiality to the Jesuits in their dispute with the seculars, with depriving of their faculties 'two of our most ancient and reverend priests . . . the special men that had longest and best deserved of our church' and who 'being greatly loved of Cardinal Allen, of pious memory, were by him honoured with special and extraordinary faculties above the rest'. Because of Blackwell's support of three Jesuits, Garnet, Lister and Jones, 'masters and servants, parents and children, husbands and wives, pastors and sheep, priests and lay people' had grown to 'a hurly-burly and mutual contention'. They accused Blackwell of 'intolerable wrongs and oppressions' and of not giving a fair hearing to those whom he condemned.

Then came an extraordinary and, from the Catholic point of view, quite deplorable new development. Some of the dissident secular clergy in England began informal negotiations with the government. The government had known for some considerable time about these

---

[1] T. G. Law, *op. cit.*, xix. January 1600.
[2] Printed in *Dodd's Church History*, edit. M. A. Tierney, III. cxxxiii ff.

divisions and was only too eager to exploit the situation. In April 1599 William Watson had presented to the Attorney General a denunciation of the Jesuits for attempting to secure the succession of a Spaniard, and Charles Paget had also given information to the English ambassador in Paris.[1] About February 1601 Thomas Bluet, who had been allowed out of prison to collect alms on behalf of other prisoners, contacted Richard Bancroft, bishop of London. Bancroft showed Bluet a collection of letters and books of Parsons and others, suggested that the Jesuits were working for a Spanish invasion, and alleged that all priests were tarred with the same brush. Bluet denied this and told Bancroft about the proposed appeal to Rome against Blackwell and the Jesuits. Bancroft realised that the situation could be exploited with advantage, and as a result of further discussions it was arranged that the appellants should be helped by the government to raise the necessary funds for their appeal, that they should be assisted in the publication of works stating their views, and that the government should help the representatives to go to Rome by 'deporting' them from England. Funds were raised and at the end of September 1601 a little group of secular priests, including Bluet and Bagshaw, left for Rome to further the interests of their appeal.[2] It seems very likely that Bluet had got this help from the government by undertaking to work in Rome for the recall of the Jesuits from England, and that the appellants hoped that once the Jesuits had been withdrawn, it would be possible for the pope to negotiate with the government to grant some kind of toleration.

A little before the priests set out for Rome the pope had in fact given a decision on their written appeal.[3] It was dated 17 August 1601. It rebuked Blackwell for the way he had exercised his powers and told him to be a shepherd of his flock, not a tyrant. The appellants' appeal for the removal of Blackwell was not granted and they were told to be charitable. The accusation of schism was not to be levelled against them and the archpriest was to forbid any further writings on the controversy.[4] Since Parsons was writing his *Brief*

---

[1] A. O. Meyer, *op. cit.*, p. 426.

[2] For further details of all this, see A. O. Meyer, *op. cit.*, p. 434 ff; T. G. Law, *The Archpriest Controversy*, R. G. Usher, *The Reconstruction of the English Church*, I. 160 ff., 'Fostering Catholic Disunion'.

[3] Printed in *Dodd's Church History*, edit. M. A. Tierney, III. cxlix ff.; A. O. Meyer, *op. cit.*, 440 ff.

[4] Philip Hughes, *Rome and the Counter Reformation in England*, p. 302 ff.

Apologie in defence of the archpriest, Blackwell deliberately suppressed the papal brief until the work had appeared. He then published it in January 1602.

Parsons *Brief Apologie* was one more contribution to the very fierce paper war which was going on among Catholics in these years. There was a very considerable literature in which the opponents launched the most outrageous charges against each other and sank very low indeed in their efforts to blacken each others characters and to mislead their readers about the true course of events. It included Bagshaw's *A True Relation of the faction begun at Wisbech* and Watson's *A Sparing Discoverie of our English Jesuits*, both of which appeared in 1601. In another pamphlet published in the same year Watson argued that the queen had in fact treated Catholics throughout her reign in a mild and gracious manner, and maintained that there was no question of Catholics having a duty to obey the pope if he ordered them to support their country's enemies. He affirmed his belief that 'we ought to have carried ourselves in another manner of course towards her, our true and lawfull queene, and towards our countrie, than hath bene taken and pursued by many catholickes, but especially by the Jesuits'.[1] In the production of these attacks on the archpriest and the Jesuits, Bishop Bancroft gave very considerable assistance to the secular priests and they were able to utilise the services of some of the most reputable printers of the day.[2]

Meanwhile the secular priests continued on their way to Rome. In Flanders they were shown the papal decision of August 1601, but three of the four nevertheless decided to continue with their mission. In Paris they were joined by another priest, John Cecil, a man with a very dubious past who now played the leading rôle in the negotiations. They reached Rome on 14 February 1602. The archpriest and the Jesuits also had representatives in Rome and there followed from February to October very lengthy negotiations. The opponents of the appellants made great play with the fact that the appellants rather

[1] A. O. Meyer, *op. cit.*, p. 436, Watson's pamphlet was entitled *Important Considerations which ought to move all true and sound catholikes who are not wholly jesuited to acknowledge that the proceedings of her Majesty . . . have been both mild and mercifull.*

[2] See Gladys Jenkins, 'The Archpriest Controversy and the Printers, 1601–1603', *The Library*, 5th series, vol. II. 1948, p. 180 ff. Mrs. Jenkins gives details of a number of the phamphlets and considers who printed them. T. G. Law, *A Historical Sketch*, p. cxxviii ff. has a bibliographical note on some of the main works produced in the controversy. See also H. R. Plomer, 'Bishop Bancroft and a Catholic Press', *The Library*, New Series, Vol. VIII, 1907, p. 164 ff; J. H. Pollen, *The Archpriest Controversy.*

than obey their superiors had preferred 'to enter into treaty with the deadly enemies of the faith'.[1] The appellants, however, had the backing of France, since their opponents, the Jesuits, were supporting a Spanish candidate for the English succession and Henry IV had no desire to see a Spaniard on the English throne.[2] The appellants had a well-prepared case which helped convince the pope that the whole question must be looked at again, and the powerful support they received from France ensured that they got very different treatment from that given to Bishop and Charnock in 1598.[3]

In a decree of 20 July 1602 the Holy Office declared that the appellants had just cause of complaint since the archpriest had treated them as schismatics, but it proposed that government by the archpriest should continue now that it had been set up. Blackwell was to be expressly forbidden from consulting with the Jesuits either in England or in Rome. He must report to the pope in person and to the Cardinal Protector on all matters concerning the English clergy. At the same time the Holy Office asked the pope to forbid under pain of excommunication 'all dealings and communications with heretics to the prejudice of catholics'—a clear condemnation of the negotiations which the appellants had in fact entered into with Bancroft and the English government.[4]

The decree of the Holy Office was not confirmed by the pope until 5 October 1602. The possibility of direct negotiation between the papacy and Elizabeth had at any rate been considered by some in high office in the Roman Church. Although Clement VIII was not willing to take the momentous step of formally recognising that heresy had come to stay in England and was certainly not prepared to concede freedom of conscience to non-Catholics, the idea of negotiation was not rejected out of hand. Bluet had urged in Rome: 'If I who am a worm and no man could prevail so much with the queen, what might not your Holiness do, with the aid of the most Christian King, towards obtaining consolation for the English Catholics?' The papal nuncio in the Low Countries had even suggested that it might be arranged for him to be taken prisoner by an English ship and taken

---

[1] A. O. Meyer, *op. cit.*, p. 443. For details of the negotiations, see T. G. Law, *The Archpriest Controversy*, II; *A Historical Sketch*, Introduction, section 7; R. G. Usher, *The Reconstruction of the English Church*, vol I.

[2] For France's rôle in all this, see John Bossy, 'Henry IV, the Appellants and the Jesuits', *Recusant History*, vol. 8, no. 2, 1965.

[3] See p. 288. [4] A. O. Meyer, *op. cit.*, p. 446 ff.

before Elizabeth. In that way negotiations could be entered into without either England or the papacy losing face.[1] Nothing came of this, and the hopes of the appellants that Henry IV would persuade Elizabeth to grant some kind of toleration to English Catholics were also disappointed.[2]

On 5 October 1602 the pope issued his final decision on the question of the archpriest.[3] Blackwell was told not to exceed his powers, which were further limited. The decision of the Holy Office forbidding him to consult with the Jesuits and ordering him to report direct to the pope was confirmed. Blackwell was told to take three of the appellants as assistants as soon as there were vacancies. Publication of controversial writing from either side was forbidden. The censures of the Church were threatened to those dealing with heretics to the prejudice of Catholics.[4]

The appellants had won a considerable triumph, but they had not got rid of the archpriest, and their hopes, which Bancroft and the government fully shared, that the Jesuits would be withdrawn from England had not been fulfilled.

The appellant party had hoped that some kind of toleration might be granted to Catholics once the hated Jesuits had gone, and the government had encouraged them in this belief because it was to its interest to keep the controversy alive. It would, of course, have won a very great victory if it had got rid of the Jesuits, for they had done much for the Catholic cause in England and their numbers in the last few years of the reign were increasing. There was, however, no serious thought on the government's part of tolerating more than one religion within the state. There was no parallel in England with the situation which led in France in 1598 to the Edict of Nantes. The Huguenots had force behind them and had fought for the concessions they obtained in a Catholic state. Except in 1569 Elizabeth had never had to face a rebellion from the Papists, and most of them were desperately anxious to act as loyal subjects of the queen.

The government's position was made plain in a Proclamation issued on 5 November 1602.[5] The queen stated that her 'desire to avoid all occasions to draw blood' had led her of late years to a greater

---

[1] A. O. Meyer, *op. cit.*, p. 448 ff.   [2] See J. Bossy, *op. cit.*, p. 85 ff.

[3] A. O. Meyer, *op. cit.*, p. 450. The pope's letter to Blackwell is printed in *Dodd's Church History*, edit. M. A. Tierney, III. lcxxxi ff.

[4] A. O. Meyer, *op. cit.*, p. 450.

[5] *Dodd's Church History*, edit. M. A. Tierney, III. clxxxiv ff.

15 A PAPIST UNDER
EXAMINATION ON
THE RACK
One of the illustrations in
Robert Parsons' *De Persecutione Anglicana Epistola*,
printed in Latin at Rouen in
1581 and translated into
English and other languages.
Both Papists and Puritans
were anxious to win sym-
pathy for their cause by
drawing attention to their
sufferings.

6 HANGING, DRAWING AND QUARTERING
One of the illustrations in Richard Verstegan's *Theatrum Crudelitatum*,
published in Antwerp in 1587, and designed to draw attention to the cruelties of Protestants in many parts of Europe. The picture is an imaginative
representation of what was involved in hanging, drawing and quartering
and does not record a particular event.

17 HIDING HOLE, SAWSTON HALL

The entrance to one of the three hiding holes at Sawston Hall, Cambridgeshire. A doorway from the Long Gallery leads into a stone turret with a stair case. At the top is a small landing, of which two of the boards lift up to give admission to a hiding hole in the thickness of the wall. The hide is 8 ft. 6 in. long, 5 ft. high, and only 1 ft. 8 in. wide. It was made by Nicholas Owen in 1592–3. See Michael Hodgetts, *Country Life*, 22 March 1962.

forbearance from the execution of the laws for the conservation of true religion and for resisting all disturbers of the same 'than the just consideration of the safety of our estate may well endure, or the examples of some other princes, where one form of religion hath ever been only allowed, do regularly approve'. She had hoped that the Romish priests sent into the realm by foreign authority to seduce her people from their obedience would be moved by this clemency not to provoke any sharper course, but they had in fact sought to ruin her and the kingdom. The Spaniards had invaded Ireland, and the secular priests and the Jesuits had invited them to do so. Their books showed that they had combined within the kingdom to help the enemy and subvert the subjects 'in that almost all the secular priests, by yielding their obedience to a new kind of subordination among them, have in effect subjected themselves to be wholly directed by the Jesuits (men altogether alienated from their true allegiance to us, and devoted with all their might to the King of Spain)'. They had thus become 'most dangerous, and more seditious' than ever before. In their books they maintained that the queen's subjects were bound to join any enemy the pope sent to subdue the queen, and they ventured in their writings 'to dispose of our kingdoms and crown at their pleasures'. If any of their sort acknowledged the leniency of the queen, they attacked them as enemies.

The proclamation stated that lately there had been much contention between the Jesuits and secular priests combined with them on the one side, and certain secular priests on the other side. There was 'a great difference of offence against us and our state' between the two groups. The Jesuits and their adherents sought the invasion of the kingdom and even the murder of the queen; the secular priests protested against this and offered to be the first to discover such treachery and to suppress it by arms and other means.

The treason of the Jesuits was much more violent than the disloyalty of the secular priests, and the queen would have liked to distinguish between them in executing the law. But those at variance with the Jesuits concurred with them in disobedience 'masking themselves under the vizard of pretended conscience (a suggestion of all other the most perilous), thereby to steal away the hearts especially of simple and common subjects from us their sovereign', and worked day and night to withdraw them from their obedience and to unite them to the queen's mortal enemy, the pope.

U

The Proclamation denied explicitly that the government had ever intended to grant toleration to Papists. It stated that possibly because of the sufferance and benignity shown to them the priests had behaved 'with so great and insolent animosity, as they do almost insinuate thereby into the minds of all sorts of people (as well the good that grieve at it, as the bad that thirst after it), that we have some purpose to grant a toleration of two religions within our realm, where God ... doth not only know our innocency from such imagination, but how far it hath been from any about us once to offer to our ears the persuasion of such a course, as would not only disturb the peace of the church, but bring this our state into confusion'.

The priests, it was alleged, were displaying audacious boldness in that 'they dare to adventure to walk in the streets at noon days, to resort to prisons publicly, and execute their functions in contempt of our laws'. Because of the mildness she had shown to them, some of her subjects 'apt to innovation and affected much to their own opinions, have broken forth ... into factious invectives in print against our present government, whereunto they repute such remissness, as if no care were had by any but a few of themselves, to preserve religion ... ' In order to avoid the inconveniences, murmurings and heart-burnings in the realm, the queen has thought it necessary to give general notice to her servants and officers how much she mislikes their remissness in taking action against secular priests and Jesuits.

The Proclamation then proceeded to make a distinction between 'all Jesuits and secular priests combined together as is before expressed' and the other secular clergy. The Jesuits and their supporters among the secular clergy are warned to leave the realm immediately. 'The other sort also of the secular priests that are at liberty, and in some things opposite into the Jesuits' were to leave the realm but were given until the 1 January 1603 to do so. Further, 'such of them as shall, in the meantime present themselves to some of the lords or others of our privy council ... or to the bishops of the dioceses, and, before them acknowledging sincerely their duty and allegiance unto us, shall submit themselves to our mercy ... ' were to be treated differently. With them the queen would 'take such further order, as shall be thought by us to be most meet and convenient'. The Jesuits and their supporters were to be dealt with according to the law, and there was to be a strict search for them in order to get rid of the danger and infection 'which is derived from their continual working upon men's consciences'.

The importance of this Proclamation of 5 November 1602 is thus twofold. It clearly states the government's policy of not tolerating two religions within the state—a policy which it had adopted in the Act of Uniformity of 1559, and at the same time it attempts to drive home the wedge splitting the Catholic priests in England by offering different treatment to those who were not adherents of the Jesuits and who would acknowledge their duty and allegiance to the queen. Those priests who were prepared to take advantage of the offer were clearly not going to be allowed to carry on their work as Catholic priests, for the Proclamation had earlier made clear that the queen considered that even those priests who opposed the Jesuits laboured 'day and night to win and withdraw them (our subjects) from their sound and due obedience . . . and to unite and knit them to our mortal enemy the pope . . . ' They were certainly not going to be permitted to spread the religion of the papal church. Presumably what they would receive if they submitted was some kind of personal protection against the law which made it high treason for them to be in England at all.

It would obviously have been an immense advantage to the government if a large number of secular priests had made the required declaration of loyalty and openly broken with the Jesuits and their adherents. In fact only 13 secular priests took advantage of the offer. In a declaration of 31 January 1603,[1] they stated that since the queen had offered clemency to them ('being all subject, by the laws of the realm, to death, by our return into the country after our taking the order of priesthood') and since she had demanded of them only 'a true profession of our allegiance, thereby to be assured of our fidelity to her majesty's person', they were willing to give such an assurance on this point 'as any catholic priest can, or ought to give unto their sovereigns'. They acknowledged that Elizabeth had as full an authority and sovereignty as any of her predecessors and affirmed that they would obey her laws in all civil causes, and they stated that this acknowledgment was 'so grounded upon the word of God, as that no authority, no cause . . . can or ought . . . to be a sufficient warrant, more unto us than to any protestant, to disobey her majesty in any civil or temporal matter'.

They stated that in the past attempts had been made to invade the

---

[1] Printed in *Dodd's Church History*, edit. M. A. Tierney, III. clxxxviii ff.

kingdom under pretence of restoring the Catholic religion by the sword—'a course most strange in the world, and undertaken peculiarly and solely against her majesty and her kingdoms, among other princes departed from the religion and obedience of the see apostolic, no less than she'. They maintained that it was because of this that the queen had ordered severer laws against Catholics than might otherwise have been the case. To reassure her Majesty, they said that they would defend her against any attempts by any foreign prelate or prince and that they would do their best to reveal any conspiracies against her. If the pope excommunicated anyone who did not support such conspiracies or invasions, they explicitly gave their opinion that 'we do think ourselves, and all the lay Catholics . . . bound in conscience not to obey this or any such like censure' and they affirmed they would defend her and their country notwithstanding the excommunication.

The thirteen priests went on to say that since they knew their action would be misrepresented to the pope they wished to assert publicly that 'in this our recognising and yielding Caesar's due . . . we depart from no bond of that christian duty which we owe unto our supreme spiritual pastor'. They acknowledge that the bishop of Rome is the successor of St. Peter and that he has 'as ample, and no more, authority or jurisdiction over us and other Christians, than had that apostle by the gift and commission of Christ, our Saviour; and that we will obey him so far forth, as we are bound by the laws of God to do; which, we doubt not but will stand well with the performance of our duty to our temporal prince . . . '

Here, then, was an explicit repudiation of the papal deposing power.[1] A. O. Meyer comments on it that it 'amounts to a revision of canon law adapted to the needs of the modern state . . . The "bloody questions" of the catholic persecution . . . were all of them answered in a manner entirely favourable to the secular power, while the papacy of the counter-reformation, as it existed from Pius V down to Sixtus V, was tacitly condemned'. He adds: 'The modern papacy indeed never formally acknowledged this revision of canon law, but in practice accepted it as time went on.'[2]

---

[1] See Philip Hughes, *The Reformation in England*, III, 392 ff.
[2] A. O. Meyer, *England and the Catholic Church under Elizabeth*, p. 456 ff. for a discussion of this Declaration. See also T. Clancy, 'English Catholics and the Papal Deposing Power', *Recusant History*, vol. 6, nos. 3 and 5, vol. 7, no. 1 (1962–3).

The position that the thirteen priests took up was substantially no different from that which most English Catholics had taken up throughout the reign—that they would accept the spiritual authority of the pope and the temporal authority of Elizabeth, except in so far as the pope urged them to overthrow Elizabeth for the good of the faith, and except in so far as Elizabeth denied them the opportunity of practising their religion. It was an illogical position to take up at a time when the government was trying to destroy Catholicism and the pope was trying by temporal as well as by spiritual means to prevent it being destroyed, but it was the only way most of them could see of trying to be both good Catholics and good Englishmen. If only thirteen out of some 400 priests were prepared to sign the Declaration, it was not because most priests were really committed to the papal deposing power, but because they must have seen that what the government was trying to do was not so much to get an assurance of loyalty from them as to divide the Catholic priesthood and to weaken its attachment to the papacy.[1]

The last years of Elizabeth were thus very troubled ones for English Catholics. The 'grand confident morning' of the 1580's had gone for ever. The bitter quarrels between 1595 and 1603 and the ferocious tone of the voluminous literature on both sides can easily lead us to paint a distorted picture of these difficult years, and make us forget that most of the laity, and possibly the majority of the priests, were not directly involved; but it seems only too clear that the savage struggle diverted from its main task the energy of a number of able men who would have been far better employed in furthering the cause of their faith, and the disputes left a legacy of serious problems which remained unsolved for many generations.

[1] A. O. Meyer suggests that 'The path of resistance, which the appellants made a show of taking, must inevitably have led them sooner or later out of the catholic church into the anglican. It was probably the instinctive feeling that such would be the result of their action that finally restrained the majority of them from coming to terms with the English state by taking the required oath of allegiance', *op. cit.*, pp. 455, 456. This seems to be going a long way beyond the evidence. The papacy still asserted its deposing power, but the deposing power was not an article of the Catholic faith, even though Catholics who questioned it would risk a conflict with Rome. If large numbers of English Catholic priests had signed the Declaration, there would presumably have been a conflict, but that would not necessarily mean that the signatories would be led into anglicanism. As it happened, no action was taken by Rome against the thirteen priests, presumably because the approaching death of Elizabeth overshadowed all other questions.

11

The Triumph of the Establishment 1590–1603: The Puritans in Disarray

IN the last twelve years of Elizabeth's reign, the Puritans, like the Papists, were faced with formidable difficulties and were unable to repeat the remarkable successes of the 1580's. The establishment maintained its counter-attack on all fronts and it was no longer possible to offer organised national resistance. Nevertheless, the Puritans continued the struggle at a number of points, and as the years went on they, like the Papists, looked forward hopefully to the accession of a new ruler who might be more sympathetic to their cause.

Whitgift and Bancroft kept up their determined drive against nonconformists and a great deal of evidence accumulated which enabled them to take legal action. John Udall, the Puritan minister at Kingston-on-Thames, had been arrested at the end of 1589. He had been in trouble with High Commission in 1586 and 1588, but he enjoyed the protection of powerful friends, including the earl of Huntingdon who had secured for him a preaching post in Newcastle. He was strongly suspected of being implicated in the production of the Marprelate Tracts. He was examined before the Privy Council in 1590 and was tried at the Croydon assizes on charges of publishing seditious books. These included *The Demonstration of Discipline; which Christ hath prescribed in his Word, for the government of the Church in all times and places, until the world's end*. It was addressed 'To the supposed Governors of the Church of England, Archbishops, Lord Bishops, Archdeacons, and the rest of that order', and it asked 'who can, without blushing, deny you to be the cause of all ungodliness; seeing your government is that which giveth leave to a man to be anything, save a sound Christian'. Udall said that it was safer in England to be a Papist, an anabaptist or a member of the Family of Love[1] than a good Christian, and he told the bishops that when they had to answer before the tribunal seat of Jesus Christ for all the souls that had gone to hell because of them, it would be no excuse to say that the queen and the council had told them to do what they had done.

Udall was found guilty and was condemned to death, but he petitioned Burghley to intercede for him and asked that he might be allowed to 'live a private life, to provide for my poor wife and children; or at least that with her Majesty's favour, I may go beyond the seas'. He said that the worst conditions would be more joyful to him 'especially that now Papists are set at liberty, and the prisons filled with God's servants, her Highness' most faithful subjects . . . ' His life was spared on condition that he went to Syria as a chaplain in the service of the Turkey Company, but he died in prison before the arrangements were completed.[2]

Whitgift and Bancroft were primarily concerned with much bigger game than Udall. In 1590 Thomas Cartwright and eight other prominent leaders were arrested and brought before High Commission.[3] The ecclesiastical authorities had accumulated a great deal of evidence about the synods and conferences held in the 1580's, and they had high hopes of getting a conviction against the ringleaders, all the more because some of those involved in the *classical* movement, including John Johnson and Thomas Stone, gave evidence for the prosecution. Cartwright and his companions, however, conducted their defence with very great skill and ingenuity. They refused to take the *ex officio* oath by which the accused was required to swear to answer truthfully to a series of questions before he knew what the questions were, and they were not prepared to incriminate others. They questioned the legality of the *ex officio* oath, and on this point they could be sure of getting a good deal of sympathy from common lawyers and others who disliked the procedure of the church courts.

Eventually in May 1591 proceedings were started against the accused in the Court of Star Chamber. There was a very long list of

---

[1] For the Family of Love, see C. E. Whiting, *Studies in English Puritanism*, p. 283 ff. The sect spread from Holland to England about 1560 and by the 1580's was giving considerable concern to the government.

[2] J. Strype, *The Life and Acts of John Whitgift*, II. 37 ff.; M. M. Knappen, *Tudor Puritanism*, pp. 294–296.

[3] For details of the case, see J. Strype, *The Life and Acts of John Whitgift*, II, chapters ii, v, vi; A. F. Scott Pearson, *Thomas Cartwright*, p. 317 ff.

charges against Cartwright in spite of the fact that Burghley, to whom Cartwright had appealed for help, had suggested to Whitgift that he should not be charged with 'old causes'. The prosecution threw in everything. Cartwright was charged with renouncing episcopal ordination and with having been ordained abroad by imposition of hands, with establishing a Presbyterian church while chaplain to the Merchant Adventurers abroad, with preaching without licence at Warwick after he had become Master of Leicester's Hospital there, with condemning the bishops and the Prayer Book, and with having knowledge of the authors, printers and dispersers of the Marprelate Tracts.[1]

The most serious charges related to the part the accused had played in the conferences, synods and meetings of the 1580's. It was argued that here was a conspiracy to alter the established religion and to replace it by a Presbyterian church with a discipline and organisation of its own, or, at the very least, to set up a rival church in opposition to the Church of England. The prosecution hoped to frighten people with a picture of a seditious movement which threatened the established order in church and state.

The attempt to suggest that there was a dangerous conspiracy was helped by the strange schemes of Hacket, Copinger and Arthington to overthrow the church and to free the prisoners. The conspirators seem to have been unbalanced. On 16 July 1591 Hacket was proclaimed the Messiah in Cheapside. The affair created a momentary stir and on 28 July Hacket was executed. Copinger starved himself to death in prison. The conspiracy was not of great significance in itself, but some of the Puritan leaders had been in touch with the group, and this helped to give the impression that their movement was dangerous.

In the course of the trial of Cartwright and his companions in the Star Chamber, a great deal of evidence was produced about the conferences and synods and about the 'discipline' which the members had tried to establish, but the accused put up a brilliant defence. They made great play with their objections to the *ex officio* oath, but their main argument was that the meetings and conferences which they had held were not in fact illegal. They were voluntary meetings at which they had discussed what they thought ought to be done, but they had not imposed their discipline on anyone, and their decisions were only 'a declaration of their judgment, leaving the determination to her Majesty and the Parliament'. On this interpretation, the alleged Pres-

[1] A. F. Scott Pearson, *Thomas Cartwright*, p. 318 ff.

byterian conspiracy became merely meetings of ministers to make suggestions to the lawful authorities about what ought to be done for the good of the church. They had no intention of withdrawing from it, they recognised its authority, but they thought it needed further reform.

It gradually became clear that the main charges could not be proved in law. The accused announced that they would appeal from Star Chamber to the Privy Council, and in anticipation of this Burghley got a legal opinion from the Attorney General, who thought that since they had resolved to have their own form of discipline only 'so far as the same might be done with the peace of the church and the laws of the land', their conduct was not illegal.[1]

As the main charges could not be proved, the government did not bring the Star Chamber case to a judgment. From January 1592 some of the accused were allowed out of prison from time to time. The prisoners had powerful friends, including Sir Francis Knollys, Lady Russell and Lady Bacon, and there were frequent appeals to Burghley to help. A form of submission was drawn up by the Attorney General, but it was not acceptable to the accused. Some time before May 1592 they were released on giving a simple acknowledgment of the royal supremacy. The lesser charges, some of which could have been proved, were not proceeded with. After eighteen months in prison, the accused were set free without having been convicted or acquitted.

In one way the outcome of the trial was a set-back for Whitgift, Bancroft and their supporters. On the other hand, their opponents had been taught a sharp lesson. They had been shown very clearly that official policy was now strongly against them and that they could no longer rely on protection from those in power. It is significant that neither Cartwright nor Travers (who had not been prosecuted) gave any more trouble. No doubt many of their followers also saw the red light and in future proceeded with great caution. National conferences might not, as Cartwright argued, have been illegal, but whether they were or not, no more were called.

A severe policy was also adopted towards the separatists, that is to say, those nonconformists who believed that they were bound in conscience to leave the established church and set up their own churches. The separatists were not numerically a very important section of the Puritans and their views were opposed by the vast majority, who wanted to reform the church but who had no desire

[1] V. J. K. Brook, *Whitgift and English Church*, p. 137.

to leave it. Nevertheless, they were significant partly because of the future history of separatism and partly because their activity helped to discredit the general image of Puritanism.

Separatists movements had a long history going back to, and beyond, the 'secret' Protestant churches of Mary's reign.[1] The organised Calvinist group which existed in London from the early years of Elizabeth's reign showed in many ways 'separatist' tendencies and resembled 'a gathered church' of the godly. There is also evidence in the 1560's and 1570's of other groups associated with Plumbers' Hall and elsewhere and with a number of ministers such as William Bonham, Nicholas Crane, and Richard Fitz.[2]

There was, however, no really important group of separatists until the appearance in the 1580's of a movement led by Robert Browne and Robert Harrison, a group to which the name 'Brownists' is often attached.[3] Robert Browne was a distant relation of Burghley. He was a graduate of Corpus Christi, Cambridge, who had become a schoolmaster and who had lost his job because of his Puritan views. Early in 1579 he had attached himself to the household of Richard Greenham, minister of Dry Drayton, near Cambridge, and he began to preach in Cambridge. He had no licence to preach, and when his brother secured one for him he threw it in the fire because he held that bishops were false teachers who had no right to license true ones. After a year he was silenced by the Council, and the man who brought him the news was Richard Bancroft.[4]

Browne then went off to Norwich to join Robert Harrison. Harrison had been at St. John's and later at Corpus Christi College, Cambridge, and he too was a schoolmaster who had been deprived for nonconformity. In 1580 he was Master of Old Mews Hospital, Norwich. Browne and Harrison decided that 'we are to forsake and deny all ungodliness and wicked fellowship . . .'[5] They formed in Norwich

[1] For 'this heavy ground-swell within English society' and 'The Lollard river, deep, murky, and quiet', see A. G. Dickens, *Lollards and Protestants in the Diocese of York 1509–1558*, 1959; and *The English Reformation*, 1964.

[2] For a short examination of these early separatist groups, see Albert Peel, *The First Congregational Churches*, Cambridge, 1920, and M. M. Knappen, *Tudor Puritanism*, Chapter XV 'Separatism'.

[3] *The Writings of Robert Harrison and Robert Browne*, edit. Albert Peel and Leland Carsen, 1953.

[4] M. M. Knappen, *Tudor Puritanism*, p. 305 ff.; H. C. Porter, *Reformation and Reaction in Tudor Cambridge*, p. 243 ff.

[5] H. C. Porter, *op. cit.*, p. 244.

a separatist church with its own liturgy and with a covenant by which the members arranged to choose their minister and entered into an agreement 'for cleaving to the Lord in greater obedience'.[1] Browne became well known as a preacher in Norfolk and apparently had congregations of over 100 in his conventicles.[2] He was sent to prison, but his relationship with Burghley gave him some protection. However, the situation became increasingly difficult, and at last 'when divers of them were againe imprisoned, thei all agreed and were fullie persuaded that the Lord did call them out of England'.[3]

The congregation went to Middleburg in Zeeland and here Browne published a number of works including *Treatise of Reformation without Tarying for anie* and *A Booke which sheweth the Life and Manners of all true Christians*. Browne took the view that the Church of England was so corrupt and superstitious that no Christian could attend it and that the true church was a voluntary gathering of true believers bound by a covenant to which they subscribed.[4] He disagreed violently with Cartwright about the possibility of reforming the Church of England and he wrote: 'They are all turned back after babbling prayers, and toying worship, after priestly preachers, blind ministers, and canon officers, after popish attire and foolish disguising, after fastings, tithings, holy days, and a thousand more abominations; and their feet do stick fast in the mire and dust of all popery, that they cannot get out.'[5] He did not think that the Christian ought to wait for the civil magistrates to reform abuses in the church. He argued ' . . . we are bought for a price, saieth Paule, and we may not be servauntes to the unlawfull commanding of men . . . Therefore the Magistrate's commaundement, must not be a rule unto me of this and that duetie but as I see it agreeth with the worde of God; so then it is an abuse of my guifte and calling, if I cease preaching for the Magistrate, when it is my calling to preach . . . And this dispensation did not the Magistrate give me but God by consent and ratifying of the Church . . . And the welfare of the whole church must be more regarded and sought than the welfare of whole Kingdomes and Countries.'[6]

---

[1] Albert Peel, *The Brownists in Norwich and Norfolk about 1580*, Cambridge, 1920.
[2] H. C. Porter, *op. cit.*, p. 244.
[3] Albert Peel, *The Brownists in Norwich and Norfolk about 1580*, Cambridge, 1920. p.11.
[4] M. M. Knappen, *Tudor Puritanism*, p. 307.
[5] H. C. Porter, *Reformation and Reaction in Tudor Cambridge*, p. 245.
[6] R. Browne, *A Treatise of reformation without tarying for anie* . . . Middleburg, 1582.

Harrison's most important work was *A Treatise of the Church and the Kingdome of Christ*.[1] He maintained that the Church of England could not be a true church and that it was filled with pollution. Its ministers were not sent by the Lord but got their authority from bishops. In a true church Christ was supreme, but in the Church of England bishops, deans, chancellors—'the pope's bastards'—had authority which came from anti-Christ. Its ministers were 'dumbe dogges, destroiers and murtherers of souls'. The sacraments were only dead signs in a false church. No one had a right to preach unless sent by God, and God did not send wicked preachers like those found in the Church of England. The true government of the church should be as in the Apostles' time with each congregation governing itself.

In *A Little Treatise on Ps. 122*,[2] published in 1583, Harrison urged his fellow countrymen to 'Looke unto your brethren of other nations rounde about which have reformed . . . ' There was no need for ordination by bishops. The duty of the magistrates was to use the civil power to reform religion and extirpate idolatry. He wanted the magistrates to remove 'the offices, rowmes, and liuinges of the Lordlie overrulers of many churches, together with Deanes & Deanaries, Prebends and Prebenshippes, Cathedralles with the Chaunters therin, and their Marmaiden musick, Bishops, Chancelors, Archdeacons, Commissaries, Proctors officials, Sumners & Questmen, whiche all do strippe ye church of her authoritie and libertie, and strippe her naked: These I say with their Courtes & Canon lawes, as also freehold Parsonages & Vicariges, which hinder the free election & deposing of the Minister . . . All these wormewoode dregges of Antichrists cupp, & whatsoever more, it appertaineth only to the office of ye civile Magistrate, to powre out and rince from the bottom'. Meanwhile God's people must keep separate from abomination and pray that the magistrates will get on with the work of reform.[3]

Browne eventually quarrelled with Harrison and in 1583 was expelled from his own church in Middleburg. He left for Scotland where

---

[1] *The Writings of Robert Harrison and Robert Browne*, edit. A. Peel and L. Carsen, p. 9 ff.

[2] *The Writings of Robert Harrison and Robert Browne*, edit. A. Peel and L. Carsen, p. 119 ff.

[3] *The Writings of Robert Harrison and Robert Browne*, edit. A. Peel and L. Carsen, pp. 10, 11.

he was imprisoned for a time, but in 1584 he returned to England and submitted to Whitgift, promising to communicate in the Church of England. In 1591 he was ordained and presented to a living in Northamptonshire.[1] After Browne's departure from Middleburg, Harrison carried on and at one time attempted to unite with the congregation to which Cartwright was minister, but he disagreed violently with Cartwright, and in 1585 he died worn out by the fierce dissensions within his own congregation. It seems that he was an able man who might have been very prominent in the history of nonconformity but for his early death.[2]

Meanwhile separatist groups continued to exist in England, particularly in Norwich and in London. The writings of Harrison and Browne were smuggled into England, and a royal proclamation was issued against them. In June 1583 John Copping and Elias Thacker were convicted at Bury St. Edmunds for spreading their works and were hanged, and William Denys was put to death at Thetford for a similar offence.[3] In London new leaders were found in two more Cambridge men—Henry Barrow of Clare[4] and John Greenwood of Corpus Christi. Greenwood had been chaplain to Lord Rich of Rochford and Barrow was a gentleman related by marriage to the Bacons.[5] Greenwood was arrested in October 1587 while holding a conventicle and when Barrow visited him he too was taken into custody, but separatism was not destroyed. A pamphlet published in 1588 refers to Browne 'the famous a(r)ch buylder of such ruinous foundations' and comments ' . . . though their ful swarme and store be (as it is most likely) in London, and the partes neare adioyning: yet have they sparsed of their companies into severall partes of the Realme, and namely, unto the West, almost to the uttermost borders thereof'. The writer urged the 'stopping that violent streame of seducing, wherein daily such numbers of the yonger and weaker sorte of Christians are carried out of our assemblies . . . ' He added 'Barrow and Greenwood nakedly discovered their profession, and are

---

[1] He gave little further trouble to the authorities for the next forty years, but when he was over eighty he struck the parish constable in a rage, was taken by cart to Northampton gaol and died there in 1633.

[2] Albert Peel, *The Writings of Robert Harrison and Robert Browne*, p. 3.

[3] *Ibid.*, p. 2; M. M. Knappen, *Tudor Puritanism*, p. 310.

[4] F. J. Powicke, *Henry Barrow, Separatist, and the Exiled Church of Amsterdam*, 1900.

[5] M. M. Knappen, *Tudor Puritanism*, p. 310.

prisoners. Browne cunningly counterfeiteth conformitie, and dissembleth with his owne soule, for libertie'.[1]

Barrow and Greenwood were in prison for some years, but they seem to have enjoyed a measure of liberty and they wrote a number of works which were published abroad. These included *A True Description of the Visible Congregation of the Saints under the Gospel* (1589), *A Briefe Discoverie of the False Church*, 1590, and *The Examinations of H. Barrow, J. Greenewood and J. Penrie* in 1593.

In his *Briefe Discoverie* Barrow argued that the people had surrendered their rights into the hands of their teachers and elders and thereby the true pattern of Christ's Testament had been overthrown. He wrote: 'The poor parish or congregation where these priests serve may not meddle or have to do with the election, administration or deposing of these their ministers; for why, they are laymen and have no skill neither ought to intermeddle with ecclesiastical affairs or with the Word of God. Be their minister never so blind, insufficient or vile a wretch, detected of never so horrible sins, yet may not they remove him; their only help is to complain to their lord ordinary.' He went on to say ' . . . my purpose is . . . to shew that every Christian congation hath power in themselves, and of duty ought, presently and publicly to censure any false or unsound doctrine that is publicly delivered or maintained amongst them . . . As for reproof by admonition, any member of the Church hath free power also to reprove the greatest elder of the Church'. He rejected popery, episcopacy and Presbyterianism when he maintained that ' . . . this power of excommunication, election, ordination etc. is not committed into the hands of one particular person, as the pope and his natural children our lord bishops now use it, nor yet into the hands of the eldership only or of pastors of many particular congregations (as the reforming preachers would have it); so much as it is given and committed to the whole Church, even to every particular congregation, and to every member thereof alike . . . '[2]

Radical views such as these were repugnant not only to the ecclesiastical authorities but to the majority of Puritans, and Barrow and Greenwood found themselves involved in a paper war with George Gifford, a Puritan minister in Essex, who attacked them as

---

[1] S. Bradwell, *The Rasing of the Foundations of Brownisme*, 1588.
[2] Quoted in G. R. Elton, *The Tudor Constitution*, pp. 445–7.

Donatists[1] who ruined the discipline of the church. Gifford commented: 'Now when the common artificer, the apprentice, and the brewer intrude themselves and they will guide the same, being ignorant, rash and headie, what worldlie wise man will not take it that discipline herself is but bedlam.'[2]

In 1593 when the government was making a drive against nonconformists and was trying to get through Parliament a bill direct against the sectaries, Greenwood and Barrow were executed for sedition. Knappen calls it an act of 'political terrorism'. These victims were certainly extremely unfortunate to receive such severe treatment, for the separatists seemed a much less formidable threat to the established order than the Presbyterians had been. Nevertheless, the government seems to have considered them very dangerous. The support for separatism was limited, but the movement was fundamentally much more revolutionary and threatened the whole basis of the Elizabethan policy of one church in one state.[3]

Another victim of the official reaction was the remarkable young man John Penry. After the Marprelate furore, Penry had fled to Scotland. He had not so far been a separatist, but Barrow's criticisms of him apparently went home, and when he returned from Scotland in 1592 he joined the London separatists and wrote in their defence.[4] He was taken in 1593. There was little hope for the man who was known to have played a leading part in the Marprelate affair and who had attacked the establishment with considerable violence. In 1590, for example, he had written ' . . . because our Council may be truly said to delight in this injury and violent oppression of God's saints and ministers; therefore, whensoever the Lord shall come to search for the sins of England with lights . . . he will surely visit our Council with a heavy plague . . . '[5] Earlier on he had written:

[1] The Donatist schism split the unity of the church in North Africa in the fourth century.
[2] M. M. Knappen, *Tudor Puritanism*, p. 311. Gifford's works included *A Short Treatise against the Donatists of England*, 1590; *Plaine Declaration that Our Brownists be Full Donatists*, 1590, and *Short Reply to the Last Printed Books of Henry Barrow and John Greenwood*, 1591.
[3] Dr. Collinson has drawn attention to various groups which were virtually churches within a church, even though they did not formally separate. Patrick Collinson, *The Elizabethan Puritan Movement*, pp. 372–82. See also Perry Miller, *Orthodoxy in Massachusetts*.
[4] M. M. Knappen, *Tudor Puritanism*, p. 312.
[5] J. Strype, *Life and Acts of John Whitgift*, II. 45.

'Of these men contained within the number of proud and ambitious Prelates, our Lord Archbishop and Bishops, godless and murdering non-presidents, profane and ignorant, idle shepherds, and dumb dogs, I will say no more in this place but this, How long, Lord, just and true, dost thou suffer thine inheritance to be polluted and laid waste by this uncircumcised generation.'

John Penry was one of the bravest and most sincere of all who opposed the established religion, and potentially he was one of the most dangerous, for he was not the kind of man who could ever come to terms with his conscience. He would not have been content to keep quiet as the holder of a lectureship or as the Master of some hospital. It might have been worth the government's while to have accepted his suggestion that he should be sent off to evangelise his native Wales rather than to put to death at the age of thirty-one this remarkable and sincere young man.

Barrow, Greenwood and Penry were martyrs for their cause. Their execution must have struck terror into the hearts of many Puritans. A number of others suffered in various ways, but there were few Puritans who were prepared to put their lives in danger for their beliefs.

The Brownists or Barrowists were not driven out of existence. The Act against Seditious Sectaries, passed in 1593,[1] gave them the option of accepting banishment if they would not conform, and the London group took advantage of this and eventually ended up in Amsterdam. A new leader turned up in Francis Johnson who had been expelled from his Fellowship at Christ's College, Cambridge, in 1589 and who had been imprisoned for his Puritan views. When he was freed he had gone to Middleburg as pastor to the Merchant Adventurers' church there and had been converted by a book of Barrow. He returned to London in 1592 and became pastor of Greenwood's congregation. He and his brother George were imprisoned with some seventy other separatists.[2] Francis was released in 1597 on condition that he went with a colonial venture to the Gulf of St. Lawrence, but his ship had to put back and he ended up in Amsterdam where he became pastor to the English congregation. It flourished and at the end of the century had nearly 300 members, but Johnson ran into

---

[1] See p. 313.
[2] M. M. Knappen, *Tudor Puritanism*, p. 313; H. C. Porter, *Reformation and Reaction in Tudor Cambridge*, p. 247 ff.

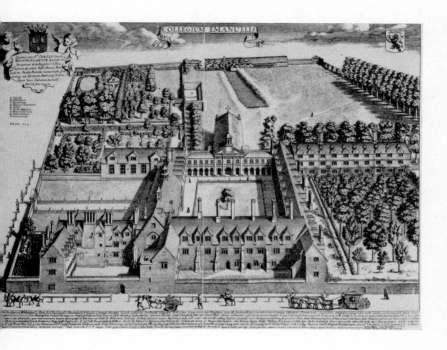

EMMANUEL COLLEGE, CAMBRIDGE

Emmanuel College, Cambridge, was founded in 1584 by Sir Walter Mildmay with the purpose of rendering 'as many as possible fit for the administration of the Divine Word and Sacraments'. Together with other Colleges in the Universities, it played a part in producing a number of ministers with Puritan tendencies who spread their views throughout the land, and acted as a 'seminary' for Puritanism with a role not altogether unlike that of the Catholic seminaries in Europe.

The illustration is Loggan's engraving of 1688 and includes a number of 17th century additions. Hammond's map of Cambridge, 1592, shows the College as it was in Elizabethan times, including the hall (a former Dominican church), the earlier chapel (left centre), the tennis court (*H*), and the fishpond (at the back of the illustration, in the centre).

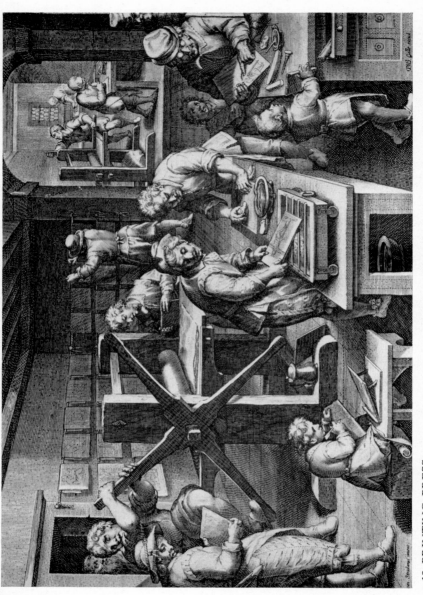

19 PRINTING PRESS
Both Papists and Puritans realised the importance of the printing press. Secret presses in England and publication of Papist and Puritan books abroad made it impossible for the Elizabethan government to

trouble, partly owing to the behaviour of his wife, Thomasine Boyes, a rich widow whom he had married in 1594. There were objections to her staying in bed on the Lord's Day until after 9 o'clock and to her 'vaunting in shop doors. Contrary to the rules of modest behaviour in the daughters of Zion'.[1] Johnson's father and brother took part in the dispute and Francis excommunicated them. There was further trouble early in the next century when separatism had a much more important rôle than it had in the Elizabethan age.

The campaign against nonconformity which resulted in the execution of Barrow, Greenwood and Penry in 1593 also had other considerable successes in the same year. In the Parliament which met in 1593 it soon became clear that the Puritans and their sympathisers were not nearly so powerful as they had been earlier. The critics of the church operated on a very limited front and raised an issue which would win the support of many M.P.s who were not Puritans. On 26 February James Morice, Attorney General of the Court of Wards, spoke about the *ex officio* oath which he described as 'an ungodly and intolerable inquisition'. He also attacked the Articles to which Whitgift required the clergy to subscribe as 'a lawless subscription'.[2] He asked: 'Where is now become the Great Charter of England?' and he asserted that: 'These extorted oaths and examinations are ungodly and unjust, invented and brought in first for none other purpose but to maintain a Romish hierarchy.' He proposed therefore to introduce two bills, one against unlawful oaths, inquisitions and subscriptions, and the other against unlawful imprisonment. The first of these would have imposed the penalties of *praemunire* on those involved, and Professor Neale remarks: 'Had the bill passed, the Church would have been helpless against Puritanism.'[3]

There was some debate, and the House called for the bills to be read, but the Speaker, Sir Edward Coke, played for time, and they were not read.[4] Whitgift had been informed of what was going on and wrote to the queen asserting that what moved Morice to act was the proceedings taken earlier against Cartwright and others 'who seek to bring in a new kind of ecclesiastical government, like unto that in Scotland, and do, as far as they dare, impugn your Majesty's authority in causes ecclesiastical . . . ' He warned the queen that 'those

---

[1] H. C. Porter, *Reformation and Reaction in Tudor Cambridge*, p. 248.
[2] J. Neale, *Elizabeth I and her Parliaments*, II. 267 ff.
[3] *Ibid.*, II. 270.   [4] *Ibid.*, II. 273.

which now impugn the ecclesiastical jurisdiction (will) endeavour also to impair the temporal and to bring even kings and princes under their censure'.[1]

The queen did not need to be told that Puritanism was potentially a political threat to her authority. She had already sent for the Speaker and instructed him to tell the House 'that they should not intermeddle at all with any other matter touching causes ecclesiastical' and that they were not to proceed with the bills. Morice was called before the Council, 'sharply chidden' and committed to prison where he remained, under honourable conditions, for just over eight weeks.[2] Robert Beale, Clerk of the Council, who was also involved, was told not to attend Parliament. The Commons took no action over all this, and it is clear that they were much more submissive and much less enthusiastic about the Puritan cause than they had been in the previous decade.

Their change of attitude to religious questions is further shown in their treatment of the government's bills concerning religion.[3] The official bill introduced into the Commons was entitled 'An Act for the reducing of disloyal subjects to their due obedience'. This was a severe measure which would primarily have affected Catholics but which could also be used against other nonconformists. In the debate Henry Finch pointed out that there were two kinds of recusants— Papists and a second sort such as the Brownists and others who 'openly pretend to be of our religion, but do neither frequent our churches nor sermons, nor communicate with us'. He did not want the second sort to be so severely treated as the Papists. He referred also to 'divers godly and zealous poor men' who had negligent or non-resident ministers and who consequently did not go to their parish church but resorted instead to some godly preacher. He claimed that such men had been cited by the bishop's officers and 'handled in more rigorous manner than any recusant Papist'. He asked that these godly men should be exempted from the penalties of the bill.

The Commons' committee considerably altered the government bill, restricted it to *popish* recusants, and, surprisingly, scaled down the proposed penalties against Papists. In the end this particular bill

---

[1] J. Neale, *Elizabeth I and her Parliaments*, II. 274.
[2] *Ibid.*, II. 275.
[3] The history of the bills is examined in great detail in J. Neale, *op. cit.*, II. 280 ff.

was dropped and another one, introduced first in the Lords, was debated instead. This new bill dealt with seditious sectaries, and after considerable debate and alteration it finally got through. It was entitled *An Act to retain the Queen's subjects in obedience*. Its preamble referred to 'the wicked and dangerous practices of seditious sectaries and disloyal persons'. If anyone over 16 years of age who refused to come to church for the space of a month should by printing, writing or express words 'advisedly and purposely practice . . . to . . . persuade any of her Majesty's subjects . . . to deny, withstand, and impugn her Majesty's power and authority in causes ecclesiastical' or should to that end move anyone to abstain from coming to church, or should be present at any unlawful assembly, conventicle or meeting, . . . then the offender was to be committed to prison until he conformed.

Anyone so offending who did not conform within three months after conviction was, after due warning from the justices, to abjure the realm. If he refused to do so, failed to go, or returned after he had gone, then he was guilty of felony and liable to the death sentence. Anyone who helped a person who obstinately refused to come to church was liable to a fine of £10 a month. Those required to abjure the realm lost all their goods and chattels and the use of their lands during their lifetime.[1]

The Act of 1593 gave the government considerable powers to use against nonconformists, for it was not limited to Brownists and other separatists, and a number of Puritans might find themselves classed as 'seditious sectaries'. The safeguards for 'godly and zealous poor men' were not inserted. Moreover Popish recusants were expressly excluded from banishment under this Act.[2] The temper of the Commons was no longer as anti-Catholic or as pro-Puritan as it had once been. As for the attitude of the government, Professor Neale remarks: 'We can only conclude that those responsible for this astonishing bias would sooner eject troublesome Protestants from the community than Catholics. To describe it as a revolution in parliamentary policy is no exaggeration; and undoubtedly its inspiration came from the Whitgift party, whom Puritans repeatedly accused of preferring Catholics to "good" Protestants.'[3]

---

[1] 35 Eliz. c. 1. *Statutes of the Realm*, IV. 841; J. R. Tanner, *Tudor Constitutional Documents*, p. 197 ff.
[2] J. Neale, *Elizabeth I and her Parliaments*, II. 297.   [3] *Ibid., cit.*, II. 297.

All this time there was coming from the printing presses a considerable amount of literature defending the established church and attacking its critics. The *ex officio* oath and the procedure of the church courts, which had come under so much fire from Puritans and from common lawyers,[1] were defended by Richard Cosin in *An Apologie of and for Sundrie Proceedings by Jurisdiction in Ecclesiasticall*.[2] Matthew Sutcliffe, dean of Exeter, was busy attacking the Presbyterian position in *De Presbyterio* written in Latin for the learned and put in a popular form in his *Treatise of Ecclesiastical Discipline*. In his *An Answere to a certaine Libel Supplicatorie* he pointed out that those who wanted a Discipline could not agree among themselves about the form it should take. He attacked those who wanted 'elders' to play a part in church government on the grounds that they 'abase the prince under the becks of a pack of clowns and clouters called church alderman'.[3] He also criticised their inconsistency about pluralism since a number of Puritans who attacked it themselves held more than one living.[4]

Yet another champion of the establishment was Thomas Bilson whose books *The Perpetuall Government of Christes Church* and *A Compendious Discourse Proving Episcopacy to be of divine Institution*, published in 1593, made very large claims on behalf of the bishops and supported the case which Bancroft had put forward earlier.

Bancroft himself made important contributions to the literary battle in his *Survey of the Pretended Holy Discipline* and in his *Dangerous Positions and Proceedings*, both of which appeared in 1593.[5] Bancroft was highly critical of the alleged scriptural basis for the Presbyterian form of government. So far was it from being clearly and definitely laid down in the scriptures that its supporters could not agree among themselves about what it ought to be. He examined the ways in which it had worked out in practice in the sixteenth century in those countries which had adopted it, and he was highly critical of

---

[1] James Morice, who was in trouble in the Parliament of 1593 (see p. 311) had attacked the oath in his *Briefe Treatise of Oaths* published in 1591 or 1592. M. M. Knappen *Tudor Puritanism*, p. 298.

[2] Published in 1591.

[3] M. M. Knappen, *Tudor Puritanism*, p. 300.

[4] We must not imagine that *all* Puritan ministers in Elizabethan England were godly and learned men with no concern for material advancement. The Puritans had their weaknesses as well as those they criticised.

[5] *Dangerous Positions* is reprinted in part in R. G. Usher, *The Presbyterian Movement in the Reign of Queen Elizabeth*.

Calvin and his successor Beza. He claimed that the 'elders' would interfere in an intolerable way with men's lives and would even seek to control the ruler. He made a detailed examination, based on the very considerable knowledge which he had accumulated during his detective work on the Puritan movement, of the ways in which the Presbyterians had sought to achieve their objectives. He made plain his view that they had meant to overthrow the established church, even though they had in the main been careful to keep within the law. His readers were meant to get the impression that there was at work a considerable underground movement subversive of the existing order in church and state.

The fierce counter-attack of Bancroft and others, and the revelation of how the opponents of the establishment had organised themselves in conferences and synods about which the public, and even the government, had known little or nothing, may well have helped to scare a number of uncommitted Elizabethans into opposing Puritanism and supporting the bishops who stood for the established order. The marked change in the religious temper of the House of Commons in the 1590's may be partly explained in these terms. The number of members who were prepared to let the Puritan leaders have their head may well have decreased as the property-owning classes realised that they had been playing with fire. 'No bishop' might mean in the end not only 'no king' but even 'no gentleman'.

Much more important in the long run than any of these ephemeral controversial works was the contribution of the great Richard Hooker who published in 1593 the first four books of his monumental apologia for the Church of England—*Of the Laws of Ecclesiastical Polity*.

We have already seen Hooker as Master of the Temple Church engaged in controversy with the Presbyterian leader Walter Travers.[1] In 1591 Hooker resigned his appointment and, with the help of Archbishops Whitgift and Sandys, worked on what was to be the most creative contribution to the literature of Anglicanism. What he produced was to be, as Professor Sisson has said, more than a magnificent piece of prose and more than a defence of the church against its Puritan critics. It was 'a manifesto to which the Church returns at every crisis to seek justification and vindication'.[2]

---

[1] See p. 229.
[2] C. J. Sisson, *The Judicious Marriage of Mr. Hooker and the Birth of the Laws of Ecclesiastical Polity*, Cambridge, 1940, p. 6.

The fact that Hooker's work turned out to be of lasting importance as a contribution to theology and to political thought must not make us forget that it was in origin a work written very much for its own time. The first four books were in fact rushed through the press in order that they might be available when the Parliament of 1593 was discussing the bill against seditious sectaries.[1]

Hooker planned a work consisting of eight books. The first four were published in 1593 and the fifth in 1597. The last three had not appeared when Hooker died in 1600. Books VI and VIII were not printed until 1648, and Book VII was not published until 1661. It is not possible here to discuss the richness, the variety and the comprehensiveness of Hooker's masterpiece, but a bald outline of his general plan will help to give some idea of what he was trying to do.

In the first Book he examined in general terms the different kinds of laws, all coming from God, the one law-giver, which affected the universe and man's part in it. Here he was concerned to establish his general position and to show that there was not merely one set of laws by which man should be guided. He was trying to show that life is in fact much more complex than the Puritans suggested. He was establishing the general principles by which he proposed to defend in detail 'the laws of the Church, whereby for so many ages together we have been guided in the exercise of the Christian religion and the service of the true God, our rites, customs and orders of ecclesiastical government'. He was defending his position against those who say that 'we are . . . men that will not have Christ Jesus to rule over them, but have wilfully cast his statutes behind their backs, hating to be reformed and made subject unto the sceptre of his discipline'.[2]

The second Book examines the position of those who urged reformation of the Church of England on the ground that 'Scripture is the only rule of all things which may be done by men', and the third Book attacks the assertion that 'in Scripture there must be of necessity be contained a form of Church polity, the laws whereof may in nowise be altered'. The fourth deals with the charge that the Church of England is corrupted with popish orders, rites and ceremonies and that it ought to follow the example of the reformed churches abroad which had got rid of these corruptions.

[1] C. J. Sisson, *op. cit.*, p. 60 ff.

[2] *The Works of that learned and judicious divine, Mr. Richard Hooker, with an account of his life and Death by Isaac Walton*, 2 vols., Oxford, 1850. I. 147.

The fifth Book, published separately in 1597, dealt at considerable length and in detail with the accusations that the Church of England still retained much superstition in its Prayer Book, its ceremonies and its methods of government.[1]

The sixth Book was meant to deal with Presbyterian claims concerning the powers of lay 'elders', the seventh with the jurisdiction of bishops, and the eighth with the power of the prince and the claims of the bishop of Rome. It seems that it was partly at least because of the controversial nature of some of Hooker's views that there was such a long delay before they were published, and even when they did appear they were not exactly as Hooker wrote them.[2]

Thus Elizabethan readers were familiar only with the first five Books of Hooker's great work. They were the most effective and authoritative defence of the established church against its Puritan critics that had so far been produced. Bishop Jewel in the 1560's had been concerned primarily with the threat from the Papists. Now, in the 1590's the really serious challenge came from within the established church, and the tone and emphasis of Hooker's work was very different from that of Jewel, to whom Hooker owed a great deal.

It is perhaps an over-simplification to say with Professor Dugmore that Hooker's work 'marks the beginning of what we now call Anglicanism', for Hooker drew on traditions which had existed earlier in the Church of England and which had been embodied in its Prayer Book and its liturgy but which had been obscured by the 'protestantising' and 'calvinising' work of the returning Marian exiles and their sympathisers. He added to these his own brilliant and original contribution in order to construct an ideal of a church which should be both scriptural and rational and which, he hoped, would attract the support of those who disliked both Popery and Puritanism. There was

[1] It was edited and annotated by Ronald Bayne, *Of the Laws of Ecclesiastical Polity: the Fifth Book*, London, 1902. See also *An Introduction to the Fifth Book of Hooker's Treatise of the Laws of Ecclesiastical Polity* by Francis Paget, Oxford, 1899.

[2] See C. J. Sisson, *The Judicious Marriage of Mr. Hooker*, p. 96 ff. 'The Suppression of Hooker's Posthumous Manuscripts'. Eighty-five pages of Book VI are missing. It seems possible that they contained passages which were too 'papistical' to be acceptable to Sir Edwyn Sandys and others concerned with the publication of Hooker's works. Professor Sisson points out (p. 107) that 'his last two Books might well fail to satisfy those in the extreme opposing wings'. He maintains that there is nothing in Hooker to serve as a foundation for episcopacy by apostolic succession and divine institution, and that when Book VII was first published in 1661 the defenders of the high Anglican position were anxious to suggest that it was not in fact the undoctored work of Hooker.

in this much on which the Laudians and 'Arminians' were able to build in the next century, but there were also views with which they were not in sympathy, any more than were the Puritans whose basic position Hooker so ably challenged. If the image of the Church of England presented by Hooker in the 1590's did not correspond to the reality as it was during Elizabeth's reign, it was nevertheless an image which was to prove increasingly attractive to future generations.

Hooker sought to convince his opponents by argument and to win their support by his sweet reasonableness. He was well aware of the difficulty of his task. He remarked: 'He that goeth about to persuade a multitude that they are not so well governed as they ought to be, shall never want attentive and favourable hearers . . . whereas on the other side, if we maintain things that are established, we have not only to strive with a number of heavy prejudices deeply rooted in the hearts of men, who think that herein we serve the time, and speak in favour of the present state, because thereby we either hold or seek preferment . . . '[1] Nevertheless, he remarked optimistically: 'I know no cause why either the number or the length of these controversies should diminish our hope of seeing them end with concord on all sides . . . [2]

Hooker accepted the basic theory of the Elizabethan church settlement—that there was in England only one church to which all must belong. He wrote: 'We hold, that . . . there is not any man of the Church of England but the same man is also a member of the commonwealth; nor any man a member of the commonwealth, which is not also of the Church of England.' He held that the sovereign was head of the commonwealth and therefore of the church, which was co-extensive with it.[3] He pointed out that of the dangers that threatened to destroy the commonwealth 'Such as arise from variety in matter of religion are not only the farthest spread, because in religion all men presume themselves interested alike; but they are also for the most part hotlier prosecuted and pursued than other strifes . . .' The deepest wounds of the church, he argued, were given it, not by poor seduced creatures like Hacket or by the scurrilous Martin Marprelate, but by more dangerous enemies who hurt the church 'more softly and closely . . . It being perceived that the plot of discipline did not only bend itself to reform ceremonies, but seek farther to erect a

---

[1] Hooker, *Works*, I. 146.
[2] *Ibid.*, I. 230.
[3] C. J. Sisson, *The Judicious Marriage of Mr. Hooker*, p. 9.

popular authority of elders, and to take away episcopal jurisdiction'. He noted that the supporters of Presbyterians had powerful allies— 'towards this destructive part they have found many helping hands, divers, although peradventure not willing to be yoked with elderships, yet contented (for what intent God doth know) to uphold opposition against bishops; not without greater hurt to the course of their whole proceedings in the business of God and her Majesty's service, than otherwise much more weighty adversaries had been able by their own power to have brought to pass'.[1]

Since the main contention of the Puritans was that the Church of England did not conform to what was laid down in the Scriptures, Hooker had to show that the Scriptures were not the only authority by which man should determine his course of action. He had argued in his first Book that there were a number of different laws binding on mankind and that man had his God-given reason to assist him. He denied in his second Book that the Scriptures were 'the only rule of all things which in this life may be done by men'.[2] He was, of course, committed to the position that the Scriptures were the final authority in matters affecting salvation, but he maintained that this rule applied only when Scripture spoke clearly and unambiguously. When it did not, reason must be allowed its say, and consideration must be given to the past—to the Fathers, the Church Councils, and Christian tradition and practice. He vigorously opposed the Puritan view that man might do only what was expressly sanctioned in the Bible. He did not think that equal weight should be attached to every passage in the Scriptures, and he was critical of those who handled the Bible in such a way that ambiguous quotations, often torn from their context, were used to support their views. Provided man did nothing directly contrary to the plain teaching of the Scriptures, he might use his reason in a very large field of religious belief and practice.

On this basis he was able to justify a great many of the beliefs and practices of the church and to answer those who accused it of preserving the relics of popery. 'The ears of the people', he wrote 'they have therefore filled with strong clamour: the Church of England is fraught with popish ceremonies: they that favour the cause of reformation maintain nothing but the sincerity of the Gospel of Jesus Christ: all such as withstand them fight for the laws of his sworn

---

[1] Hooker, *Works*, I. 418–20.
[2] Hooker, *Works*, I. 229 ff.

enemy, uphold the filthy relics of Antichrist, and are defenders of that which is popish.'[1] These alleged popish relics, Hooker argued, were perfectly reasonable and were not forbidden by God. He proceeded to defend them in great detail and with great ability.

Hooker saw the different churches of Europe not in terms of Christ and Antichrist, but as different parts of the one Church of Christ. He wrote: 'The Church of Christ which was from the beginning is and continueth unto the end; of which Church all parts have not always been equally sincere and sound . . . Not withstanding so far as lawfully we may, we have held and do hold fellowship with them.'[2]

Even the Church of Rome taught a measure of truth and was not to be equated, as many Puritans equated it, with Antichrist. In a remarkable ecumenical passage, he wrote 'with Rome we dare not communicate concerning sundry her gross and grievous abominations, yet touching those main parts of Christian truth wherein they constantly still persist, we gladly acknowledge them to be of the family of Jesus Christ, and our hearty prayer unto God Almighty is, that being conjoined so far forth with them, they may at length (if it be his will) so yield to frame and reform themselves, that no distraction remain in anything, but that we "all may with one heart and one mouth glorify God the Father of our Lord and Saviour" whose church we are'. He would have welcomed the Second Vatican Council.

On the burning issue of the day—the question of church government—Hooker argued that there was not a clear-cut form of church government laid down once and for all in the New Testament, and he seems to hold that the form of church government need not be the same in every part of the church.[3] He knew very well that there were many Protestant churches which were not governed by bishops and which the Church of England nevertheless recognised as 'true churches'.[4] Professor Sisson points out that, in his defence of episco-

---

[1] Hooker, *Works*, IV. 359.

[2] See J. S. Marshall, *Hooker and the Anglican Tradition*, 1963, p. 39.

[3] V. J. K. Brook, *Whitgift and the English Church*, p. 151, argues that later Hooker does insist that the three orders of the church go back to Apostolic times and 'had their beginning from Christ and his blessed Apostles themselves'.

[4] Mr. Brook notes that although Whitgift had urged against Walter Travers that he had received orders abroad (not from a bishop), there does not seem to have been as yet any final decision by the Church of England that such orders were inadequate for office in the Church of England and that such decision was not legally enacted until the time of Charles II (V. J. K. Brook, *op. cit.*, p. 108).

pacy as it existed in the Church of England, Hooker put the stress on
the need for law and order rather than apostolic succession and the
sacramental function of the priesthood, but he adds that the sacramental aspect of the Christian life was very much in Hooker's mind
and that Travers was not alone in his suspicions of Hooker's Protestant orthodoxy.[1]

Although there is no doubt about the tremendous importance of
Hooker's work in the long run, it is more difficult to assess its impact
on Elizabethans. Certainly Whitgift, Sandys and others recognised its
value, but it seems that the 1593 edition of the first four Books was
not exhausted until 1606, nor the 1597 edition of Book Five until 1610,
in spite of the fact that they were very moderately priced at 3s. and
3s. 6d. respectively, and that the number of copies in each edition was
probably only 1,200.[2] What conclusions should be drawn from this
is not clear. It may be that contemporary interest in the controversies
was dying down. It is also possible that there was as yet no large
audience sympathetic to Hooker's point of view.[3] Whether this is so
or not, it is evidence of the changed fortunes of Puritanism that the
fundamental and profound criticisms which Hooker made of the
Puritan position were not effectively answered. Earlier on there would
have been a spate of books and pamphlets challenging Hooker, but
now Field was dead, Cartwright and Travers had given up the battle,
and other Puritan leaders like Perkins were directing their energies
into less controversial paths and did not choose to enter the lists
against this formidable champion of the established church. Mr.
Knappen notes that the only reply to Hooker was *A Christian
letter of Certaine English Protestants* published in 1599 which charged
Hooker with attacking Calvinism and teaching the doctrine of free
will.[4]

In the 1590's Puritanism suffered yet another setback on an intellectual front in which it had hitherto been securely entrenched. The
issues were very complicated and turned on the question of grace and
free will, on the proper interpretation of predestination, on what was
meant by the statement that Christ died for all men, and on whether

---

[1] C. J. Sisson, *The Judicious Marriage of Mr. Hooker*, p. 11.

[2] *Ibid.*, p. 66 ff., 'The Book and the Book Trade'.

[3] For the difficulty which Hooker experienced in getting his masterpiece published
at all, and for a contemporary printer's view that 'bookes of that Argument and on that
parte were not saleable', see C. J. Sisson, *op. cit.*, p. 49 ff., 'The Contract for Printing'.

[4] M. M. Knappen, *Tudor Puritanism*, p. 301.

the 'elect' could fall from grace and forfeit eternal life.[1] The debates were the English contribution to an intellectual battle between Calvinism and its critics which was being fought in Europe in the second half of the sixteenth century. In the English setting, they raised the question of what was the orthodox theology of the Church of England and what was the meaning of the Thirty Nine Articles.

Even before the 1590's, Calvinism, although the predominant theology in intellectual circles in England, had not been unchallenged. Anthonio de Corro, for example, who had lectured at Oxford in the 1570's and become a canon of St. Paul's and later of Lichfield, had been an opponent of Calvinism and had been called by Walter Travers the spiritual predecessor of Hooker.[2] John Overall, a future bishop, had preached that Christ died for all men,[3] and Peter Baro, a French refugee who had been ordained by Calvin himself and who had become one of the most respected figures in Cambridge, had been very critical of his master Calvin, maintaining that 'God's purpose and decree taketh not away the liberty of man's corrupt will'.[4] There was, then, a powerful undercurrent of anti-Calvinist views in existence in intellectual circles a considerable time before the disputes came to a head in the mid 1590's.

The crisis arose because in 1595 a number of Heads of Houses in Cambridge decided to take action against William Barrett, a young chaplain of Gonville and Caius, who had preached that no one 'can of necessity be assured of his salvation' and that sin is the true, exclusive and first cause of damnation (as opposed to the Calvinist teaching that God had for his own inscrutable reasons from the very beginning predestined some to salvation and others to damnation).[5]

Such views were not novel, but evidently the predominantly Calvinist group in the university felt that a stand must be made against the spread of what it regarded as false doctrine, and on 10 May 1595 Barrett was forced to read a recantation. He did so, it was claimed, in a very irreverent, profane and impudent manner.[6] There followed

---

[1] There is an excellent discussion of the theological issues in H. C. Porter, *Reformation and Reaction in Tudor Cambridge*.

[2] H. C. Porter, *op. cit.*, p. 283. de Corro was a Spanish monk who fled to France in 1558 and later settled in England.

[3] *Ibid.*, p. 285 ff.

[4] *Ibid.*, pp. 376–7. Baro had been ordained by Calvin in 1560. He came to England in 1572 and was elected commoner of Peterhouse, Cambridge, in 1573.

[5] H. C. Porter, *op. cit.*, p. 344 ff.

[6] *Ibid.*, p. 346.

appeals to Whitgift and to Burghley, the Chancellor of Cambridge, in which the Calvinist Heads of Houses asserted that their doctrines were 'the truths of religion publicly and generally received' and that they had never been 'openly impugned amongst us but by some persons of late', that is, by Barrett and his supporters.[1] William Whitaker, the Regius Professor of Divinity, argued that Barrett had contradicted 'the religion of our church publicly received, and always held in her Majesty's reign', and which was maintained 'in all sermons, disputations and lectures'. In his recantation, Barrett had been required to say that he believed 'concerning the doctrine of election, and reprobation, as the Church of England believeth and teacheth in the book of articles of faith in the article of predestination'. This meant that the Heads of Houses in Cambridge were asserting that their interpretation of the teaching of the Thirty Nine Articles on the subject of predestination was the only possible orthodox interpretation.

A lengthy dispute followed in the course of which Barrett retracted his recantation. Whitgift decided that he was not himself prepared to give unqualified support to the Cambridge Calvinists, even though he was in fairly general agreement with their position. In November 1595 he received from Whitaker and others a statement of their views on the issues in dispute, but only after he had made considerable modification was he prepared to accept their document as 'sound doctrine . . . uniformly professed in this Church of England, and agreeable to the Articles of Religion . . .'[2]

In spite of Whitgift's alterations these nine Lambeth Articles were strongly Calvinist in tone, although not as strong as the Calvinists wished. The first of them, for example, unlike the Thirty Nine Articles, stated that God from eternity had not only predestined some men to life but had reprobated some to death, and the ninth article stated that it was not in the will of each and every man to be saved.[3]

The Lambeth Articles were not the official teaching of the Church of England, and the archbishop made it clear to the Vice-Chancellor of Cambridge that although nothing was to be publicly taught to the contrary in Cambridge, they were only his private judgment.[4] He was anxious that these questions should be discussed with moderation,

[1] H. C. Porter, *op. cit.*, p. 314.
[2] H. C. Porter, *Reformation and Reaction in Tudor Cambridge*, p. 364 ff., 'The Lambeth Articles'.
[3] The Articles are printed in H. C. Porter, *op. cit.*, p. 371.
[4] *Ibid.*, p. 372.

and the Lambeth Articles were not officially published. The queen was even more anxious to prevent theological controversy, and on December 1595 Whitgift was told that 'she mislikes much that any allowance hath been given by your Grace and the rest of any points to be disputed of Predestination, being a matter tender and dangerous to weak ignorant minds . . . '[1] She required him to stop any further disputation.

The dispute did not at once die down because in January 1596 Baro preached a sermon directly contradicting part of the Lambeth Articles. There was a fuss about this and he was in trouble in the Consistory Court in Cambridge, but eventually the case against him was dropped. There were other disputes also in the late Elizabethan period, and in 1599 John Overall, Regius Professor of Divinity since 1595, was involved in another argument about predestination, but the matter did not reach a conclusion.

These complicated and difficult theological disputes, which have been touched on only very briefly here, are a further illustration of the fact that in the realm of theology the Calvinist Puritans were being challenged and that their calm assumption that what they believed was in fact the orthodox teaching of the Church of England was no longer unquestioned in the late Elizabethan period.

The Puritan case was further weakened by the efforts which Whitgift and others were making to remove some of the abuses which had made the church so vulnerable earlier on. The financial difficulties under which the church laboured were too great to be overcome, short of really drastic measures which the queen would certainly not have supported and which would have aroused fierce resistance from the laity, but something could be done in other directions. In 1591, for example, in an attempt to deal with the 'dissoluteness in manners and ignorance in the common sort', the archbishop urged his bishops to make the clergy catechize the children, preferably in the presence of their parents, and to admit to confirmation only those who knew the catechism.[2] In 1593 at the queen's command he held an enquiry into the educational attainments, preaching ability and standard of conduct of all the clergy, and in 1594 there was an examination of abuses in clerical courts. When the queen summoned parliament in 1597, Whitgift laid before Convocation a long list of abuses in the church which needed reforming.

[1] H. C. Porter, *op. cit.*, pp. 373–4. [2] V. J. K. Brook, *Whitgift and the English Church*, p. 154.

The parliament of 1597 was also concerned with ecclesiastical affairs but not in the carefully planned and premeditated manner of the 1580's.[1] There had been some very serious scandals concerning the granting by the ecclesiastical authorities of licences to marry without calling the banns, and the House proposed to legislate against abuses. The queen intervened and asked the House to collect evidence on which she herself would take action. The Commons set up a committee with much wider terms of reference—'to receive information of the grievances touching ecclesiastical causes',[2] and on 22 November they produced a bill concerning marriage licences, in spite of the fact that the queen had indicated her intention to handle the matter herself. A few days later there was introduced a bill against excessive fees in church courts, and a little later still a Puritan member introduced a bill which would have made it easier for Puritan ministers to accept the Act of Uniformity and the Thirty Nine Articles. The bills got no further, and Sir John Neale suggests that although the Puritans in the House were able to get a temporary majority on these questions they could no longer command enough support to press the issues to a conclusion. He adds that both the archbishop and the queen showed their healthy respect for parliamentary agitation by passing through Convocation a series of 'constitutions' dealing with some of the grievances.[3]

Parliamentary pressure as well as criticism from other sources no doubt help to explain the passing of the Constitutions of 1597, but it is less than just to Whitgift's very genuine reforming efforts to see these reforms simply as defensive action. Rather should they be seen as evidence of his 'unremitting determination to deal with the shortcomings of the church'.[4] The Constitutions supplemented the Canons of 1585 and dealt with a considerable range of problems, including the selection and appointment of suitable men for the ministry, the abuses of pluralism, excessive use of excommunication, excessive fees in church courts, and abuses in the granting of marriage licences.[5]

---

[1] J. Neale, *Elizabeth I and her Parliaments*, II. 356.
[2] *Ibid.*, p. 357.
[3] *Ibid.*, p. 358.
[4] V. J. K. Brook, *Whitgift and the English Church*, p. 168.
[5] The Constitutions of 1597 are printed in E. Cardwell, *Synodalia*, I. 147 ff. For marriage licences, see Patrick McGrath, 'Notes on the History of Marriage Licences' in *Gloucestershire Marriage Allegations, 1637–1680*, edit. Brian Frith, Records Section of the Bristol and Gloucestershire Archaeological Society, 1954.

To the very end, Elizabeth's parliaments continued their attempts to deal with matters concerning religion. In 1601 there was a bill for the better observance of the sabbath which was eventually whittled down to a bill prohibiting the keeping of fairs and markets on Sundays. It passed the Commons, was read twice in the Lords, and after that no more was heard of it.[1] Another bill 'against wilful absence from divine service upon the Sunday' was introduced by the last surviving member from among the Marian exiles. It proposed to make it easier to collect the 1s. fine by substituting prosecution before Justices of the Peace for the laborious and costly procedure of indictment at the assizes, and it made husbands liable for their wives' recusancy. The bill was defeated by 140 to 137 votes. It was a changing world when a bill against Papists could not get a majority. A new and less severe bill was introduced by Sir Francis Hastings, but this was lost by 105 to 106 votes. Finally, there was a bill to restrict pluralism. Unlike an earlier bill in the Parliament of 1589, this allowed no exceptions for existing holders of more than one living if their livings exceeded £8 in value. It got a first reading, but no more was heard of it.[2]

It is clear, then, that the strong religious passions of earlier years had died down in the House of Commons and that members were no longer prepared to fight on issues which once would have stirred them to enthusiasm and to anger. It was but one more indication that Puritanism as a militant creed had lost ground and that the Elizabethan age had come to an end before the death of Elizabeth.

All this does not mean that Puritanism must be written off as a lost cause in the later Elizabethan period. The Presbyterian movement and its national organisation had been destroyed, but Puritanism in many other forms still went on. At local although not at national level, it can be argued that Puritan organisation was not so much dead as dormant and that the well-organised campaign of the Puritans in connection with the Millenary Petition of 1604 showed that the Puritans had not been eliminated but only subdued.[3] Dr. Collinson points out that there were still plenty of opportunities for informal meetings of

---

[1] J. Neale, *Elizabeth I and her Parliaments*, II. 394. Both Houses had passed a bill for the better observance of the Sabbath in 1584–5, but the queen vetoed it. In 1601 the word Sabbath in the original bill was changed to Sunday. Great Yarmouth was excepted from the law.

[2] J. Neale, *op. cit.*, II. 406 ff.

[3] Patrick Collinson, 'The Puritan Classical Movement', p. 1148 ff.

like-minded Puritan ministers at Quarter Sessions, at the assizes, at visitations and even in religious 'exercises', and he maintains that in almost every district where the Puritan movement had been represented in the 1580's there is some trace of locally organised movements of Puritan ministers in the period 1592–1603.[1]

In these years when agitation for changes in the church was difficult and even dangerous, many Puritans turned their energies in other directions. Much of the effort that earlier had gone into arguing about methods of church government or into carrying out elaborate surveys of the ministry was now directed into pastoral work, into giving men practical instruction on how to lead the Christian life, on how to deal with problems of conscience and how to assure themselves that they were among the 'elect'. The Puritan preachers began to come into their own and to develop their special style of preaching.[2]

Perhaps the most outstanding of this kind of preacher and pastor in the late Elizabethan age was the great William Perkins. He had come from Warwickshire to the University of Cambridge in 1577 and he had become an extremely influential and persuasive preacher and writer. Although he occasionally got into difficulties with the ecclesiastical authorities and was at one time implicated in the 'classical' movement, he was able, as Haller puts it, 'by careful avoidance of controverted questions in his public discourses, to keep his pulpit undisturbed until his death at forty-four in 1602'.[3] He was a first-rate scholar, but he also had a great capacity of putting his arguments across to the less educated. In the Preface to his collected works, published posthumously in 1608, the printer remarks: ' . . . as for the matter of his doctrine, he contenteth and satisfieth the most learned; so for the manner of his delivering the same, he condescendeth to the capacitie of the meanest of God's children'.[4]

Perkins was a prolific and very popular writer. His *Armilla Aurea*, which appeared in English in 1591 as *A Golden Chain*, went through

[1] Patrick Collinson, *op. cit.*, p. 1197. For a full examination and discussion of the evidence, see *ibid.*, p. 1144 ff., and *The Elizabethan Puritan Movement*, p. 437 ff.

[2] The development of a 'new' kind of Puritanism in the late Elizabethan period has parallels in the growth of a new kind of 'Anglicanism' and in the changes in English Catholicism.

[3] William Haller, *The Rise of Puritanism or, the Way to the New Jerusalem as set forth in Pulpit and Press from Thomas Cartwright to John Milburne and John Milton, 1570–1643*, New York, 1947, p. 64.

[4] *The Works of William Perkins*, 3 vols., 1608. I. Breward, 'The Life and Theology of William Perkins', Manchester Ph.D. thesis, 1963.

Y

at least 3 Latin and 9 English editions by 1600. It was a detailed study, complete with chart, of the processes by which a man made his way to heaven or to hell. Perkins' sermons made a tremendous appeal, and the practical nature of their teaching is illustrated by such titles as *How to Live and That well: in all estates and times. Specially, when helpes and comforts fail* or by *A Case of Conscience, the Greatest that ever was: how a man may know whether he be the childe of God or no.* There were a considerable number of Elizabethans, even in sophisticated university congregations, who wanted assurance that they were children of God, and Perkins preached to packed churches. A seventeenth-century church historian summed him up when he wrote: 'An excellent Chirurgeon he was at joynting of a broken soul, and at stating of a doubtfull conscience', and again: 'The Scholar could heare no learneder, the Townsman plainer Sermons.'

Perkins was one of the most distinguished of the 'godly Puritan preachers'. Haller maintains that it was from him probably more than from any other that the members of the brotherhood learned to put abstract doctrine into practical terms and to work out a method of spiritual self-help.[1] The preacher must himself experience the work of the spirit within him. 'Can he', asked Perkins, 'commend the state of grace to another, and never felt the sweetness thereof in his own soule? Dare he come to preach sanctification with polluted lips, and out of an unsanctified heart?'[2] In his *Art of Prophecying* he urged the minister to preach so that 'all, even ignorant persons and unbelievers may judge that it is not so much he that speaketh, as the Spirit of God in him and by him'.[3] Elsewhere he warns ministers that they must not be like cooks who prepare a banquet but who eat none of it because their stomachs are cloyed with the smell and taste of it, and he points out that 'it may come to passe, that the minister which dresseth and provideth the spiritual food, may eate the least of it himselfe; and so, labouring to save others, hee may be a reprobate'.[4] In their teaching, ministers must 'observe an admirable plainnesse and an admirable powerfullnesse' so that the unlearned man might be able to perceive his own faults and the unregenerate will be moved to exclaim that God speaks in the preacher.[5] Men must be admonished

---

[1] William Haller, *The Rise of Puritanism*, p. 92. For a general consideration of Puritan Preachers, see I. Morgan, *The Godly Preachers of the Elizabethan Church*. For Elizabethan preaching in relation to earlier preaching, see J. W. Blench, *Preaching in England in the late 15th and 16th centuries*, 1964   [2] William Haller, *op. cit.*, p. 93.
[3] *Ibid.*, p. 131.   [4] William Perkins, *Works*, I. 359.   [5] William Haller, *op. cit.*, p. 130.

'that they use most painfull diligence in working their salvation' and taught to 'presse on to the straight gate with maine and might' so that 'with all violence (they) lay hold on the kingdome of heaven'.[1] In *The Warning against the Idolatrie of the last times*, dedicated to Lord Hastings, Perkins laments that, although God had bestowed on us the treasures of the Gospel for more than forty years under our gracious queen, ' . . . alas in respect of the greatest number, we are a nation very unthankefull: yeelding small obedience to the gospell of life'. The ignorant multitude must be informed touching the true worship of God for 'the remainders of Poperie yet stick in the minds of many of them, and they thinke, that to serve God, is nothing else but to deale truly with men, and to babble a few words morning and evening, at home or in the Church, though there be no understanding'.[2] It was the business of the preacher to stir up men's consciences. Perkins remarks that 'some say, that if they should frequent sermons, they should be accounted precise, and be mocked', but if a man is ashamed of Christ, his heavenly father will be ashamed of him.[3]

Perkins was very suspicious of those who argued 'that our religion and the Religion of the present Church of Rome are all one for substance: and that they may be re-united as (in their opinion) they were before', and he asserted 'let men in shew of moderation, pretend the peace and good estate of the Catholike Church as long as they will, this union of the two religions can never bee made, more than the union of light and darknesse . . . ' Rome for him was and is the whore of Babylon.[4]

Perkins also disliked witches and in his *Discourse of the Damned Art of Witchcraft*, printed in 1609 and dedicated to Sir Edward Coke, he advocated putting to death 'all Diviners, Charmers, Juglers, all wizzards, commonly called wise men and wise women; yea, whosoever doe anything (knowing what they doe) which cannot be effected by nature or art'.[5] He was also opposed to sports on Sundays, stage plays and 'painting and colouring, thereby making themselves seeme

---

[1] William Perkins, *Works*, I. 361.

[2] *Ibid.*, pp. 650, 651.

[3] *Ibid.*, p. 695. In his writing on the Lord's Supper, Perkins appears to be teaching that Christ is received in a purely spiritual manner and seems to repudiate both transubstantiation and consubstantiation.

[4] *Ibid.*, I. 549 ff. in the dedication of 'A Reformed Catholike'.

[5] *Ibid.*, III. 650. On this subject, see J. L. Teall, 'Witchcraft and Calvinism in Elizabethan England', *Journal of the History of Ideas*, xxiii, 1962.

that which they are not'. He seems to hold the view that after the Fall the human body became shameful and that 'The ende of attire is, to hid the shamefull nakedness of the body from the sight of men'.[1]

But for all that he seems to display on occasions some of the characteristics of the stage Puritan,[2] Perkins was undoubtedly a most important and influential religious thinker. Dr. Porter suggests that he is perhaps the first systematic English theologian. His theology was basically Calvinist. He maintained that 'God doth take certain men which are to be created, into his everlasting love and favour, passing by the rest', and this is done, 'of the sole will of God, without respect either of good or evil in the creature'.[3] Again, he says: 'God would not have all men called unto Christ', and he asserts that 'the greatest part of the world hath ever been out of the covenant of grace.'[4] Yet with him, as with most of the godly preachers, there seems to have been an implicit assumption that all pious hearers of the word were elect.[5] One of his works was entitled *A Treatise tending unto a declaration, whether a man be in the estate of damnation, or in the estate of Grace: and if he be in the first, how he may in time come out of it: if in the second how he may discerne it, and persevere in the same to the end.* In practice, if not in theory, there would seem to be some hope of avoiding damnation for those who diligently followed the teaching of the godly preacher.

Another man who is often used to illustrate the work of a godly Puritan minister is Richard Greenham who from 1571 to 1591 was rector of Dry Drayton near Cambridge.[6] Haller regards him as one of those who sought 'to effect by preaching and by the example of their own lives that moral and religious reform which they could not for the time being accomplish by direct control over the establishment'.[7] He had given some support to Cartwright when he first fell foul of the authorities and he was later in the Cambridgeshire *classis*,[8] but he avoided controversy. He was only once in trouble for nonconformity and was quickly let off.[9] At Dry Drayton he preached

[1] William Perkins, *Works*, II. 138.
[2] See W. P. Holden, *Anti-Puritan Satire 1572–1642*, Yale, 1954
[3] H. C. Porter, *Reformation and Reaction in Tudor Cambridge*, p. 298.
[4] *Ibid.*, p. 309.   [5] *Ibid.*, p. 310.
[6] See H. C. Porter, *Reformation and Reaction in Tudor Cambridge*, p. 216 ff.; W. Haller, *op. cit.*, p. 25 ff.
[7] W. Haller, *op. cit.*, p. 48.
[8] H. C. Porter, *op. cit.*, p. 216.   [9] W. Haller, *op. cit.*, p. 26.

twice every Sunday, catechised his parishioners and engaged in charitable works. His aim was to help the spiritually sick and to minister to the troubled mind.[1] And he acted as a spiritual director for a number of Cambridge men. Looking back on his long ministry at Dry Drayton he saw himself as a failure. As Dr. Porter puts it: 'Dry Drayton remained, in spite of his tears and his preaching, ignorant and obstinate'[2]—a reminder that we must not assume that the godly ministers always carried their flocks with them. He left for London in 1591 and spent the last three years of his life there, dying of the plague in 1594. His works were collected by his friend Henry Holland and were published in 1599. They went through five editions by 1612.[3] His career, practically untroubled by the ecclesiastical authorities, is one more reminder of the difficulty of defining a 'Puritan'. The kind of activity in which a 'godly preacher' like Greenham was engaged was not such as to bring him into conflict with the establishment. There was room with the Church of England for ministers concerned with pastoral work and with this particular approach to the spiritual life, provided they accepted the Prayer Book and the system of government of the Church in which they ministered.

Another such man was Henry Smith, whose step-mother was Burghley's sister. He was a disciple of Richard Greenham, and in 1587 Burghley's influence helped him to secure a lectureship at St. Clement Danes in London. When Bishop Aylmer tried to silence him for preaching without licence, Burghley intervened to help him. Smith became an extremely popular London preacher. In his biography Thomas Fuller calls him 'silver-tongued' and comments: 'His Church was so crowded with Auditors, that Persons of good quality brought their own Pues with them, I mean their legs . . . Their ears did so attend to his lips, their hearts to their ears, that he held the rudder of their affection in his hands, so that he could steer them whither he pleased.'[4] He too was a physician of souls. In a sermon called 'The Sinfull Mans Search', he said: 'In a sicke and evill affected body . . .

---

[1] W. Haller, op. cit., pp. 27, 28.
[2] H. C. Porter, op. cit., p. 218.
[3] W. Haller, op. cit., p. 26. Haller comments that Henry Holland's preface to Greenham's work is 'possibly the earliest of the long series of spiritual portraits of Puritan divines and others of the elect which were to play so important a part in Puritan propaganda'. Their importance, however, lay in the seventeenth century, not in the sixteenth.
[4] Quoted in W. Haller, The Rise of Puritanism, p. 30.

we usually see preparatives ministered, that the maladies may bee made more fit and pliable to receive the wholesome medicines. The like, yea, and greater regard ought we to have of our soules, which being not crasie only, or lightly affected with sinne, but sicke even unto death, had need to bee prepared with threates and exhortations, comforts and consolation, one way or another that they may bee made fit, not to receive the preparative, but the perfection of happie salvation.'[1] Smith died very young, but from 1592 onwards there were numerous editions of his sermons.[2]

Two other ministers whose writings are often used to exemplify the 'Puritan spirit' are Richard Rogers and Samuel Ward, both of whom left diaries which tell us a good deal about them.[3] Rogers was the son of a Chelmsford joiner. He was born in 1551, and in 1566 went up to Christ's College, Cambridge, which produced a number of distinguished Puritans including William Perkins. He took an M.A. in 1574 at Caius College, and a year or two later he is found at Nethersfield in Essex, seven miles east of Braintree, where he was 'Preacher of the Word of God', acting either as a lecturer, or as a curate, to John Ludham who held the living from 1570 to 1613. He married twice, had a large family and survived till 1618. He was a member of the Dedham *classis* and he was suspended and silenced for a time when he refused to subscribe to Whitgift's Three Articles of 1583. He describes with some satisfaction how '(The Archbishop) protested none of us should Preach without conformity and subscription. I thanke God I have seen him eat his Words as Greate and as Peremptory as he was. For after Thirty Weeks I was Restored by Dr. Aylmer, Bishop of London, to whome Sir Robert Wroth Writ in favour of me, and bad me Preach and he would beare me out, and so I have continued about 20 yeares to the end of Archbishop Whitgifts life who deceased the first of March 1604'.[4] Nevertheless, after this incident Rogers spent a great deal of time worrying lest he should again be stopped from preaching. He was in some trouble again in 1604–5, but for most of his life he was in fact unmolested.

Rogers had a considerable reputation as a godly preacher, a spiritual adviser and a holy man. In 1603 he published a work with

---

[1] *The Sermons of Master Henry Smith*, London, 1609.
[2] W. Haller, *op. cit.*, p. 30 ff.
[3] *Two Elizabethan Puritan Diaries*, edit. M. M. Knappen, American Society of Church History, 1933.
[4] M. M. Knappen, *op. cit.*, p. 29.

the lengthy title of *Seven Treatises, Containing such Direction as is gathered out of the Holie Scripture, leading and guiding to true happines, both in this life, and in the life to come; and may be called the practize of Christianitie. Profitable to all such as heartily desire the same: in the which, more particularly true Christians may learne how to leade a godly and comfortable life every day.* Every day the Christian must humble himself by self-examination and be raised up by the assured hope of forgiveness promised by God. He must prepare his heart to seek the Lord, he must arm himself against evil and sin, he must nourish his fear and love of God, he must watch and pray for steadfastness and keep his peace with God.[1]

Rogers seems to have taken students as lodgers and to have acted as spiritual adviser to many who were troubled in spirit. He used to spend about two hours a day in prayer and meditation and from nine to ten hours in study and he also strove to be 'fruitful' in pastoral work. He tried to organise a group of parishioners for devotional purposes but was not very successful. He was an expert at self-examination in order that he might 'know mine own hart better . . . and to be acquainted with the diverse corners of it and what sin I am most in daunger of and what diligence and meanes I use against any sin and how I goe under any affliction'.[2] In his diary he engaged in spiritual book-keeping. Thus he notes on 30 September 1587: 'Declineinges this first week I have sensibly found in my selfe from that staidnes in a godly life in which I lately determined a new to continue.' On 30 October 1587 he thanks God for his blessings, including 'goodwill and a good name with the godlier sort, communion with them and such manifold comfort in my life and with his people, with liberty in my ministery'.[3] He also thinks that 'God besides all this hath been very mercifull to me in my sermons. For either in my med(itation) of them or utteringe of them to the people, sometimes in both, I have been veary well moved and have seen the same in others'. On 22 December 1587 he notes: 'The 6 of this month we fasted betwixt our selve min(isters), to the stirringe upp of our selves to greater godliness . . . and then we determined to bringe into writinge a direction for our lives, which might be both for our selves and others.'

---

[1] M. M. Knappen, *Two Elizabethan Puritan Diaries*, p. 7; W. Haller, *op. cit.*, p. 36 ff.

[2] M. M. Knappen, *op. cit.*, p. 62; H. C. Porter, *Reformation and Reaction in Tudor Cambridge*, p. 220.

[3] *Ibid.*, p. 61.

The other diarist was Samuel Ward, a Durham man, who came to Christ's College, Cambridge, in March 1589 and who greatly admired William Perkins. Ward became a Fellow of Emmanuel College in 1598. Subsequently he did very well indeed for himself in the University and in the church, moving in the course of his career from a radical to a conservative position. He too used his diary to keep a check on his spiritual life. Thus he notes on 13 May 1595: 'My desire of preferment over much. My adulterous dream. Think thow how that this is not our home in this world, in which we are straungers . . . Think how bad a thing it is to goo to bed without prayer, and remember to call on God at goyng to our prayers in the Chappell . . . ' On 1 June 1595 he notes: 'My late rising in the morning to sanctify the Sabaoth. My negligence all that day, and idleness in performing the dewtyes of the Sabaoth . . . My by talk in the bed, of other matters than are meet to be talked of on the Sabaoth. My ill dream.' On other occasions he was troubled by 'My thought of pride att reading of Greek, concerning the teaching of my auditors the Greek accentes . . . ' and by 'My immoderate dyet in eating cheese, very hurtful for my body att 3 aclock' and by 'My unfruytfull spending of money that day I went downe the river to Chesterton . . . ' More serious than his 'immoderate eating of walnutes and cheese after supper' on 3 October 1595 was his conduct on 8 September 1596 when he noted: 'My goynge to the taverne with such lewd fellowes, albeyt I knew them not. How little greived was I att ther swearing and othes and wyld talk.' In June 1598 he rather surprisingly noted: 'My negligence in commending the medicine for my nose to Godes blessing.'

Another diary written at the turn of the century also illustrates those features which are commonly taken to be characteristic of the 'Puritan' way of life.[1] This is the work of Lady Margaret Hoby of Hackness in Yorkshire who took as her third husband Sir Thomas Posthumous Hoby. Margaret seems to have been brought up in the household of Catherine countess of Huntingdon, the wife of the strongly Protestant third earl, and Sir Thomas's mother was one of the five brilliant daughters of another strong Protestant, Sir Anthony Cooke of Gidea Hall in Essex. Sir Thomas was thus related to Burghley and to the Bacon family.

Lady Hoby's Diary reveals her as someone who is very fully, and perhaps rather self-consciously, engaged in the practice of her reli-

[1] *Diary of Lady Margaret Hoby 1599–1605*, edit. Dorothy M. Meads, 1930.

gion, in prayer, meditation, reading the Bible and making a daily examination of her conscience. Thus in one of the early entries in 1599 we find her writing: 'After I was redie I betooke my selfe to priuat praier, wherin it pleased the Lord to deall mercifully . . . after, I went about the house, and instructed Tomson wiffe in som principles of relegion, and then eate my breakfast, and then walked about tell all most: 11: of the Clock: and after I had read: 2: chapters of the bible, I went to diner: after diner I went to worke, at which Contenewed tell: 4:, then I took order for supper . . . went to praier and to writ some notes in my testament, from which I was Called to walk with Mr Hoby . . . and so to supper: imediately after praer and Lector, for the diligent attencion of which the Lord did heare my praier by remouing all wanderinges which vse to hvrt me so that I receiued much Comfort, I went to bed.'[1] Again on another typical day she writes: 'In the morninge, after priuat praier, I Reed of the bible, and then wrought till 8: a clock, and then I eate my breakfast: after which done, I walked in to the feeldes tell: 10 a clock, then I praied, and, not long after, I went to dinner: and about one a clock I geathered my Apeles tell: 4: . . . and then I went to priuat praier and exemenation, in which it pleased the lord to blesse me: and besiech the lord, for christ his sack, to increase the power of his spirite in me daly Amen Amen: tell supper time I hard Mr Rhodes read of Cartwright, and sonne after supper, I went to prairs, after which I wrett to Mr Hoby, and so to bed.'[2]

On one occasion she records that she 'neclected my custom of praier, for which, as for many other sinnes, it pleased the Lord to punishe me with an Inwarde assalte: But I know the Lord hath pardoned it because he is true of his promise and, if I had not taken this course of examenation, I think I had for gotten itt'.[3]

The following extract is typical of the way Lady Hoby spent her Sundays: 'After priuat praers I reed and then went to the church: after, I Came home and praied and then dined: after diner I talked of the sarmon, and read of the bible with some Gentlewomen . . . after, I praied, walked and went to the church againe, and after I walked a whil: and so I spent some time in writings on my sarmon book and at prainge, and, after, I went to supper and, sonne after,

[1] *Diary of Lady Margaret Hoby*, p. 62.
[2] *Ibid.*, p. 67.
[3] *Ibid.*, p. 70.

I hard publeck praers and, lastly, when I had praied priuatly, I went to bed.'[1] Lady Hoby's Diary illustrates some of those features which Mr. Hill considers characteristic of the new Puritanism of the 1590's. He sees William Perkins as the high priest of 'a Puritanism not committed to a presbyterian system or organization but emphasizing ever more strongly preaching, household discussion and education, the sanctity of the Sabbath'. It was a Puritanism which stressed 'an individual pietism, with the household as its essential unit rather than the parish'.[2] Lady Hoby certainly observed the Sabbath in a way which would have won the approval of Richard Greenham, whose *Treatise of the Sabbath Day* was composed in the early 1590's, and of his son-in-law Nicholas Bownde, whose *Doctrine of the Sabbath* was published in 1595.[3]

The 'Puritan' diarists were clearly very much concerned with leading a well-ordered religious life. They spent a good deal of time in self-examination so that they might know their own weaknesses and avoid the occasion of sin in future. Prayer, meditation, reading the Scriptures, preaching or hearing sermons, play a major part in their religious life, and the sacraments seem to be of less importance. Mr. Knappen comments on the two diaries which he edited that there is in them an overwhelming predominance of the ethical element, of concentration on the good life, and that there is an anxiety to suppress the flesh. He thinks it doubtful if the writers spent much time thinking about the future life and he notes that they do not seem particularly worried about securing assurance that they are 'elect'. He questions whether the doctrine of predestination had much influence on the writers and points out that they seemed to think they had free will. He suggests that they show an intense desire to experience spiritual

[1] *Diary of Lady Margaret Hoby*, p. 131.

[2] Christopher Hill, *Society and Puritanism*, p. 502.

[3] Mr. Hill maintains that Sabbatarianism which had hitherto been part of the common Protestant heritage, became from the 1590's 'the shibboleth of the Puritans' (*op. cit.*, p. 501). For further discussion, see Christopher Hill, *Society and Puritanism* ('The Uses of Sabbatarianism'); M. M. Knappen, *Tudor Puritanism* ('Sabbatarianism'); W. B. Whitaker, *Sunday in Tudor and Stuart Times*, 1933; Patrick Collinson, 'The Beginning of English Sabbatarianism', in *Studies in Ecclesiastical History*, I, Ecclesiastical History Society, 1961. There were of course non-Puritans such as Lancelot Andrewes who wanted a stricter observance, and Andrewes had a great influence on Greenham and Bownde. In 1599 Whitgift called in the copies of Bownde's book but it was reissued early in the next century. It is nevertheless true that those who supported stricter observance were not necessarily Puritans.

joys *in this world*.[1] There does not seem to be any great stress on love of God for his own sake, or on the love of Jesus Christ, even though the writers recognise that they are saved through the merits of his passion and death.

It is important to remember that in this meditation, prayer and self-examination, and in these attempts to lead the godly life, there is a great deal which is not exclusively 'Puritan'.[2] These things have, after all, been basic characteristics of Christian practice throughout the history of Christianity. Moreover, the Puritans were hardly the first to stress the temptations presented by the world, the flesh and the devil. There is nothing peculiarly 'Puritan' in self-examination, and the Roman Church had brought it to a fine art in connection with the sacrament of Penance. The need for prayerful reading of the Scriptures was accepted by all sixteenth-century Protestants who believed that the Scriptures contained all that was necessary for salvation.

But if the Puritan spirit and way of life was not as original or as exclusive as is sometimes suggested, it is nevertheless true to say that in later Elizabethan England there were a number of 'godly' preachers and their followers who laid particular stress on certain elements in Christianity to the exclusion, or at least the diminution, of other elements. They developed a way of life in which preaching and hearing the Word played a very large part and the sacraments a much smaller one, and in which the individual was much more conscious of himself as an individual Christian or as one of a select band of godly brethren than as a member of a nation-wide Christian church.

The Puritans of the later Elizabethan age were no longer launching vigorous attacks on the established church.[3] The aggressive fighting spirit of earlier times found its outlet now in a pastoral and pietistic Puritanism in which the enemies were the world and the flesh rather than the archbishops and bishops. Nevertheless, the Puritans had not yet abandoned hope of reforming the church, and early in James I's

[1] M. M. Knappen, *op. cit.*, p. 14.
[2] See I. Morgan, *The Godly Preachers of the Elizabethan Church*; particularly Chapter V, 'New Monks?'
[3] Some of the Puritans hoped to find a leader in the earl of Essex. Penry in 1593 appealed to him to lead the godly party, Bownde's book on the Sabbath was dedicated to him, Cartwright was in correspondence with him and 'the whole pack of Puritans' were said to have flocked to him just before his abortive rising in January 1601. See Patrick Collinson, 'The Puritan Classical Movement', p. 1200 ff. A number of Catholic malcontents were also associated with Essex at the time of his rebellion. See D. N. De Luna, *Jonson's Romish Plot*, Oxford, 1967, pp. 98–102.

reign they made one more effort to do so. They showed then by the Millenary Petition of 1604 that they had not lost the capacity for organisation,[1] but their earlier defeats no doubt help to explain why their demands were now pitched in a much lower key. When their efforts were again unsuccessful some sought escape by emigration, but many were prepared to content themselves with following their own way of life within the established church and with trying to get moderate concessions through Parliament. It was not until the Arminian party began to dominate the leadership in the church that really serious conflict once more arose.

[1] See p. 340 ff.

12

Epilogue: The Hampton Court Conference and the Gunpowder Plot

THE accession of James VI of Scotland to the English throne was regarded with hope by Puritans and Papists alike, for both groups believed that they would fare much better than in the days of Elizabeth. The Puritans had great expectations from a king who had been brought up in one of 'the best reformed churches'—the Presbyterian Church of Scotland. The Papists were optimistic about a ruler who had already been in negotiation with the papacy and who was understood to have said that he would not persecute any Papist merely because of his religious beliefs. One excessively optimistic lady went so far as to say: 'We had a late Queene and she was a blodye Queene ... and now we have a Kinge who ys of our religion and will restore us to our rightes ... '[1]

The most apprehensive religious group was that of the leaders of the established church, for there was no certainty that James would not want to 'reform' the Church of England, and if he did, it would be impossible to stop him. It was indeed fortunate for the Church of England that James had had more than enough of Presbyterianism in Scotland. If he had been a Presbyterian zealot, the whole course of English history might well have been fundamentally changed. As it was, the uncertainty about his intentions and his willingness to give the Puritans a hearing were extremely worrying to Whitgift and Bancroft.

The Puritans were quick to take advantage of the opportunity given them by the change of rulers, and at first they played their hand very

---

[1] *Historical MSS Commission: Various Collections*, I. 73. The lady was Katharine Gawan, gentlewoman, wife of Thomas Gawan of Hurcott, Oxfordshire. By Whitsun 1605 she had changed her views. She said she had rejoiced at the King's coming and 'had bestowed many charges in bonefires and otherwise to shew her joy at his coming, but it is a King indeed as good as no King'. *Ibid.*, pp. 77, 78,

skilfully. They presented to James in 1603 the so-called Millenary Petition which was alleged to have the support of nearly a thousand ministers.[1] They claimed that they were 'neither as factious men affecting a popular parity in the Church, nor as schismatics aiming at the dissolution of the state ecclesiastical' but faithful servants of Christ and loyal subjects longing for 'the redress of divers abuses of the Church'. They asserted that although hitherto they had for various reasons subscribed 'rather than the Church should have been deprived of their labour and ministry' they were now 'groaning as under a common burden of human rites and ceremonies' and were asking for relief.

With regard to church services the Millenary Petition asked that the sign of the cross in baptism should be abolished, that in the service questions should not be put to infants, that baptism should not be administered by women, that the cap and surplice should not be insisted upon, and that there should be an examination of prospective communicants before communion. The sacrament was to be administered with a sermon, the terms *priests* and *absolution* and some other words used in the Book of Common Prayer were to be corrected[2] and the ring was not to be used in the marriage ceremony. The 'longsomeness' of the service was to be abridged.[3] Church songs and music were to be 'moderated to better edification'. The Lord's Day was not to be profaned, and the rest upon holy days was not to be so strictly urged. There was to be 'an uniformity of doctrine prescribed'. Popish opinions were not to be taught or defended. Ministers were not to teach their people to bow at the name of Jesus, and only the canonical scriptures were to be read in church.[4]

Only able and sufficient men were to be admitted as church ministers, and they were to preach diligently, especially on the Lord's Day. Non-preachers were to be removed or else forced to maintain preachers. Non-residency was to be forbidden. The statute of Edward VI allowing marriage of ministers was to be revived.[5] Ministers were

[1] Printed in Thomas Fuller, *The Church History of Britain*, edit. J. S. Brewer, Oxford, 1845, V. 305 ff.; J. R. Tanner, *Constitutional Documents of the Reign of James I*, Cambridge, 1930, p. 56 ff.

[2] The term *priest* suggested the sacrificing priesthood of the Church of Rome and *absolution* might seem to be connected with the popish sacrament of penance.

[3] The intention was to allow more time for the essential work of preaching.

[4] That is to say, the Apocrypha was to be cut out.

[5] 2 & 3 Edward VI c. 2. (1549). This had been repealed under Mary and had not been revived under Elizabeth, so that the legality of ministers' marriage was not clearly established.

not to be required to subscribe to anything except, in accordance with the law, to the Articles of Religion and the Royal Supremacy.[1]

The Millenary Petition also made a number of proposals about clerical livings and the maintenance of ministers. Pluralities were to end, impropriations attached to bishoprics and colleges were to be demised to incumbent preachers 'for the old rent', and there was to be a tax of one-sixth or one-seventh on lay impropriations in order to maintain a preaching ministry.[2]

With regard to church discipline, the Puritans asked that 'discipline and excommunication may be administered according to Christ's own institution; or, at the least, that enormities may be redressed'. There was to be no excommunication in the name of lay officials or 'for trifles and twelve penny matters'. No one was to be excommunicated without the consent of his pastor.

In addition, the petitioners requested that officers in church courts should not charge unreasonable fees and that the *ex officio* oath should be 'more sparingly used'. The 'longsomeness of suits' in church courts was to be restrained. Various 'Popish canons', such as those forbidding marriage at certain times, were to be removed, and licences for marriage without banns were to be more cautiously granted.

The petitioners maintained that they could show that these and other abuses in the Church of England were not agreeable to the Scriptures, and they stated that they were ready to do so if the king would give them further hearing, or would allow them to put their case in writing, or would agree to these questions being resolved 'by conference among the learned'. They believed that the king himself was able 'to judge the equity of this cause'. They were sure he would do what was acceptable to God and profitable to the church, which would be thereby increased, since ministers would be 'no more suspended, silenced, disgraced, imprisoned for men's traditions'. They asserted that the petition represented the views of more than a thousand ministers 'that desire not a disorderly innovation but a due and godly reformation'.

---

[1] This would have made impossible the kind of subscription to the Prayer Book and the Articles which Whitgift had tried to insist upon.

[2] Usher points out that this was the first time that Puritan critics publicly faced the fact that the problem of an 'insufficient' ministry was closely related to economic difficulties and made proposals which would have affected laymen as well as the wealthier clerics and the two universities. *Reconstruction of the English Church*, I. 291.

Many historians have stressed the moderate nature of the demands made by the Puritans in the Millenary Petition, and the widespread belief that it had the signatures of something like a thousand ministers of the Church of England has been used to support the claim that the Petition had the backing of a formidable minority among the clergy. It is therefore important to remember that the Petition was not in fact signed by the hundreds of ministers who were alleged to support it, and that we do not in fact know how many read it and gave it their blessing.[1]

It is hardly surprising that the Millenary Petition made only relatively moderate demands for reform, and we cannot assume that this was the most that the Puritan leaders really wanted. They were at this stage proceeding very cautiously. They wanted to get as much support in the country as they could, they hoped to get a sympathetic hearing from the king, and they were likely to get more favourable consideration if they stressed obvious deficiencies in the church rather than put the emphasis on their own positive demands for fundamental alterations in the establishment. By attacking abuses in the church they put the bishops on the defensive. If they could only get a hearing, then there might be a chance to bring forward their real views. They could suggest how the episcopal system, which had resulted in so many abuses, might be modified.

Although the Millenary Petition was a very cautious document, it was not in fact quite so moderate as has sometimes been suggested. It did not limit itself to asking simply for a few minor changes and for the reform of obvious abuses. The request that 'discipline and excommunication may be administered according to Christ's own institution' and that no man should be excommunicated 'without the consent of his pastor' would, if granted, have profound consequences for the whole structure of church government.[2] For the more radical

---

[1] See S. R. Gardiner, *History of England from the Accession of James I to the outbreak of the Civil War*, 1905, I. 148. Fuller later said that only 750 ministers signed it, but Gardiner points out that there were no signatures at all. He suggests that those who drew it up probably got only seven hundred and fifty letters of assent and left the original words standing either accidentally or as believing that the sentiments of at least two hundred and fifty out of those who had not come forward were represented in the petition. Gardiner's conjecture *may* be right, but the fact remains that we do not really know how many ministers backed the Petition.

[2] R. G. Usher, *The Reconstruction of the English Church*, I. 291, argues that 'these seemingly innocuous requests' could import only one thing—the introduction of the Book of Discipline which was the only form accepted as of 'Christ's own institution'. It

Puritans the Millenary Petition was the thin end of a wedge which they hoped in due course to drive home.

By presenting what appeared to be very moderate and reasonable demands the Puritans achieved a great tactical success. To the alarm of his bishops the king was prepared to give the Puritans a hearing and to examine their case. He agreed to call a conference under his own chairmanship at which both sides were to state their position. He was genuinely interested in theological questions about which he had considerable knowledge, he was very anxious to establish unity in the church, he thought there was a *prima facie* case made out that abuses existed within it, and he was an enthusiastic supporter of the idea of a learned and preaching ministry. For these reasons he was prepared to hear the issues discussed in his presence by both sides, and the Puritans thus received a measure of official recognition such as they had never received under Elizabeth.

This initial success encouraged the more radical Puritans to agitate for further concessions even before the conference met. They began once more to organise and to agitate as they had done in the 1580's. Presumably even in the dark days of the 1590's a number of the leaders had kept in touch with each other by correspondence and other means, and an organisation which had been dormant now once more stirred into activity. The work of drawing up and getting support for the Millenary Petition must already have done much to revivify the propaganda machinery, and this could now be used to win support for further and more radical demands. In May 1603 a number of leaders, including very active Henry Jacob and Stephen Egerton, the Puritan minister of Blackfriars, London, put out a plan of campaign in a document entitled *Advice tending to Reformation*.[1] This was said to be based on the advice of 'some of creditt and neere

---

would also seem that the requests that communion should be administered with a sermon and that the use of the words *priest* and *absolution* should be corrected have theological implications. Professor Knappen (*Tudor Puritanism*, p. 321) seems to be playing down too much the significance of the Puritan demands when he claims that this 'studiously moderate petition' represented on the whole 'a return to the Grindal program' of reform of the ecclesiastical courts, the end of non-residence and pluralism and of an ignorant, non-preaching underpaid ministry. Dr. Collinson also comments on the Petition's 'general moderation' (*The Elizabethan Puritan Movement*, p. 452), but even 'after a careful reading of the text', doubts still remain about whether it was quite as 'moderate' as is suggested.

[1] M. M. Knappen, *Tudor Puritanism*, p. 322; R. G. Usher, *Reconstruction of the English Church*, I. 294 ff.

Z

to his Majesty'.[1] The *Advice* suggested that all should 'complaine of corruption and desire reformation in severall petitions signed with as many hands of everie sort as may be procured'. There were to be 'sundrie petitions of ministers of sundrie partes', but the wording of the draft petition was to be varied and only a few were to sign each petition to avoid any suspicion of conspiracy. All the petitions were to insist on the need for 'reformacion to be according to the woord and all reformed churches about us . . . ', but they were not to ask explicitly for the abolition of bishops. In addition, evidence was to be collected about the enormities and sins of the hierarchy, and ministers were to 'stirre up the people to a desire or a liking of reformation' by preaching against 'the superstitions ceremonies and tirannie of Prelates'. Lawyers were to be encouraged to prepare draft statutes abolishing abuses and establishing true religion, and there was to be a diligent enquiry into the state of the ministry.[2]

The Puritan propaganda machine swung into action. As Professor Knappen puts it, 'Once more Puritans rode, consulted, drafted, and signed, as in the pre-Armada days, and it was soon possible for the party to make a rather formidable showing'.[3]

There was, however, division within the Puritan ranks about what should be demanded in the petitions and at the conference. Henry Jacob and Stephen Egerton wanted to ask for the reform of the church according to God's holy word and the example of other reformed churches which 'have restored both the Doctrine and Discipline, as it was delivered by our Saviour, Christ and His Holy Apostles'. At a meeting in London in July 1603 they seem to have got their proposal adopted, but the moderates reserved the right to leave out this straightforward demand for Presbyterianism and to substitute instead a list of specific grievances.[4]

The Puritan agitation produced some strong reactions. In May 1603 Archbishop Whitgift instructed the bishops to collect informa-

---

[1] It is suggested that they may have been the Scottish Presbyterian minister Patrick Galloway who had come to England with James, and Lewis Pickering, a Northamptonshire Puritan gentleman who had attached himself to the Court.

[2] R. G. Usher, *op. cit.*, I. 294, 295.

[3] M. M. Knappen, *op. cit.*, p. 322. For a report on 'The Lamentable Estate of the Ministry in Staffordshire', see A. Peel in the *English Historical Review*, 1911. See also *The State of the Church in the Reigns of Elizabeth and James I*, edit. C. W. Foster, Lincoln Record Society, 1926.

[4] R. G. Usher, *op. cit.*, I. 296. Patrick Collinson, *The Elizabethan Puritan Movement*, pp. 454–5.

tion about the number and qualifications of the preachers in their dioceses so that he would be in a better position to meet criticisms about an unlearned and non-preaching ministry. In June he asked for statistics about communicants, recusants, pluralists, non-residents and impropriators. The universities of Oxford and Cambridge condemned the Millenary Petition. Cambridge forbade its members to find fault publicly with the doctrine and discipline of the church, and Oxford used Jacob's letters and petitions to support the allegation that the Puritans 'tell us plainly They wil never have an end, till either they have set up the Presbitery, Or else be out of Authority'. The university put the rhetorical question 'Were we perswaded that their Discipline, their Presbytery, the life and being of their Discipline, were indeede of Christ's institution . . . could we be contented to be without it?' It argued that by their demand that excommunication should not take place without the consent of the pastor, the Puritans were 'thereby intending the utter overthrow of the present Church government, and in steede thereof the setting up of a Presbytiry in every parish . . . '[1]

In July the king caused some concern in the ranks of the establishment by informing the vice-chancellors of Oxford and Cambridge that he intended to devote all royal impropriations to improving the income of livings. He expressed the hope that the universities would do likewise. He had thus recognised that one of the major obstacles to establishing a learned, preaching ministry was the very low income attached to many livings, and he was proposing to do something to deal with the problem by giving up some of the ecclesiastical income which had come into the hands of the crown. The bishops, however, hastened to point out that university impropriations were in fact being used to encourage and help learned ministers. The laity, including the Puritan laity, had so far shown no enthusiasm for surrendering any of their income from impropriations, and the bishops may have felt that there was no reason why the universities, which were at least doing something to provide a learned clergy, should be singled out to make sacrifices while the laity got off scot free. In the end James did not take action over royal impropriations and nothing more was heard about the proposal.[2]

[1] R. G. Usher, op. cit.; I. 299–300; S. R. Gardiner, op. cit., I. 150.
[2] S. R. Gardiner, History of England, I. 151, seems to do less than justice to the archbishop when he wrote: 'Whitgift immediately took alarm and drew up a statement for

Meanwhile, the Puritan agitation continued, and petitions were organised on the lines suggested by the leaders. In Sussex, for example, 1,285 signatures were obtained on 9 different petitions. These included 40 ministers, a dozen gentlemen, and some 1,200 people whom Usher describes as 'peasants'.[1] In Northamptonshire, Cartwright was persuaded to approach Justice Yelverton to get his assistance in preparing a petition.[2] This agitation was condemned by the opponents of the Puritans, and the Privy Council alleged that there had been a 'raising of tumults for the settling of fancies'. On 24 October 1603 James was persuaded to issue a proclamation against 'such as seditiously seek reformation in Church matters' in which he said that 'since we have understood the form and frame (of the Church of England), we are persuaded that both the constitution and doctrine thereof is agreeable to God's word and near to the condition of the primitive Church'.[3] It seems that the Puritans had damaged their case by the methods they had adopted and by disclosing prematurely their more extreme demands.

The Hampton Court Conference had originally been called for 1 November 1603 but for various reasons it was postponed until 14 January 1604. The traditional accounts of this conference have been questioned by Professor Mark Curtis who has raised serious doubts about the older views that the conference was a failure and that James was personally responsible for its failure.[4] A brief examination of the course of events is necessary in order to make the situation clear.

The first session was held on Saturday, 14 January 1604. There

---

the King of the inconveniences which were likely to result'. Whitgift was not a supporter of spoilation of the church or of an ignorant underpaid ministry, but he saw dangers in the limited action which the king proposed. The economic problems of the church could not be solved without a drastic overhaul of the whole system, and this would certainly arouse lay opposition.

[1] R. G. Usher, *op. cit.*, I. 307.

[2] M. M. Knappen, *Tudor Puritanism*, pp. 323, 324.

[3] R. G. Usher, *op. cit.*, I. 308, 309.

[4] Mark H. Curtis, 'Hampton Court Conference and its aftermath', *History*, xlvi, 1961. Professor Curtis points out that the account of the conference given by William Barlow, dean of Chichester, which has been used as the main source, was a piece of work sponsored by Bancroft and that its purpose was to make the Puritan case look weak and futile. It stressed the points of conflict between the Puritans and the king, it played down the differences between James and the bishops, and it passed over points about which James and the Puritans were in agreement. Professor Curtis stresses the importance of other material which has been unduly neglected.

were in attendance the archbishop of Canterbury, 9 bishops, 7 deans and 2 other clerics. The chief speakers chosen to put the case for the Puritans were Reynolds, Chaderton, Sparks and Knewstub who represented fairly moderate views, but the total number of Puritans present was over thirty and they included a number of men who were far more extreme than the main speakers.[1]

At the first session the king called in only the bishops and deans. He explained why he had called the conference and instructed them to tell him what needed reforming in the church. Whitgift and Bancroft fell on their knees and begged him to preserve the church from any alteration in government and liturgy. They said that if he made changes in the church after it had been in existence for over forty years, the Papists would complain that they had been wrongfully oppressed in the past. James very sensibly replied 'It was no reason that because a man had been sick of the poxe 40 years, therefore he should not be cured at length',[2] and he raised a number of questions about the Book of Common Prayer, the ecclesiastical courts and the state of the clergy. He refused to accept the bishops' plea that he should not give a hearing to charges which the Puritans might bring, and there was a four-hour discussion about the points at issue.[3] The bishops supported a number of changes and reforms, and James instructed them to draw up proposals for the next meeting.

Professor Curtis argues convincingly that James and the bishops had different views about what ought to be done. The king held the bishops responsible for some of the abuses in the church and he was in a sense putting them on trial. He had in a number of respects an open mind about reform. He was genuinely anxious to strengthen the unity of the church and he was prepared to make some concessions to the Puritans, particularly in the matter of reforming proved abuses and removing errors.[4]

The second session was held on 16 January 1604 when the Puritan representatives led by Dr. John Reynolds of Corpus Christi College,

[1] Usher stated that the original idea seems to have been to have 8 bishops and 8 Puritans, but Cartwright died in December 1603 and three others originally selected were for one reason or another removed from the list. These were Hildersham, Egerton and Fen whose views were thought to be too radical (R. G. Usher, *op. cit.*, I. 312–13). Patrick Collinson gives a somewhat different account (*The Elizabethan Puritan Movement*, p. 455 ff.) The larger body consisted of delegates meeting at the conference but not in the palace. *Ibid.*, p. 456.

[2] Mark H. Curtis, *op. cit.*, p. 8.

[3] *Ibid.*, pp. 8, 9.   [4] *Ibid.*, pp. 5–8.

Oxford, met Bancroft, bishop of London, and Bilson, bishop of Winchester, and several deans in the presence of the king and Council. The king explained that he did not propose to bring in innovations, but that his aim was 'to settle an uniform order through the whole Church, secondly, to plant unity for the suppressing of Papistes and enemies to Religion; thirdly, to amend abuses'.[1] The Puritans were then given an opportunity to put their case. In a brief which had been drawn up in preparation for the conference they had decided to ask for a learned ministry 'able to teach, diligent in teaching, and of unblameable life'. They intended to ask for the avoidance of dispensations, pluralities, non-residence and *commendams*.[2] They wanted to ask for a competent maintenance for ministers to be achieved by uniting small parishes, preventing unjust commutation of tithes, and increasing the allowance made to ministers by impropriators. They hoped to press for a revision of the Thirty Nine Articles, the abolition of obnoxious ceremonies, the correction of the liturgy, the revision of the canon law, the preparation of a more satisfactory catechism, and for the more reverend observation of the Sabbath. Subscription to the Thirty Nine Articles was to be limited to those articles which concerned faith. They hoped for a restoration of 'prophesyings' and for a recognition of 'ministers' rights' in ordination. Individual clergy were to have powers of censure over the laity, and the bishops were to take no action against nonconformists until all these questions had been decided by king and parliament.[3]

In the course of the discussion at the second session the Puritan leaders were able to put a considerable number of points to the king who gave them a hearing in spite of attempts by Bancroft to stop proceedings on the grounds that the Puritans were schismatics who ought not to be heard against their bishops. The traditional story that James broke up the conference with an angry speech when the word 'presbytery' was mentioned seems to rest on questionable evidence. Professor Curtis argues that 'Contrary to what is generally believed he did not deny out of hand everything proposed by Rainolds'.[4] He apparently agreed about the need to eliminate non-resident clergy, to

---

[1] R. G. Usher, *op. cit.*, p. 320.

[2] A benefice given in charge or trust until a proper incumbent was provided. Bishops and other dignitaries were often permitted to hold livings for life in this way in addition to their own preferment.

[3] R. G. Usher, *The Reconstruction of the English Church*, I. 313–15.

[4] Mark H. Curtis, *op. cit.*, p. 9.

improve the quality of the ministers and to establish a preaching ministry. He was willing to allow an improved catechism to be prepared and to make certain changes in the Prayer Book. He was prepared to consider a proposal to include in the Thirty Nine Articles the Calvinistic Lambeth Articles.[1] He was agreeable to changes in the confirmation service designed to show that confirmation was not a sacrament, but he did not approve of a proposal that every minister should be allowed to confirm. He was not prepared to abolish the use of the sign of the cross in baptism or the compulsory wearing of the surplice, unless the Puritans could show him that these things were contrary to scripture.[2]

The Puritans at the Conference were not pressing for the abolition of episcopacy, but they had in mind the possibility of limiting the powers of bishops by associating them with 'grave ministers'. In connection with a request for the revival of 'prophesyings' Reynolds suggested that disputed points should be referred to bishops assisted by grave and learned 'Presbyteri'. It was this reference to presbyters which aroused the king's anger and led him to make his much-quoted remark 'No Bishop, no King'. He thought the Puritans were aiming at a Scottish Presbytery 'which agreeth as well with a monarchy as God and the devil'. He added 'then Jack and Tom, and Will and Dick, shall meet, and at their pleasure censure me and my Council and all our proceedings. Then Will shall stand up, and say, "It must be thus"; then Dick shall reply, and say, "Nay, marry, but we will have it thus . . . "'.' He told Reynolds 'Stay, I pray you, for one seven years, before you demand that from me, and if then you find me pursy and fat, and my windpipes stuffed, I will perhaps hearken to you . . . But, Dr. Reynolds, until you find that I grow lazy, let that alone.'[3]

Traditionally this meeting on the second day is represented as ending in an angry scene with James saying as he left the Conference: 'If this be all they have to say, I shall make them conform themselves, or I will harry them out of the land, or else do worse.'[4] The bishops would certainly have liked it to end in this way and it would have suited their purpose very well to suggest that the king had swept aside the Puritan case as contemptible, but Professor Curtis raises serious

---

[1] See p. 323.
[2] Mark H. Curtis, *op. cit.*, pp. 9, 10.
[3] S. R. Gardiner, *History of England*, I. 156.
[4] *Ibid.*, p. 157.

doubts about whether the meeting did come to this abrupt and angry conclusion. One of the sources suggests that James did in fact stay on to decide some other points in favour of the Puritans, and Toby Matthew, bishop of Durham, relates that at the end of the discussion the king 'favourablie dismissed them (the Puritans) for that tyme'. What is even more significant is that the events of the third day show that James was prepared to make quite important concessions to those whom he is alleged to have dismissed with such contempt.

The Conference met for the third time on 18 January 1604 when there was a full session at which were present the representatives of the church and 32 Puritan ministers. The members listened to a speech from the king pointing out the importance of unity. The Puritans were urged to obey their bishops, but the bishops were also told to treat the Puritan ministers with consideration 'and more gently then ever they had done before'. The decisions announced by the king showed that the Puritan demands had not in fact been completely swept aside.[1]

There were to be some modifications in the Book of Common Prayer in order to remove ambiguities. Absolution was henceforth to be called 'absolution or general remission of sins', confirmation was to be called 'confirmation, or further examination of the children's faith'. Private baptism was to be administered by ministers and curates only and not by lay people or women. Readings from the Apocrypha were not to be included in the Lessons. There was to be one uniform translation of the Bible. The Articles of Religion were to be explained and enlarged, and no man was to preach against them. The law about receiving communion once a year was to be enforced.

In ordaining, suspending, degrading or depriving ministers, bishops were not to act alone but were to be assisted by deans and chapters or by some grave ministers. High Commission was to be reformed. Chancellors, officials and commissaries of bishops were to lose their powers of excommunication. There were to be improvements in parish livings in order to encourage a learned ministry, the abuses of pluralism and non-residence were to be controlled, and preachers were to be planted in Ireland, Wales and the Northern Borders. There was to be control over the import of popish books. The details of these reforms were to be worked out by commissions of privy councillors

[1] R. G. Usher, *The Reconstruction of the Church*, I. 328 ff.; Mark H. Curtis, *op. cit.*, p. 9.

and bishops. In ceremonies and things indifferent, grave, sober and peaceable people were not to be too far urged at first.[1]

What was granted may seem small in relation to what the Puritans had hoped to achieve, but it is clear that the Conference was far from being a complete failure. James was certainly not prepared to make fundamental alterations in the doctrine and government of the church, but he was ready to make some concessions, and he was not anxious to play the rôle of a persecutor. Chaderton's request that specially favourable consideration should be given to the Puritan clergy of Lancashire, where the Papists were numerous, was sympathetically received by the king, although he was not ready to grant a similar concession to the Suffolk Puritans.[2] Chaderton, who was Master of Emmanuel College, gave his assurance that the College would conform. Not all the Puritan leaders felt that the king was offering them impossible terms.

Two classical writers on the subject—Samuel Rawson Gardiner and Roland G. Usher—were both convinced that the Hampton Court Conference failed and that it produced little except a new translation of the Bible—the famous authorised version of 1611. Gardiner believed that James was presented with an opportunity to reconcile the Puritans with the established church and that he failed to take it. Gardiner quotes approvingly the words of one of his heroes, Sir Francis Bacon, who had written: 'It is good we return unto the ancient bonds of unity in the Church of God, which was, one faith, one baptism; and not, one hierarchy, one discipline.'[3] Dealing with the clash on the second day, Gardiner wrote of James ' . . . in two minutes he had sealed his own fate and the fate of England for ever. The trial had come, and he had broken down. He had shut the door, not merely against the Puritan cry for acceptance of their own system, but against the large tolerance of Bacon. The essential littleness of the man was at once revealed. More and more the maxim, "No Bishop, no King", became the rule of his conduct.'[4] With a somewhat exaggerated idea of the weight of learning and piety behind the Puritan movement, Gardiner went on to say 'many a man who cared nothing for minute points of doctrine and ritual . . . would feel his

---

[1] For these decisions, see Mark H. Curtis, *op. cit.*, pp. 11, 12; S. B. Babbage, *Puritanism and Richard Bancroft*, p. 66. ff.

[2] S. R. Gardiner, *History of England*, I. 158.

[3] *Ibid.*, I. 146, 147.

[4] *Ibid.*, I. 157.

heart swell with indignation when he heard men whose fame for learning and piety was unsurpassed by that of any Bishop on the bench, had been treated with cool contempt by men who were prepared to use their wit to defend every abuse, and to hinder all reform'.[1]

Usher, like Gardiner, believed that the king had already decided against the Puritans before the Conference, but for Usher James's great mistake was that he had raised the hopes of the Puritans by showing a certain sympathy with their demands and by delaying for nearly a whole year a public statement of his commitment to the doctrine and government of the Church of England. During that time of uncertainty the Puritans gathered strength and under cover of fairly moderate demands worked for 'some other method of church government than that maintained by the established institution'.[2] The king, however, had seen the light in time. For him, the Hampton Court Conference was not intended to be an equal contest at which he was to hear both sides before deciding the fate of the church. He never intended it to take on the importance which was in fact attached to it. For him there was nothing remarkable in listening to theological arguments, for he did it frequently in Scotland. What he intended to do was simply to hear what the Puritans had to say for themselves and then to take steps to put right a few abuses in the church.[3] Nevertheless, Usher thought, the king had made a great mistake in calling a joint conference of bishops and Puritans. The Puritan hopes had been raised, and their disillusionment was all the greater when James came out publicly for episcopacy and finally made clear that 'The Church was to be reorganised, not transformed, and there was to be no more toleration for nonconformity'.[4]

Professor Curtis suggests that the Conference was much more successful than used to be believed. After summarising the decisions made by the king he remarks that a Conference which achieved so much was hardly a failure. He points out that the reactions of the Puritans were mixed but that on the whole they were favourable. Some of them thought that the success at the Conference was 'but the beginning of reformation; the greater matters were yet to come'.[5] He argues that if the Conference was in the long run looked upon as a

[1] S. R. Gardiner, *History of England*, I. 158.
[2] R. G. Usher, *Reconstruction of the English Church*, I. 248.
[3] R. G. Usher, *op. cit.*, I. 309–10.
[4] *Ibid.*, p. 331.
[5] Mark H. Curtis, *op. cit.*, p. 12.

failure it was because the bishops, who were members of the commissions which were set up to put the king's recommendations into effect, managed to sabotage them and to prevent them being implemented. Frustration at having a measure of success snatched from them annoyed the Puritans far more than the deprivations of 1605 and 1606 and led to the sudden upsurge of separatism.[1] Professor Curtis thinks that if Whitgift and Bancroft had shown good faith in carrying out the agreements of Hampton Court 'they might have forestalled the events which brought about a combination of religious and secular opposition to the Stuart régime'.

It nevertheless remains true that for the radical as distinct from the moderate Puritans, the Hampton Court Conference constituted a major setback. The king might be willing to make a considerable number of concessions but he had destroyed any hopes the Puritans had of introducing some form of modified episcopacy and Presbyterian Discipline. The decision in the last resort lay with him, and after an interval of nearly a year since his accession he publicly and firmly came out on the side of the establishment on these fundamental questions. We shall never know what would have happened to the Church of England if James had decided otherwise.

On 9 February 1604 letters patent were issued authorising the printing of a revised Book of Common Prayer. This contained a few amendments but not nearly as many as the Puritans had expected to be made as a result of the Conference. On 5 March a proclamation was issued requiring everyone to conform to 'the only form of serving God established and allowed to be in this realm'.[2] The proclamation stated that the king had found 'mighty and vehement informations supported with so weak and slender proofs, as it appeared to us and our council, that there was no cause why any change should have been made at all in that which was most impugned, the Book of Common Prayer'. The Puritans would sooner or later have to decide whether or not they could accept the uniformity in religion which the king intended to impose.

There was still hope that something more satisfactory could be achieved through parliament which met on 19 March 1604. In his opening speech the king professed his personal adherence to the 'One

---

[1] Mark H. Curtis, *op. cit.* p. 16.
[2] R. G. Usher, *Reconstruction of the English Church*, I. 336. The proclamation is printed in Thomas Rymer, *Foedera*, 1704, XVI. 574.

Religion . . . publickly allowed and by the Law maintained'. He pointed out that there existed two groups which did not conform to the established religion—the Papists and those whom he called 'a Sect, rather than a Religion', namely 'the Puritans and Novelists, who do not so far differ from us in Points of Religion, as in their confused Form of Policy, and Parity; being ever discontented with the present Government, and impatient to suffere any Superiority, which maketh their Sect unable to be suffered in any well-governed Commonwealth . . . '[1] It is interesting to note that the king did not apparently object to the Puritans primarily on theological grounds. His own doctrinal background was calvinistic and he was in many ways nearer to the Puritans in doctrine than he was to Bancroft and a number of other bishops of the Church of England. What worried him were the Puritan views on church government with their political implications. It was because of this that they could not be tolerated in any well-ordered commonwealth. The question was whether parliament would follow the royal lead.

It was some time before the House of Commons got round to considering religion, but on 16 April Sir Francis Hastings asked for a committee to consider 'the confirmation and re-establishing of the religion now established within the Kingdom; as also of the settling, increasing and maintaining a learned ministry, and of whatsoever else may incidentally bring furtherance thereunto'. The committee obviously had very wide terms of reference and this would present the Puritans with an opportunity for proposing sweeping changes. James asked the House to confer about these matters with Convocation. It refused to do so, but agreed to confer with the bishops as Lords of Parliament, and a conference was arranged for 18 May 1604.

Meanwhile Convocation was in session at the same time as Parliament and was at work on a fundamental revision of the canon law. Archbishop Whitgift had died on 29 February 1604 and Convocation was under the able and powerful leadership of Richard Bancroft. He had tried to anticipate a probable attack by the Commons on the church and had got Convocation to appoint a committee to convey to the Commons the grievances of the clergy against the laity as well as to hear the laity's complaints. He also had to fend off Puritan attacks in Convocation itself, for a number of Puritan ministers petitioned the bishops to provide the church with a 'sufficient ministry'

[1] *Journals of the House of Commons*, I. 144.

and 'to ease it of its courtes and censures Ecclesiasticall'.[1] On 2 May there was another Puritan petition to Convocation asking for reform of the recently revised Prayer Book.[2] There was also a Puritan attempt to hold up proceedings by getting the Commons to charge Bancroft with high treason for his dealings with the Catholic appellants and by getting the prolocutor of Convocation arrested for debt.[3]

On 18 May 1604 the king presided over the conference between the bishops and the representatives of the Commons. The Commons' Committee requested, with reference to the Thirty Nine Articles, that ministers should be required to subscribe only to the articles relating to doctrine and the sacraments and not to those relating to episcopacy. The Articles were to be 'explained, perfected and established' and not only ministers but all heads of households were to be required to subscribe to them. There were a number of proposals for establishing a learned ministry. Only university graduates and such as were approved by six preachers of the country where they lived were to be admitted to benefices. There were to be no more dispensations for pluralism and non-residence. The income of benefices worth less than £20 a year was to be increased 'as shall be thought convenient'. This was to be achieved partly at the expense of the higher clergy. 'Such faithful ministers as dutifully carry themselves' were not to be deprived or silenced for refusing to agree to such things as the use of the surplice or of the sign of the cross in baptism.[4]

The Lords showed little or no enthusiasm for supporting the demands made in the House of Commons, and the Commons decided to proceed on their own. In June two bills were passed—one against pluralism and the other to provide for a learned and godly ministry. The bills went to the Lords but made no progress there. Convocation reacted against the Commons by passing a resolution that religion was no business of theirs.[5]

In the *Form of Apology and Satisfaction* drawn up in 1604 the Commons attempted to explain to the king what lay behind their religious policy. They stated that they had not come 'in any Puritan or Brownist spirit to introduce their parity, or to work the subversion of the State ecclesiastical . . . we disputed not of matters of faith and

[1] R. G. Usher, *Reconstruction of the English Church*, I. 343, 344.
[2] *Ibid.*, I. 345.   [3] *Ibid.*, I. 346–7.
[4] S. R. Gardiner, *History of England*, I. 179, 180; R. G. Usher, *Reconstruction of the English Church*, I. 348, 349.
[5] S. R. Gardiner, *op. cit.*, I. 80. R. G. Usher, *op. cit.*, I. 351 ff.

doctrine, our desire was peace only, and our device of unity, how this lamentable and long-lasting dissension amongst the ministers (from which both atheism, sects, and ill-life have received such encouragement, and so dangerous increase) might at length, before help come too late, be extinguished . . . ' They asked 'that in this Parliament such laws may be enacted as by relinquishment of some few ceremonies of small importance, or by any better way, a perpetual uniformity may be enjoined and observed'. They asserted 'Our desire hath been also to reform certain abuses crept into the ecclesiastical estate even as into the temporal; and, lastly, that the land might be furnished with a learned, religious, and godly ministry, for the maintenance of whom we would have granted no small contribution, if in these (as we trust) just and religious desires we had found that correspondency from others which was expected'.[1]

The reform programme which the House of Commons advocated in 1604 was indeed very moderate,[2] and it contained much that could be supported by non-Puritans. The king and the bishops were certainly not opposed to the establishment of a 'learned and godly ministry'. The bishops had done much to raise standards under Elizabeth and they were continuing their efforts in the new reign.[3] They were certainly not advocates of pluralism and non-residence, although they were well aware of the difficulties in the way of reform. They, too, wanted to end 'the lamentable and long-lasting dissensions among the ministers'. But they were not convinced that the divisions arose simply because of 'some few ceremonies of small importance'. James and his bishops might on the face of it seem to be driving Puritans out of the church over trivial issues, but not unjustifiably they feared that the Puritan demands threatened the whole basis of that religious uniformity which Elizabeth had for more than forty years striven to maintain. The apparently modest requests in 1604 seemed like the thin end of a potentially very dangerous wedge which might split the religious and political unity of England.

The decisions taken by the king in 1604 meant that sooner or later the Puritans would have to make up their minds about their relations

---

[1] S. R. Gardiner, *History of England*, I. 184.

[2] For a recent reassessment of the significance of the *Apology* of 1604, see G. R. Elton's contribution to *From the Renaissance to the Counter-Reformation*, edit. C. H. Carter, 1966.

[3] Soon after Whitgift's death in 1604 they had met to discuss plans for establishing able ministers in every parish. R. G. Usher, *op. cit.*, I. 337 ff.

with the established church and decide whether they could conform. Before the confrontation came, the Church of England had taken measures to define its teaching and to consolidate its position. Under Elizabeth its doctrine and its law had developed in a very haphazard and unco-ordinated way. A considerable and often unrelated collection of parliamentary statutes, royal injunctions, Articles of Religion, canons, constitutions and episcopal orders had come into being, often in response to particular crises rather than as a result of careful planning. It was far from easy to know precisely what the law was both for clergy and laity. There were plenty of disagreements about what was 'true doctrine' and about what was 'essential' and what was 'indifferent'. There was no really satisfactory definition about what constituted membership of the Church of England. The Puritans, apart from the Separatists, insisted that they were members of the church, even though they disagreed with the bishops and their supporters about a wide range of important doctrinal and liturgical questions.

The Canons of 1604 were an elaborate and systematic attempt to clarify the position and to establish whether the Puritans were, as Bancroft put it, 'either joined with them or severed from them'.[1] They were based on earlier legislation and practice, but they also contained a good deal that was new. The Church of England had been in process of developing its doctrine and its liturgy for forty years, it had been in conflict both with Papists and with Puritans, and now it attempted to make clear where it stood in relation to its numerous critics.[2]

The most significant aspect of the Canons of 1604 in relation to the question of Puritanism was the attempt in the first twelve canons to state the opinions which could not be held by those who claimed to belong to the church. The first two canons asserted the royal supremacy in causes ecclesiastical, repudiated all usurped and foreign power, required all ecclesiastical persons to teach and preach against foreign jurisdiction, and declared excommunicated anyone who impeached the royal supremacy.

The third canon excommunicated anyone who affirmed 'that the Church of England...is not a true and apostolical church, teaching and maintaining the doctrine of the apostles...', and the fourth did

---

[1] *Journals of the House of Commons*, I. 304.
[2] See R. G. Usher, *The Reconstruction of the Church*, I. 359 ff. for a chapter on 'Genesis of the Canons of 1604'. The Canons are printed in *Synodalia*, edit. E. Cardwell, I. 245 ff.

likewise with those who affirmed that 'the form of God's worship in the Church of England . . . and contained in the Book of Common Prayer and Administration of Sacraments, is a corrupt, superstitious, or unlawful worship of God, or containeth anything in it that is repugnant to the scriptures'. Canon V excommunicated anyone who held that the Thirty Nine Articles 'are in any part superstitious or erroneous, or such as he may not with a good conscience subscribe unto', and Canon VI condemned anyone who held 'that the rites and ceremonies of the Church of England are wicked, anti-christian, or superstitious, or such as . . . men, who are zealously and godly affected, may not with any good conscience approve them, use them . . . or, as occasion requireth, subscribe unto them . . . '

The seventh canon excommunicated those who affirm 'that the government of the Church of England under his majesty by arch-bishops, bishops, deans, archdeacons, and the rest that bear office . . . is anti-christian, or repugnant to the word of God', and the eighth condemned those who affirmed 'that the form and manner of making and consecrating bishops, priests, or deacons, containeth any thing in it that is repugnant to the word of God, or that they who are made bishops, priests, or deacons, in that form, are not lawfully made'.

Canons IX–XI condemned those who separated from the Church of England or who held unlawful meetings, and Canon XII was directed against those who maintained that it was lawful 'for any sort of ministers and lay persons, or either of them, to join together, and make rules, orders, or constitutions in causes ecclesiastical, without the king's authority . . . '

The next section (XIII–XXX) dealt at length with Divine Service and the Sacraments. Ministers must observe the form of service laid down in the Book of Common Prayer without 'either diminishing in regard of preaching . . . or adding anything in the matter or form'. When the name of Jesus was mentioned there was to be 'due and lowly reverence . . . by all persons present, as it hath been accustomed'. Every lay person was to receive holy communion three times a year and parishioners were to be duly warned. All masters, fellows and scholars in the universities were to communicate at least four times a year 'kneeling reverently and decently upon their knees'. The regulations requiring the use of copes and surplices were reaffirmed. Canon XXX gave a very lengthy explanation, designed to satisfy Puritans, of why the sign of the cross was to be used in baptism. It explained that it had been 'purged from all popish superstition and error' and that its use was commanded by public authority.

The next group of Canons (XXXI–LXXVI) dealt with the ordination, functions and duties of ministers. No man was to be ordained unless he had the necessary qualifications and unless there was a living available for him. Those admitted to the ministry were required to subscribe to the Three Articles[1] in terms which left no room for ambiguity about what they were accepting. There were regulations to prevent simony; pluralism was to be allowed only on strict conditions, and an attempt was made to insist on residence. Every beneficed preacher was to preach one sermon every Sunday, and those who could not preach must arrange for a sermon to be preached every month. There were regulations about the licensing of preachers. No one might impugn or confute any neighbouring preacher without permission from the bishop. Licensed preachers who refused to conform to the laws, ordinances and rights of the Church were, after due warning, to lose their licences. Beneficed ministers, readers, preachers and catechizers must administer the sacraments of baptism and the Lord's Supper according to the Book of Common Prayer at least twice a year.

Canon LVII stated that 'divers persons, seduced by false teachers, do refuse to have their children baptized by a minister that is no preacher, and to receive holy communion at his hands . . . as though the virtue of those sacraments did depend upon his ability to preach . . . ' These practices were condemned and the sacraments were not to be refused from non-preaching ministers. The official Holy Days and fasting days were to be proclaimed by every parson, vicar, or curate at the appointed times. Those who obstinately refused to come to divine service were to be openly denounced and excommunicated.

Canons LXXII and LXXIII laid down that ministers should not without the bishop's direction 'appoint or keep any solemn fasts' or 'hold any meetings for sermons, commonly termed by some prophecies or exercises'. No one was to hold secret meetings in private houses 'to consult upon any matter or course . . . which may any way tend to the impeaching or depraving of the doctrine of the Church of England, or the Book of Common Prayer, or of any part of the government and discipline now established in the Church of England'.

[1] See p. 213.

The appropriate clerical dress for public and private use was laid down and the hope expressed that 'in time newfangleness of apparel in some factious persons will die of itself . . . ' It was explained that this was not intended 'to attribute any holiness or special worthiness to the said garments, but for decency, gravity, and order'.

Then followed regulations concerning schoolmasters; ornaments and other things required in churches; the proper placing of the communion table; the repair of churches; the duties of churchwardens and sidesmen.

There were a great many orders concerning church courts, court officials and the fees to be charged. Provisions were made for presentment of schismatics, Papists, disturbers of divine worship, and non-communicants.

Finally, Convocation which had drawn up the canons protected itself against attack from its potential critics. Canon CXXXII excommunicated 'whosoever shall hereafter affirm, That the sacred synod of this nation, in the name of Christ and by the King's authority assembled, is not the true Church of England by representation . . . ' Those who denied that clergy and laity were subject to the canons were likewise excommunicated. The king had given his assent and every subject was required to obey. Every minister must read the canons in his church once a year and every parish must buy a copy.

The canons of 1604 explicitly condemned a wide range of beliefs some or all of which were held by the many different kinds of Puritans. Since they were the official views of the Church of England, solemnly adopted in Convocation and approved by the king as Supreme Governor, they presented the Puritan clergy with the serious problem of whether they could continue to remain members of a church which held such rigid views.[1] It remained to be seen how many were prepared to leave the church for conscience' sake.

The issue was clearly presented in a Proclamation of 16 July 1604.[2] The king reminded his subjects of his pains to settle the affairs of the Church of England 'in an uniformity as well of doctrine as of government, both of them agreeable to the Word of God, the doctrine of the

---

[1] The problem was rather less serious for the laity. Early in 1607 the Commons passed a bill 'to restrain the execution of canons ecclesiastical not confirmed by Parliament'. It was defeated in the Lords, but this bill later was used as a basis for the argument that ecclesiastical canons were not binding on the laity unless confirmed by Parliament. J. R. Tanner, *Constitutional Documents of the Reign of James I*, pp. 230–1.

[2] Printed in J. R. Tanner, *op. cit.*, p. 70 ff.

primitive Church, and the laws heretofore established . . . ' He had
held a Conference at Hampton Court at which 'no well grounded
matter appeared to us or our said Council why the state of the
Church here by law established should in any material point be
altered'. He added that 'those that before had seemed to affect such
alteration, when they heard the contrary arguments, (did) not greatly
insist upon it, but seemed to be satisfied themselves, and to undertake
within reasonable time to satisfy all others . . . ' Nevertheless, in the
recent meeting of Parliament 'there wanted not many that renewed
with no little earnestness the questions before determined, and many
more as well, about the Book of Common Prayer, as other matters
of Church-government . . . ' These people, too, when they had heard
the royal speeches and conferred with the bishops, had desisted from
further action and were content with the steps which the King and
Council intended to take for the furtherance of religion and the
establishment of a ministry fit for the same. There was no good
reason why the Book of Common Prayer or church discipline should
be changed, and particular abuses could be remedied without general
alterations. The king's subjects were admonished to conform 'without
listening to the troublesome spirits of some persons who never receive
contentment, either in civil or ecclesiastical matters, but in their own
fantasies, especially of certain ministers who, under pretended zeal of
reformation, are the chief authors of divisions and sects among our
people'. The king hoped such people would on reflection see their
errors and 'join in one end, that is, the establishing of the Gospel and
recovering of our people seduced out of the hands of the common
adversaries of our religion . . . '

The king went on to say that his duty to God required 'that what
untractable men do not perform upon admonition they must be compelled unto by authority . . . ' So that they might have sufficient warning and admonition he gave them until 30 November 1604 to decide
what to do, 'either to conform themselves to the Church of England
and obey the same, or else dispose of themselves and their families
some other ways'. Meanwhile the ecclesiastical authorities were to
endeavour by conferences, arguments, persuasions, and by all other
means of love and gentleness, to reclaim all to obedience to the
church, and magistrates and gentlemen were not to countenance
factious ministers in their obstinacy.

On 4 December 1604 Richard Bancroft was consecrated archbishop of Canterbury. On 10 December the Council instructed him to proceed against nonconformists, and on 22 December he issued directions that all curates and lecturers should be required to subscribe to the Articles as laid down in the Canons of 1604. Beneficed clergy who refused to conform were to be deposed. Those who would conform but who refused to subscribe were to be left alone. In 1605 the work of depriving nonconforming ministers began.[1]

The number of ministers who were prepared to resist was remarkably small. There is some division of opinion about the number actually deprived. It has been put as high as 300,[2] but Usher thought that the figure of 300 probably referred to the number of men who thought they were threatened. He thinks that in the end only about 60 were deprived, and about 100 suspended, silenced and admonished. Of those who were deprived, a number subsequently made their peace with the church, and a final return of deprived ministers in 1609 put the figure at 49.[3]

A number of important Puritan ministers were treated very leniently. Arthur Hildersham, who had been prominent in the *classis* movement and in the agitation about the Millenary Petition, was suspended and deprived but was once more preaching in his own pulpit in Ashby de la Zouche by 1608; Richard Rogers was suspended but was saved from deprivation by Lord Knollys. Reynolds who conformed but would not subscribe was left alone. Knewstub, Chaderton, Ward and a number of other leaders were not molested. Usher denies that royal policy excluded from the church 'the cream of the English clergy for piety and learning' and affirms that those who were deprived or suspended cannot be said to be the very best among the Puritan clergy.

The failure of the Puritan ministers to offer really effective resistance to the uniformity which James and his bishops were attempting to impose does not, of course, mean that all the ministers except about fifty became fully committed members of the establishment. Puritanism in various forms lived on, and, when occasion offered, it struggled to bring about this or that reform which might help it in the efforts to establish a godly church. A certain amount could be done through

---

[1] S. R. Gardiner, *op. cit.*, I. 196 ff.   [2] *Ibid.*, I. 197.
[3] R. S. Usher, *op. cit.*, II. 3 ff. Dr. Babbage put the number of beneficed clergy who preferred deprivation to conforming at not more than 90. *Puritanism and Richard Bancroft*, p. 217

parliament, and much more could be achieved by 'godly preachers' encouraging Puritan piety and a Puritan way of life on the lines which we have seen developing in the later Elizabethan period.

For those who could not conform there was always the road of separatism leading at first to Amsterdam and Leyden and later to North America, but for the most part the Puritans decided to remain within the establishment. Professor Knappen sums up the situation thus: 'Though the moderates writhed and protested, though they continued to grasp at legal straws and fill books with theological arguments, they bowed their necks to the yoke.'[1] They tried as best they could to swallow the Prayer Book, the Thirty Nine Articles and the Canons of 1604. Such were 'The reluctant Puritans who were swept back into the official fold by the disciplinary measures of 1605–6' and who 'constituted a powerful Low Church wing of the establishment ... Through such agencies Puritan theological ideas, piety and moral attitudes could be communicated to the masses.'[2]

James I's religious problems were not solved by the decisions of 1604, and the various Puritan undercurrents within the church were to give him plenty of trouble, but fundamentally he had been right in his calculation that few would make an open stand against the outward uniformity which, like Elizabeth, he sought to impose on all the subjects. The once militant Puritanism was now content to pursue within the church a way of life which avoided open conflict with the establishment, and those who could not conform were forced to pursue their activities outside England. It was not until Arminianism became a powerful force within the Church of England that the King was faced with another serious crisis in religious affairs.

* * *

The opening years of the reign of James I were an important turning point in the history of the Puritans. They made one more bid to modify the nature of the established church and they failed in their attempt. The situation of the Papists was very different. It had become only too obvious to most of them in the last years of Elizabeth's reign that there was no longer any prospect of the restoration of Roman Catholicism in England, and that the most they could hope for was some measure of toleration.

The hopes of Papists, like those of the Puritans, had been raised

[1] M. M. Knappen, *Tudor Puritanism*, p. 329.
[2] *Ibid.*, p. 336.

by what were believed to be the views of the new king. On 16 April Garnet wrote to Parsons reporting that the accession of James had brought to the recusants 'a golden time of unexpected freedom . . . '[1] Moreover, Papists were at last released from the embarrassing situation of having a temporal ruler who had been excommunicated by the pope, but their troubles were by no means over, and the variations in the government's policy regarding the enforcement of the penal laws were to produce some very unfortunate consequences.

As James moved south, an English priest named Hill presented him at York with a petition alleged to be drawn up 'in the name of the Catholics of England'. It asked for full revocation of the penal laws and it compared the Catholics with the Israelites who asked King Jeraboam for relief and when they failed to get it took 'just occasion to leave their due obedience'. James had the priest arrested. When the king got to London a much more tactful petition alleged to represent the views of 'The Lay Catholics of England' was presented to him, and copies were also distributed. It asked for freedom of religion 'if not in publike churches at least in private houses, if not with approbation yet with toleration, without molestation'. This Catholic appeal for toleration provoked replies stressing that 'discord and rebellion are the chiefest virtues of your new false Catholike Romish religion'.[2]

Early in the reign a large number of imprisoned priests had been released, but in May 1603 it was announced that the recusancy fines would still be exacted, and the secular priest, William Watson,[3] who had been so prominent in the archpriest controversy and who had assured his fellow Catholics that James would grant toleration, became involved in what is known as the Bye Plot. The complicated relationship between the Main and the Bye Plot need not concern us here.[4] Three priests—Watson, Clarke and Copley—and a number of Catholic gentry were in varying degrees involved in a scheme to seize the king's person and to force him to grant toleration to Catholics.[5] The schemes of Watson were condemned by both seculars and Jesuits,

---

[1] Quoted in A. J. Loomie, 'Toleration and Diplomacy: The Religious Issue in Anglo-Spanish Relations 1603–1605', *Transactions of the American Philosophical Society*, New Series, vol. 53, Part 6, 1963, p. 13.

[2] A. J. Loomie, *op. cit.*, p. 14.   [3] See pp. 286, 292 and note 1.

[4] The Bye Plot was alleged to be a subsidiary of the Main Plot in which Sir Walter Raleigh and Lord Cobham were involved.

[5] R. G. Usher, *Reconstruction of the Church*, I. 302 ff. A number of the documents in the case are printed in *Dodd's Church History*, edit. M. A. Tierney, IV, appendix.

and information about the plot was first given to the government by a secular priest. Watson and Clarke were executed.

The scare of the Bye Plot did not stampede James into violent action against the Papists. He was pleased at the loyalty of his Catholic subjects who were prepared to give information against fellow Catholics engaged in treason. He was, moreover, about to enter into peace negotiations with Spain, and in September 1603 there arrived in England the embassy of Don Juan de Tassis to open informal discussions. One of the purposes of the mission was to see what could be done, directly and indirectly, to lighten the burden on English Catholics.[1]

Before parliament met in March 1604 James took steps to placate its probable anti-Catholic views. On 22 February 1604 he issued a Proclamation, based on that of 5 November 1602, ordering all priests to leave England. The 'late conspiracy' was alleged as a justification. A Catholic secret press responded by publishing John Colleton's *Supplication to the Kinges most Excellent Maiestie* to be 'read and pondered by the Lords, Knights and Burgesses of the Present Parliament' asking for toleration to worship in private, as in parts of Germany, France and Poland 'where diversitie of religion is licensed by supreme authoritie, and the like have found peace wrought and established thereby . . . ' This, too, provoked replies, and it was agreed that James could not tolerate blasphemy and that it was therefore out of question for him to tolerate popery.[2]

In his speech to parliament on 19 March 1604 the king referred to those 'falsely called Catholicks, but truly Papists' who constituted 'a private Sect, lurking within the Bowels of this Nation'.[3] He made his own profession of faith but said that he was not violent or unreasonable in it. He acknowledged the Roman Church 'to be our Mother Church, although defiled with some Infirmities and Corruptions . . . ' He did not want it destroyed but rather purged, and he added ' . . . My Mind was ever so free from Persecution, or Thralling of My Subjects in Matters of Conscience, as, I hope, that those of that Profession, within this Kingdom, have a Proof'. He made a distinction between clergy and laity. The laity were further divided into 'quiet and

---

[1] A detailed study of the lengthy negotiations is given in Albert J. Loomie, 'Toleration and Diplomacy', *Transactions of the American Philosophical Society*, 1963.
[2] *Ibid.*, p. 28.
[3] *Journals of the House of Commons*, I. 144.

well-minded men' who were old and brought up in the popish religion or young and misled by their teachers, and another group of 'factious Stirrers of Sedition, and Perturbers of the Commonwealth'. James was prepared to give a measure of toleration to the laity who behaved themselves as good subjects, and he suggested the desirability of examining the penal laws to modify them in cases where the judges had interpreted them more vigorously than had been intended.

As for the clergy, as long as they maintained that the pope had 'an Imperial Civil Power over all Kings and Emperors' and held that an excommunicated sovereign could lawfully be deposed or put to death, they could not be allowed to remain in the kingdom.

James nevertheless warned the lay papists not to presume on his lenity 'as thereupon to think it lawful for them daily to increase their Number and Strength in this Kingdom; whereby, if not in My Time, at least in the Time of my Posterity, they may be in hope to erect their Religion again . . . ' He assured parliament 'I could not permit the Increase and Growing of their Religion, without first Betraying of Myself and mine own conscience'.[1]

The House of Commons did not share James's tender feelings towards the Papists, and the king himself seems to have become concerned at their increase in numbers, for on 17 May 1604 he complained of their growth to the House of Commons and recommended the preparation of laws 'to hem them in'.[2] A bill for the due execution of the statutes against Jesuits, Seminary Priests and Recusants was introduced into the Lords on 4 June and was eventually passed by both Houses, receiving the royal assent on 8 July 1604.[3] It enacted that all the Elizabethan statutes against Jesuits, seminary priests and recusants should be put into due and exact execution. Stricter regulations were introduced to ensure the payment of the fines of £20 a month. Anyone going themselves or sending a child abroad to any Catholic college to be strengthened in the popish religion was liable to a fine of £100 for every offence; and everyone going beyond the seas for this purpose was to forfeit rights to property and goods in England. Any trust arrangements made on behalf of such people were to be void. Any subject of the king at present beyond the seas for such

---

[1] *Journals of the House of Commons*, I. 144, 145; S. R. Gardiner, *History of England*, I. 166 ff.

[2] *Journal of the House of Commons*, I. 214; S. R. Gardiner, *History of England*, I. 202.

[3] 1 & 2 Jac. 1. c. 4. Printed in part in J. R. Tanner, *Constitutional Documents of the Reign of James I*, pp. 83–5.

purposes who did not return within a year was subject to the like penalties, but could avoid them by obeying the laws of the Church of England and repairing to church. No woman or child under 21 was to go overseas without licence, and officials and ship owners who carried unlicensed passengers were liable for various penalties.

The law thus became still more severe as far as Papists were concerned, but James did not in fact enforce the penal code for the time being. Some of the judges, however, were less lenient, and there were three executions in July and August. On 5 September 1604 commissioners were appointed to preside over the banishment of priests and a number were deported. The £20 a month fine was exacted from a few Catholic gentlemen.[1]

So far the attitude of the government had been tolerant, particularly as far as laymen were concerned, but in February 1605 there was a change of policy. The king addressed the Council and protested 'his utter detestation' of the 'superstitious religion' of the Papists. He said that he was so far from favouring it that 'if he thought his son and heir after him would give any toleration thereunto, he would wish him fairly buried before his eyes'.[2] The bishops and judges were told to take action and to enforce the law.[3] There followed a considerable drive against recusants, and over 5,500 Papists were convicted of various offences.

This renewed persecution in 1605 was the most important factor in bringing to a head the most memorable conspiracy in English history—the famous gunpowder plot. This is not the place to examine the details of the attempts made by a very small group of English Catholics to overthrow the government by force. The whole affair bristles with problems. There is no doubt that there was a plot, but there has been considerable controversy about the truth of the government's official account, the extent of its previous knowledge of what was going on and the use made of the affair to discredit Papists in general and Jesuits in particular.[4]

---

[1] S. R. Gardiner, *History of England*, I. 222–4.
[2] J. R. Tanner, *Constitutional Documents of the Reign of James I*, p. 83.
[3] S. R. Gardiner, *op. cit.*, I. 227.
[4] The very considerable literature includes: David Jardine, *A Narrative of the Gunpowder Plot*, 1857; *A Narrative of the Gunpowder Plot* written by the contemporary Fr. John Gerard and edited by J. Morris, 1871; John Gerard, *What was the Gunpowder Plot?*, 1897; S. R. Gardiner, *What Gunpowder Plot was*, 1897; John Gerard, *The Gunpowder Plot and the Gunpowder Plotters*, 1897; John Gerard, *Thomas Winter's Confession*

The significance of the plot in the history of English Catholicism is that it planted even more firmly in the minds of many Englishmen the conviction that Catholicism was of its very nature identified with treason and that Jesuits were arch-conspirators. The fact that Henry Garnet, the Jesuit Superior in England, had known of it only under the seal of confession and had done all in his power to stop the conspirators was irrelevant, and the government used with great ability the splendid propaganda opportunity with which it was presented.

The immediate repercussions of the Gunpowder Plot were disastrous for the Papists. Henry Garnet, who had directed the operations of the Jesuits in England with such ability for nearly twenty years, was at last taken and was the central figure in a trial designed to show that the Jesuits were implicated in the plot. Nicholas Owen, the maker of hiding holes, was captured and so severely tortured in an attempt to extract information that he died as a result. John Gerard who had continued to work in England after his famous escape from the Tower of London was hotly pursued but managed to make his way abroad.

Early in 1606 parliament passed two new penal laws against Catholics. The first of these was an Act for the better discovering and repressing of Popish recusants.[1] This stated that many of his Majesty's subjects who 'adhere in their hearts to the Popish religion' were so perverted by the infection drawn from it and by the 'wicked and devilish counsel of Jesuits, seminaries and other like persons' that they were ready to entertain any treasonable conspiracies 'as evidently appears by that more than barbarous and horrible attempt to have blown up with gunpowder the King, Queen, Prince, Lords, and Commons in the House of Parliament assembled . . . ' This was undertaken 'by the instigation of Jesuits and seminaries . . . by their scholars taught and instructed by them to that purpose'. The Act went on to say that 'divers persons Popishly affected do nevertheless, the better to cover and hide their false hearts and with the more safety to attend the opportunity to execute their mischievous designs'

---

and the Gunpowder Plot, 1898; H. R. Williamson, The Gunpowder Plot, 1951; Henry Garnett, Portrait of Guy Fawkes, 1962; Philip Caraman, Henry Garnet and the Gunpowder Plot, 1964. B. N. De Luna, Jonson's Romish Plot, Oxford, 1967. For earlier disturbances in Herefordshire and Monmouthshire in June and July, 1605, see Roland Mathias, Whitsun Riot, 1963.

[1] 3 & 4 James I, c. 4. Statutes of the Realm, IV. 1071. Printed in part in J. R. Tanner, Constitutional Documents of the Reign of James I, p. 86 ff.

repair sometimes to church to escape the penalty of the law. To discover such persons, it was laid down that every Popish recusant who had been convicted and who subsequently conformed and went to church should be required in future to receive the blessed sacrament of the Lord's Supper at least once a year. The penalty for not doing so was to be a fine of £20 in the first year, £40 in the second year, and £60 in each succeeding year.

Churchwardens and constables were to present to Quarter Sessions every year the names of all popish recusants absent from church, the names and ages of their children over 9, and the names of their servants, and these were to be recorded.

Justices of Assize and Justices of Peace were to enquire into all offences under this Act and under earlier Acts against those who did not go to Church, and were to order the offenders to be taken into custody before the next Assize or Sessions. If the offender did not appear his default constituted 'sufficient a conviction in law' as if he had actually been tried.

Every recusant once convicted for not going to church and ordered to pay £20 a month must continue to pay this sum monthly without need for further indictment. It was in future to be at the king's discretion whether to accept the fine of £20 a month or to take into the hands of the crown two-thirds of the recusant's estates.[1]

Section VIII of the Act made provision for 'the better trial how his Majesty's subjects stand affected in point of their loyalty and due obedience'. Bishops and Justices of the Peace were empowered to require known or suspected recusants to take the oath of allegiance laid down in the Act.[2] It was to the effect that the king was lawful and rightful sovereign of the realm and that the pope had no power or authority to depose him or to discharge any of his subjects of their allegiance. The recusant was required to say 'Also I do swear from my heart that notwithstanding any declaration or sentence of excommunication or deprivation made ... by the Pope or his successors ... I will bear faith and true allegiance to his Majesty his heirs and successors, and him or them will defend to the uttermost of my power against all conspiracies and attempts whatsoever ... And I do further swear, that I do from my heart abhor, detest, and

---

[1] Hitherto the crown had power to seize two-thirds of the estate only in cases where the recusant defaulted on payment of £20 a month.
[2] The oath is printed in full in J. R. Tanner, *op. cit.*, pp. 90–1.

abjure, as impious and heretical, this damnable doctrine and position, that princes which be excommunicated or deprived by the Pope may be deposed or murdered . . . And I do believe and in my conscience am resolved that neither the Pope nor any person whatsoever hath power to absolve me of this oath . . . '. The penalties for refusing to take the oath when required were those of Praemunire.

Another clause in the act made it felony to go overseas to serve a foreign prince without having taken the oath. Anyone who persuaded any of the king's subjects to withdraw from their allegiance, to be reconciled to the see of Rome or to promise obedience to a foreign prince, and anyone so persuaded, was guilty of High Treason.

Those who did not go to church might be brought before the justices who could then give a warrant to the churchwarden to levy the twelve-penny fine and to commit the offender to prison in default of payment. There were new provisions regarding the levying of fines on those who kept in their houses servants or sojourners who did not attend church.

The other statute dealing with Papists was An Act to prevent and avoid dangers which may grow by popish recusants.[1] It began by stating that Jesuits, seminaries and popish priests were daily withdrawing his Majesty's subjects from the true service of Almighty God to the Romish religion and encouraging them to commit most damnable treasons. To prevent this, people who gave information leading to the conviction of such priests, including where they said mass and who was present, were not only freed from any danger of the law themselves but were to have a third of any sums levied in fines up to a maximum of £50. Popish recusants were not to come to the Court without special order, and they were not to dwell within ten miles of London unless their livelihood was there or unless they had no other dwelling-place. New regulations were introduced concerning the licensing of Papists who wished to travel more than five miles from their homes.

Clause VI laid down that no convicted recusant should practise the Common Law as counsellor, clerk, attorney, or solicitor, nor the Civil Law as advocate or proctor. Convicted recusants were not to practise physic nor use the trade of apothecary, nor act as officials in any court. They were not to bear office as captain, lieutenant, cor-

---

[1] 3 & 4 James I. c. 5. *Statutes of the Realm*, IV. 1077. Printed in part in J. R. Tanner, *Constitutional Documents of the Reign of James I*, p. 94 ff.

poral, sergeant, ancient-bearer in any troop of soldiers, nor were they to hold office in the king's ships or in royal fortresses. The fine for offenders was £100. Convicted recusants, or those having wives who were convicted recusants, were disabled from holding any public office. Wives who were convicted recusants were to forfeit to the king two-thirds of their jointure and two-thirds of their dower. Recusants were to be treated as excommunicated and were to suffer the legal disabilities which followed from excommunication.

Since popish recusants were not usually married or buried according to the rites of the Church of England and did not have their children christened according to those rites, it was laid down that if they were married outside the Church of England they should forfeit many of the important property rights that followed from a legal marriage, and they were liable to a fine of £100. There was also a fine of £100 for recusants who did not have their children baptised in the parish church within one month of their birth, and a fine of £20 for executors and others who arranged burials of popish recusants in any other place than the church or churchyard and without the rites of the Church of England.

If children were sent abroad without licence, they were not to have the benefit of any gift or conveyance of lands, leases or goods until they were eighteen years of age and took the oath of allegiance. In the meantime the next of kin who was not a popish recusant might have the lands, leases and goods so conveyed, but in such cases he was to account for and to repay the profits to the child if the child conformed. The penalty for sending children overseas without licence was a fine of £100. Similar regulations were applied to those already overseas if they did not return within six months and take the oath.

Convicted Popish recusants were disabled from presenting to any benefice, prebend, or ecclesiastical living or to any Free School or Hospital, and the rights so forfeited were granted to one or other of the universities.

Clause XIV stated that convicted recusants were not fit to be executors or to have the education of their own or other people's children. They were therefore disabled from acting as executors or administrators or from exercising the rights of wardship or guardianship of any child.

It was forbidden to bring from abroad or to print, sell or buy 'any Popish primers, Lady's psalters, manuals, rosaries, Popish catechisms, missals, breviaries, portals, legends and lives of saints, containing superstitious matter . . . ' upon pain of forfeiting 40s. for every such book. One-third of the fine went to the king, one-third to the informer, and one-third to the poor of the parish where the books were found. Justices were authorised to search the houses of convicted recusants and of every person whose wife was a convicted recusant for popish books and relics of popery. If any altar, pyx, beads, pictures, or suchlike relics, or any popish books, were found, they could be defaced and burnt. If 'a crucifix or other relic of any price' was discovered, it was to be defaced at Quarter Sessions and then restored to the owner.

Popish recusants were also to be deprived of armour, gunpowder and munitions, except such weapons as the Justices of the Peace thought necessary for the defence of their persons and houses.

Thus for the Papists the early years of James I's reign saw the rise and fall of their hopes that better days had come with the new ruler. Their public image had suffered tremendous damage as a result of the Gunpowder Plot, and within three years of James's accession there had been placed on the statute book penal laws which increase the range and ferocity of the Elizabethan statutes directed against them. The existing divisions within their ranks were made even wider by the new oath of allegiance, for there were differences of opinion about whether it might be taken with a good conscience. The oath was condemned by Rome in 1606, but when the archpriest Blackwell was captured by the government he took the oath himself and was deposed by the pope. The problems of relations between the regular and the secular clergy still remained and were to prove a fruitful source of trouble in the years ahead.

In 1606 the outlook for Papists seemed very black indeed. In fact the future was not nearly so gloomy as might have been expected. Priests and those who helped them were put to death from time to time, and some 25 died on the scaffold under James I, but after 1618 there were no further executions until 1628. The long drawn-out negotiations for a Spanish marriage and the successful negotiations with France, which gave England a Catholic queen in 1625, helped to ensure a considerable measure of toleration for Papists in spite of the penal laws, and James I was not anxious to persecute. Not without cause did the Parliaments of the early Stuarts complain bitterly about the increase of Papists and the failure to enforce the law. There were converts in high places and Catholicism more and more came into the open. The number of priests grew, and before James died in 1625 there were over 140 Jesuits in England and there was once again a Catholic bishop. Fr. Caraman has labelled the period from James I to Cromwell 'The Years of Siege',[1] but for a great deal of the time the besieged Papists were able to relax and to mingle freely with the besieging Protestants. Indeed, the spread of popery and its influence at Court often gave the impression to Puritans and committed Protestants that it was they and not the Papists who were being encircled.

[1] Philip Caraman, *The Years of Siege: Catholic Life from James I to Cromwell*, 1966.

13

Like and Unlike: Some General Considerations

IT would be much easier to assess the importance of the Papists and the Puritans in Elizabethan England if we knew how many of them there were. Various attempts have been made to provide estimates of numbers, with widely differing results. Mr. Brian Magee concluded that Catholics were a majority of the nation up to the time of Armada and that after that they still formed a very large minority.[1] Mr. Trimble argued that they were too few and too powerless either to prevent disestablishment at the beginning of the queen's reign or to have a voice in the selection of her successor at the end. He pointed out that the records of taxation and of censuses of recusants in the 1570's and 1580's prove that the Catholics were of the minor gentry in wealth, status and influence and 'formed sizable aggregations only in certain counties'.[2] Professor Dickens showed that even in the major Catholic district of Yorkshire a very careful census of recusants made in 1604 put their number at less than 3,500 in a total of more than 300,000 and that even this small figure included several hundred who attended matins and evensong, although they refused communion.[3] A. O. Meyer thought that the Catholics from about 1580 onwards were between 2 and 3 per cent of the total population,[4] but R. G. Usher put the figure a good deal higher. In one place he expressed the view that the number of 'avowed Catholics' was perhaps 5 per cent

---

[1] Brian Magee, *The English Recusants*, 1938.
[2] William R. Trimble, *The Catholic Laity in Elizabethan England*, p. 264.
[3] A. G. Dickens, *The English Reformation*, p. 312. See also A. G. Dickens, 'The Extent and Character of Recusancy in Yorkshire in 1604', *Yorkshire Archaeological Journal*, XXXVII; A. G. Dickens and John Newton, 'Further Light on the Scope of Yorkshire Recusancy in 1604', *ibid.*, XXXVIII; A. G. Dickens, 'The First Stages of Catholic Recusancy in Yorkshire', *ibid.*, XXXV.
[4] A. O. Meyer, *England and the Catholic Church under Elizabeth*, p. 65.

of the nation,[1] and elsewhere he wrote: 'The only scholarly position to assume . . . is to acknowledge that we do not know at all how many Catholics there were in England but, if we might hazard a guess, there were very likely 750,000 or 1,000,000 . . .'[2]

Similar problems arise in estimating the number of Puritans and 'Anglicans'. We must not forget that there was a very large group of people who, as the Puritan ministers put it in 1604, did 'greatly regard not of what religion they be'.[3] Usher thought that in the early seventeenth century 75 per cent of the population was 'utterly indifferent to all forms of church government or details of ceremonies'. Of the remainder, he put the zealous followers of the establishment at 18 per cent and the 'avowed Catholics' at perhaps 5 per cent, and he suggested that the Puritans were possibly as few as 2 per cent of the total.[4] Professor Knappen was inclined to agree with Usher that 75 per cent of the people were 'either religiously indifferent or without any opinions on religious questions', but he was very critical of Usher's estimate concerning the strength of the Puritans. He argued that during Elizabeth's reign Puritanism had grown into 'a powerful force, which . . . was supported by the great majority of serious-minded Protestants, and even at the end of the queen's reign was regularly able to command a majority in the House of Commons, the nearest thing to a truly representative body which England then possessed'. Of the 22 per cent which remains after deducting the indifferentists and the Papists, he thought that 'at a very rough guess' at least 15 per cent were Puritans by the middle of Elizabeth's reign, with the proportion towards the end of the century declining somewhat but 'not so much as to deprive the Puritans of their clear numerical preponderance over the Anglican party'.[5]

There are, then, very considerable differences in the estimates of the total numbers in each group and of the relative sizes of the different groups. This is unfortunate. Obviously the influence of a group in a community is not determined simply by its size, but our general

---

[1] R. G. Usher, *Reconstruction of the English Church*, I. 269.

[2] R. G. Usher, *op. cit.*, p. 159. We are not even sure of the number of priests in the country. A. O. Meyer and Philip Hughes give figures of about 300 seculars and a dozen Jesuits in the country at the end of Elizabeth's reign, but the archpriest in 1608 reported to the pope that there were nearly 500. See E. I. Watkin, *Roman Catholicism in England*, 1957, p. 59.

[3] Historical Manuscripts Commission: *Montagu of Beaulieu*, p. 37.

[4] R. G. Usher, *op. cit.*, I. 269.

[5] M. M. Knappen, *Tudor Puritanism*, pp. 333–4, and note 24.

conclusions about religion and religious policy in Elizabethan England are bound to be very different if we think of Papists and Puritans as very small minorities from what they would be if we think, for example, that the Puritans enjoyed a 'clear numerical preponderance over the Anglican party' or that the Papists were a majority in the nation up to the time of the Armada.

A measure of agreement among historians on these vital questions is clearly desirable, but it is not likely to be attained. One difficulty is the limitation of the available evidence. Although a great deal is known about those who came in conflict with authority, we lack the materials for making anything approximating to a religious census of the nation as a whole. We have to fall back on contemporary estimates and conjectures, often made by men who were influenced by their own hopes and fears, and we have to try to reach conclusions based on our own general impressions of the period. This at once raises the difficulty, which we have noted earlier, of deciding precisely what constitutes a 'Puritan', an 'Anglican' or a 'Papist'.[1] As we have seen, there were many different kinds of 'Puritans', and the divergences and the different degrees of commitment within the 'Puritan' ranks must raise serious doubts about whether all those who have been given the label can be meaningfully included in the one general heading of 'The Puritans'.[2] Because a man lined up with the Puritans on this or that particular issue he did not thereby become a committed Puritan, and in fact such people were often highly selective in their attitude to Puritan programmes. The wide differences in the estimates of the Puritan numbers are to some extent explained by the fact that those making the estimates are attaching different meanings to the same term.

The Papists, too, present similar problems. As Professor Dickens pointed out, there is a vast difference between recusancy, which is 'a concrete, and usually a recorded, phenomenon' and 'mere religious conservatism'.[3] The existence of an unknown number of 'Church Papists' is a further complication, and Dr. Bossy's most valuable examination of the nature of Elizabethan Catholicism is an additional

---

[1] See chapter 2, p. 27 ff.

[2] R. G. Usher, *op. cit.*, I. 251, thinks that '. . . there were probably not ten conscientious men, in all England in 1603, who approved of the Church precisely as it stood', but in his view their disapproval did not automatically make them 'Puritans'.

[3] A. G. Dickens, 'The First Stages of Catholic Recusancy in Yorkshire', *Yorkshire Archaeological Journal*, XXXV.

reminder that the label 'Roman Catholic' can conceal extremely wide differences of outlook within an apparently homogeneous group.[1]

There is a great deal more which could be found out about the Papists and the Puritans, or rather about that limited number of them who found their way into the records, but even if we could arrive at a moderately satisfactory estimates of the totals they would be largely illusory unless they could be broken down into numerous categories showing the general outlook and degree of commitment of those included in them.[2]

In order to assess the influence of the different religious groups we also need to know more about the way in which they were distributed throughout the country. In 1910 Usher produced maps showing the distribution of Catholic laymen and of Puritan ministers in 1604.[3] A good deal of work has been done since then with relation to particular regions,[4] but much more needs to be found out before it will be possible to make anything like a satisfactory picture. The situation was, of course, continually changing during the forty-four years of the reign, and once again the limitations of the evidence and the problems of definition mean that all that could be provided would be a rough-and-ready guide to a highly complex situation.

Catholicism and Puritanism were widespread phenomena in Elizabethan England, and in some degree all English counties were affected by them. Nevertheless, there were a number of particularly important concentrations. Catholics were, for example, very strong in the dioceses of Chester (which included Lancashire), York, Coventry and Lichfield, Durham, Hereford and Winchester, while Puritanism was particularly flourishing in certain counties such as Essex, Suffolk,

[1] John Bossy, 'The Character of Elizabethan Catholicism', *Past and Present*, no. 21, 1962.

[2] R. G. Usher pointed out that in a list of 281 names of Puritan ministers which he compiled, 206 were not much more than names and less than 50 were prominent men. Only 105 out of 281 had first degrees. Of the 50 or so who were prominent, he wrote: 'These are, in fact, the men of whom we read, who make the plans and execute them, who write the tracts, who draw the petitions and procure the signatures to them.' *Reconstruction of the English Church*, I. 254. Usher minimised unduly the strength of Puritanism, but nevertheless his point is relevant.

[3] See pp. 402, 403 and Appendices 1 and 2.

[4] Dr. Collinson's work has added new dimensions to the history of Elizabethan Puritanism. There are a number of extremely valuable distribution maps in his thesis. The latest addition to the regional studies of Papists is Hugh Aveling, *Northern Catholics*, 1966. For other studies, see bibliography: M. O'Dwyer, J. E. Paul, J. S. Leatherbarrow, H. Aveling, A. G. Dickens.

Northamptonshire, Norfolk and Sussex, and in a number of towns such as Coventry, Leicester, Bury St. Edmunds, Northampton and Cambridge.[1] Nevertheless, we must be very careful not to label particular counties 'Puritan' or 'Catholic', for the religious patterns of Elizabethan England seem to have been in fact very variegated. 'Catholic' Lancashire had its Puritan pockets; in the North of England the bishop of Durham, the dean of Durham and the third earl of Huntingdon did much to ensure that the influence of 'the old religion' was opposed by vigorous Puritan preachers; the Puritanism of parts of Suffolk was counter-balanced by the Catholicism of an important group of gentry, and if Essex was to some extent a major Puritan centre, there were also flourishing groups of Papists.

The extent to which the government could enforce its policy of religious uniformity depended on a number of factors which varied greatly from one part of the country to another. Counties which were remote from the seat of government or which were not easily accessible were more likely to go their own way than those near at hand, and they might well have a tradition of independence and conservatism that made them regard with suspicion decisions made in London. In the 'dark corners of the land'[2] it was often possible to fight delaying actions against the advance of the Protestant Reformation, and there might be 'a conspiracy of support' among the local authorities to render ineffective an unpopular religious policy. Much depended on the energy and determination of the government's representatives in the locality. It has been suggested that one of the main reasons for the growth of recusancy in Lancashire in the period 1569–78 was the apathy and indifference of the earl of Derby and the bishop of Chester and that when Lancashire did eventually get a 'hammer for recusants' in the person of bishop William Chadderton it was too late to undo all the damage.[3] In East Anglia, Bishop Freke, driven to distraction by his wife and by the aggressive Puritans, even went so far as to ally with some of the Papist gentry. On the other hand, a really determined and dedicated official like the third earl of Huntingdon could achieve a great deal even in the conservative north, and a Puri-

[1] For Usher's figures, which are of some help as giving a rough-and-ready indication of distribution of Papists and Puritans, see pp. 399–401.

[2] See Christopher Hill, 'Puritans and "The Dark Corners of the Land" ', *Transactions of the Royal Historical Society*, 5th series, XIII, 1963, p. 177 ff.

[3] J. Stanley Leatherbarrow, *The Lancashire Elizabethan Recusants*, Chetham Society, 1947.

tan town council could make its influence felt in the surrounding countryside. Generalisations are dangerous in a society where the apostacy of a Catholic gentleman, the personal commitment of a Puritan nobleman, the influence of an able preacher or the energy of a courageous priest could have widespread consequences for a whole district.

Catholicism and Puritanism clearly owed much of their success to the support they received from some of the nobility and gentry. Professor Lawrence Stone maintains that ' . . . it was resistance to government orders by a handful of magnates on either side which allowed Catholicism and Puritanism to dig in and take root within this tepidly conformist society'. He concedes that others had a vital rôle to play, including Puritan ministers and Catholic missioners, city artisans and pious country gentlewomen, but he thinks that 'if the peers and leading squires had distributed their support in a different way between 1558 and 1588, the religious configuration of seventeenth-century England would undoubtedly have looked very different . . .'[1]

It would not be difficult to provide a host of illustrations of the all-important support and patronage which such men as the earl of Leicester, the earl of Huntingdon, Lord Grey of Wilton, Lord Rich of Rochford, Lady Bacon, the duchess of Suffolk and Lord Burghley himself gave to Puritan ministers and 'godly preachers'. The lay patrons did not for the most part supply the ideas, but the work of the ministers would have been drastically curtailed if their supporters among the nobility and gentry had not provided them with the livings, the lectureships, the chaplaincies and the appointments of one sort or another which gave them an income and a platform, nor could they have operated so successfully if they had not received considerable protection from their patrons against royal and ecclesiastical attempts to enforce uniformity. The Catholic peers and gentry had a similar if sometimes more dangerous rôle to play. Without the protection afforded by innumerable country houses scattered throughout the country, the seminary priests and the Jesuits would soon have been hunted down.

---

[1] Lawrence Stone, *The Crisis of the Aristocracy*, p. 729. Professor Stone suggests that the formation and preservation of a substantial minority of religious dissidents on either flank of the Established Church depended in very large measure on the patronage of 'a few dozen dedicated magnates and leading squires', and adds 'Had it not been for this powerful protection, it is more than likely that official persecution would have succeeded, as elsewhere in Europe, in creating a monolithic state church . . .' *Ibid.*, p. 741.

Dr. Bossy has stressed the importance of this 'household religion' as far as the Papists were concerned.[1] The Catholic gentleman with his circle of Catholic friends, his relationships by marriage, his Catholic servants and tenants, his private chapel and his private chaplain, often regarded his religion as his own business and not a matter in which the central government ought to interfere. His attitude was admirably expressed by Lord Vaux who when he was presented for not coming to church in 1581, together with 'his household and familiars and divers servants', justified himself on the ground that he 'did claim his house to be a parish by itself'.[2] A very similar situation existed in the households of many Puritan gentry where the family, their guests, and their servants assembled for prayers, and where a chaplain or local minister preached to the assembled company, catechised the dependants and children, and co-operated with the master of the house in organising a 'godly life' for the whole establishment.[3]

The stress which historians have laid in recent years on the rôle of the layman must not lead us to minimise the part played by the priest and the minister. For the Papists, the priest had unique functions which could not be performed by anyone else. He could be made a priest only by ordination by a bishop. Without him the central act of Catholic worship—the mass—could not be celebrated. He alone was the means by which the Catholic could receive the sacrament of Penance and obtain formal absolution for his sins. Without him Catholicism would wither and die, and the defection of the vast majority of the priests in the early Elizabethan period struck an almost mortal blow at English Catholicism. It survived primarily because a number of Marian priests did not conform to the establishment, and its main strength was on the estates of the Catholic nobility and gentry.

In a very stimulating article on the character of Elizabethan

[1] John Bossy, 'The Character of Elizabethan Catholicism', *Past and Present*, 1962.

[2] See John Bossy, *op. cit.*, p. 40.

[3] See, for example, Lord Rich of Rochford whose chaplain Robert Wright catechised all and sundry in the great hall and held services, although he had never been ordained by a bishop and never used the Book of Common Prayer. L. Stone, *The Crisis of the Aristocracy*, p. 735. For an examination of the part played in the Puritan movement by various kinds in 'Meeting of the Godly', see Patrick Collinson, *The Elizabethan Puritan Movement*, pp. 372–82. Dr. Collinson writes: 'There was an extensive area of corporate religious experience within the establishment over which the official Church had little control and which is still for the most part unexplored and unmapped.'

Catholicism Dr. Bossy suggests that this early pattern of 'household' or 'seigneurial' Catholicism was changed, and in some measure disrupted, by the arrival from abroad of missionary priests whose conception of the rôle of the cleric was very different from that of the Marian priest or the tame domestic chaplain of the Catholic gentleman. He argues that few of the new priests were gentry or came from the parts of the country where 'seigneurial' Catholicism was strong. They were 'clerks first and last' and their religion did not mean conformity to traditional forms of belief and behaviour but 'a conversion, a religion individual and interior'. They were men of action, not prepared to compromise with error, and they had the Puritan ideal of 'a people purified by truth'. Dr. Bossy points out that we do not know very much about how they were financed, but it is clear that they depended on means of supply which were not wholly provided by the Catholic gentry. As a result of all this, the importance of 'the clerk' or the priest was considerably increased and the dominance of the 'seigneurial' social structure of English Catholicism was for a time greatly reduced.[1]

We must also be careful not to minimise the rôle of the minister in the development of Puritanism. It seems clear that the Puritans owed even more to lay patronage than did the Papists, and recent work has tended to emphasise this aspect of the movement.[2] Indeed, Professor Stone argues that Puritanism differed from Catholicism in that the initiative came in the first place from the laity which demanded, and finally got, a clerical wing which spread the movement throughout the populace at large.[3] This could easily lead us to underestimate the importance of the Puritan clergy. Even in the early stages they provide the ideas and the drive, and although they relied on lay support, they

[1] John Bossy, 'The Character of Elizabethan Catholicism', *Past and Present*, 1962. This is a very important article and it raises a number of issues which cannot be examined here. Dr. Bossy stresses the elements of conflict in the two different conceptions of Catholicism, but he agrees that for twenty years or so after the foundation of Douay the dynamism of the clerks succeeded on the whole in carrying the gentry with it (although there were, as Parsons put it, 'domestical difficulties'). (p. 50.) It does not seem to be clearly established that the divisions in the Catholic body in the late Elizabethan period can be primarily explained in terms of conflict between 'the religion of the clerks' and 'seigneurial Catholicism'.

[2] Dr. Collinson has produced a great deal of new evidence on lay patronage of Puritanism, and Professor Stone lays much emphasis on the work of a group of the nobility and gentry in fostering and protecting the movement (*The Crisis of the Aristocracy*, p. 734 ff.).

[3] *The Crisis of the Aristocracy*, p. 734.

were never in the pockets of the laity. As Michael Walzer puts it in *The Revolution of the Saints*, 'From the days of the Marian exile, the minister was its central figure. He had both patrons and allies among the gentry and even among the great noblemen, but Puritan ideology was entirely a clerical creation. Until the 1630's no important lay authors can be counted among the English Calvinists',[1] and again, 'The Puritan ministers remained, despite considerable support from titled families and encouragement from members of the Privy Council, an isolated group. The tone of their literature and the modes of their association, at least until the 1590's, were those of a radical intelligentsia, narrowly constituted, totally committed, doctrinaire, with what must have seemed the most tenuous of connections to Renaissance England.'[2]

There would, then, seem to have been the same possibilities of conflict between minister and layman in the Puritan movement as there were between the Catholic gentleman and the missionary priest, but conflict was for the most part avoided. The more radical of the 'godly ministers' pursued their ends through organisations which they themselves controlled. The lay sympathisers were required not so much to make policy as to help and protect those who made it and to organise propaganda in support of it. The rôle of the layman in the 'classical' movement and in the 'prophesyings' was very limited.

The 'godly minister' did not play the unique part in the Puritan scheme of salvation that the priest played in the Catholic system, but he was nevertheless a man with a special calling from God whose job was to preach the Word, and he was prepared if necessary to rebuke the unrighteous—even if they happened to be his social superiors. He often received from the laity the respect due to a man sent from God. Edward Dering and John Field were certainly not in the pockets of any layman, and the earl of Leicester, the great patron of the Puritans, and for that matter even Lord Burghley himself, were prepared on

[1] Michael Walzer, *The Revolution of the Saints*, 1966, p. 115. See *ibid.*, p. 114 ff., section on 'The Puritan Clergy'. Professor Walzer compares the Puritan ministers with the Papist priests but he thinks that the priests 'were closely bound to the traditional social order and were most often willing to work within the limits of the feudal connection of Lord and chaplain' (p. 131). On this point he does not take into account Dr. Bossy's views concerning the conflict between 'seignorial' Catholicism and the religion of 'the clerks'.

[2] Michael Walzer, *ibid.*, p. 116–17. See also M. M. Knappen, *Tudor Puritanism*, p. 353.

occasions to listen with quite surprising patience and humility to rebukes from godly ministers.[1]

It might be argued that although the support of the nobility and gentry was essential for the survival of Catholicism and Puritanism, this support also acted as a brake on both movements. The Catholic gentleman with his house and lands, his family and his friends and his desperate concern to show his loyalty to the queen, was often reluctant to risk everything for the sake of his religion and he did not always fully share the missionary zeal of the seminary priest. There were limits also to the support which the Puritan patron was prepared to give to the cause of godliness.[2] The government recognised where the real danger lay by directing its main efforts not against the lay sympathisers but against the Catholic priests and the Puritan ministers who would not conform.

One great advantage which the Puritan minister enjoyed over the Catholic priest was that he was often able to operate openly both in the country and in the town. Outside London it was very difficult for the Catholic priest to operate at all except from the base of a gentleman's house, and his sphere of influence tended to be limited to the gentry and their dependants. The Puritans who were presented to livings by sympathetic patrons had captive audiences on which they could work in their own parishes, and they were able to entrench themselves not only in rural areas but also commercial and industrial centres. Small oligarchic groups of town councillors, working hand-in-hand with Puritan ministers who had been appointed to livings, lectureships and masterships of hospitals, could do much to transform their towns into 'little Genevas', and a sympathetic gentry in the areas around these towns could also lend a helping hand in the process. Dr. Collinson has stressed this coincidence of industrial and mercantile activity with Puritanism in such towns as Norwich, Northampton, Coventry, Newcastle and London; in textile centres like Cranbrook and Ashford in Kent; in the river valleys of the Suffolk–Essex border; in industrial Wales, Gloucestershire and the West Riding; and Mr. Hill has drawn attention to the pockets of

---

[1] *Letters of Thomas Wood*, edit. Patrick Collinson, pp. xvi ff., 1, 2; Conyers Read, *Lord Burghley and Queen Elizabeth*, p. 113 ff.

[2] Professor Walzer comments: 'By the 1580's the politically significant aristocracy was already a court aristocracy, caught up in the cult of Gloriana', and again, 'Courtiers like Leicester sought Puritan support . . . but they were in no position to act consistently against the wishes of the Queen . . .' (*The Revolution of the Saints*, pp. 115, 116).

Puritanism in the industrial areas of Yorkshire, Lancashire and Tyneside such as Halifax, Manchester and Newcastle, and to its strength in towns on the Welsh Marches such as Worcester, Hereford, Shrewsbury and Chester.[1]

Nevertheless, the main strength of Elizabethan Puritanism did not lie among the townsmen and the urban middle classes nor among 'the industrious sort of people', and it is doubtful whether in the Elizabethan period Puritanism made a more powerful appeal to them than it did to other sections of the community. It made headway in some urban centres, but there were many others where it had no great success. Professor Dicken's generalisation that 'We might reasonably claim that it flourished most as a social religion among townsmen ...' may possible be true of Puritanism looked at as a whole over a long period, but it is questionable whether it can safely be applied to Elizabethan England.[2]

There is no simple answer to the question why a considerable number of Elizabethans chose to be Papists or Puritans rather than accept the religious settlement imposed by the state. Within any large religious group there are bound to be people of varying degrees of commitment, and the motives of individuals are often very mixed. There were many non-religious reasons why men and women chose as they did, but there is no doubt that both the Catholic and the Puritan groups showed a capacity to attract support from the comparatively small body of people with really deep religious convictions, people who were so sure that they had the truth that they were ready to accept serious inconveniences and danger rather than relinquish it. Professor Dickens remarks that 'When we have finished our efforts to

[1] Patrick Collinson, 'The Puritan Classical Movement', p. 772; Christopher Hill, 'Puritans and "The Dark Corners of the Land" ', *Transactions of the Royal Historical Society*, 5th series, XIII, pp. 86–7.

[2] A. C. Dickens, *The English Reformation*, p. 318. When Mr. Hill remarks (*Society and Puritanism*, p. 511) that 'To understand Puritanism we must understand the needs, hopes, fears and aspirations of the godly artisans, merchants, yeomen, gentlemen, ministers and their wives, who gave their support to its doctrines' we are bound to ask whether *in relation to Elizabethan England* the supporters are placed in the correct order of importance and whether the godly artisans and merchants are not getting undue stress as a result of being put first in the list. M. M. Knappen (*Tudor Puritanism*, p. 353) states that it 'throve best among the merchants, lawyers and small landowners', but adds 'there is little, however, to indicate that Puritanism . . . was predominantly a middle-class movement. Rather . . . it was a Protestant clericalism, a system in which the organized intelligentsia, whoever their allies might be, played the role of the senior partner. When laymen definitely secured the upper hand, Puritanism soon ceased to be Puritanism.'

modernise and secularise Puritanism, it remains an obstinately religious phenomenon . . . ',[1] and this is also true of Catholicism. What gave both groups their energy and their dynamic was in the last resort the conviction of their fully committed members that they were right about a vital issue—the proper relationship between God and man.

The fact that the committed Puritan and the committed Papist both believed that the commandments of God were more important than the commandments of men, and that the future life mattered more than life on this earth, meant that the two movements had many characteristics in common, in spite of their fundamental doctrinal differences. The energy and enthusiasm of the Marian exiles and their supporters finds a parallel in the work of the Catholics who went into exile at Louvain and elsewhere rather than accept what they believed to be a false religion. The Puritan drive of the 1580's had its counterpart in the reformed Catholicism brought into England by those who had gone abroad for the sake of religion and who returned with a missionary enthusiasm as great as that of Field or Cartwright or Travers. The burning zeal for truth shown by Penry is basically very similar to that shown by Campion. The Puritans, it is true, suffered a great deal less than did the Catholics, but for a number of them the road they chose to follow was difficult and at times dangerous. If men like Field, Cartwright, Campion and Parsons had gone with the tide, their abilities would have secured them high office within the establishment, but their religious convictions required them to suffer persecution for the sake of the truth.

The insistence of the committed Puritan that the things which are God's must come first is admirably illustrated by a speech of Tristram Pistor in the parliament of 1571. Pistor was speaking about Strickland's bill for the reformation of the Prayer Book.[2] He is reported as saying that the cause of religion was a matter 'stretching further and higher to everyone of us than the monarchy of the whole world . . . Those causes he showed to be God's. The rest are all but terrene; yea, trifles in comparison. Call ye them never so great, or pretend ye that they import never so much: subsidies, crowns, kingdoms, he knew not, he said, what they were in comparison of this'.[3] The spirit which moved Tristram Pistor was not so different from that which moved

---

[1] A. G. Dickens, *The English Reformation*, p. 319.
[2] See p. 128.
[3] J. Neale, *Elizabeth I and her Parliaments*, I. 199.

Parsons to put God's cause first, even though, as he saw it, this meant the restoration of true religion by force of arms.

Since Catholicism and Puritanism both insisted so strongly that this life was only a preparation for union with God, both displayed certain common characteristics in the methods by which they sought to reach their heavenly goal. In spite of their theological differences, they both saw the special need to develop their spiritual resources in the face of the challenge from the world around them. Both Puritan and Papist spirituality stressed the importance of prayer and meditation, and the need to bring the flesh into subjection to the spirit. Fasting was of value to the Puritan, even though he insisted it was not the superstitious fasting of the Papist. The self-examination of the Puritan and the comfort to the troubled spirit offered by godly ministers like Greenham or Perkins was not without some resemblance to the self-examination of the Papist in the confessional and the comfort he received from the priest who resolved his 'cases of conscience' and gave him absolution in the name of God. There were similarities in results, if not in methods, between the Puritan strengthening his spiritual life by listening to the godly preacher and the Papist drawing on the resources offered him in the mass and the sacraments. We must not forget that both groups recognised the same saviour Jesus Christ. It was not altogether surprising that a pirated and edited version of Parsons' *Christian Directory* should be produced by a Puritan minister and should enjoy a considerable sale in Elizabethan England.[1]

Since there was so much religious vitality in Catholicism and in Puritanism, it is understandable that each group saw in the other a particularly dangerous rival. The fierce anti-popery of the Puritans and their continual insistence on the menace of the Whore of Babylon arose not only from the detestation of the errors of the Church of Rome, but also from their realisation that Catholicism, after its initial defeats at the time of the Reformation, was now vigorously counter-attacking with considerable success. They felt that instead of harassing Protestants, the establishment ought to be busy fighting its real enemy. Similarly, a number of Catholic writers thought that their most formidable opponents were Puritans, whom they saw as 'the hotter sort of Protestants' and as 'a later and more fresher sort of Calvinists than the English Protestants are'. Nicholas Sander claimed that the

---

[1] See p. 188.

English government had been so busy suppressing Catholics that it had let the Puritans get out of hand, and he thought that 'the ministers of the new sect, under the pretence of avoiding superstition, would by degrees destroy in Church and State all order, good manners, policy and civilization itself—yea, and even their own religion—by their savage rudeness if the civil power did not put some check on them.'[1] Robert Parsons recognised his own vitality in others when he said: 'The Puritan parte at home in Ingland, is thought to be the most vigorouse of any other, that is to say, most ardent, quick, bold, resolute ... ' The religious enthusiasts on both sides were well aware that men who know what they love and love what they know can often exercise an influence out of all proportion to their numbers.

Although there was a hard core of fully committed men and women in both religious groups, other factors besides religious enthusiasm and religious conviction played a part in determining people's religious allegiance. The Papists were helped by the deep-seated reluctance of many people to abandon traditional habits and practises, and 'popish superstitions' took a remarkably long time to eradicate. Dislike of government interference with what men considered to be their own affair, family loyalties, the attachment of tenants and servants to a particular nobleman or gentleman, the climate of opinion in a particular area, all helped men to remain faithful to the 'old religion' in the face of government pressure and in spite of the financial and physical dangers it might involve. When the earlier traditions were weakening, the missionaries injected into the Catholic body a new vitality and built up new loyalties on the ruins of the old order.

If the pattern of Catholic loyalties was by no means as simple as is sometimes suggested, the motives, other than religious conviction, which made men Puritans or supporters of Puritanism were even more complex. There were so many different kinds of Puritans that no one explanation can satisfactorily cover them all. The Puritanism of a Leicester was poles apart from the Puritanism of a Field; the highly respectable Lady Hoby moved in a different world from that of the hunted Penry; and William Perkins, the much admired preacher in Cambridge, was not the kind of man to have any sympathy with the writers of the Marprelate tracts. There were many who liked listening to 'godly' sermons but who had no intention of getting into trouble with the authorities.

---

[1] T. H. Clancy, *Papist Pamphleteers*, p. 23.

The situation was further complicated by the fact that the Puritan programme was often attractive from a worldly point of view. It offered certain material advantages to the gentry and to the middle classes of a kind that Catholicism was certainly not in a position to offer. Mr. Hill has demonstrated at considerable length the nature of these non-religious factors which brought men to a greater or lesser degree within the Puritan ranks. Men's motives are often mixed, and it was certainly an advantage if one found that one's religious convictions also coincided with one's material interests.

Due weight must certainly be given to the benefits in this life which Puritanism offered, or appeared to offer, to its supporters, but man does not live by bread alone, and the appeal of Puritanism cannot be explained merely in economic terms. Recently Professor Walzer has attempted to dig beneath the surface in order to find the deep-seated psychological factors which made some men Puritans,[1] and he concluded that English Puritanism was 'one possible response to the experiences of disorder and anxiety' in a changing world. Some men felt a 'need for the self-control and godly government that sainthood offered', and Puritanism seemed to them 'a way out of anxiety'. He conceded, however, that 'There were both merchants and gentlemen ... who obviously enjoyed the very freedoms that frightened the saints so much—mobility, extravagance, individuality, and wit ... ', and since men in the same classes of society were not all affected in the same way he decided that 'All that can be said is that some of the men living in this age of social transformation found what was for them a suitable response in Calvinist ideology. In England, Puritanism was their effort to capture control of the changing world and their own lives—hence the insistent concern of the saints with order, method and discipline.'[2]

Although the attachment of certain men and women to Puritanism or to Catholicism cannot be fully 'explained', it might be suggested that among the many different attractions which these religions offered was the fact that both provided their adherents with a clear-cut explanation of the meaning and purpose of man's life on this earth. Moreover, the ascetical and other-worldly elements which both contained had a conscious or unconscious appeal to those who were dissatisfied with the materialism of the society in which they lived.

---

[1] Michael Walzer, *The Revolution of the Saints.*
[2] *Ibid.*, p. 309.

Lady Hoby living her well-ordered life of prayer, meditation and self-examination had basically a good deal in common with those who made the Spiritual Exercises of St. Ignatius.

Among the many problems which faced the Papists and the Puritans in Elizabethan England was the perennial question of the proper relationship between Christians and the civil power. Both groups found themselves to a greater or lesser degree in conflict with the state, because they shared the view that in the last resort the state could not justly override the claims of 'true religion'. The Papist who believed that the Church of Rome was the one true church and the Puritan who saw the Church of England as an imperfect church with doctrines and practices not warranted by Scripture were, if they followed their beliefs to their logical conclusion, bound in conscience to resist the attempts of the government to impose on the nation doctrines and forms of worship which they believed to be false. Further, they were committed to the view that the 'true church' had an independent rôle to play and that, although ideally the state should support 'true religion', if there was a conflict spiritual authority was superior to secular authority. Theoretically, the Christian could not be content merely with passive resistance to the state when it attempted to impose error on its subjects, since the true believer had a duty to his neighbour and to God to preach the gospel to every creature.

In practice, many Papists and Puritans were extremely reluctant to face the logical consequences of the position they had taken up. Personal loyalty to the queen, respect for authority, the difficulty in deciding at what point a stand must be made, the hope that sooner or later the situation would improve—all this helped to weaken resistance to the government's attempts to impose religious uniformity. The loyalty of the Catholic gentry in spite of the bull of excommunication and their unwillingness to become involved in the schemes of the papacy and the emigrés to restore the true church by force of arms made the government's task much easier than it would have been if there had been a serious threat from a large Catholic fifth-column. The uncertainty of Puritans about what could or could not be tolerated, their fear that if they deserted their flocks the people would fall prey to Romish wolves, their dreams of reforming the church from within and their belief that Elizabeth was 'a godly prince' helped to ensure that Elizabethan Puritanism, in spite of the fears of Whitgift and Bancroft, never became a seditious movement[1] and that the great majority of its adherents never thought of separating from the Church of England.

Although Papists and Puritans both resisted the religious settlement imposed by the state, they did not champion the right of the individual conscience, since they held a common belief that religious truth could be known with certainty and that it was the duty of the state to suppress false teaching. For Cartwright, as for Parsons during most of his life,[2] 'error had no rights' and the government had an obligation to put false prophets to death. Nevertheless, when they began to realise that their cause was not likely to triumph in the immediate future, both Catholics and Puritans began to ask for a measure of toleration for themselves, even though they did not believe in toleration for others and would certainly not have conceded it as a right if they had been in power.

In the field of organisation and method there were inevitably a number of parallels between the two movements since both had to take steps to preserve themselves against attack and to spread their message in spite of official disapproval. It was much easier for the Puritans to do this than it was for the Papists, since their beliefs did not of their very nature bring them into conflict with authority in the way that allegiance to the Pope brought a Papist into conflict with the law. The Puritan worked from within the church and it was only very slowly that the official dividing lines between 'orthodoxy' and 'nonconformity' were clearly drawn. It was from the start obvious that Catholicism and Protestantism differed fundamentally from each other, but to the end there was uncertainty about the position of 'Anglican Puritans'. Thus Puritans long enjoyed opportunities for infiltrating the establishment both in state and church, and they were able to further their cause from the pulpits of the parish church and through sympathisers in the Privy Council, in parliament and among the local authorities. An earl of Leicester or an earl of Huntingdon could without difficulty use his patronage to put men of Puritan sym-

---

[1] Professor Hurstfield points out that in the ecclesiastical system the bishops were the last line of defence before the monarchy. When they came under fire 'Elizabeth began now to strike harshly at the critics . . . because she believed she was fighting for monarchy itself', and, again, 'Whatever happened to Calvinistic puritanism in practice, in theory it was democratic'. *Elizabeth I and the Unity of England*, pp. 159, 160.

[2] Parsons modified his position in later years. See Thomas Clancy, *Papist Pamphleteers*, p. 153 ff.

pathy in positions of influence. Field for the most part was able to exercise his genius for organisation without coming in conflict with the law. The influential 'prophesyings' enjoyed the protection of a number of bishops and long escaped the attention of the government, and the 'classical' movement flourished for many years before the reaction association with Whitgift and Bancroft brought its leaders— unsuccessfully—before a court.

Although the Puritans could always plead that what they were doing was not illegal, they did not go out of their way to attract the attention of the authorities to their organisation, and the effect produced by the apparently spontaneous demands for reform from many parts of the country was all the greater because the influence exercised by such novel religious 'pressure groups' was as yet little understood.

The Papists had to operate under much greater difficulties and their opportunities for influencing people were much more restricted. Unlike the Puritans, they could not work openly. They could not lobby M.P.s or exercise influence on Privy Councillors and they could not meet in 'prophesyings' or 'classes'. To be involved in any Catholic organisation inevitably exposed a man to a charge of treason or sedition. But in spite of the danger, they were compelled to take steps, on a local and *ad hoc* basis, to ensure that the seminaries were supplied with candidates for the priesthood, that Catholic children were educated abroad, that girls who wished to live the religious life found their ways to foreign convents,[1] and that priests were brought safely into the country and provided with the means of carrying on their work once they had arrived. That much of their organisation was imperfect and unco-ordinated is only too clear, but considering the difficulties, their achievement was remarkable. Activity of this kind seems to have acted as a stimulus to Catholicism, just as the organising of meetings and the preparation of petitions and propaganda acted as a stimulus to Puritanism.

Both Papists and Puritans were keenly aware of the importance of propaganda in the battle for men's minds and both realised the influence of the printed word. The Puritans had the advantage that they could publish a great deal at the officially approved presses. Influence in high places enabled them, at least until Whitgift and Bancroft triumphed, to get past the censors much that might otherwise have been

[1] See for example, *The Chronicle of the English Augustinian Canonesses in Louvain*, edit. Adam Hamilton, 1904.

CC

banned as contrary to official policy. There were, however, limits to what could be done publicly, and the more radical Puritan books and pamphlets had to be printed at secret presses within the country or by foreign printers. The Papists, of course, were unable to get their works printed by licensed printers and were driven on occasions to set up secret presses of their own. The parallels between the history of the Marprelate tracts and that of Parsons' Greenstreet House press are too obvious to need stressing. But for the most part the Papists had to rely on foreign presses and were compelled to undertake the costly and dangerous task of smuggling books into the country and distributing them in the face of formidable difficulties. Like the Puritans they achieved some remarkable successes.

There were other means of spreading the gospel and influencing men's minds. In a society which was only partly literate and in which there were no newspapers, broadcasting or television, preaching was of tremendous importance, and here the Puritans enjoyed an immense superiority. They attached special value to preaching as 'the ordinary means of salvation', and they had among their numbers some of the ablest preachers in the country. The Papists, on the other hand, were starved of sermons and could hear them, if at all, only with great difficulty and danger. The Puritan preachers were produced in large numbers in the universities, but the priests had to be trained abroad, and their numbers were very limited. It was rather late in the day before the establishment woke up to the need to produce preachers who would be not only 'learned' and 'godly' but also conforming members of the Church of England. It paid a heavy price for allowing its critics to capture the pulpits and for the queen's under-valuation of preaching as a means of propaganda.

Both Puritans and Papists were well aware of the importance of education as a means of spreading their views.[1] The Puritans were able to operate within the universities of Oxford and Cambridge where they could work out many of their ideas in relative security and train a considerable number of 'godly' ministers. Emmanuel College, founded by Sir Walter Mildmay in 1584, and Sidney Sussex College, established in 1596 with funds left by Frances Sidney, dowager countess of Sussex, provide two notable illustrations of the Puritan concern for higher education in relation to the spread of religious

[1] See M. M. Knappen, *Tudor Puritanism*, Chapter XXVI, 'Learning and Education' A. C. F. Beales, *Education under Penalty*.

truth, and this same concern on another level is to be found in the insistence of Puritan clergy and schoolmasters on the importance of catechising children and servants. The Papists worked under much greater difficulties, but the establishment of a Catholic centre at Louvain, the efforts of Allen to provide at Douay a substitute for Oxford and Cambridge, and the training of an educated clergy in the seminaries abroad show that they too realised the importance of learning as a weapon in the religious struggle. A number of the nobility and gentry sent their children to be educated at schools and convents abroad, and within England itself Catholic tutors and schoolmasters strove to bring up a younger generation in 'The old religion'. Robert Parsons displayed both his own understanding of the situation and the special interest of his Society in education when he suggested that in an England which had once more been reconquered for Catholicism there should be an increase in schools and the establishment of a third university.[1]

The government's task of trying to impose religious uniformity in the face of determined and intelligent resistance was not an easy one, and it was made even more difficult by the fact that neither Catholicism nor Puritanism was a purely English phenomenon which could be dealt with inside the boundaries of the national state. The impact of Europe on English Catholicism is perhaps more obvious than the influence of Europe on English Puritanism, for Catholicism was of its very nature an international religion. English Catholics were not free to compromise on questions of doctrine. They were, moreover, directly affected by the policy of the papacy, the actions of Catholic princes, and by the ideas and energy of the Counter-Reformation. The seminaries for the training of priests, the schools for the education of a Catholic élite, the places of refuge for the exiles and the presses for the printing of Catholic controversial and devotional literature were outside the control of the English government, and the fate of that government depended in no small measure on European international politics.

The development of English Puritanism was also related closely to what was happening in other countries. The influence of Calvinism, although it was by no means confined to Puritans, is too obvious to call for further comment. The Marian exiles bringing back to England what they had learnt in Germany and Switzerland provided one

See p. 273 note 3.

of the great formative influences in the religious life of Elizabethan England, and the English Puritans had always before their minds the examples of 'the best reformed churches' in Switzerland, Germany, Scotland and elsewhere—churches which, as they saw it, had removed the relics of popery and approached much closer to the ideal of the true church than had the Church of England. For Puritans, as for Papists, European theological writers were of great importance. Europe provided ideas and offered in the last resort a refuge for those who found it impossible to remain any longer in England.

The religious differences within the Elizabethan state not only complicated international relations but also had profound effects on political and constitutional developments in England itself. In order to further their aims Puritans made great use of the House of Commons. As Professor Neale puts it, 'by skilful exploitation of propitious circumstances they were able to shake Crown, Church, Council and Parliament... Indeed, the art of opposition, which might be considered the outstanding contribution of the Elizabethan period to parliamentary history, was largely learnt from them or inspired by them'.[1] These conflicts or so-called 'lovers' quarrels' between the queen and her faithful Commons were not, of course, limited to questions of religion, but on the numerous occasions when there was disagreement about religious policy angry feelings were the more easily aroused because a number of members felt that 'true religion' was being sacrificed to political expediency.

The Papist contribution, on the other hand, was mainly indirect. Catholics achieved very little in the Parliaments of 1559 and 1563, and after that they were excluded from the House of Commons. Nevertheless, the attempt of the queen to make her religious settlement acceptable to as many people as possible meant that the church established in 1559 retained many beliefs and practices which the Puritans condemned as 'popish' and which they strove hard to remove. The queen persistently and successfully resisted such attempts to interfere with what she held to be her own business, but she was unable to deal as severely with the Puritans as she would have wished because she and her advisers knew that they were her most determined and zealous supporters in the struggle against the Papists.

When the queen died Catholicism and Puritanism were much less serious threats than they had been in the 1580's, but the religious

[1] J. Neale, *Elizabeth I and her Parliaments*, II. 436.

uniformity for which Elizabeth had struggled so long had not been achieved. She had sought to persuade all Englishmen to give their allegiance to one church, but many able and sincere men and women had found themselves unable to support it. The Elizabethan national church was the poorer as a result, and the state had been in some measure weakened by the need to spend so much physical and mental energy in a task which in the end proved to be more than it could accomplish.

The Elizabethan Age was one of the most important periods in the history of Catholicism and Puritanism, for what happened then was not only significant in itself but was to have very great influence on the future. For English Catholics this was the Heroic Age, and the memory of so many who suffered fines, imprisonment and death for the sake of their faith was to become part of the English Catholic tradition. Because of the enterprise and endurance of the Elizabethans, the Catholic religion managed to survive as a force of significance in in English life. The memory of the martyrs remained long after the less satisfactory aspects of the period—the attempts of Spain and the papacy to overthrow the government by force, the intrigues of the exiles, the fierce quarrels over the archpriest and the appellants—had faded from men's minds.

Under the Stuarts conditions were to become a good deal easier, and although there were difficult times, Catholics found themselves much freer to practise their religion, but in this gentler atmosphere English Catholicism seems to have lost much of its earlier drive. Dr. Bossy remarks that what gave vitality to English Catholicism was 'a refusal to accept the accomplished fact, "an alarm spiritual", a demand for reformation'. He thinks that 'Its dominant expression was action', and he finds great significance in the revival of the Benedictine order in the early seventeenth century—'the reappearance of the monks'. Here was the religion of contemplation rather than of action, and he sums up the position with the comment that 'The history of Elizabethan Catholicism is a progress from inertia to inertia in three generations'.[1] It may be that this minimises unduly the achievements of seventeenth-century Catholics, but it seems clear that by the late Elizabethan period the missionary drive had lost much of its impetus and that the Catholic community was directing its effort not so much

[1] J. Bossy, 'The Character of Elizabethan Catholicism', *Past and Present*, No. 21, pp. 56, 57.

to bringing about the conversion of England as to trying to obtain the right to live quietly within a predominantly Protestant society.

The significance of Puritanism in the religious life of the country is difficult to assess because it was such a complex phenomenon and included so many diverse elements. In so far as Elizabethan Puritanism can be considered in its own right and not merely as a prologue to what happened later, its contribution was both negative and positive. It failed in its attempts to impose on the Church of England an exclusively Calvinist doctrine and a Presbyterian or semi-Presbyterian discipline, it forced the church in self-defence to define its theology and its practice on more rigid and more exclusive lines, and it helped promote the growth of that 'Anglicanism' which will always be associated with the great work of Richard Hooker. But although it did not succeed in seizing control of the church, it did not separate from it, and it nourished within the framework of the establishment a strongly 'Protestant' tradition and a way of life that can conveniently, if not very precisely, be described as 'Puritan'.[1]

One's judgment on the long-term importance of Elizabethan Puritanism will depend on how one sees it in relation to Stuart Puritanism. If one regards Puritanism as a homogeneous and continuous movement gathering momentum from the early years of Elizabeth and reaching a triumphant climax in the Puritan Revolution, then clearly the Elizabethan Age was the great formative period when the seed was sown and the first fruits were gathered of what was to be in due course a most abundant harvest, both in England itself and in the North American colonies.

That there was continuity between Elizabethan Puritanism, Jacobean Puritanism and Caroline Puritanism, no one would deny, but there were, too, highly important differences, and one must beware of the temptation to see Elizabethan Puritanism as leading inevitably to a Puritan Revolution. Both Elizabeth and James had considerable success in their attempts to keep Puritanism under control, and when the confrontation came in the mid-seventeenth century, it was only partly the result of attitudes which had developed under Elizabeth. Although their creed may have had revolutionary implications, Elizabethan Puritans were not in fact revolutionaries. It was only in the very different circumstances of the seventeenth century that Puritans

[1] For a detailed discussion of the intellectual, social and cultural aspects of Puritanism, see M. M. Knappen, *Tudor Puritanism*, pp. 339–480.

reluctantly reached the conclusion that they must take up the sword in defence of good government and true religion.

It was once the fashion to stress the 'rise of the middle classes' in the sixteenth and early seventeenth-century England and to see Puritanism as the creed which made a special appeal to the growing 'capitalist spirit' which in 1642 came in conflict with 'feudal society'. While there were certainly a number of elements in Puritanism which appealed to the material interests of both the landowning class and the bourgeoisie, there were other elements which were directly opposed to the growth of 'capitalism'. As Professor Dickens puts it, 'Looking at the whole movement we see an essentially other-worldly religion, dominated not only by an almost morbid moral sensitivity but by a real distrust of "modern" capitalist tendencies'.[1] No one would deny what Mr. Hill has so convincingly shown—that in the Elizabethan and in the early Stuart period there were many non-religious reasons why Puritanism attracted support from some of the landowning, commercial and industrial classes, but Elizabethan Puritans and their sympathisers cannot be held responsible for the violent courses which were adopted, in very different circumstances, by those who came after them.

It is also necessary to be cautious in assessing the debt to the Elizabethans of those who established Puritanism across the Atlantic. It is true that many of them had been bred in Elizabethan England and imbibed there 'the spirit of Puritanism' which under the Stuarts they took to the American colonies, but American Puritanism was not the direct product of the main Elizabethan movement, for the great majority of Elizabethan Puritans did not approve of separating from the Church of England.

In the early years of the reign Edwin Sandys had preached that liberty for men openly to profess diversity of religion was dangerous to the commonwealth, and Grindal had prayed 'May God at length grant that we may all of us think the same things'. Elizabeth had worked for over forty years to bring about the 'conformity and unity in religion' which she hoped would be 'as a wall of defence unto this realm'. She had succeeded to the extent that by 1603 the majority of Englishmen were prepared to give at least passive consent to the Church of England, but there still remained the formidable minority of people who wished to worship by other forms of religion altogether

---

[1] A. C. Dickens, *The Reformation in England*, p. 317.

or to make fundamental changes in the church established by law. We shall never know whether the queen would have had even greater success if she had established her church on a different basis. As far as the Papists were concerned, there was not much that she could have done to make the national church acceptable to them, since they were committed to the belief that there was only one church founded by Christ—the Church of Rome. As for the Puritans, they might have been less critical if she had established a more 'Protestant' church instead of what they regarded as 'a crooked halting betwixt two religions', but in such a church there would have been no room for the 'Anglicanism' which attracted men like Hooker, and the 'discipline' of a godly reformed church might have alienated the loyalty of the large number of Elizabethans who were religious indifferentists.

R. G. Usher believed that 'the cleavage of religious parties in England at the close of the sixteenth century was the result of deep fundamental causes and not the product of slight misunderstandings between men who agreed in all essentials'.[1] Not everyone will accept this view, but there is at least a possibility that in the religious conflicts of the Elizabethan Age we have an illustration of Cardinal Manning's claim that 'all great quarrels between men are at bottom theological'.

[1] R. G. Usher, *Reconstruction of the Church*, I. 89.

Appendix 1

CATHOLIC RECUSANTS IN 1603

The following table, which is printed in R. G. Usher, *The Reconstruction of the English Church*, I. 158, is based on a return of Catholic recusants made by the bishops in 1603. Although it is not of much value as a guide to the *total* number of Catholics, it is useful for providing a very rough-and-ready indication of the relative strength of Catholicism in the different dioceses.

Diocese	Men	Women	Total
Chichester	109	153	262
Bristol	89	124	213
Peterborough	13	83	96
Exeter	44	55	99
Gloucester	33	31	64
Hereford	152	279	431
Coventry and Lichfield	231	419	650
Bangor	11	21	32
St. Asaph	100	150	250
Canterbury	18	20	38
Peculiars of Canterbury	5	13	18
Rochester	11	7	18
London	166	152	318
Norwich	147	177	324
Oxford	93	141	234
Bath and Wells	50	52	102
Winchester	149	249	398
Worcester	102	168	270
Salisbury			171[1]
Ely			19[1]
Llandaff			381[1]
St. Davids			145[1]
Lincoln			295[1]
York	300	420	720
Durham	211	315	526
Chester	922	1,560	2,482
Carlisle	30	44	74
Total number	2,986	4,633	8,630

[1] The returns do not give separate figures for men and women.

399

Appendix 2

PURITAN MINISTERS *c.* 1600–10

R. G. Usher, *Reconstruction of the English Church*, I. 250, gave the following estimates of the numbers of Puritan clergy. He based the figures in the first column on 'as exhaustive a list . . . as could

	Tabulation of actual names	Calculations of numbers threatened 1605	Calculations in the 'Abridgement' 1605
London and Middlesex	35	22	30
Essex	43	43	57
Suffolk	33	50	71
Norfolk	20	—	28
Northamptonshire	29	⎧ —	51
Hertfordshire	9	⎨ 40	17
Rutland	3	⎩ —	—
Lincoln	12	—	33
Leicestershire	9	—	57
Huntingdon	1	—	—
Bedfordshire	3	32	16
Buckinghamshire	9	—	33
Nottinghamshire	5	—	20
Oxfordshire	6	9	9
Sussex	18	30–40	47
Lancashire	17	—	21
Warwick	3	27	44
Kent	1	—	23
Wiltshire	3	—	31
Surrey	2	—	21
Devon and Cornwall	6	41 (?)	51
Hampshire	2	—	—
Worcestershire and Monmouth	2	—	—
Dorsetshire	—	—	17
Stafford and Derby	—	—	34
Somerset	—	—	17
Cheshire	—	—	12
Total number	281	297	746

possibly be made of those found in England during the years 1600–1610' compiled from 'petitions, tracts, letters, Diocesan archives, and printed books'. For the tests which he applied to decide whether or not a minister should be listed as a Puritan, see *ibid.*, I. 249–50. He compiled the second column from various contemporary estimates of ministers thought to be in danger of deprivation in 1605. The figures in the third column, which are much larger than those in the other two, are based on Puritan propaganda tract of 1605—*An Abridgement of that booke which the Ministers of Lincoln Diocess delivered to his Maiestie upon the first of December last* . . .

Usher was aware that his list of names of ministers was incomplete, but he nevertheless thought that 'perhaps a total of three hundred or three hundred fifty would represent with substantial accuracy the full number of the Puritans who declared themselves'.

Many historians think that Usher's definition of a Puritan was much too narrow. The tables nevertheless provide a rough-and-ready indication of the relative strength of Puritanism in different parts of the country.

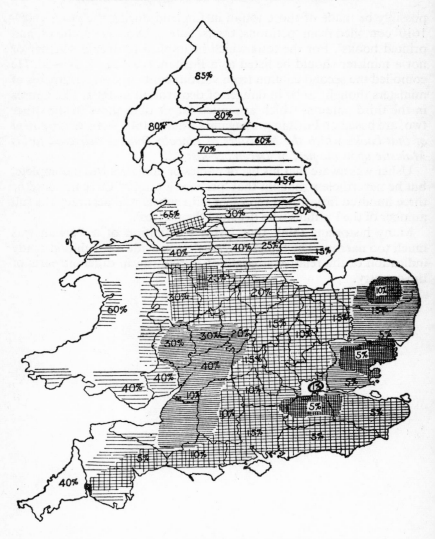

Reproduced from R. G. Usher, *The Reconstruction of the English Church*, Vol. 1, 1910. The shading was intended to show the relative density of the population and the figures were meant to show what proportion of the population were open or secret Catholics in 1603. See Appendix 1.

Reproduced from R. G. Usher, *The Reconstruction of the English Church*, Vol. 1, 1910.
The single crosses were intended to represent the location of one minister; the double and
triple crosses, the location respectively of three and five (or more) ministers beneficed in
the same place. Where the minister's location could not be definitely determined, he was
not represented at all, for the map was intended to show the maximum of exact information then available. See Appendix 2.

Books and Articles

There is a vast literature dealing with Papists and with Puritans, and a full-length bibliography would be out of place here. Further information can be found in the section on Ecclesiastical History in the standard *Bibliography of British History: Tudor Period*, edited by Conyers Read, Oxford, 1959, pp. 150–212. Many of the works listed below contain their own bibliographies.

The following is not a selected bibliography but a list, arranged alphabetically under authors and editors, of books and articles referred to in the footnotes. Cross-references and sub-titles are given where appropriate. The place of publication is London unless otherwise stated.

Acts of the Privy Council, edit. J. R. Dasent, 32 vols. 1890–1907.

Admonition to the Parliament, see *Puritan Manifestoes*.

Allen, William, Cardinal, *A True, Sincere and Modest Defense of English Catholics*, see Kingdon, R. A. *Letters and Memorials*, see Knox, T. F.

Allison A. F. and Rogers, D. M., *A Catalogue of Catholic Books in English, printed abroad or secretly in England, 1558–1640*, 2 vols. Arundel Press, Bognor, 1956.

Anstruther, Godfrey, *Vaux of Harrowden, a recusant family*, Newport, 1953. *Elizabethan Seminary Priests 1558–1603*, Dominican Priory, Leicester, 1966.

Arber, Edward, *An Introductory Sketch to the Martin Marprelate Controversy*, 1879.

Arber, Edward (edit.), *Admonition to the People of England by Thomas Cooper*, English Scholars' Library, no. 15, 1882. *The Epistle by Martin Marprelate*, English Scholars' Library, no. 11., 1880.

Aveling, Hugh, *Post Reformation Catholicism in East Yorkshire*, East Yorkshire Local History Society, 1960. *The Catholic Recusants of the West Riding of Yorkshire, 1558–1790*, Leeds Philosophical and Literary Society, 1963. *Northern Catholics: The Catholic Recusants of the North Riding of Yorkshire, 1558–1790*, 1966.

Ayre, J. (edit.), *The Sermons of Edwin Sandys*, Parker Society, Cambridge, 1841.

Babbage, S., *Puritanism and Richard Bancroft*, 1962.

Bald, R. C. (edit.), *An Humble Supplication to Her Maiestie by Robert Southwell*, Cambridge, 1953.

Bancroft, Richard, *Dangerous Positions*. See Usher, R.G.

Beales, A. C. F., *Education under Penalty*, 1963. *A Biographical Catalogue of Catholic Schoolmasters in England*, Part I, 1558–1603, in *Recusant History*, vol. 7, no. 6, 1964.

Birt, H. N., *The Elizabethan Religious Settlement, a study of contemporary documents*, 1907.

Black, J. B., *The Reign of Elizabeth 1558–1603*, Oxford History of England, 2nd edition, 1959.

Blench, J. W., *Preaching in England in the late 15th and 16th centuries*, 1964.

Bossy, J. 'The Character of Elizabethan Catholicism', *Past and Present*, Vol. 21, 1962. 'Rome and the Elizabethan Catholics: A question of Geography', *The Historical Journal*, vol. 7, no. 1, 1964. 'Henry IV, the Appellants and the Jesuits', *Recusant History*, vol. 8, no. 2, 1965.

Booty, J. E. (edit.), *An Apology of the Church of England by John Jewel*, Cornell University Press, 1963.

Bowler, Hugh, *Recusant Roll No. 2, 1593–1594*, Catholic Record Society, vol. 57, 1965.

Bradwell, S., *The Rasing of the Foundations of Brownisme*, 1588.

Breward, I., 'The Life and Theology of William Perkins', Manchester Ph.D. thesis, 1963.

Brook, V. J. K., *Whitgift and the English Church*, 1957. *A Life of Archbishop Parker*, Oxford, 1962.

Browne, Robert, *A Treatise of reformation without tarrying for anie* . . . Middleburg, 1582. See also Peel, A. and Carsen, L. (edit.) for *The Writings of Robert Harrison and Robert Browne*.

Bruce, J. and Perowne, T. (edit.), *Correspondence of Matthew Parker*, Parker Society, Cambridge, 1853.

Caraman, Philip, *The Other Face: Catholic Life under Elizabeth I*, 1960. *Henry Garnet and the Gunpowder Plot*, 1964. *The Years of Siege: Catholic Life from James I to Cromwell*, 1966.

Caraman, Philip (edit.), *William Weston: The Autobiography of an Elizabethan*, 1955. *John Gerard: The Autobiography of an Elizabethan*, 1956 edition. Also published as a Fontana paperback under the title of *The Hunted Priest*.

Caraman, Philip, and Walsh, James, *Martyrs of England and Wales 1535–1680*, a chronological list, 1960.

Cardwell, E., *Synodalia*, 2 vols. Oxford, 1842.

Cecil, William, *The Execution of Justice in England*, see Kingdon, R. M.

Chadwick, Owen, 'The Sixteenth Century' in *The English Church and the Continent*, edit. Dodwell, C. R. 1959.

Challoner, Richard, Bishop, *Memoirs of Missionary Priests and other Catholics of both sexes that have suffered death in England on religious accounts from the year 1577 to the year 1684*, 1741–2. Also edited by J. H. Pollen, 1 vol., 1923.

Clancy, T. H., *Papist Pamphleteers*, Chicago, 1964. 'Notes on Persons' *Memorial for the Reformation of England* (1596)' in *Recusant History*, vol. 5, no. 1, 1959. 'English Catholics and the Papal Deposing Power', *Recusant History*, vol. 6, nos. 3, 5; Vol. 7, No. 1 (1962–3).

Collinson, Patrick, *The Elizabethan Puritan Movement*, 1967. 'The Puritan Classical Movement in the Reign of Elizabeth I', unpublished London Ph.D. thesis, 1957. *A Mirror of Elizabethan Puritanism: The Life and Letters of Godly Master Dering*, Dr. Williams' Trust, 1964. 'John Field and Elizabethan Puritanism' in *Elizabethan Government and Society*, edit. S. T. Bindoff, J. Hurstfield and C. H. Williams, 1961. *The Letters of Thomas Wood, Puritan, 1566–1577*, Bulletin of the Institute of Historical Research, Special Supplement no. 5. November, 1960. 'The beginnings of English Sabbatarianism', *Studies in Church History I*, Ecclesiastical History Society, 1961.

Cooper, Thomas, see Arber, Edward.

Couper, W. J., *Robert Waldegrave King's Printer for Scotland*, Scottish Typographical Journal, Glasgow, 1916.

Cross, F. L., see More, P. E.

Cross, M. Claire, *The Puritan earl: the life of Henry Hastings, third earl of Huntingdon 1536–1595*, 1966. 'Noble Patronage in the Elizabethan Church', *The Historical Journal*, vol. III, no. 1. 1960. 'The Third Earl of Huntingdon and Trials of Catholics in the North 1581–1595', *Recusant History*, vol. 8, no. 3, 1965.

Curtis, M., *Oxford and Cambridge in Transition 1558–1642*, Oxford, 1959. 'Hampton Court Conference and its aftermath', *History*, xlvi, 1961.

Davies, Daniel Horton, *The Worship of the English Puritans*, 1946.

De Luna, B. N., *Jonson's Romish Plot*, Oxford, 1967.

Devlin, Christopher, *The Life of Robert Southwell*, 1956.

D'Ewes, Simonds, *The Journal of all the Parliaments during the Reign of Queen Elizabeth*, 1682.

Dickens, A. G., *Lollards and Protestants in the Diocese of York, 1509–1558*, 1959. *The English Reformation*, 1964. 'The First Stages of Catholic Recusancy in Yorkshire', *Yorkshire Archaeological Journal*, XXXV, 1941. 'The extent and character of recusancy in Yorkshire in 1604', Yorkshire Archaeological Journal, XXXVII, 1948. (With Newton, John) 'Further Light on the Scope of Yorkshire Recusancy in 1604', *Yorkshire Archaeological Journal*, XXXVIII, 1955.

Dodd, Charles, *The Church History of England, with Notes, Additions and a Continuation by M. A. Tierney*, 5 vols., 1839–1843.

Dodwell, C. R. (edit.), *The English Church and the Continent*, 1959.

Douglas, C. E., see Frere, W. H. and Douglas, C. E. *Puritan Manifestoes*.

Driscoll, J. P., 'The Supposed Sources of Persons' Christian Directory', *Recusant History*, vol. 5, no. 6, 1960.

Dugmore, Owen, 'Richard Bancroft's Submission', *Journal of Ecclesiastical History*, iii, 1952.

Edwards, Francis, *The Dangerous Queen*, 1964.

Elton, G. R., *The Tudor Constitution: Documents and Commentary*, Cambridge, 1960. 'A High Road to Civil War' in *From the Renaissance to the Counter-Reformation: essays in honour of Garrett Mattingly*, edit. C. H. Carter, 1966.

Foley, Henry (edit.), *Records of the English Province of the Society of Jesus*, 8 vols., 1877–1883.

Foster, C. W. (edit.), *The State of the Church in the Reigns of Elizabeth and James I*, Lincoln Record Society, 1926.

Frere, W. H., *The English Church in the reign of Elizabeth and James I*, 1924.

Frere, W. H. and Douglas, C. E. (edit.), *Puritan Manifestoes: a study of the origin of the puritan revolt, with a reprint of the Admonition to the Parliament, etc. 1907*. Another edition with new preface, 1954.

Fuller, Thomas, *The Church History of Britain*, edit. J. S. Brewer, 6 vols. Oxford, 1845.

Gardiner, S. R., *History of England from the Accession of James I to the outbreak of the Civil War*, 10 vols. 1905 edition. *What Gunpowder Plot was*, 1897.

Garnett, Henry, *Portrait of Guy Fawkes*, 1962.

Garrett, C. H., *The Marian Exiles, A Study in the Origins of Elizabethan Puritanism*, Cambridge, 1938.

Gee, H. and Hardy, W. J., *Documents illustrative of English Church History*, 1910.

George, Charles and Katherine, *The Protestant Mind of the English Reformation 1570–1640*, Princeton, 1961.

Gerard, John, *A Narrative of the Gunpowder Plot*, edit. Morris, J., 1871. *Autobiography*, see Caraman, P.

Gerard, John, *What was the Gunpowder Plot?* 1897. *The Gunpowder Plot and the Gunpowder Plotters, Thomas Winter's Confession and the Gunpowder Plot*, 1898.

Gillow, Joseph, *A literary and biographical history, or bibliographical dictionary, of the English Catholics from the breach with Rome to the present time*, 5 vols. 1885–1903.

Green, V. H. H., *Religion at Oxford and Cambridge*, 1964.

Guilday, Peter, *The English Catholic Refugees on the Continent 1558–1795. Vol. I, the English Colleges and Convents in the Catholic Low Countries, 1558–1795*, London, 1914.

Hall, Basil, 'Puritanism: the Problem of Definition', in *Studies in Church History, II*, edit. G. J. Cuming, Ecclesiastical History Society, 1965.

Hardy, W. J., See Gee, H. and Hardy, W. J.

Haller, W., *The Rise of Puritanism or, the Way to the New Jerusalem as set forth in pulpit and press from Thomas Cartwright to John Lilburne and John Milton, 1570–1643*, New York, 1938.

Harris, P. R., 'William Fleetwood, Recorder of the City, and Catholicism in Elizabethan London', *Recusant History*, vol. 7, no. 3, 1963.

Harrison, Robert, See Peel, A. and Carsen, L. *The Writings of Robert Harrison and Robert Browne*.

Hicks, L., *An Elizabethan Problem*, 1964. 'An Elizabethan Propagandist: the career of Soloman Aldred', *The Month*, May–June, 1945. 'The Strange Case of Dr. William Parry—the Career of Agent-Provocateur', *Studies*, Dublin, 1948. 'Father Robert Persons S.J., and the Book of Succession', *Recusant History*, vol. 4, no. 3, 1957.

Hicks, L. (edit.), *Letters and Memorials of Father Robert Persons to 1588*, Catholic Record Society, vol. 39, 1942.

Hill, Christopher, *Economic Problems of the Church from Archbishop Whitgift to the Long Parliament*, Oxford, 1956. *Society and Puritanism in Pre-Revolutionary England*, 1964. 'Puritans and "The Dark Corners of the Land"', *Transactions of the Royal Historical Society*, 5th series, XIII, 1963.

Historical Manuscripts Commission, *Various Collections I*, 1901. *MSS. of the Marquis of Bath*, 1903. *Montagu of Beaulieu*, 1900.

Hoare, H. W., *Our English Bible*, 1911.

Hoby, Lady Margaret, see Meads, D. M.

Hodgetts, Michael, 'Priests' Hiding Holes', *The Venerabile*, XIX, no. 3 November 1959. 'Nicholas Owen in East Anglia', *The Month*, new series, vol. 26, 1962. *Country Life*, 22 March 1962. 'The Priest Holes at Harvington Hall', *Transactions of the Worcestershire Archaeological Society*, XXXIX, 1962.

Holden, W. P., *Anti-Puritan Satire 1572–1642*, Yale, 1954.

Hooker, Richard, *The Works of that learned and judicious divine, Mr Richard Hooker, with an account of his life and Death by Isaac Walton*, 2 vols. Oxford, 1950. *Of the Laws of Ecclesiastical Polity: the Fifth Book*, edit. R. Bayne, 1902. See Paget, Francis; Sisson, C. J.

Hughes, Philip, *Rome and the Counter-Reformation*, 1942. *The Reformation in England*, vol. III, 1954.

Hurstfield, Joel, *Elizabeth I and the Unity of England*, 1960.

Janelle, Pierre, *Robert Southwell the writer*, 1935.

Jardine, David, *A Narrative of the Gunpowder Plot*, 1857.

Jenkins, Gladys, 'The Archpriest Controversy and the Printers 1601–1603', *The Library*, 5th series, Vol. II, 1948.

Jessopp, Augustus, *One Generation of a Norfolk House*, 2nd edition, 1879.

Jewel, John, see Booty, J. E.

Journals of the House of Commons

Klarwill, Victor von (edit.), *Queen Elizabeth and Some Foreigners*, 1928.

Kearney, H. F., 'Puritanism and Science: Problems of Definition', *Past and Present*, No. 31, 1965.

Kingdon, Robert M. (edit.), *The Execution of Justice by William Cecil and A True, Sincere and Modest Defense of English Catholics by William Allen*, New York, 1965.

Knappen, M. M., *Tudor Puritanism*, Chicago, 1939. Reprinted, 1963. *Two Elizabethan Puritan Diaries*, American Society of Church History, 1933.

Knox, S. J., *Walter Travers: Paragon of Elizabethan Puritanism*, 1962.

Knox, T. F., *The First and Second Diaries of the English College, Douay*, 1878. *Letters and Memorials of William Cardinal Allen*, 1882.

Langston, J. N., 'Robert Alfield, schoolmaster, of Gloucester, and his Sons', *Transactions of the Bristol and Gloucestershire Archaeological Society*, vol. 56, 1934.

Law, T. G., *A Historical Sketch of the Conflicts between Jesuits and Seculars in the Reign of Queen Elizabeth*, 1889. *The Archpriest Controversy*, 2 vols, Camden Society, 1898. See also Vaux, Laurence.

Leatherbarrow, J. S., *The Lancashire Elizabethan Recusants*, Chetham Society, 1947.

Levine, Mortimer, *The Early Elizabethan Succession Question 1558–1568*, Stanford University Press, 1966

Lewis, David, see Sander, Nicholas.

Loades, D. M., *Two Tudor Conspiracies*, Cambridge, 1965.

Loomie, A. J., *The Spanish Elizabethans: The English Exiles at the Court of Philip II*, New York, 1963. 'Toleration and Diplomacy: the Religious Issue in Anglo-Spanish Relations 1603–1605', *Transactions of the American Philosophical Society*, vol. 53, part 6, Philadelphia, 1963.

Marchant, R., *The Puritans and the Church Courts in the Diocese of York 1560–1642*, 1960.

Marprelate, Martin, see Arber, Edward; Pierce, W.

Marshall, J. S., *Hooker and the Anglican Tradition*, 1963.

Mathew, David, *The Celtic Peoples and Renaissance Europe*, 1933.

Mathias, Roland, *Whitsun Riot*, 1963.

Mattingly, Garrett, 'William Allen and Catholic Propaganda in England', *Travaux d'Humanisme et Renaissance*, XXVII, 1957.

McGinn, D. J., *The Admonition Controversy*, New Brunswick, 1949.

McGrath, P. V., 'Notes on the History of Marriage Licences' in *Gloucestershire Marriage Allegations*, edit. Brian Frith, Bristol and Gloucestershire Archaeological Society, 1954.

McGrath, P. V., and Rowe, J., 'The Recusancy of Sir Thomas Cornwallis', *Proceedings of the Suffolk Institute of Archaeology*, XXVIII, Part 3, 1961.

Meads, Dorothy M. (edit.), *Diary of Lady Margaret Hoby 1599–1605*, 1930.

Meyer, A. O., *England and the Catholic Church under Queen Elizabeth*, translated by J. R. McKee, 1915.

Meyer, Carl S., *Elizabeth I and the Religious Settlement of 1599*, St. Louis, 1960.

Miller, Perry, *Orthodoxy in Massachusetts, 1630–1650*, Cambridge, Massachusetts, 1933.

More, P. E. and Cross, F. L., *Anglicanism*, 1935.

Morgan, Irvonwy, *The Godly Preachers of the Elizabethan Church*, 1965

Morris, J., *The Troubles of our Catholic Forefathers*, 3 vols., 1872–7.

Munday, Anthony, *The English Roman Life* in *Harleian Miscellany*, VII, 1746.

Neale, J., *Elizabeth I and her Parliaments*, 2 vols., 1953, 1957.

New, John F. W., *Anglican and Puritan, The Basis of their Opposition 1558–1640* 1964.

Newton, John, see Dickens, A. G.

O'Connell, Marvin R., *Thomas Stapleton and the Counter Reformation*, Yale University Press, 1964.

O'Dwyer, M. 'Catholic Recusants in Essex c. 1580–c. 1600,' unpublished London M.A. Thesis, 1960.

Paget, Francis, *An Introduction to the Fifth Book of Hooker's Treatise of the Laws of Ecclesiastical Policy*, Oxford, 1899.

Parker, Matthew, see Bruce J. and Perowne, T.

Parsons, Robert, S. J., Memoirs, see Pollen, J. H. (edit.) *Letters and Memorials*, see Hicks, L. (edit.) *Annals of the English College, Seville*, see Hicks, L. (edit.)

Pastor, Ludwig von, *The History of the Popes*, edit. R. F. Ker, vols. XV, XVI, 1928.

Paul, J. E., 'Hampshire Recusants in the time of Elizabeth I, with special reference to Winchester', *Proceedings of the Hampshire Field Club*, xxi, Part II, 1959. 'The Hampshire Recusants in the Reign of Elizabeth', unpublished Ph.D. thesis, Southampton, 1958.

Pearson, A. F. Scott, *Thomas Cartwright and Elizabethan Puritanism*, Cambridge, 1925.

Peel, Albert, *The Brownists in Norwich and Norfolk about 1580*, Cambridge, 1920. *The First Congregational Churches*, Cambridge, 1920. 'The Lamentable Estate of the Ministry in Staffordshire', *English Historical Review*, 1911.

Peel, Albert (edit.), *The Seconde Parte of a Register, Being a Calendar of Manuscripts under that title intended for publication by the Puritans about 1593, and now in Dr Williams' Library, London*, 2 vols., Cambridge, 1915. *Tracts ascribed to Richard Bancroft*, Cambridge, 1953.

Peel, Albert and Carsen, Leland, *The Writings of Robert Harrison and Robert Browne*, 1953.

Perkins, William, *Works*, 3 vols., 1608.

Petti, Anthony G. R., 'A Study of the Life and Writings of Richard Verstegan', unpublished London M. A. Thesis, 1957. *The Letters and Despatches of Richard Verstegan*, Catholic Record Society, vol. 52, 1959. 'A Bibliography of the writings of Richard Verstegan', *Recusant History*, vol. 7, no. 2, 1963.

Pierce, W., *An Historical Introduction to the Marprelate Tracts*, 1908.

Pierce, W. (edit.), *The Marprelate Tracts*, 1911.

Plomer, H. R., *A Short History of English Printing 1476–1898*, 1900. 'Bishop Bancroft and a Catholic Press', *The Library*, new series, vol. VII, 1907.

Pollen, J. H., *The Institution of the Archpriest Blackwell*, 1916. *The English Catholics in the Reign of Queen Elizabeth*, 1920.

Pollen, J. H. (edit.), *The Memoirs of Father Robert Persons*, Catholic Record Society, vol. 2, 1905; vol. 4, 1907. *The English Martyrs 1584–1603*, Catholic Record Society, vol. 5, 1908. *Annals of the English College, Seville, with an account of four other foundations from 1589 to 1595, an unfinished Memoir written by Father Robert Persons, S.J. in 1610*, Catholic Record Society, vol. 14, 1914. See also Challoner, Richard.

Porter, H. C., *Reformation and Reaction in Tudor Cambridge*, Cambridge, 1958.

Powicke, F. J., *Henry Barrow, Separatist, and the Exiled Church of Amsterdam*, 1900.

Puritan Manifestoes, see Frere, W. H. and Douglas, C. E.

Raine, A. (edit.), *York Civic Records Vol. VII*, Yorkshire Archaeological Society, 1950.

Read, Conyers, *Mr. Secretary Walsingham and the Policy of Queen Elizabeth*, 3 vols. Oxford, 1925. *Lord Burghley and Queen Elizabeth*, 1960.

Renold, P. (edit.), *The Wisbech Stirs 1595–1598*, Catholic Record Society, vol. 51, 1958.

Robinson, Hastings (edit.), *The Zurich Letters, comprising the correspondence of several English Bishops and others with some of the Helvetian Reformers during the early part of the reign of Queen Elizabeth*, Cambridge, 1842. *The Zurich Letters*, second series, Parker Society, Cambridge, 1845.

Rogers, D. M., see Allison, A. F. and Rogers, D. M.

Rowe, J., see McGrath, P. V. and Rowe, J.

Rowse, A. L., *Tudor Cornwall*, 1941. *The England of Elizabeth: The Structure of Society*, 1950.

Rymer, Thomas, *Foedera*, 20 vols., 1704.

Salmon, J. H. M. *The French Religious Wars in English Political Thought*, Oxford, 1959

Sander, Nicholas, *Rise and Growth of the Anglican Schism*, trans. and edit. David Lewis, 1877.

Sandys, Edwin, see Ayre, J.

Sharpe, Cuthbert, *Memorials of the Rebellion of 1569*, 1840.

Simpson, Richard, *Edmund Campion*, 1896.

Sisson, C. J., *The Judicious Marriage of Mr. Hooker and the Birth of the Laws of Ecclesiastical Polity*, Cambridge, 1940.

Smith, Henry, *Sermons*, 1609.

Southern, A. C., *Elizabethan Recusant Prose, 1559–1582*, 1950.

Southgate, W. H., *John Jewel and the Problem of Doctrinal Authority*, Harvard University Press, 1962.

Southwell, Robert, *An Humble Supplication*, see Bald, R. C. *An Epistle of Comfort*, see Waugh, Margaret.

Squiers, Granville, *Secret Hiding Places*, 1934.

Statutes of the Realm

Stone, Lawrence, *The Crisis of the Aristocracy, 1558–1641*, Oxford, 1965.

Strype, John, *The Life and Acts of Matthew Parker*, 3 vols. Oxford, 1821. *The History of the Life and Acts of the Most Reverend Father in God, Edmund Grindal*, Oxford, 1821. *The Life and Acts of John Whitgift*, 3 vols. Oxford, 1822. *Annals of the Reformation*, Oxford, 1824. *Historical Collections of the life and acts of John Aylmer*, Oxford, 1821.

Sykes, Norman, *Old Priest and New Presbyter*, Cambridge, 1956.

Tanner, J. R., *Constitutional Documents of the Reign of James I*, Cambridge, 1930. *Tudor Constitutional Documents*, Cambridge, 1948.

Teall, J. L., 'Witchcraft and Calvinism in Elizabethan England', *Journal of the History of Ideas*, xxii, 1962.

Tierney, M.A., see Dodd, Charles.

Trevor-Roper, H. R., *Historical Essays*, 1957.

Trimble, W. R., *The Catholic Laity in Elizabethan England*, Cambridge, Massachusetts, 1964.

Usher, R. G., *The Presbyterian Movement in the Reign of Queen Elizabeth as illustrated by the Minute Book of the Dedham Classis, 1582–1589*, Camden Society, 1905 (includes extracts from Richard Bancroft's *Dangerous Positions*). *The Reconstruction of the English Church*, 2 vols., 1910.

Vaux, Laurence, *A Catechisme of Christian Doctrine necessarie for Children and ignorante people . . .* edit. T. G. Law, Chetham Society, Vol. 4, new series, 1885.

Veech, T. N., *Dr. Nicholas Sander and the English Reformation 1530–1581*, Louvain, 1935.

Verstegan, Richard, see Petti, Anthony.

Walker, F. X., 'The Implementation of the Elizabethan statutes against Recusants 1581–1603', unpublished London Ph.D. thesis, 1961.

Walsh, James, see Caraman, Philip, and Walsh, James.

Walzer, Michael, *The Revolution of the Saints: A Study in the Origins of Radical Politics*, 1966.

Watkin, E. I., *Roman Catholicism in England from the Reformation to 1950*, 1957.

Waugh, Evelyn, *Edmund Campion*, 1935.

Waugh, Margaret, *Blessed Nicholas Owen. An Epistle of Comfort*, by Robert Southwell, 1960 (edit.)

Weston, William, see Caraman, Philip.

Whitaker, W. B., *Sunday in Tudor and Stuart Times*, 1933.

White, F. O., *Lives of the Elizabethan Bishops of the Anglican Church*, 1898.

White, Helen, *Tudor Books of Saints and Martyrs*, Wisconsin, 1963.

Whiting, C. E., *Studies in English Puritanism from the Restoration to the Revolution 1660–1688*, 1931.

Williamson, H. R., *The Gunpowder Plot*, 1951.

Wilson, J. Dover, 'Richard Schilders and the English Puritans', *Transactions of the Bibliographical Society*, xi, 1909.

Wood, Thomas, *Letters*, see Collinson, Patrick.

Zurich Letters, see Robinson, Hastings.

Index

Date Due

MAY 30 '89			
NOV 25 1974			
JA 09 '78			
MY 10 '82			
OC 18 '82			
DE 6 '82			
FE 14 '83			
JE 20 '83			
APR 21 1985			